THE PAINTED
art journal

24 Projects for Creating Your Visual Narrative

Jeanne Oliver

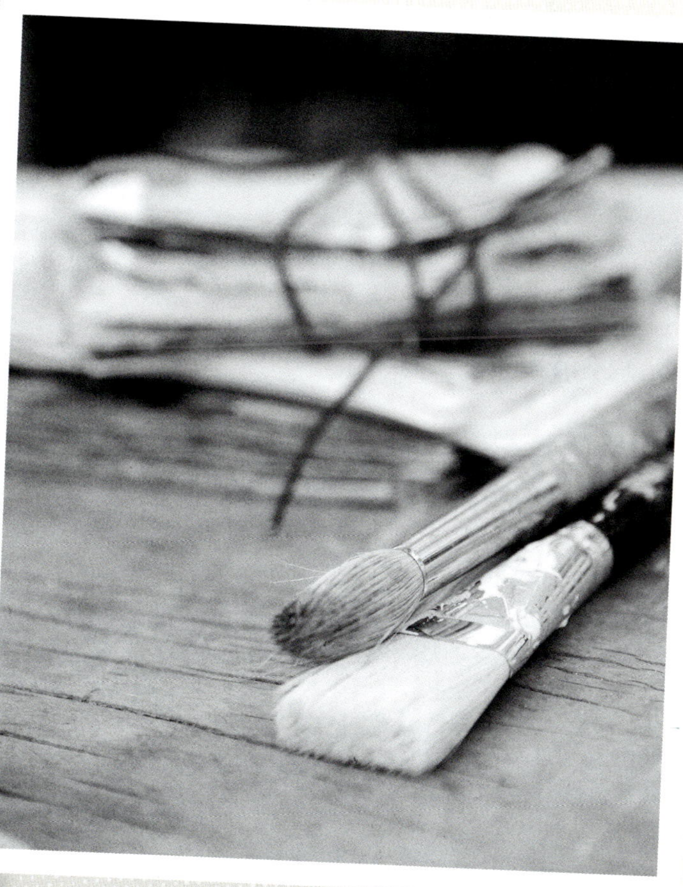

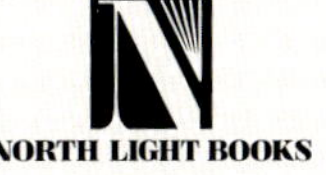

NORTH LIGHT BOOKS

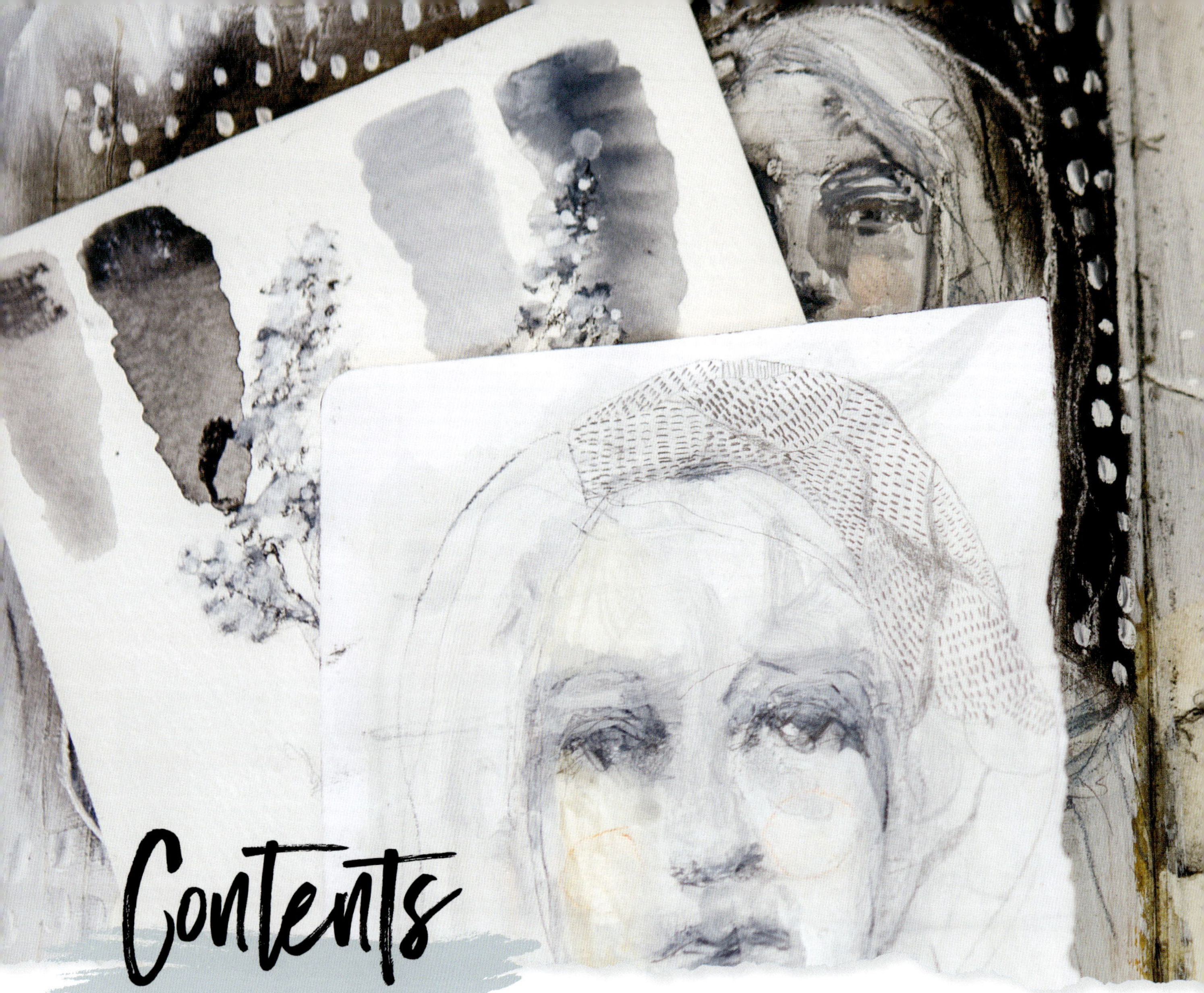

Contents

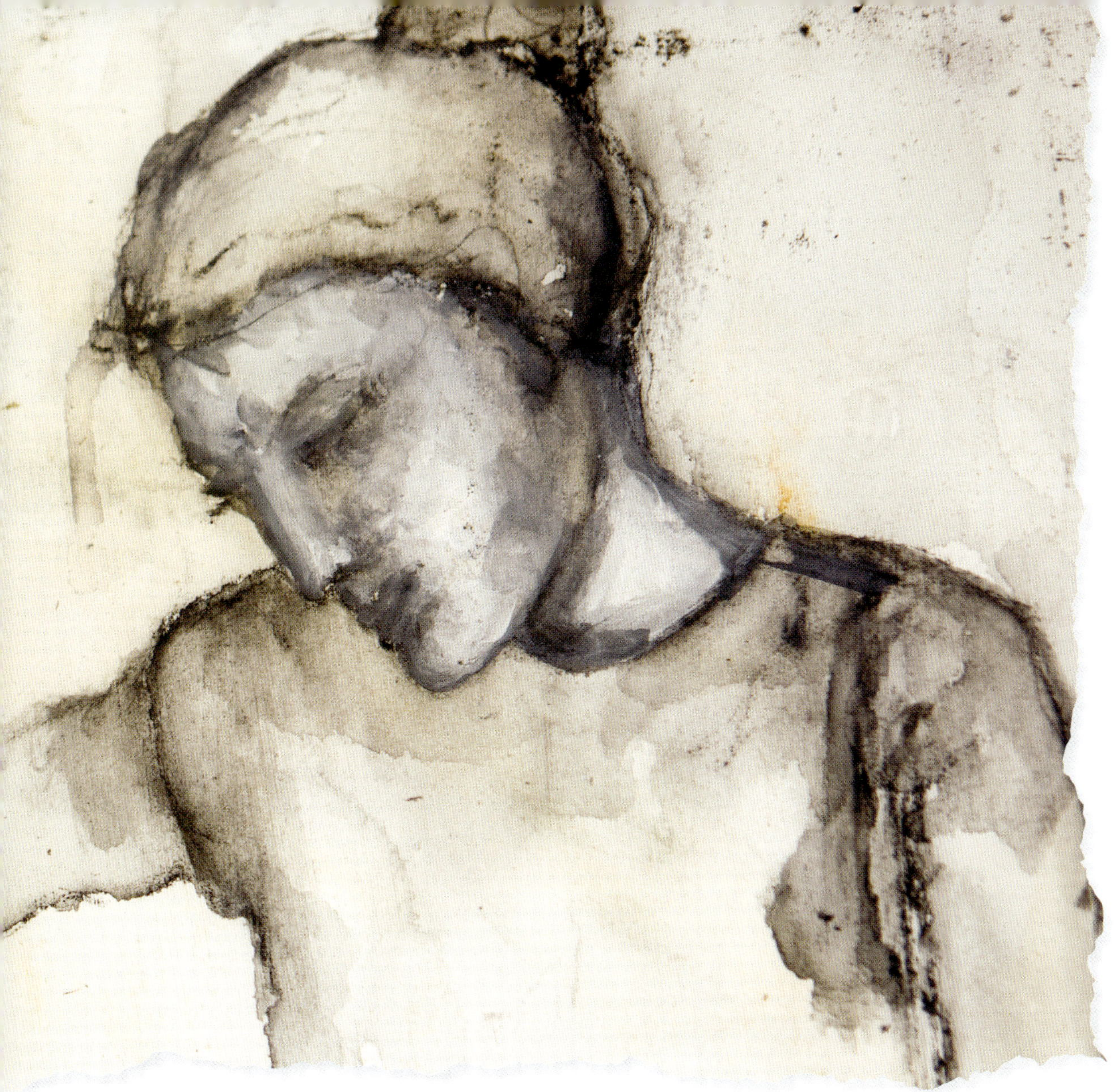

Introduction

The Painted Art Journal was born from my own discovery about my authentic self and the journey I am on. I believe it is a journey we are all on: to discover who we really are and how to tell that story within our art. I had a deep desire to create art that authentically looked like me and told a story only I could tell.

It was during this time of honoring my gifts and intentional quiet that memories started to flood my mind of Illinois woods, dirt roads, floral wallpaper, my grandparents, cornfields, old farmhouses, sheets drying on the clothesline, silos, small town main street, the home I grew up in, my childhood dreams, the joys and pains from growing up, our brokenness and our joys . . . so many of the images and memories that make up who I am. As these reflections came rushing back, I asked myself why wasn't I sharing the most authentic stories about who I am, where I came from and where I wanted to go? They had been there right in front of me the whole time, and I had ignored their significance and dishonored the importance of the road I had traveled.

I finally saw that my story was good enough. I had all the stories in me to create deeply authentic art. Seeing and honoring our stories sets us free to discover the art we have longed to create. We have the freedom to walk forward and boldly watch our creativity unfold.

The storytelling and techniques in this book are active exercises in truly looking at your life and story, documenting it and what that means for you and your art. It becomes a part of your legacy and what you give to those around you and yourself. As you begin to gather your story, you will also begin to discover your color palette, imagery, mark making and patterns.

If we have our eyes over someone else's shoulders, and we are looking at what they are creating and the story they are telling, we will inevitably get lost. We go off our own path and far away from our own story and storytelling. In the process our authentic art never gets made.

When I started to see my own stories as meaningful and significant, my art began to change. When I could look back and find my own timeline and defining moments, I was able to start digging deeper as an artist and my creating became more of a time of remembering, honoring, forgiving, healing and celebrating. It made me more intentional about where I wanted to go creatively and how I wanted to share my story and my art.

IF YOU THINK YOUR STORY ISN'T GOOD ENOUGH, YOU ARE MISTAKEN.

IF YOU ARE AFRAID TO TELL YOUR STORY, MAYBE IT IS TIME TO FIND FREEDOM.

IF YOU HAVE NEVER TOLD YOUR STORY, IT IS TIME.

IF YOU WANT TO CREATE AUTHENTIC ART THAT NO ONE ELSE CAN CREATE—LET'S GET STARTED.

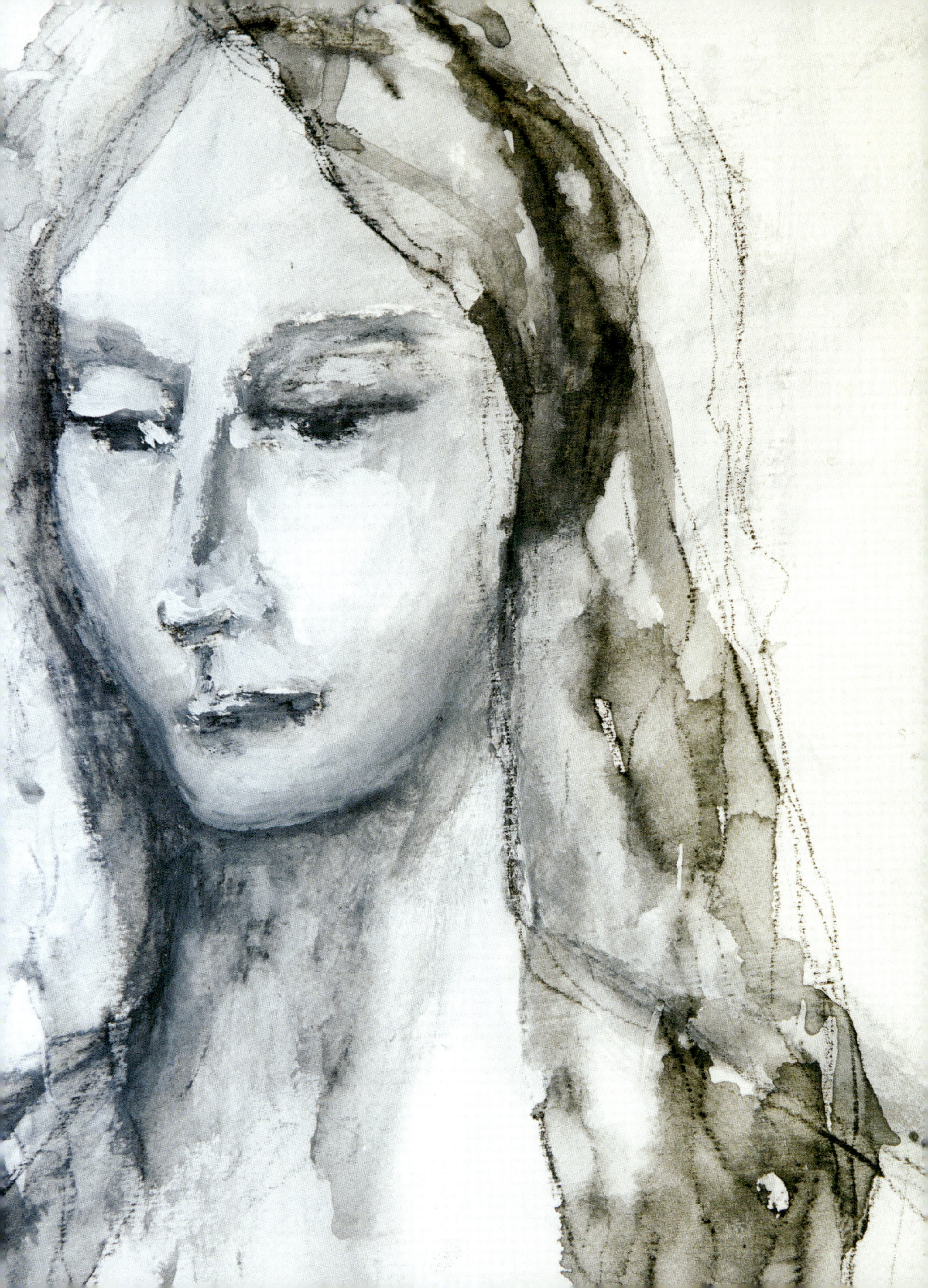

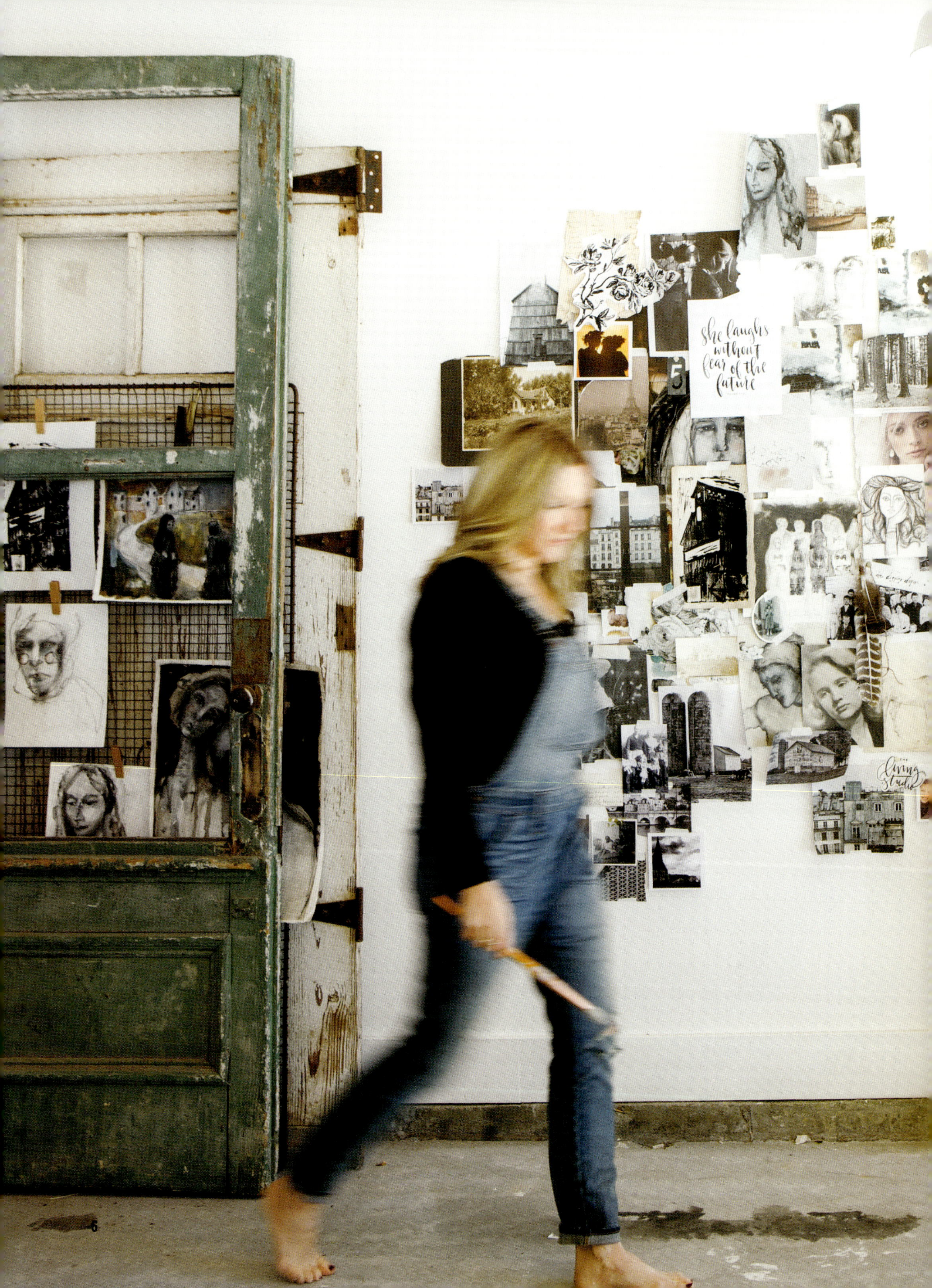

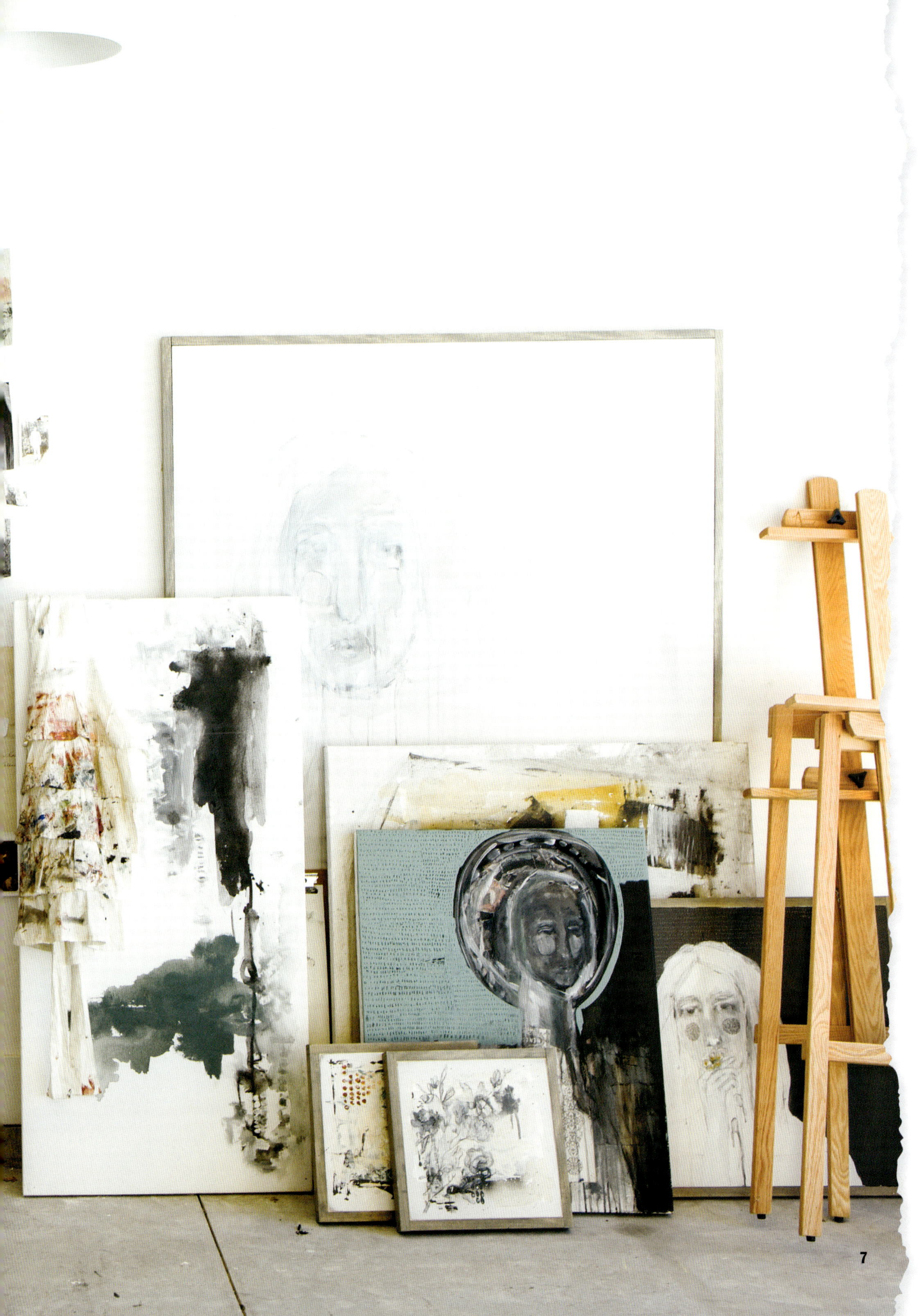

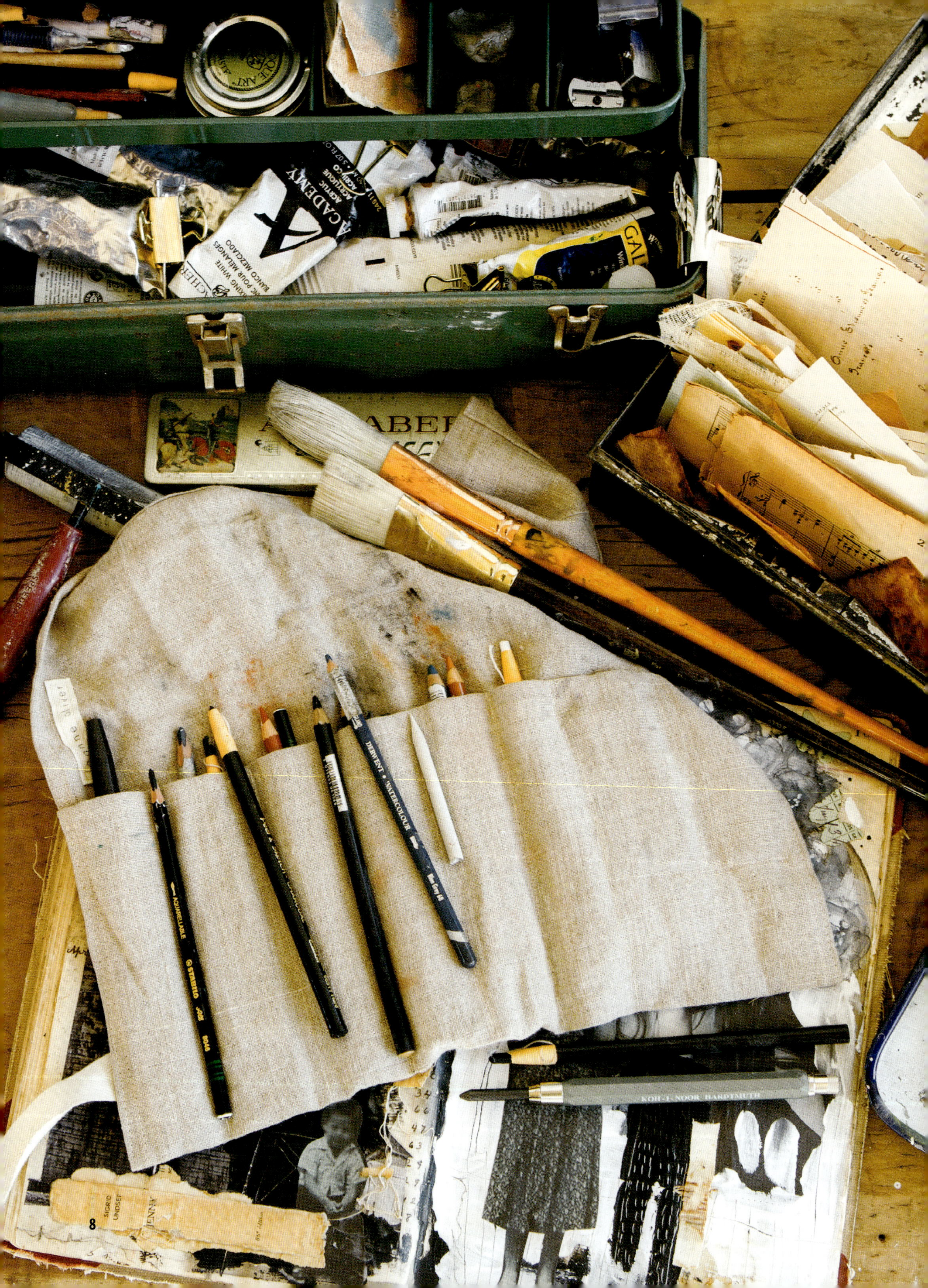

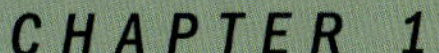

CHAPTER 1

Tools and Basic Supplies

THE MORE YOU CREATE AND GET TO KNOW how you like to use your tools (and the different ways your tools work on different substrates and mixed with other mediums), the more freedom you will also have in your art and storytelling. Most creatives love to get new supplies and we also want to learn what other artists are using. With any art form we are drawn to the supplies and creativity of those around us whom we admire. I would only caution you to not buy any new supplies mentioned in this book until you first see if something you already have will do the job.

I do not want you to have to run out and buy art supplies that you may not use, nor do I want to confuse you into believing buying art supplies is essential to making art. With most of our projects, if I use a Daniel Smith watercolor stick in Yellow Ochre, you could substitute it with a watercolor pencil, water-soluble crayon or even acrylics in the same color. It is more important for you to use the tools in your color palette and to find the techniques that connect with your style than to worry about using the exact same supplies.

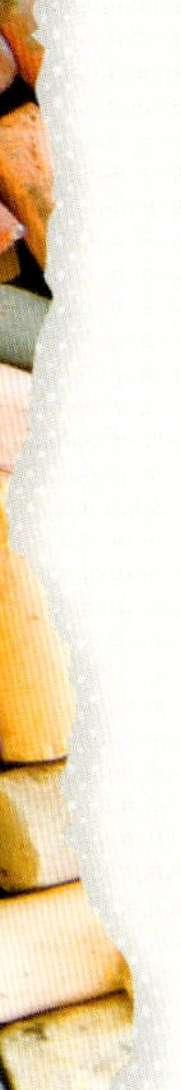

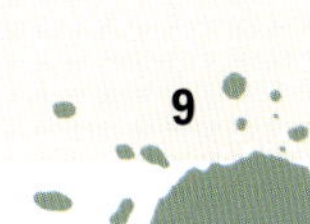

Here are some of the materials you'll encounter frequently in the projects in this book.

Acrylic Paints

Acrylic paints are fast-drying paints made of pigment suspended in acrylic polymer emulsion. They are water-soluble, but become water-resistant when dry. There is a wide range of pricing and quality you have to choose from. The nicer the quality of paint, the higher the pigment. Because we are working in art journals, you can get away with a lower quality of paint.

Alcohol Ink, Walnut Ink, Black Calligraphy Ink

These inks bring pigment and transparency to your work. The dropper will allow you to add mark making in a semicontrolled technique.

Carbon Paper

A thin paper coated on one side with a dark waxy pigment, often containing carbon, that is transferred by the pressure of writing onto the copying surface below.

Caran d'Ache Neocolor II Artist Crayons

These are water-soluble crayons with beautiful pigments. They blend easily and are a portable alternative to watercolors. These can also be made permanent by mixing with clear or white gesso.

Charcoal

If there is a medium that I am deeply in love with, it is charcoal. This is one of my go-to tools, and I use many varieties. Some of my favorite forms are a charcoal pencil (easy to take on-the-go and not messy), willow charcoal for sketching and warming up, and Derwent XL charcoals for the size, colors and ability to help me get out of my comfort zone and create large.

Charcoal is such a versatile medium and can be mixed with water and gesso to bring about different effects.

Coffee and Tea

Listing coffee and tea in the supply section may sound odd, but I have found that both work well for painting and creating layers in my work. It is much more subtle than ink and is readily available. Try different strengths and see how you like it in your work. They are also both wonderful for instantly aging ephemera.

Ephemera

In my art I like to include vintage ephemera from my travels, wallpaper, spines of old books, old tea bags and words cut from magazines and newspapers. I love how the vintage papers bring so much interest and texture into my creating.

Gesso

White, clear and black gesso are all staples on my table. Each one is a primer coat that you can apply to any substrate (any surface you paint on). Gesso prevents your mediums from absorbing into your substrate and becomes the first layer you build upon. It can also be mixed with different water-soluble mediums, and once dry, it becomes permanent. This allows you to build upon your creation without the layers blending. My favorite brand is Liquitex because of the grit, or tooth, of the clear and the fluidity of the white.

Glue

My glue of choice is Liquitex matte medium. It is the only adhesive I use because I have found that it doesn't bubble, and it gives me the best final product. I also use the matte medium to seal collage work and for image transfers. Always use what works for you.

Journal

All of the projects shared in this book will be in an art journal or vintage ledger, but you can also create them on canvas, cardboard, wood or the substrate of your choice. If I'm using a manufactured journal, I like to choose a journal that has mixed-media paper or watercolor paper so the pages can take more medium. Some of my favorite store-bought journals are Dylusions by Ranger or Moleskines. Other choices include the handmade journal in Chapter 6, a vintage ledger or old book such as you'll see in Chapter 5 or another store-bought journal.

Laser and Ink-Jet Images

Using your laser printer, print out images of your family, architecture, imagery from your story and more. We will use these images to do image transfers. If you don't have a laser printer, you can go to a local library to make copies of your images. I don't encourage you to go to a copy shop because their toner will be too high quality and your images will not transfer as well. We will also be photographing our work throughout the book and then printing those photos out on a laser or ink-jet printer and using them in other projects. This is a perfect way to use your art over and over again, and each time yields new results. It also encourages you to use sketches and mark making from previous work in your new work.

Linoleum Cutting Tools

Creating your own stamps is so fun in mixed media, and you can create exactly what your mind imagines. This is a fun and relatively easy way to bring your mark making into your work in a way that can be duplicated again and again. Buy a simple beginning set and you will probably find that you will never need to buy more.

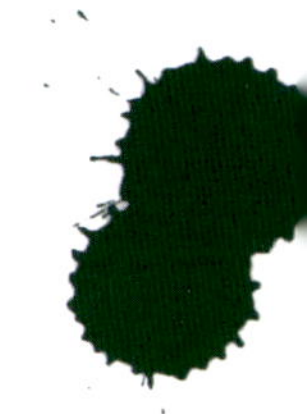

Mark-Making Tools

These are tools that you can use in your art to create marks by scratching into dry or wet mediums. Some of my favorite tools are skewers, a craft knife and sculpting tools.

Mechanical Pencil

I bring in a mechanical pencil for mark making, quick contour sketches and journaling. I prefer a .05mm or .07mm lead size.

Natural Fabrics

I like to have different natural fiber fabrics on hand to include in my mixed media and especially my journal making. Muslin, flour sack or cheesecloth are inexpensive and also wonderful absorbers of coffee, tea and rust dyeing.

Paintbrushes

I have both nice and inexpensive brushes and I am not good at taking care of any of them, so I do not spend a ton on brushes. I use a no. 4 round long-handled brush the most out of all of my brushes for journal and smaller work. If I use different brushes on a project, I will always share the size.

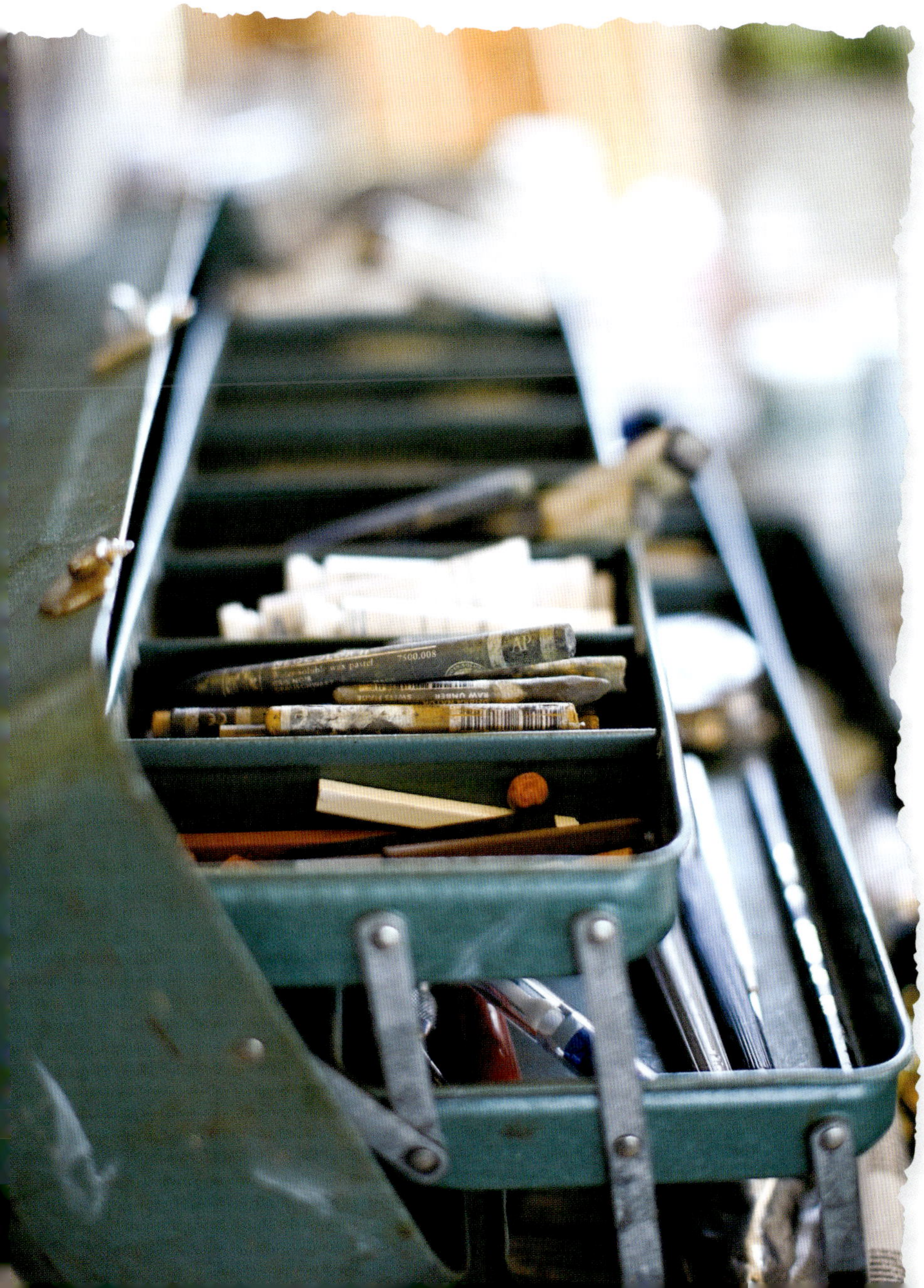

Small Rusty Items

It is time to go through your junk drawers and garage because those rusty items are going to make the most amazing rust-dyeing tools. After you do some rust dyeing, you will never look at rust the same. Look for nails, screws, odd-shaped items and even broken-off pieces. All of it will be useful and will yield unique results.

Soft Pastels

I prefer soft pastels for easy mark making and blending. They are created with pure powdered pigment and a binder. My favorites are hand rolled and higher quality because they will have more pigment and blend beautifully. I recommend purchasing these individually and not in a set, so you get only the pigments you will use.

Stabilo

The Stabilo All pencil is also another tool that is always with me, and there is rarely a piece that doesn't include this versatile tool. The Stabilo comes in many colors, is water-soluble and can write on almost anything (hence, the name). There are pieces that I have "painted" with only a black Stabilo plus water and have been able to create beautiful values and emotion.

Watercolors

Daniel Smith watercolors are my favorite because of the pigment and quality. But I also use the Daniel Smith watercolor sticks, watercolor markers, watercolor pencils and pan sets. Use what you can afford and slowly add to your collection. I buy only the colors I will use and never buy supplies in a set.

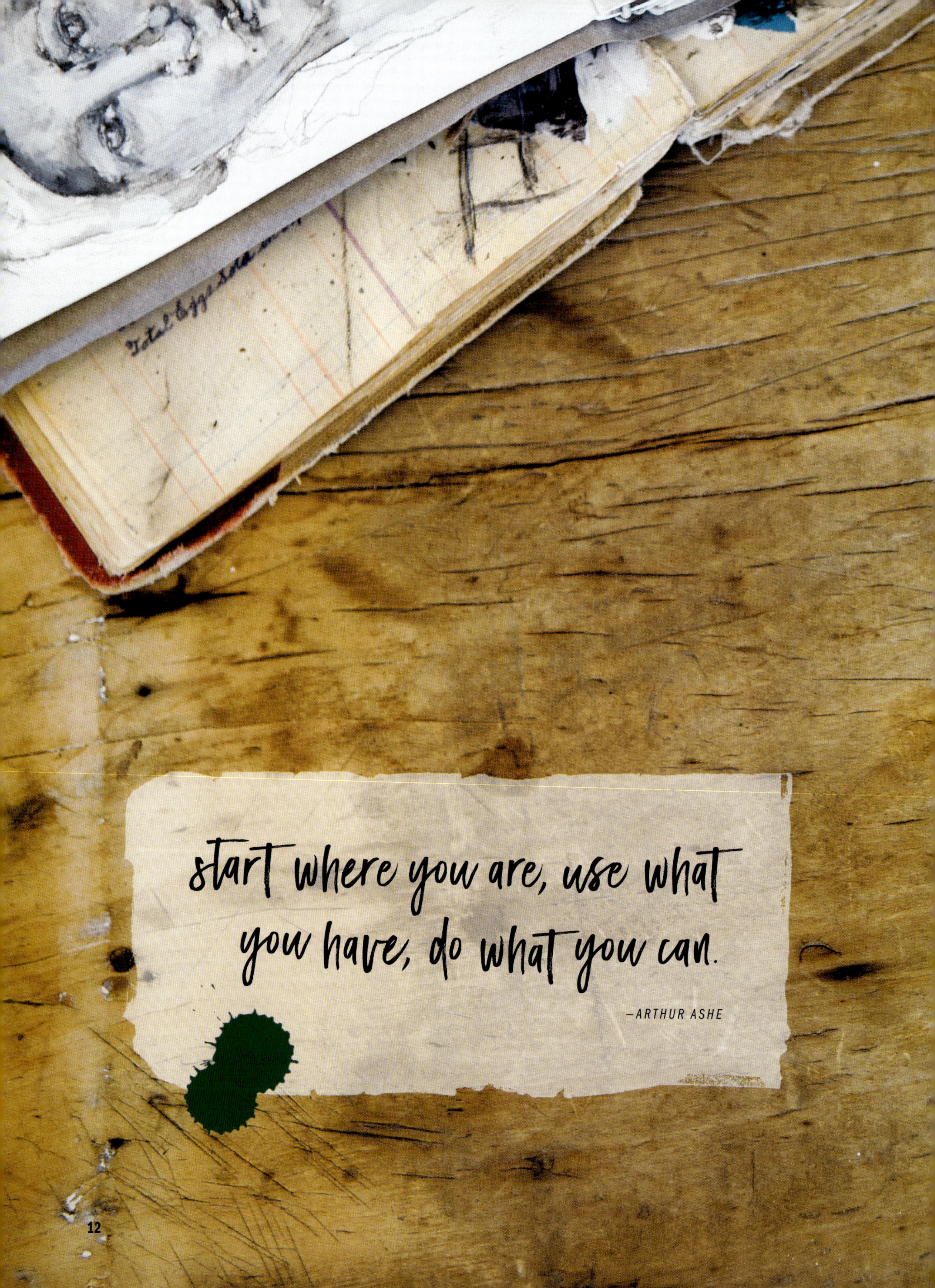

start where you are, use what
you have, do what you can.

—ARTHUR ASHE

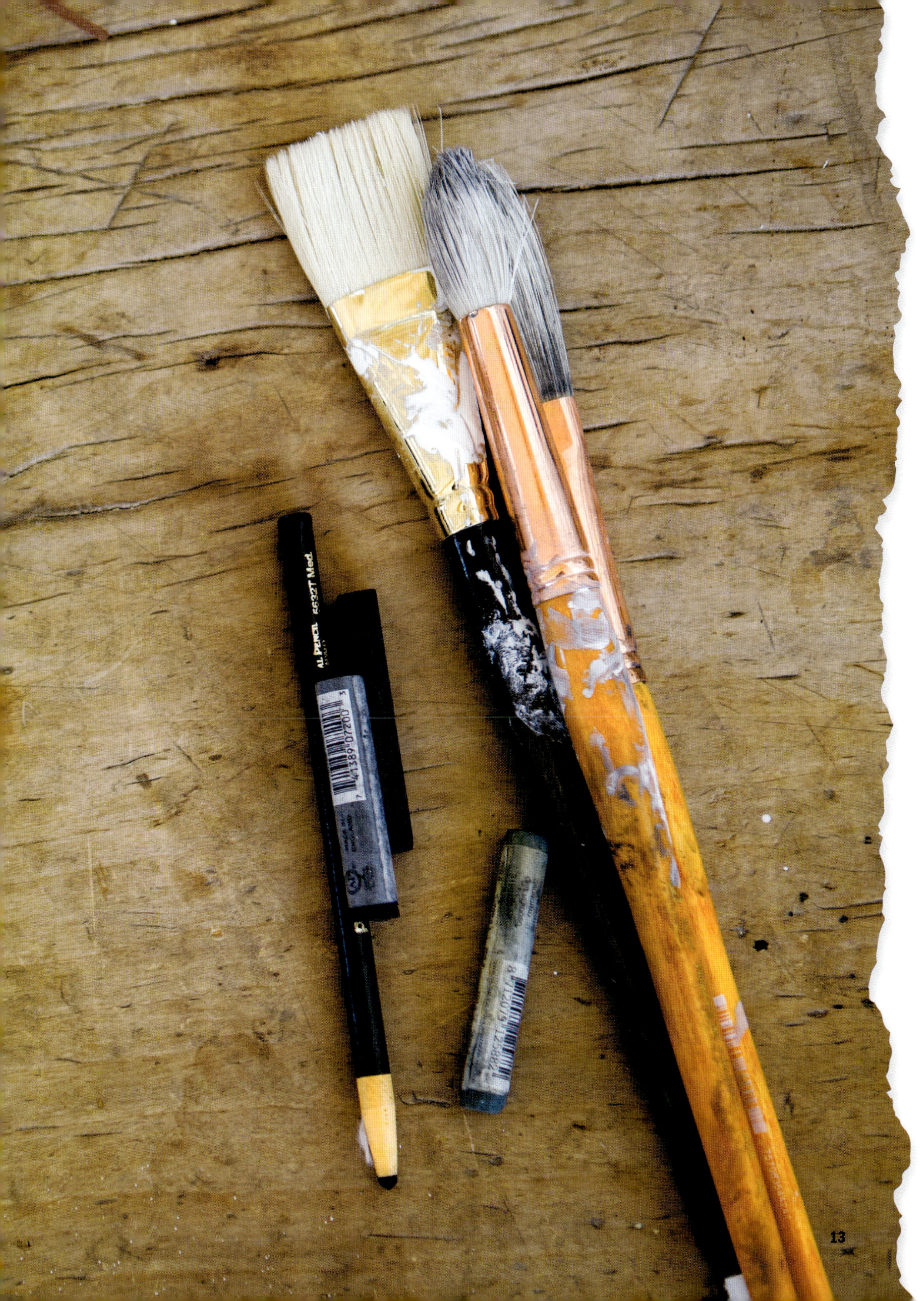

The Story

FOR SOME, THE IDEA OF FINDING THEIR STORY can be daunting, and for others, it is clear and exciting. It is a process, and, like anything else worth your time and energy, it may not come easily. Not everyone wants to tell all of their story and there may be parts you skip over. That is as it should be. There may be others who don't know the full extent of their story because of life experiences, and to those I say: Your story can even be imaginary and what you want it to be. Don't let not having all of the facts or having areas that are too painful keep you from telling your story. Honoring your story doesn't always mean telling it as it was. It is honoring you and your process. Be content with what that looks like.

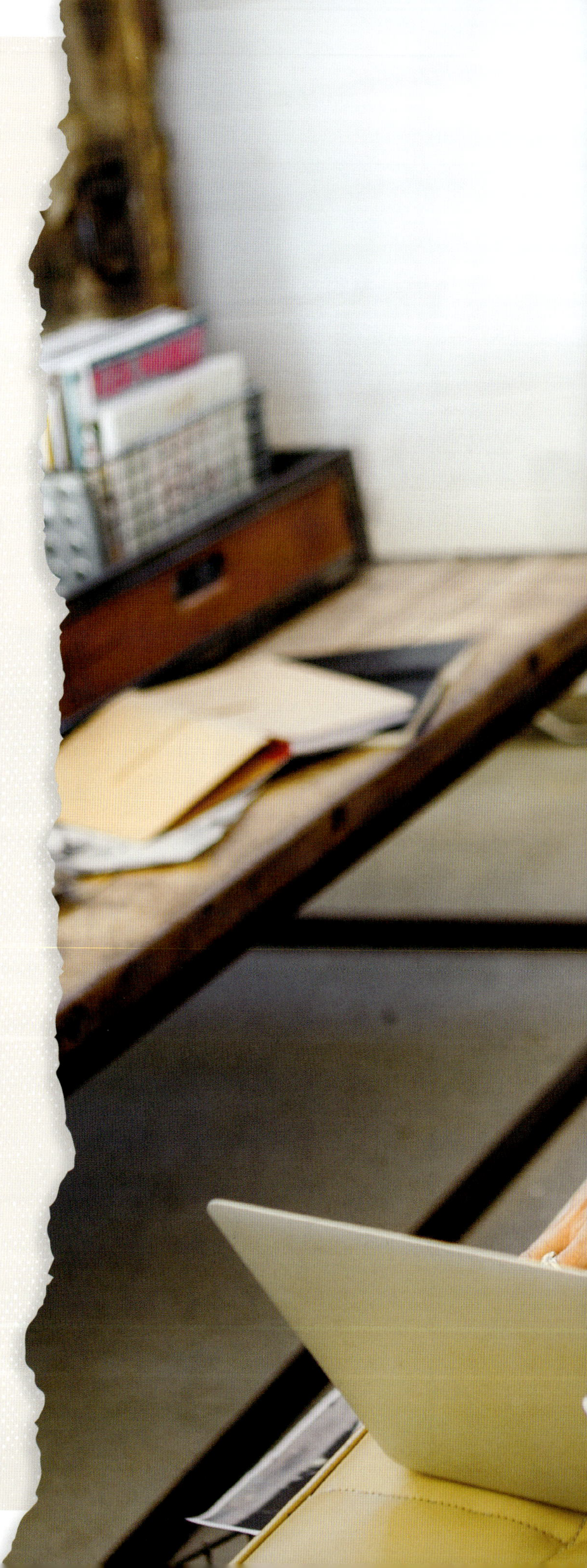

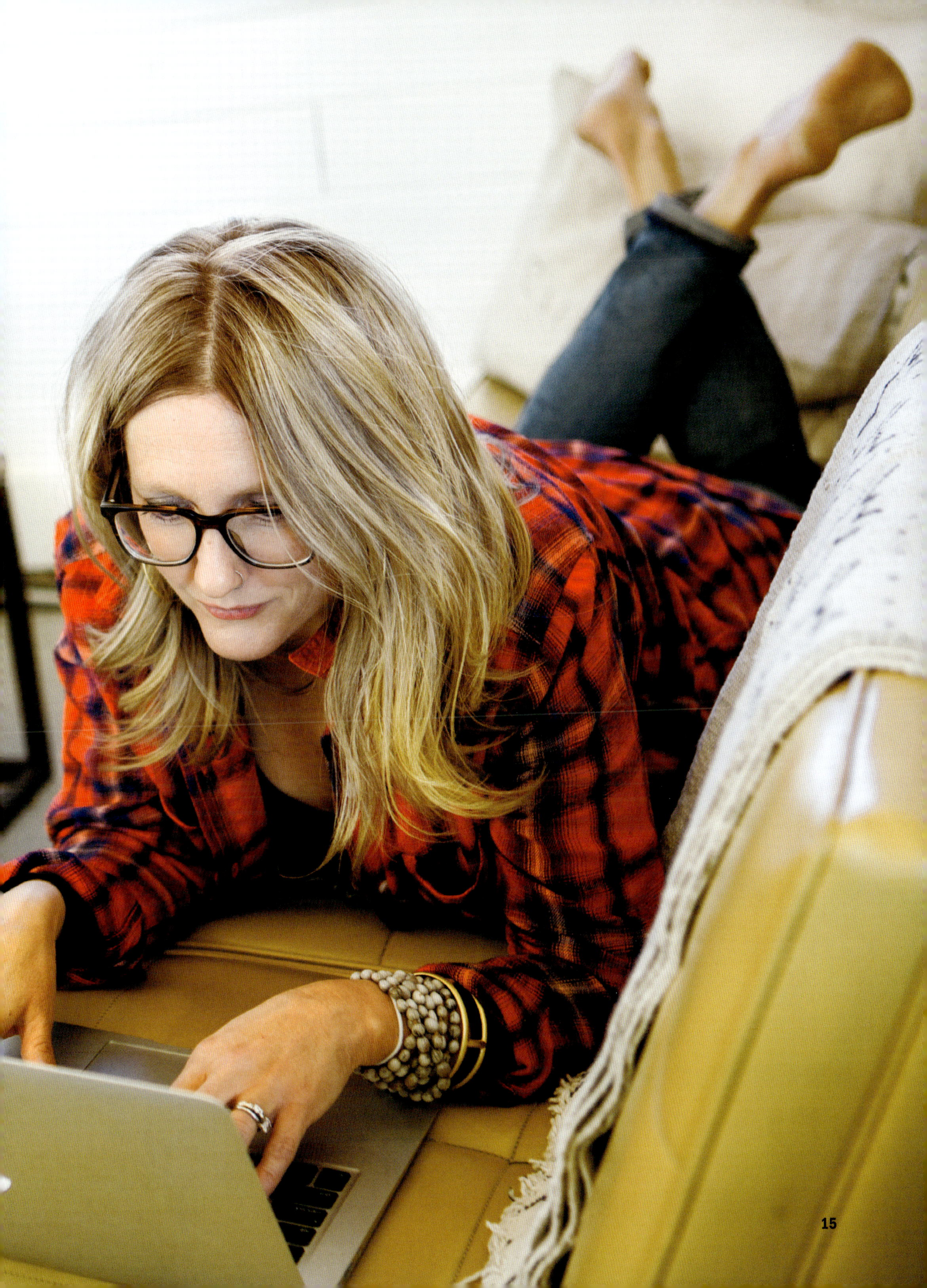

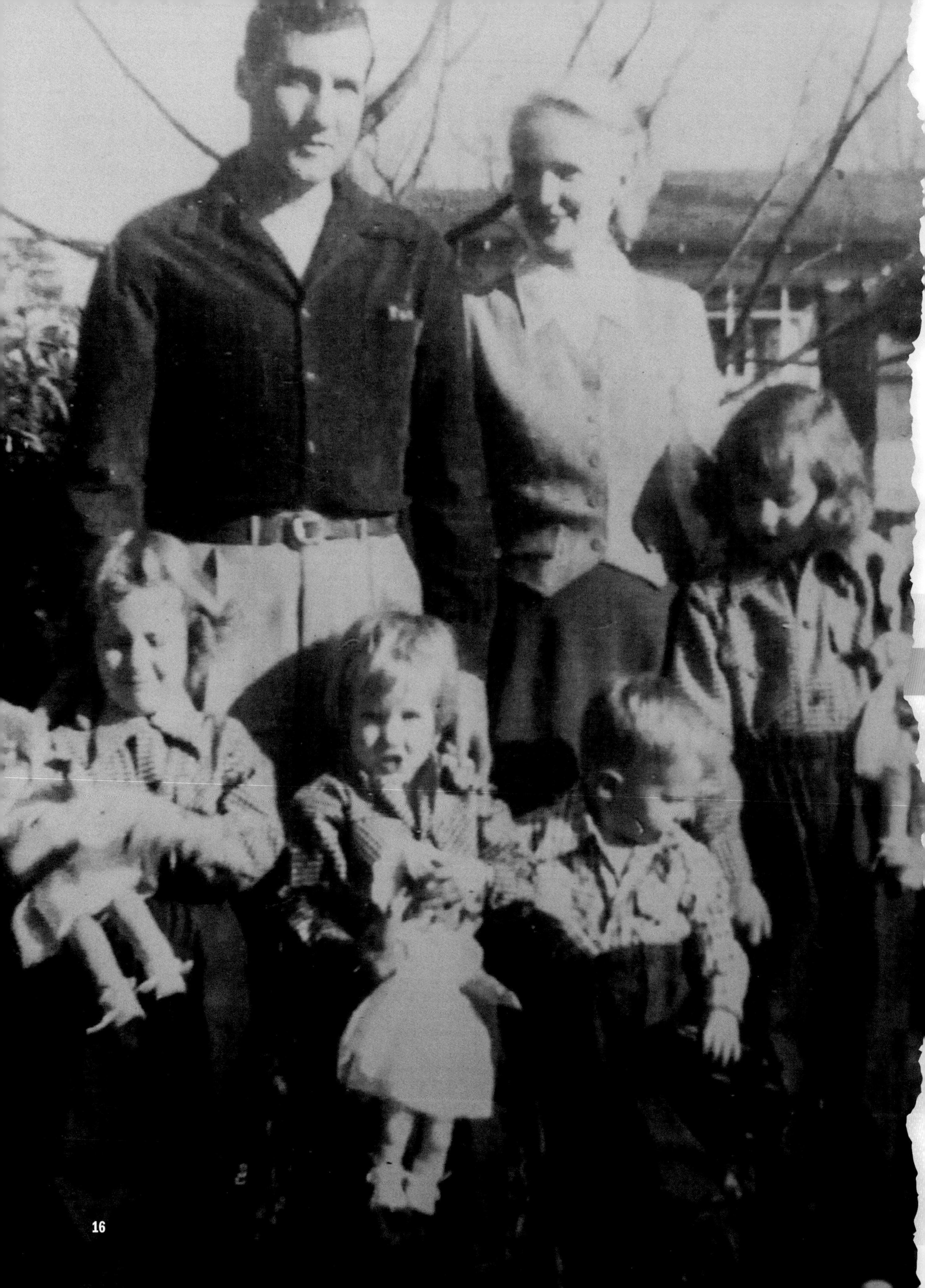

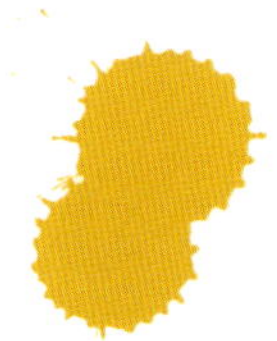

—UNKNOWN

There is not one way to tell your story, and as you begin I believe you will find the process that fits your creativity and personality. I love research, gathering, note taking, collecting and organizing before I begin my storytelling. I pull from many different areas and then keep only what speaks to me the most. I see clearly only when it is all out in front of me, and then my creativity is set so free that it can be hard to rein it in.

When I first began being intentional about my story, it began with simple note taking and sketches. As I was drawn deeper into the research of my story, I began to pull out not only symbolism, imagery, stories and photos, but also emotions and thoughts I had long ignored or forgotten. Each piece—joyful, indifferent or painful—became a treasure. Whether or not I chose to share them, I was still changed. I was remembering and honoring that part of who I am and where I came from.

There is no one way to tell your story

So, how do you begin finding your story and what you want to include in your art? These are some suggestions to get you started:

> Find a quiet place and set a timer for fifteen minutes and write as many things as you can remember about your life. Start chronologically if that is your personality or just write in any order.

> Brainstorm ideas of what you wish you would have done differently in major moments of your life or what you believe were defining moments.

> What imagery can be represented from your story? Some examples of mine are cornfields, farmhouses, dirt roads, farmers, cows and barns.

> If your memories are painful, then come up with the places, moments, imagery, architecture that bring you joy and peace now.

> If you do not have photos of where you grew up or where you are living now, do general Internet searches and begin collecting stories and photos.

> Join a site like Ancestry.com to trace your genealogy.

> If you have access to photo albums, go through them and photograph the photos, architecture and imagery you are most drawn to. You can later print these images out to use as reference.

> Take a road trip by yourself or with a close friend and go in search of your story. Make it an adventure! Record your thoughts, take photos, interview friends and family, videotape the journey.

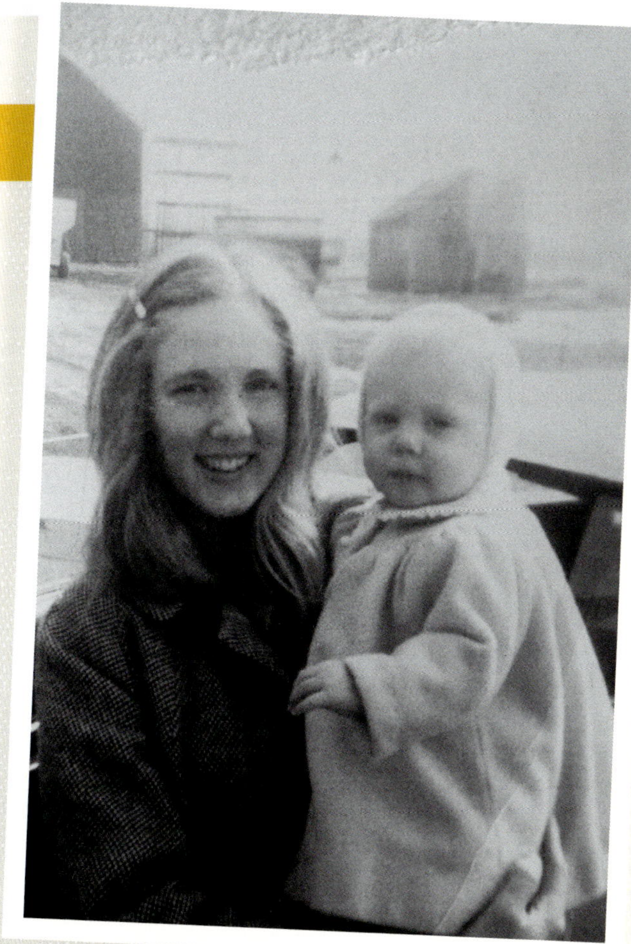

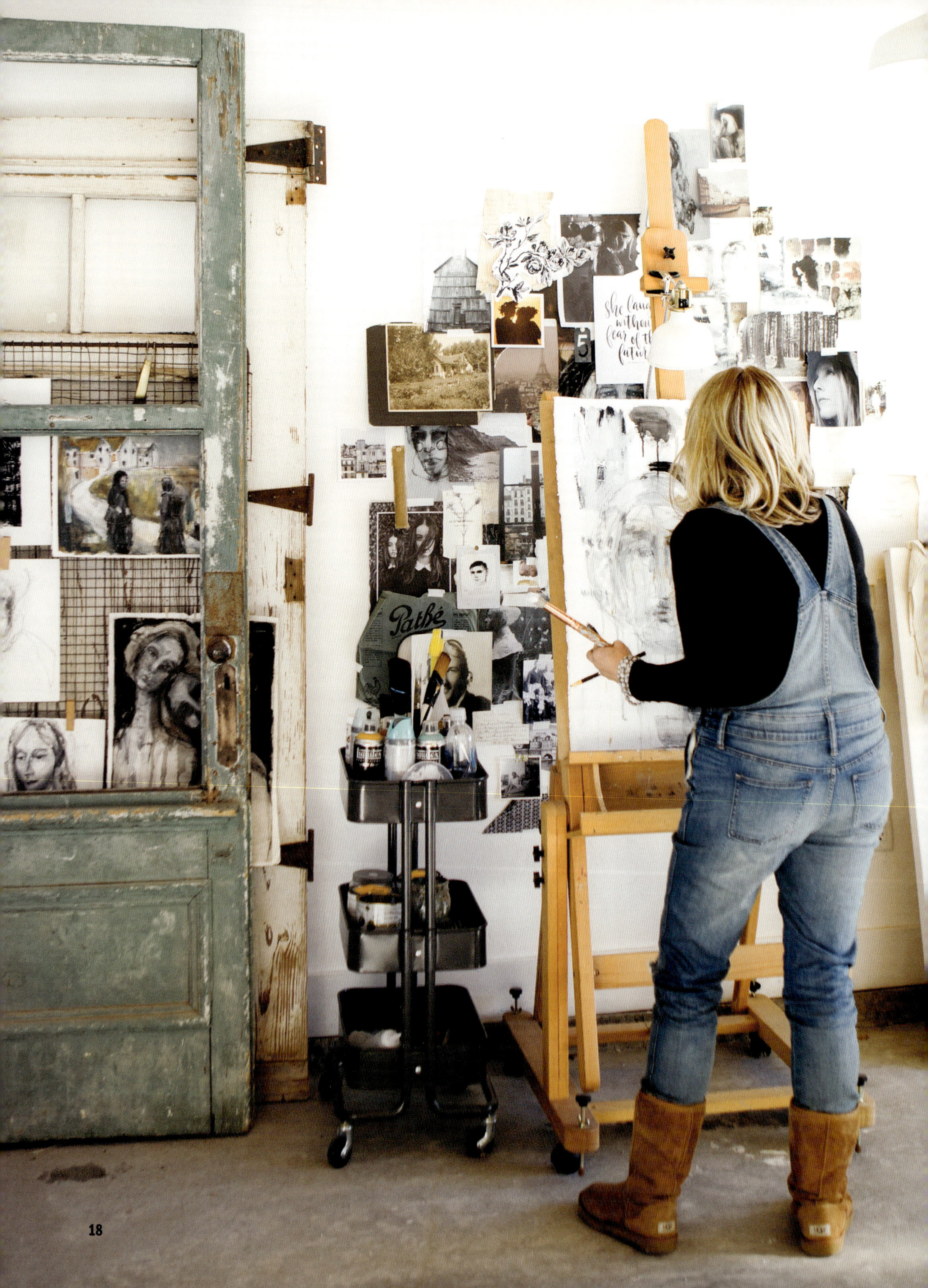

CHAPTER 3

Creative Rituals

HAVE YOU EVER THOUGHT ABOUT HOW CRUCIAL IT IS TO PREPARE your heart, mind and space for creating? For years I ignored this fact and would find myself disappointed with my creative time for one reason or another. Maybe I had only thirty minutes, or it had been a hard day with the kids, or my creativity was at an all-time low, or a million other reasons why our time creating is not treated as sacred and honored. We are busy, and, if you are anything like me, it can be hard to jump back and forth between the different parts of who you are. There was a time when I would skip creating altogether because I was afraid of the failure that would come out of my efforts or lack of time.

No matter what your spiritual beliefs are, I think we all can agree . . . Art is spiritual. No matter where you believe the creativity comes from, we know that when we give ourselves the time to connect and create that we are connected to something bigger than ourselves.

My time in the studio changed when I acknowledged the creative force (I believe in the Holy Spirit) and made room. I come into my space and slow down. I put on music that helps me to slow down. I change the scent of the space to slow down. I stretch and breathe and follow a ritual that reminds my heart and mind that I have come to create. I encourage you to develop a creative ritual that lets your spirit know you have come to create. This is no different than stretching before an athletic event or warming up your fingers before a piano competition. It is being intentional with yourself and honoring the time you are about to give . . . no matter the results.

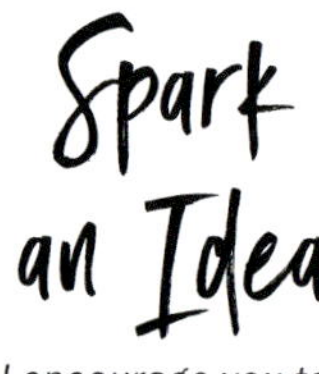

Spark an Idea

I encourage you to develop a creative ritual that lets your spirit know you have come to create.

Start a Creative Ritual

Here are some examples of ways you can start your own creative ritual:

> Music

> Candles or essential oils

> Notice how you breathe and take deep breaths.

> Speak out loud the work you want to produce that day.

> Meditate or pray.

> Organize your space as you warm yourself up to create.

> Review some of the printable art prompts I have included in the back of the book.

> Begin practicing to warm up with one of the audio art prompts I have included in the links at the back of the book.

> Your ritual can also be jumping jacks and loud music! Whatever connects you with your creative force and reminds your heart, mind and spirit that you are serious about this thing called your creativity!

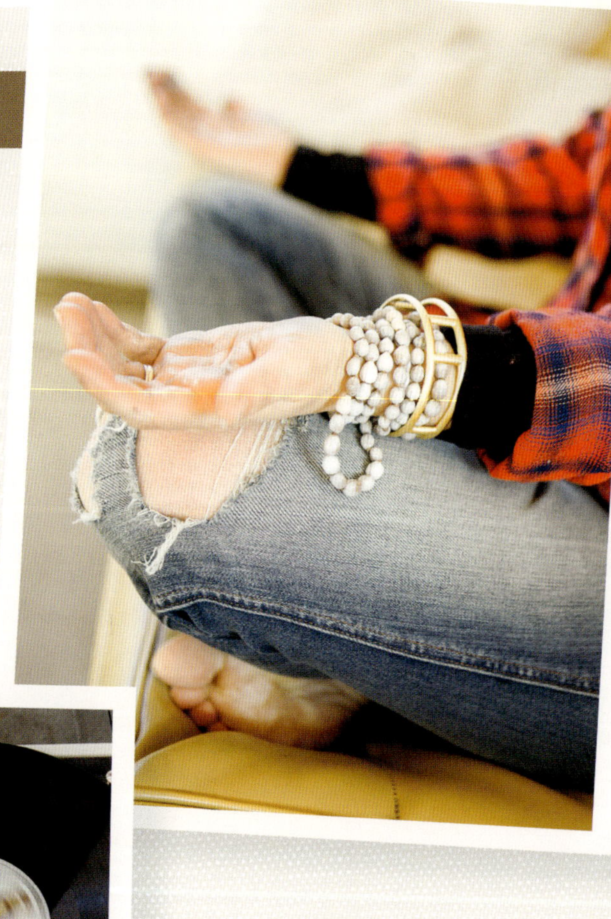

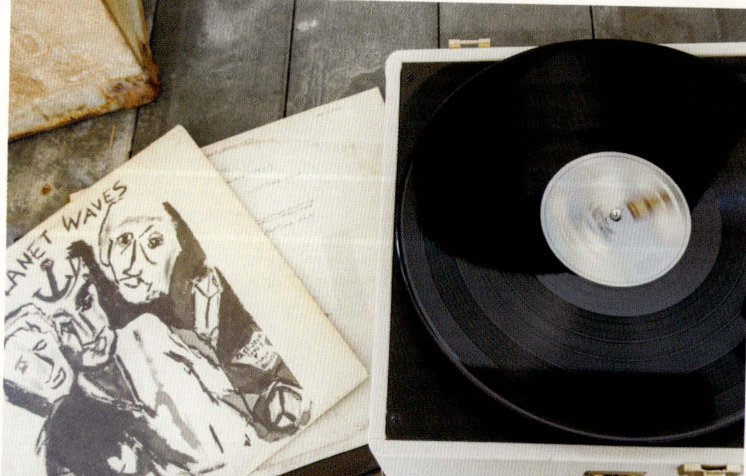

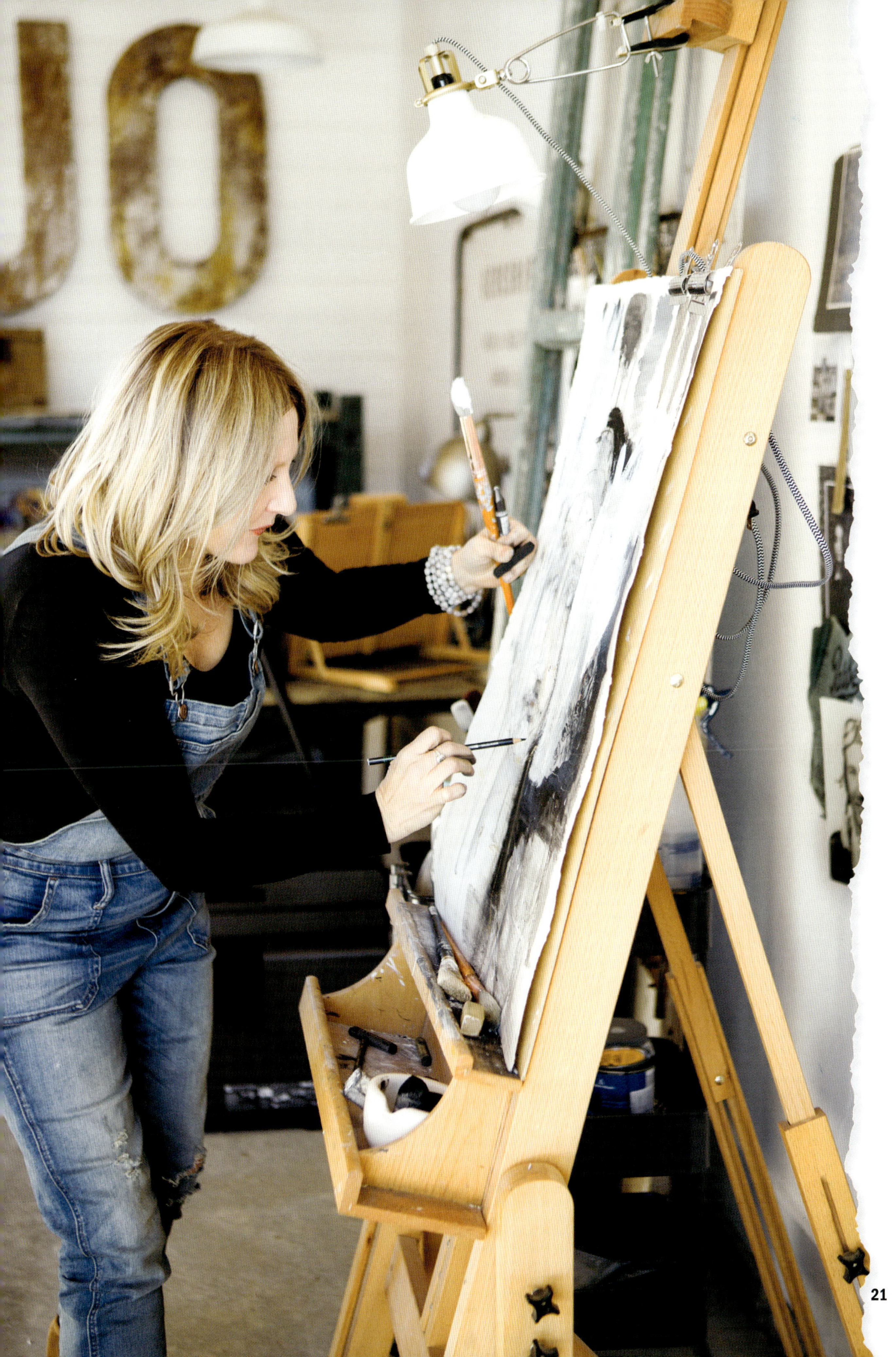

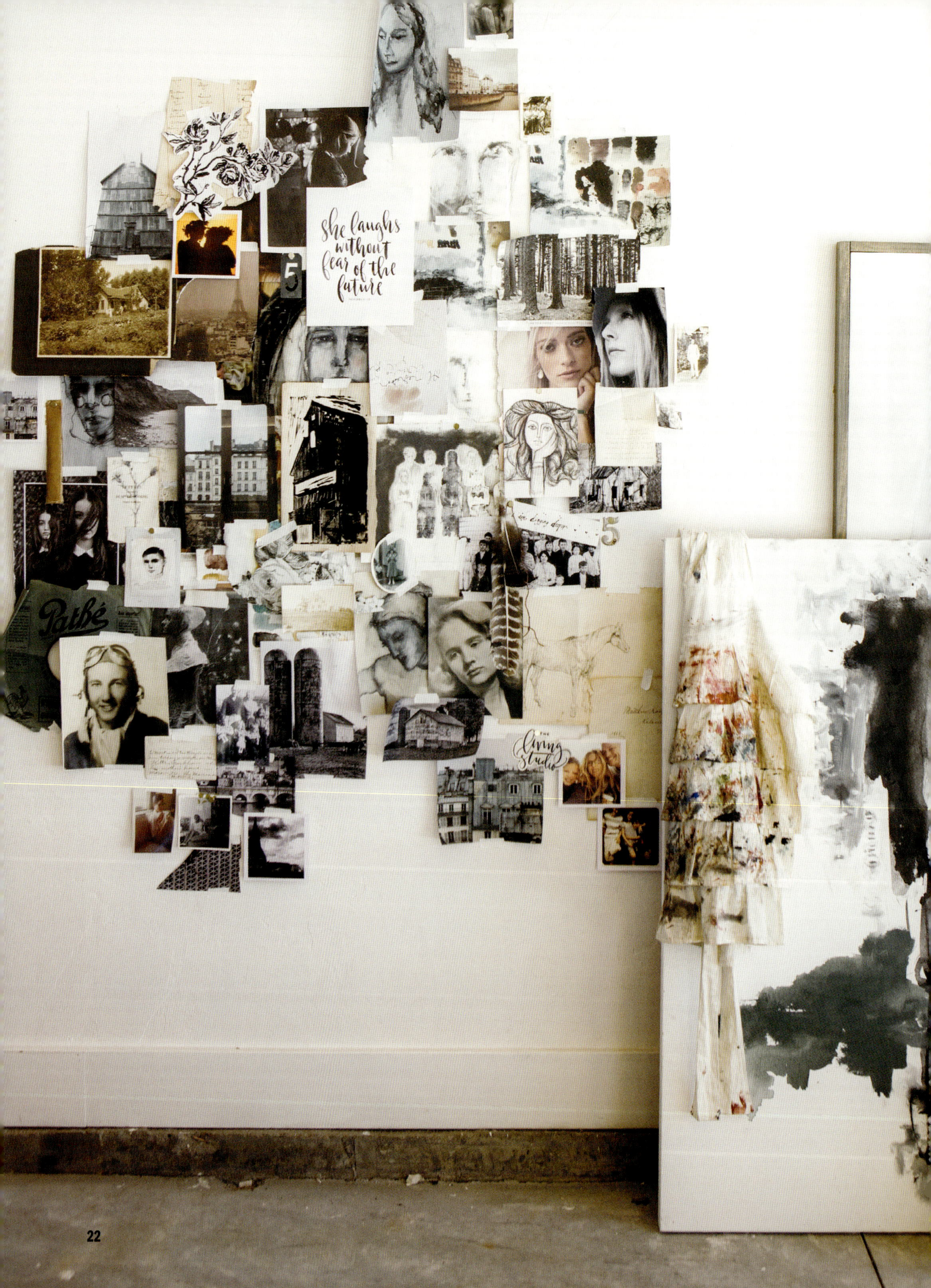

she laughs
without
fear of the
future
Pathé
THE
living
studio

Gathering Your Story Elements

EACH OF OUR STORIES IS SO DIFFERENT, LOVELY AND BROKEN IN ITS OWN WAY.
Being an artist and a very visual person, I enjoy the act of gathering. I like to collect, sort and curate the beautiful things around me. I like to be intentional. It helps me see clearly. Over the years I have found that by gathering and then intentionally sifting through the bits that I have collected that I have come to understand myself better, the art I want to make, the palette that authentically calls to me and even the lines and designs that are waiting for me to reach out and create.

The act of gathering and creating a storyboard will help you narrow down what is really calling to you. As you begin this journey to discover your stories, I believe you will be surprised with all the beautiful and broken parts that make up your story that you may not regularly consider. This exercise gives you the opportunity to pull together the story that is already all around you . . . you just need to see it.

Collecting Your Story

Your board will not look like anyone else's, and it is a reflection of whatever you choose to focus on. Your storyboard can be general and include a little bit of everything, like mine, or you can make is as specific as you wish. As you gather for your storyboard, remember: This is just for you.

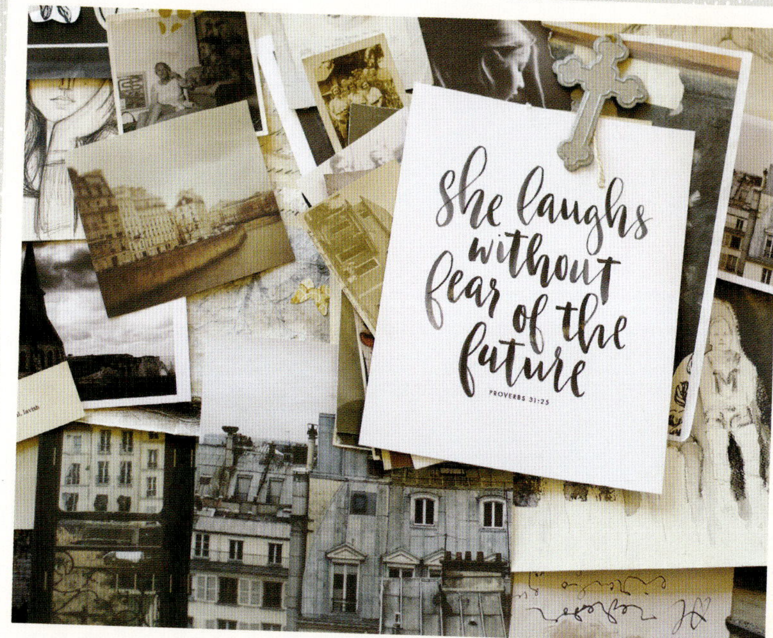

GATHER THIS
– *As you begin to gather items for your own storyboard, here are a few suggestions to get you started: colors, textures, images, art, quotes, magazine pages, objects, travel, architecture, history, family, vintage ephemera, fabrics and online searches regarding people or places.*

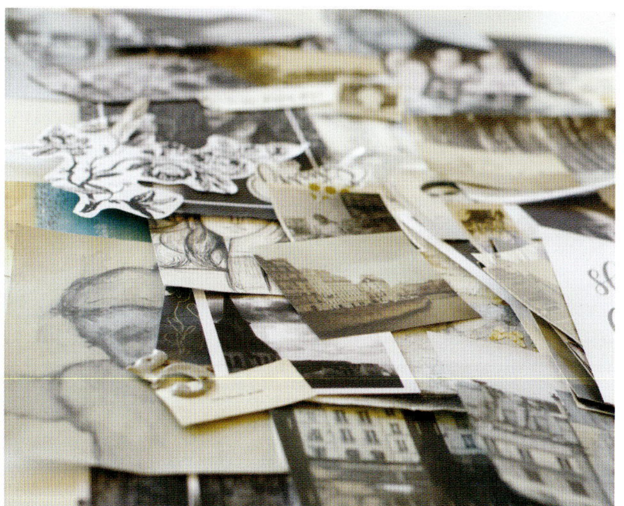

1 Use whatever space and tools you have on hand to display your board. This will be based upon whether you create a large storyboard or one in your art journal, on cardboard or on corkboard. There comes a time when you need to stop collecting and begin creating. Just like any form of supplies it can become a procrastinating tool if we aren't honoring of the process.

I find the gathering part of this exercise extremely relaxing and meditative, and it is fun to bring together all of these collections.

The real voyage of discovery consists not in seeking new landscapes but in having new eyes.

—*MARCEL PROUST*

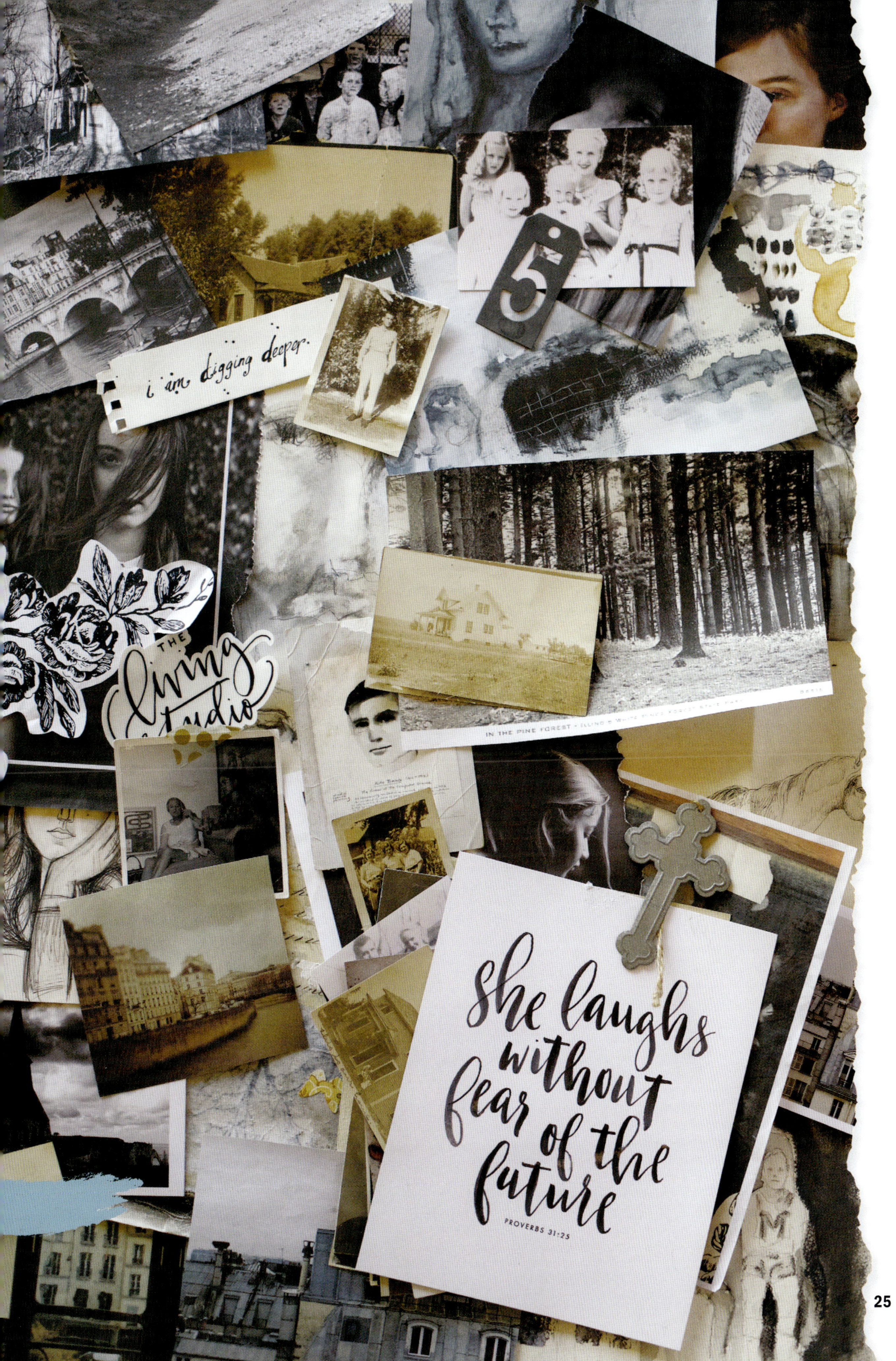

i am digging deeper.
THE living studio
5
she laughs without fear of the future
PROVERBS 31:25

Displaying Your Story

Find a place where you can display your storyboard whether it is a large wall or an art journal. Enjoy the process of choosing from what you have gathered and seeing your story come to life before you. This exercise can be one of the most beautiful ways to honor your research about your history, present and future. I found it became the archaeology of me, and it has been one of the most art-changing experiences of my creative life.

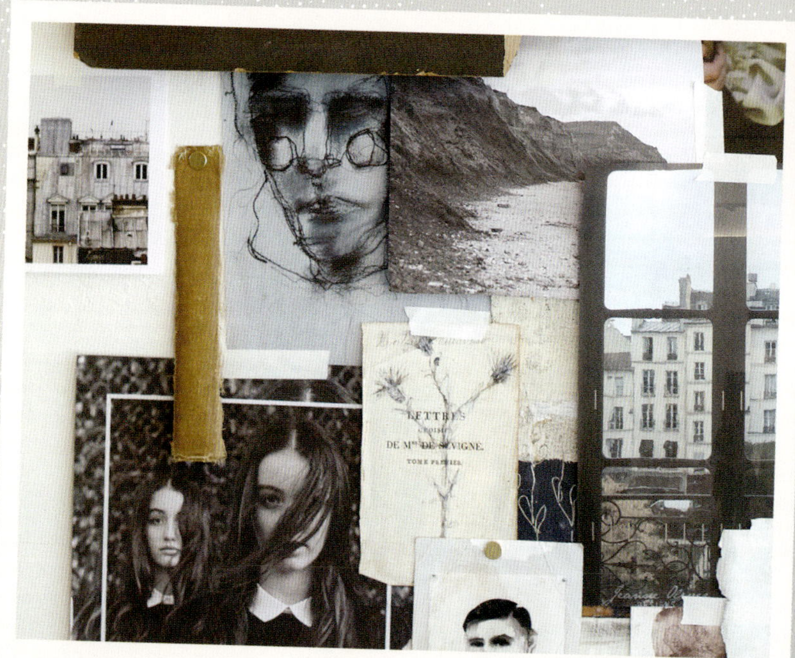

WHAT YOU NEED
- *Bulletin board (or wall)*
- *Gathered storyboard elements*
- *Paperclips*
- *Stapler*
- *Tape: washi, artist or masking*
- *Thumbtacks*

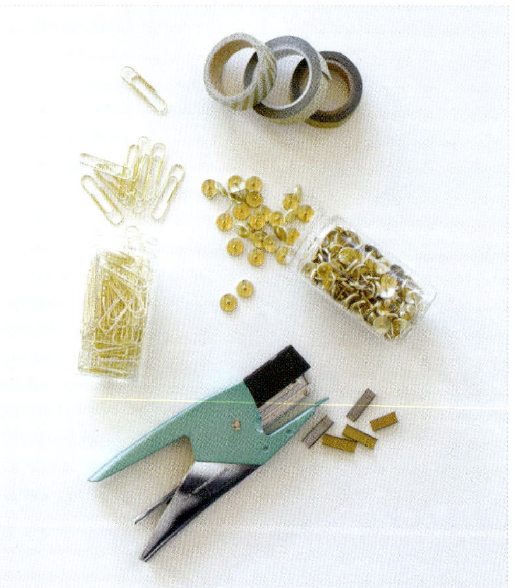

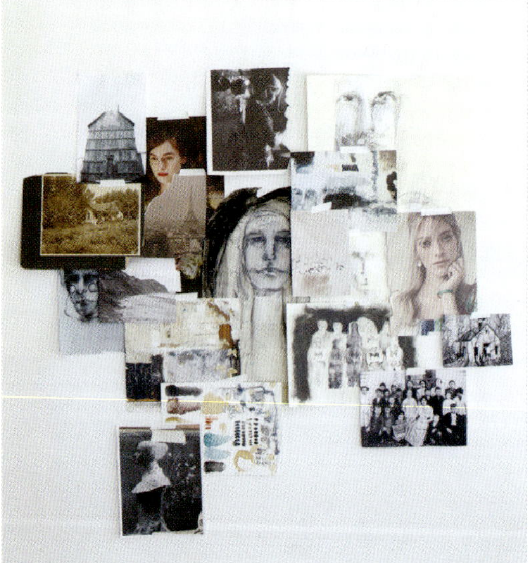

1 The first step in creating your storyboard is deciding on a location. I chose a wall in my studio because I intend to keep it up for ongoing inspiration. Artist's tape and thumbtacks work well for displaying the papers and images you're going to pull together. Decide whether you'll use an existing wall or a bulletin board. If you are limited by space, use cardboard or your journal.

2 Sort through what you've gathered, selecting images that speak to you most, and begin arranging them as you feel inspired. There were many images and objects I eventually did not include, yet still, when I look over my storyboard, I see bits of my story throughout. Play around with your elements and the arrangement until it feels good to you and reflects your own story.

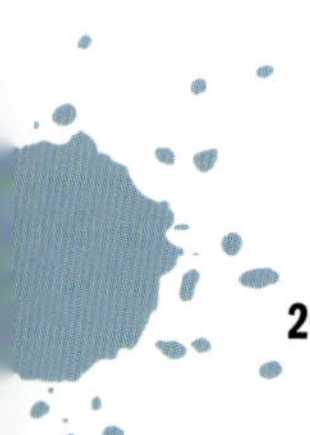

What does your storyboard show you?

> What is your color palette?

> What images are you most drawn to?

> Is there something in your past or present that you have never considered painting, sketching or incorporating into your art?

> What mark marking can be found?

> Could there be new inspiration for your art that is right in front of you?

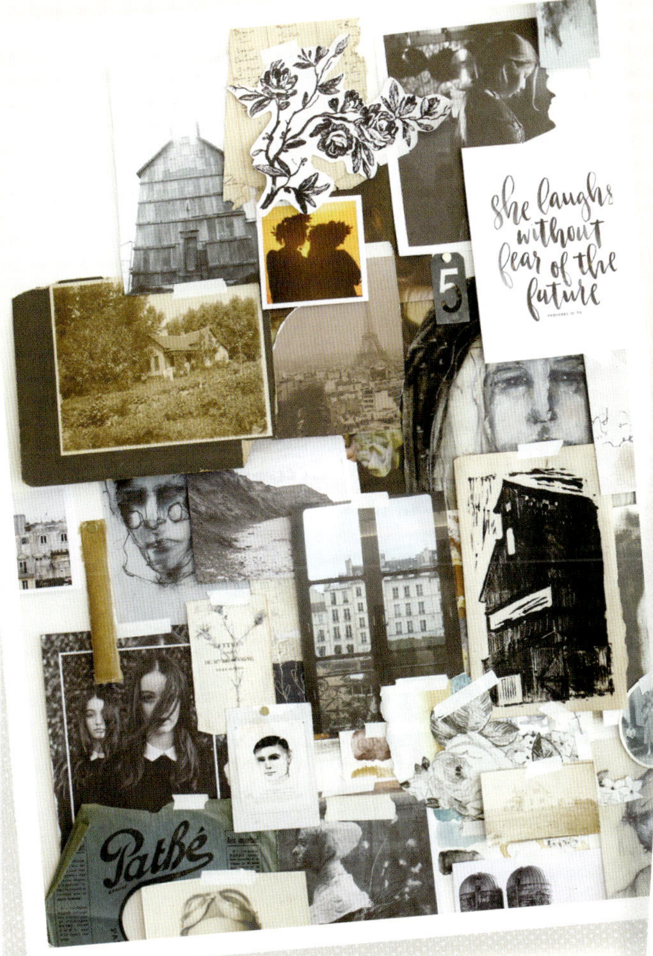

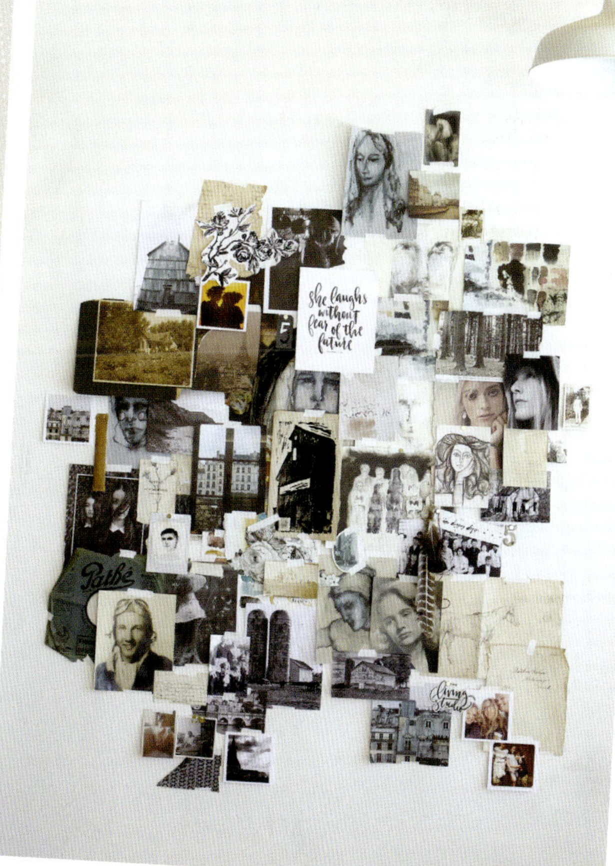

Here I'm able to see my love of type, vintage ephemera, travel, family, portraits, faith, mark making and the simple knowledge that sometimes I like things just because they are pretty. What do you see when you look at your board? Does anything surprise you?

When you feel stuck in your art, turn first to your storyboard and see if your creative block vanishes. You may be like me and decide to keep your storyboard up in your creative space long after the projects in this book are complete, so you can keep adding new inspiration to it and rearranging it when you feel it's necessary.

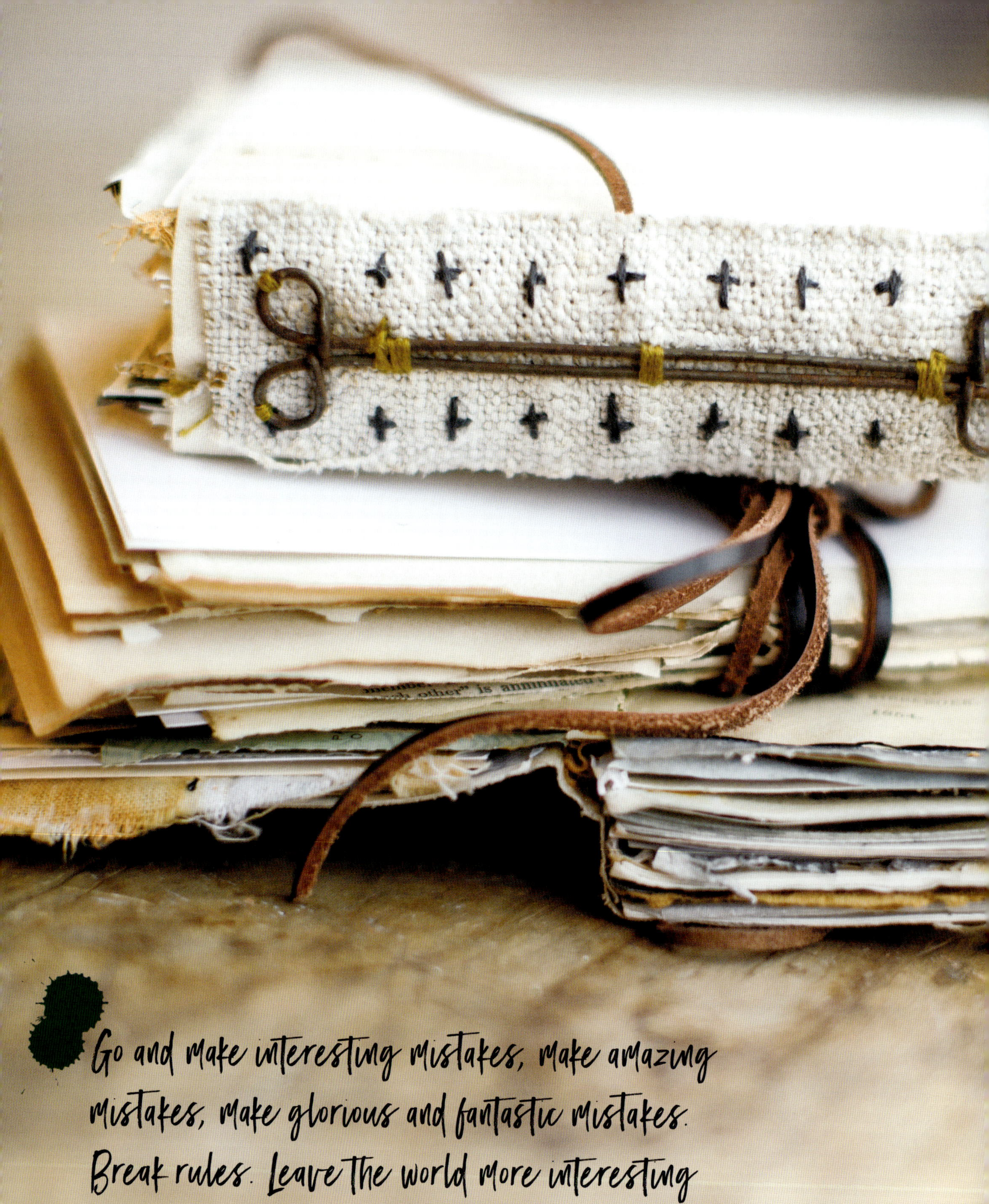

Go and make interesting mistakes, make amazing mistakes, make glorious and fantastic mistakes. Break rules. Leave the world more interesting for your being here. Make. Bad. Art.

—NEIL GAIMAN

CHAPTER 5

Alternative Journal Options

OFTEN WE MIGHT FIND OURSELVES EQUATING THE PURCHASE OF MORE and more art supplies with making more art. Throughout this book, I will encourage you to use what you have, know the tools you use and practice all the time.

Have you ever waited to start a new project until you found the perfect journal, and once you found that perfect journal you were afraid to make one mark on those perfect pages? I think we have all found ourselves there at one time or another. When I began thinking outside of the box in regards to what I could use as an art journal, I saw my fear of the blank page disappear.

I love history, stories and pieces with a past. It is no surprise to me that I would be drawn to vintage papers, books and ledgers. I have found these vintage gems to be the most freeing tools. When you have an alternative art journal that already has the perfect patina and often gorgeous script, then it is not as scary to put down that first mark.

You may find that you already have an old book on hand that you will not miss if you choose to transform it into your newest art journal. Let's talk about how to prep some of my favorite alternative art journals—vintage books and ledgers—and why.

If you feel you would prefer using a new journal, there are several wonderful, affordable new journals that I love and use. I have sourced them in the materials section.

Setting up a Vintage Book as Your Journal

Using a vintage ledger or hardbound book is not only an economical option for your journal, it's also a beautiful way to connect to and suggest a sense of history. There are just a few steps you'll want to take to prepare your chosen book for painting, and we'll go over those three things in this section.

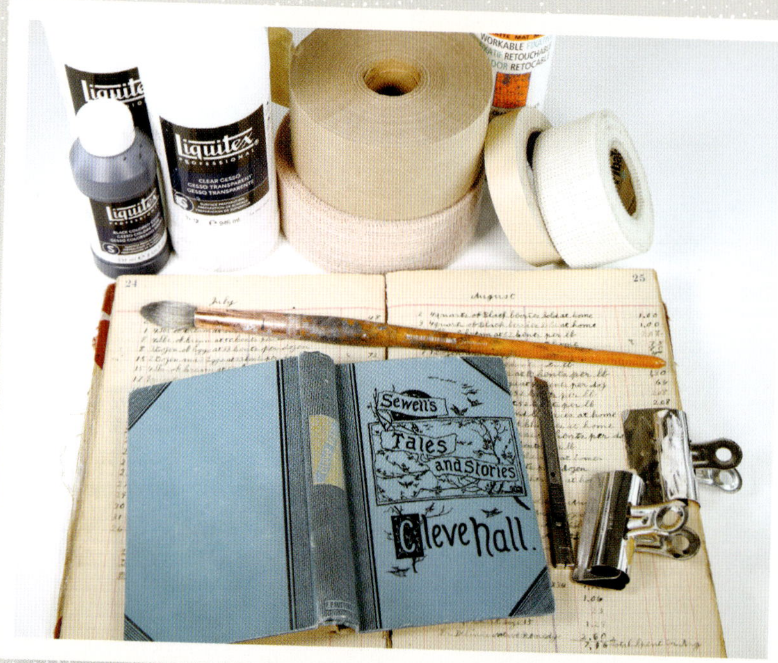

WHAT YOU NEED

- Binder clips

- Craft knife

- Gesso: black, clear or white

- Paintbrush: medium or large

- Scissors

- Spray fixative (optional)

- Tapes, assorted (drywall, masking, brown packing, etc.)

- Vintage book or ledger

REMOVING PAGES

When using a vintage book as an alternative art journal, you may need to create room within the book for your art. This is simple to do by cutting out some of the pages throughout the book. This will not only allow more room for your mediums but also help the book close more easily.

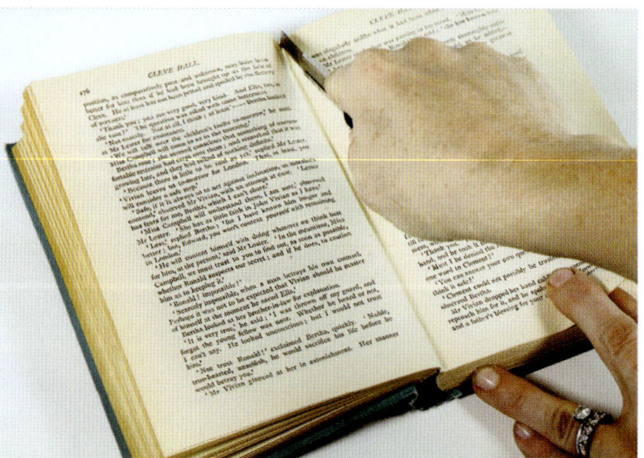

1 Randomly go through your vintage book and, using a craft knife, cut out five to twenty pages at a time by running the knife along the spine. Cut out ¼ of the book to start, then remove more as needed. Don't worry about perfection. Allow the randomness and imperfections to add to the beauty of your journal.

Gesso, paints and other mediums can add a lot of bulk to your pages. As you create, you may find that you need to cut out additional pages over time. Vintage book art journals are worth the extra time and effort.

Tip

If you are using a vintage ledger that has handwriting in ink, you may want to test a small corner with the gesso to make sure the ink will not bleed. If you find that the ink is beginning to smear, I suggest spraying a workable fixative, such as Grumbacher matte workable fixative, over the pages, allowing it to dry and then proceeding with your gesso.

MAKING REINFORCEMENTS

Often when working with vintage papers, books and ledgers you will find loose pages, broken spines and lack of structural integrity. I think this can add to the beauty of your art journal if you embrace the age and imperfection and add support throughout with an assortment of drywall tape, brown packing tape and even artist's tape or masking tape. Each of these choices will later become a beautiful layer in your work and add stability to your journal.

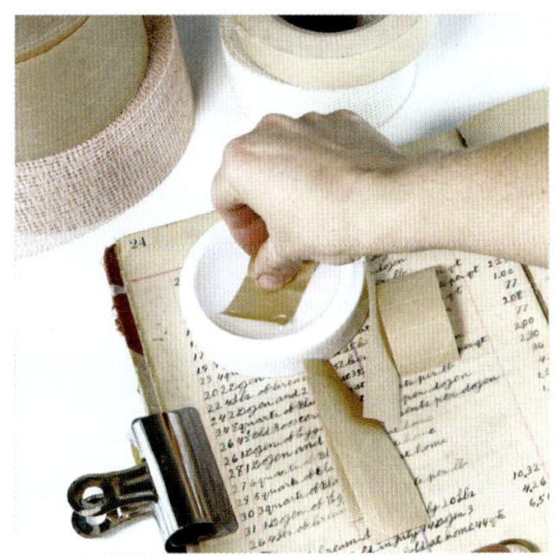

1 Brown packing tape is an excellent way to reinforce your pages. Wet the strips and apply them where you need extra strength.

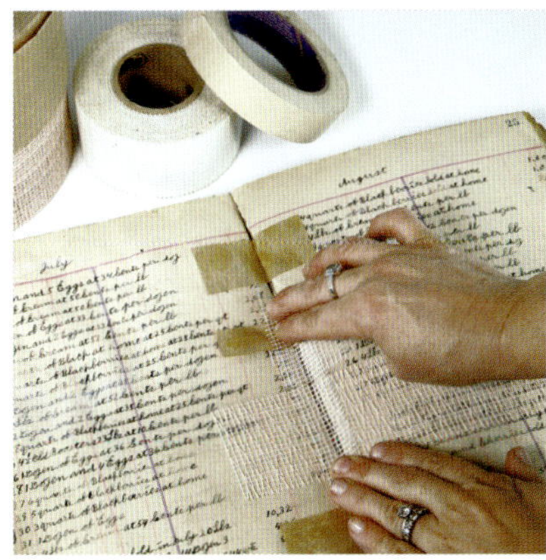

2 Don't be afraid to use multiple kinds of tape. Mix masking tape, brown packing tape and even drywall tape for strength and interest on your pages.

APPLYING GESSO

When you are working on any substrate that can absorb your mediums, you will want to prime them with gesso. Gesso will be the foundation to allow layers of several mediums.

Gesso comes in clear, white or black and can be used to prime almost any surface. For this demonstration, we will be priming vintage book and ledger pages to prepare them for various mediums.

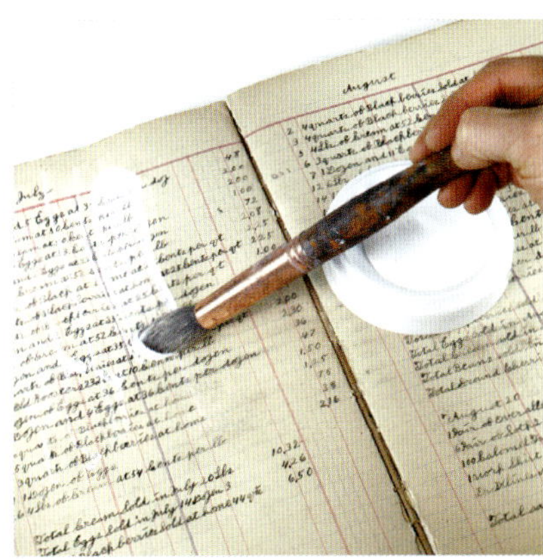

1 I use clear gesso often because I love the grit that it brings to the page and also because it allows me to see the detail of the vintage pages below. It dries quickly, and my page has the primer it needs to not absorb my medium.

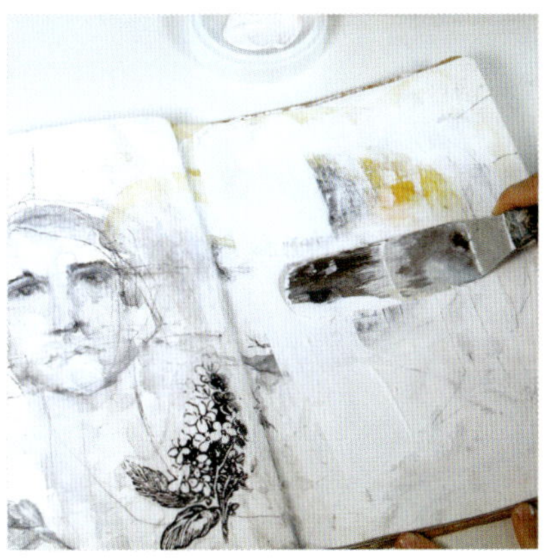

2 Just like clear gesso, white gesso is a primer but with pigment.

White gesso is also the perfect tool when you are not in love with a piece of your practice and want to cover all or some of it. You can apply the white gesso and then scrape parts of it off while it is wet to reveal parts of the work below. Once it dries, you have a page ready for you to begin again or to add to a part that you were connecting with.

White gesso is also a medium I use with many of my water-soluble tools. We will explore this medium and alternative ways to use it later in the book.

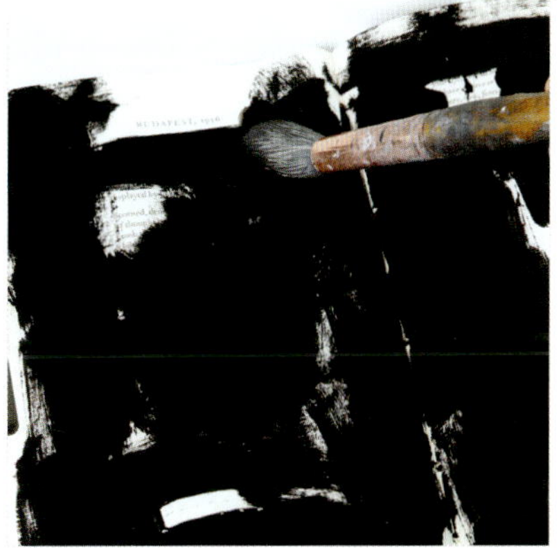

3 Black gesso allows you to prime but with black pigment and depth. This is the perfect primer for when you want to completely cover the pages underneath or to bring more emotion to your piece even on the first layer.

Hand-Binding a Journal

One of the most relaxing parts of my creative process is the gathering. I love gathering words from newspapers and magazines, images that speak to me, color palettes, quick sketches of patterns I find while exploring, marks and art that I have made, photos and, of course, vintage papers and book spines. These are treasures to me. As much as I love gathering, I also don't want to surround myself with inspiration I don't use, so this gathering, for me, is a tool. In the process of gathering I figure out where my next piece will go, what is inspiring me right now, what palette I will use and what I need and want to say through my art.

I have found that one of most satisfying ways to transform these collected pieces

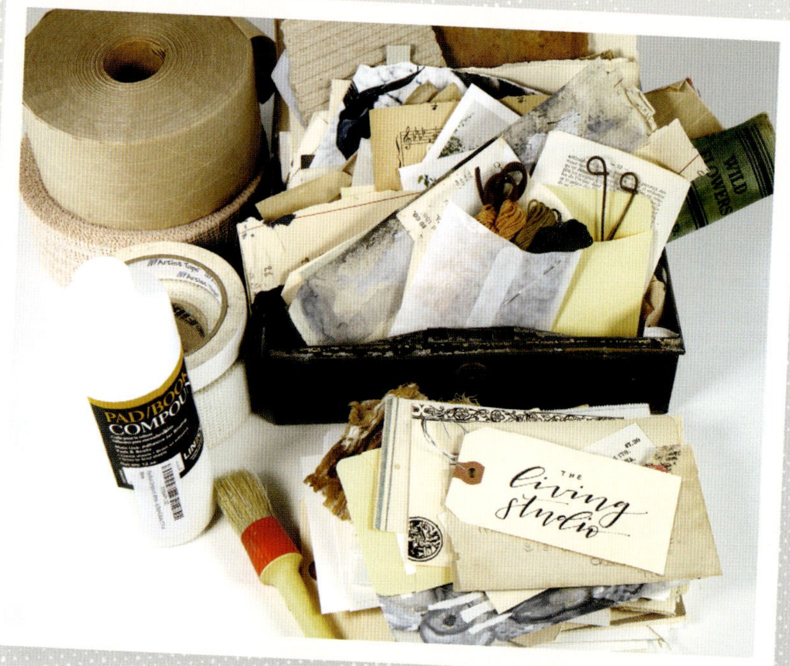

is to create small handmade journals that feed my bigger story.

When we bring together a pool of beautiful bits and pieces, we create a larger view into what we find lovely. This is just for you. No one else has to get it or confirm for you what catches your heart and eye. When you are finished putting together

this hand-bound journal, you will hold in your hands a book full of ready-to-use canvases for journaling on that are instantly a reflection of things you love. Something so loved holds no intimidation and only peace to begin your more in-depth forms of expression.

WHAT YOU NEED
- Book adhesive (PVA or similar compound)
- Embroidery thread
- Glue gun
- Fabric
- Leather cord, 36" to 60" (91cm to 152cm)
- Paintbrush, medium (inexpensive for gluing)
- Pencil
- Ruler
- Rusty pieces (nails, wire or other)
- Scissors
- Sticky-back canvas
- Watercolor paper cut to 4" × 6" (10cm × 15cm) pieces

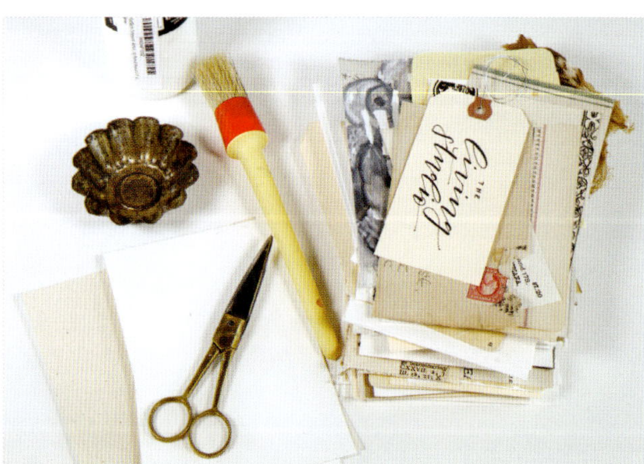

1 Begin by cutting the items you've gathered to generally the same size. 4" × 6" (10cm × 15cm) is a nice size to start with. If you have smaller pieces, don't hesitate to include them; it's OK to have a few smaller pieces in the mix as they will make wonderful mini canvases throughout your journal.

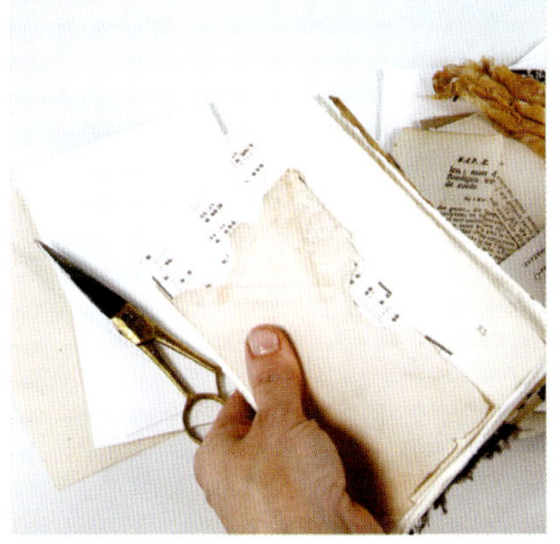

2 Organize all of your items in the order that you want them. Feel free to place them upside down, some closer to the top and others to the bottom, and don't forget to incorporate the small pieces to give your journal more interest. Put a heavier front and back cover on your stack of papers. I used watercolor paper.

Ideas to include in your hand-bound journal

- > vintage papers
- > watercolor paper
- > mixed-media paper
- > charcoal paper
- > handmade papers
- > fabric
- > photos
- > deli paper

- > your art cut into pieces
- > library index cards and pocket holders
- > tracing paper
- > dried tea bags
- > gauze
- > images printed out on tracing paper
- > sketches

- > kraft paper
- > large paper tags
- > photocopies of photographs or your art
- > postcards
- > envelopes
- > letters
- > cheesecloth

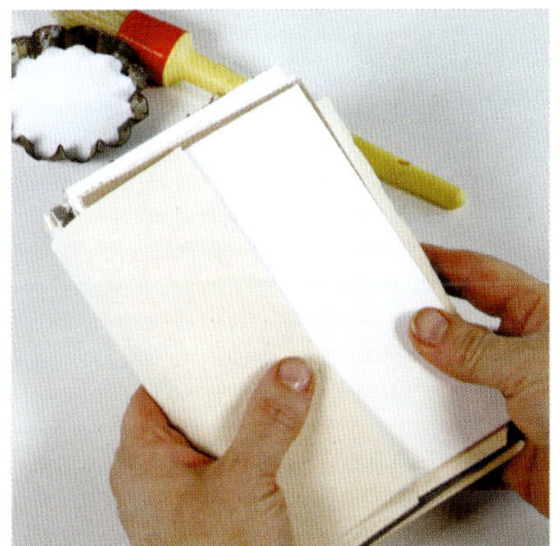

3 Cut sticky-back canvas to 6" × 6" (15cm × 15cm). With your whole pile of papers together, place the spine side of the pile in the center of the sticky canvas (with the backing paper still intact). This will allow you to judge where you want to attach the canvas to the front and back covers. Place a small mark on the front and back covers where the edge of the canvas will be, and then take the pile of papers away. Remove the wax paper from the back of the canvas and attach the canvas to both covers where marked.

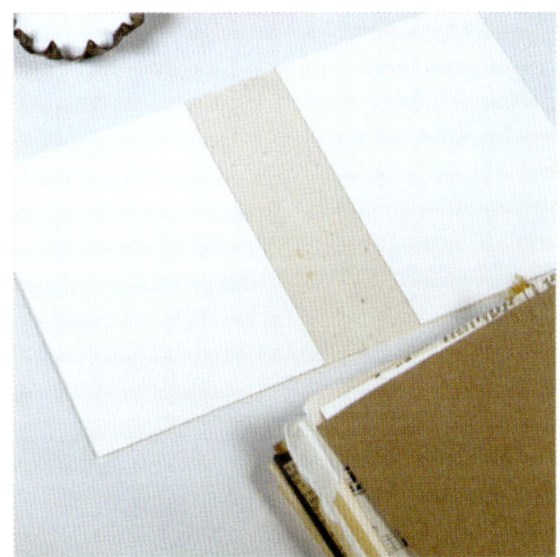

4 Lay the covers and canvas sticky side up on the table. Pour some binding compound into a small container and have a medium-sized, inexpensive paintbrush ready.

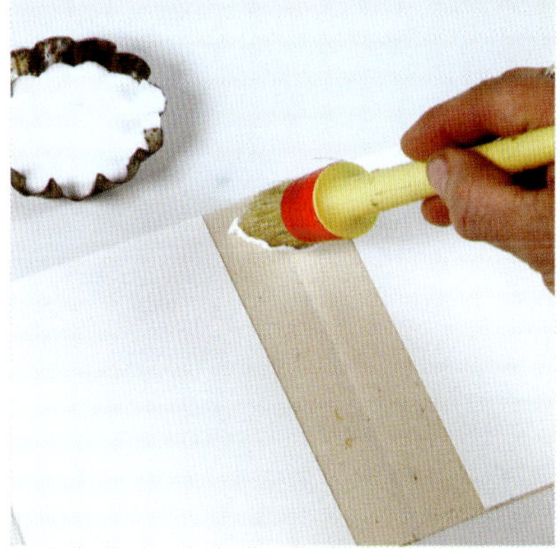

5 Apply a nice layer of glue to the canvas. The glue should be opaque enough without being so thick it drips.

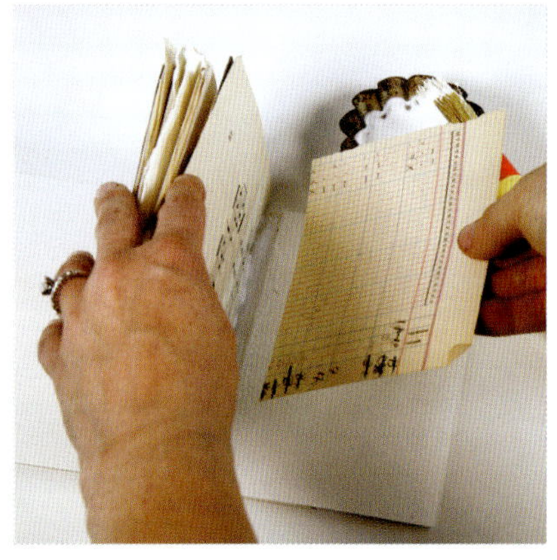

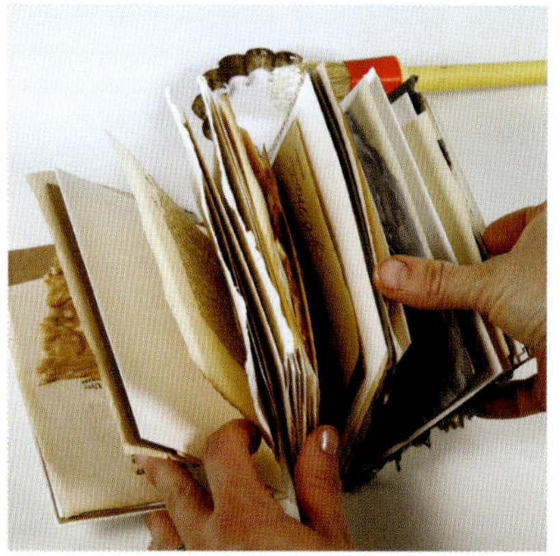

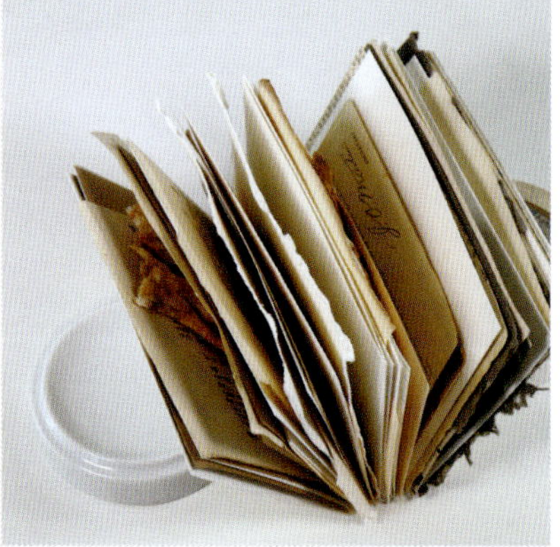

6 Working from the left to the right side of the spine, add your collection of papers and other findings. Be careful not to hold the papers tight while gluing and prevent the book from opening fully once dry.

7 Add more glue as needed but be careful to not add too much glue; that will end up with glue moving up the papers and result in pages sticking together. We are primarily trying to glue down the spine edge of the papers, but if 1/16" (2mm) or so of the pages stick together, it will be OK.

8 Once all papers/fabrics, etc., have been glued down, prop up both sides of your journal with small objects to allow the glue to dry while the journal is on its spine.

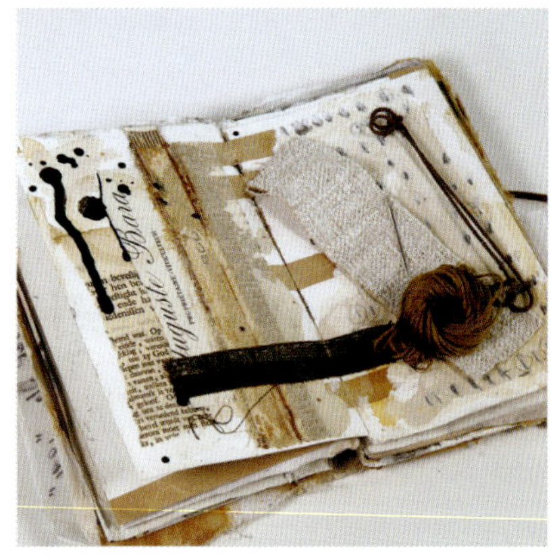

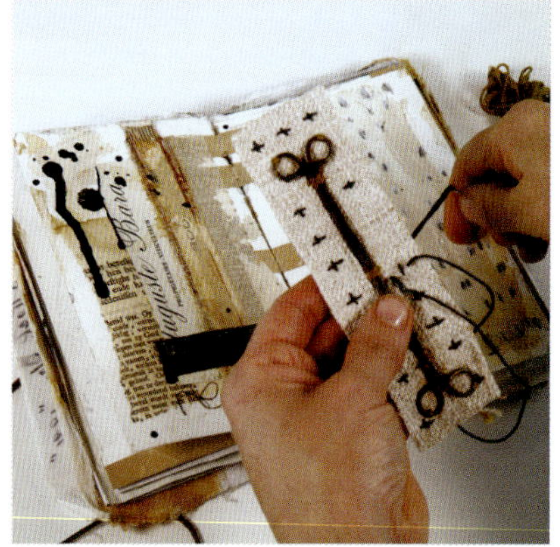

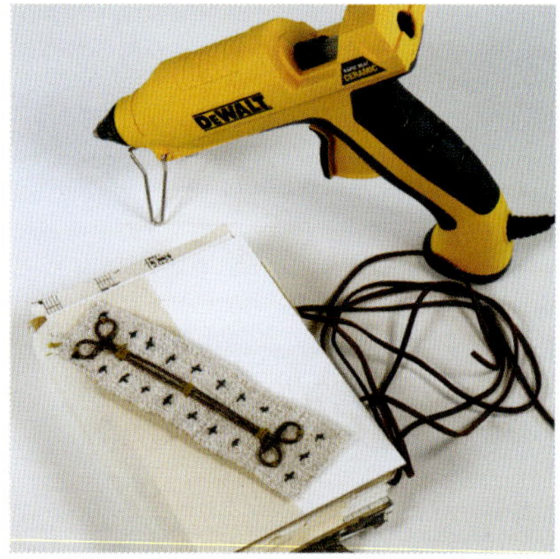

9 While your journal is drying you can create your decorative spine. Gather a glue gun, fabric (I am using vintage French linen), rusty found metal pieces, embroidery thread and leather cord. Once again, look around and find what you have on hand already. Cut fabric or canvas to 5½" × 1¾" (14cm × 4cm).

10 Using embroidery thread, attach your rusty pieces and create marks on the fabric using simple stitches. I made simple cross marks. Look around you for marks and patterns in your daily life.

11 Once the glue has dried in your journal and you have created your altered fabric spine, it is time to bring all the pieces together.

An awake heart is like a sky that pours light.

—HAFEZ

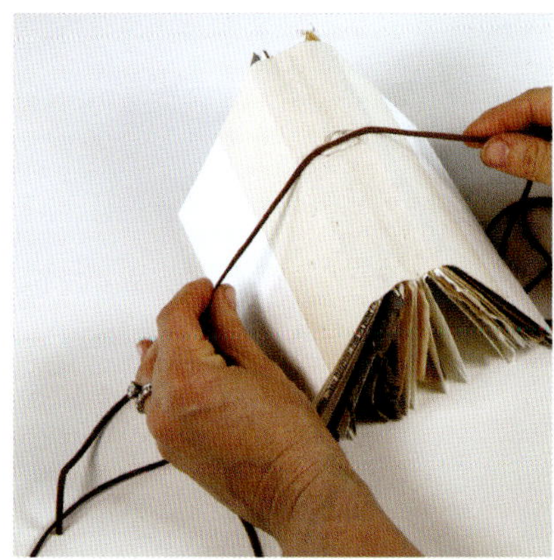 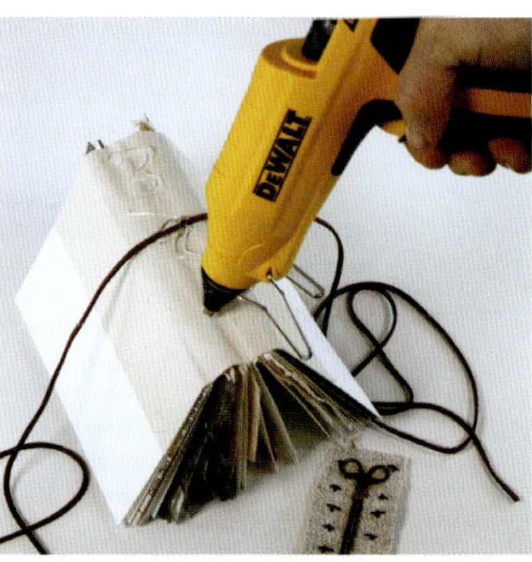 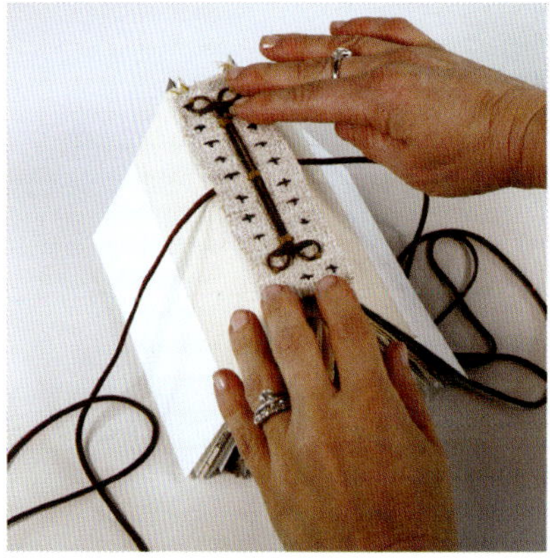

12 Cut the leather cord to a length that will allow you to wrap it around the journal multiple times. My cord was 60" (152cm) long. Using hot glue, adhere the center of the cord to the center of the spine.

13 Apply binding compound or hot glue to the spine.

14 Adhere your altered fabric spine on top of the leather strip. Allow to dry.

Your hand-bound journal is now ready for your first sketch!

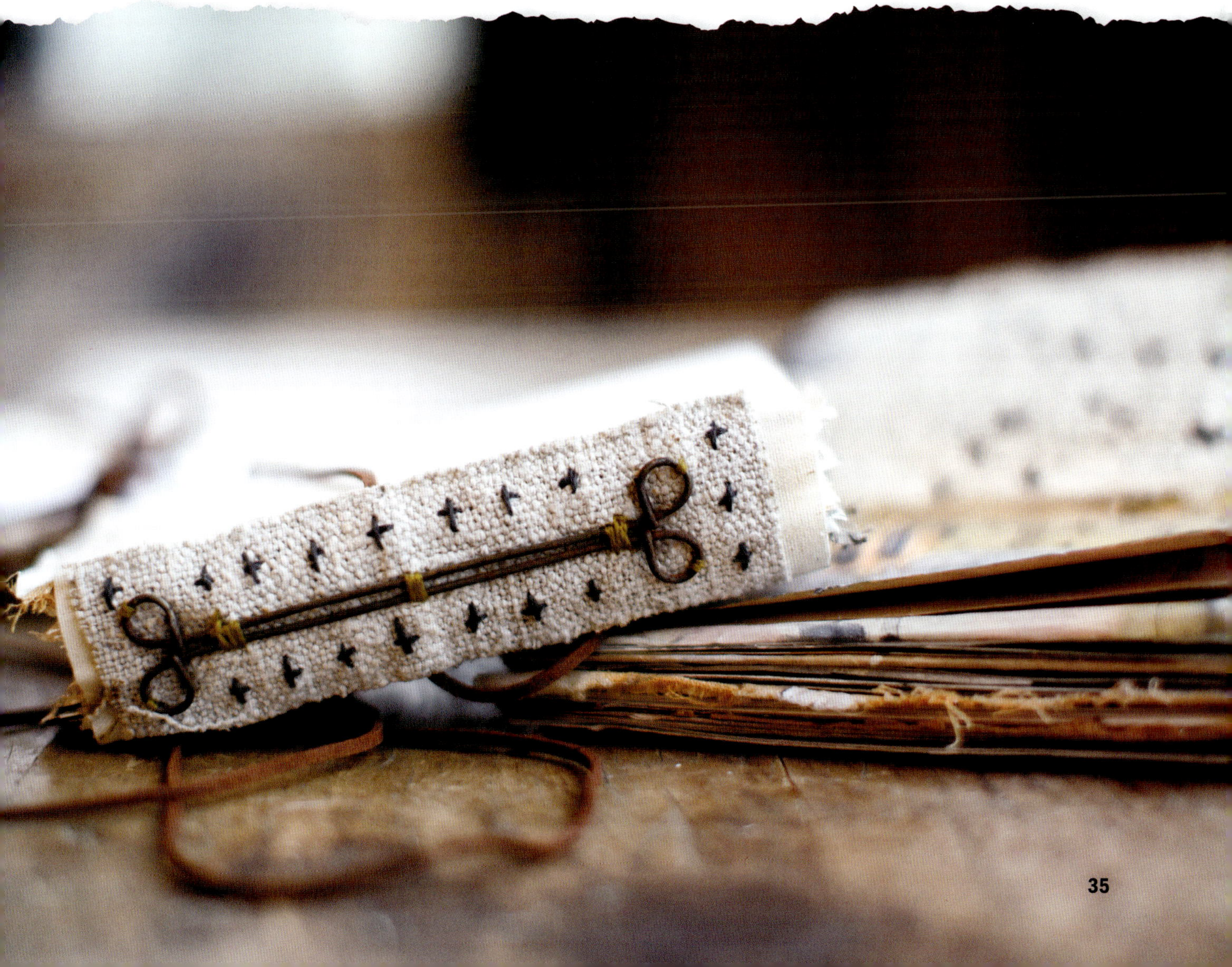

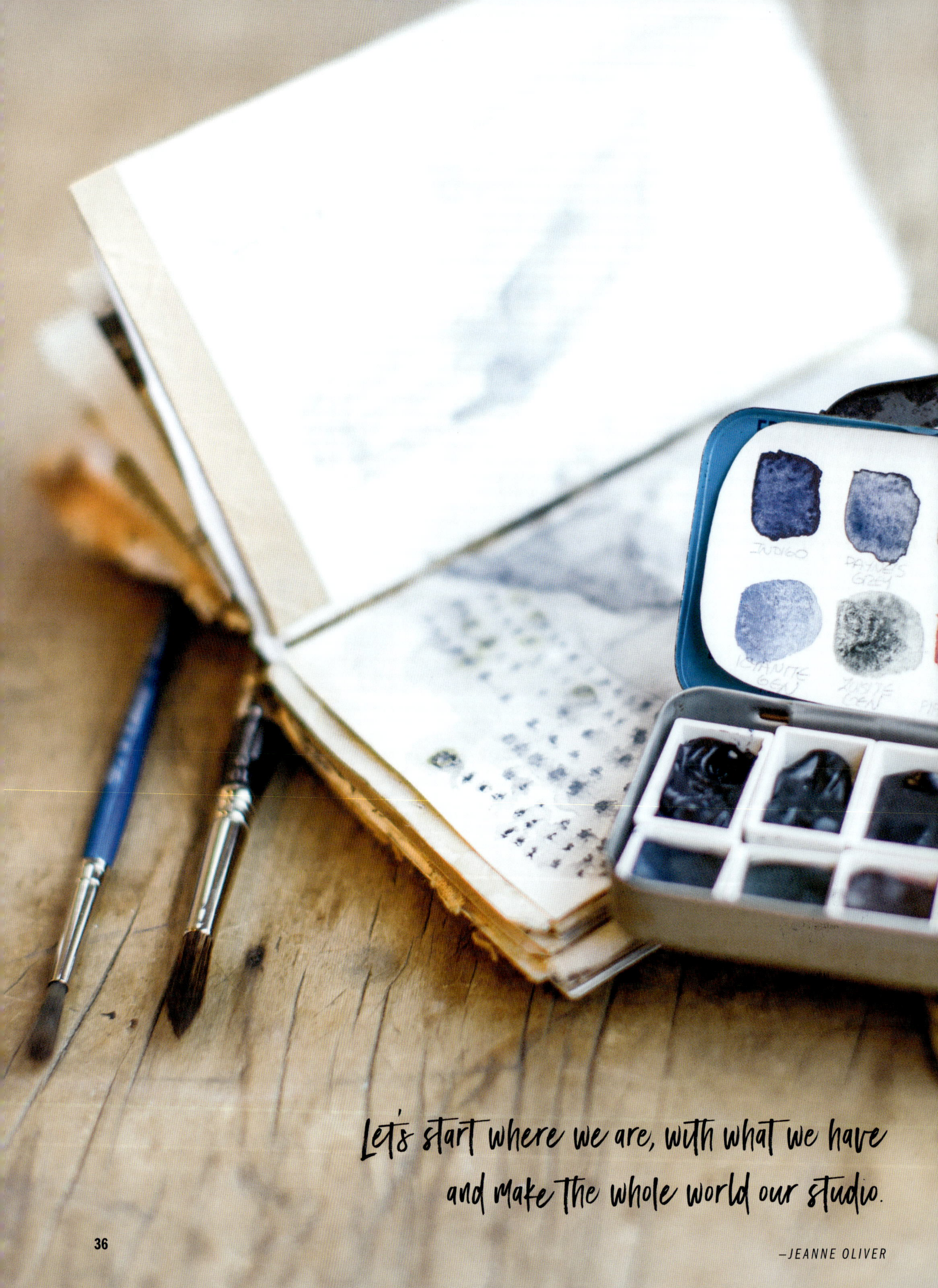

Let's start where we are, with what we have
and make the whole world our studio.

—JEANNE OLIVER

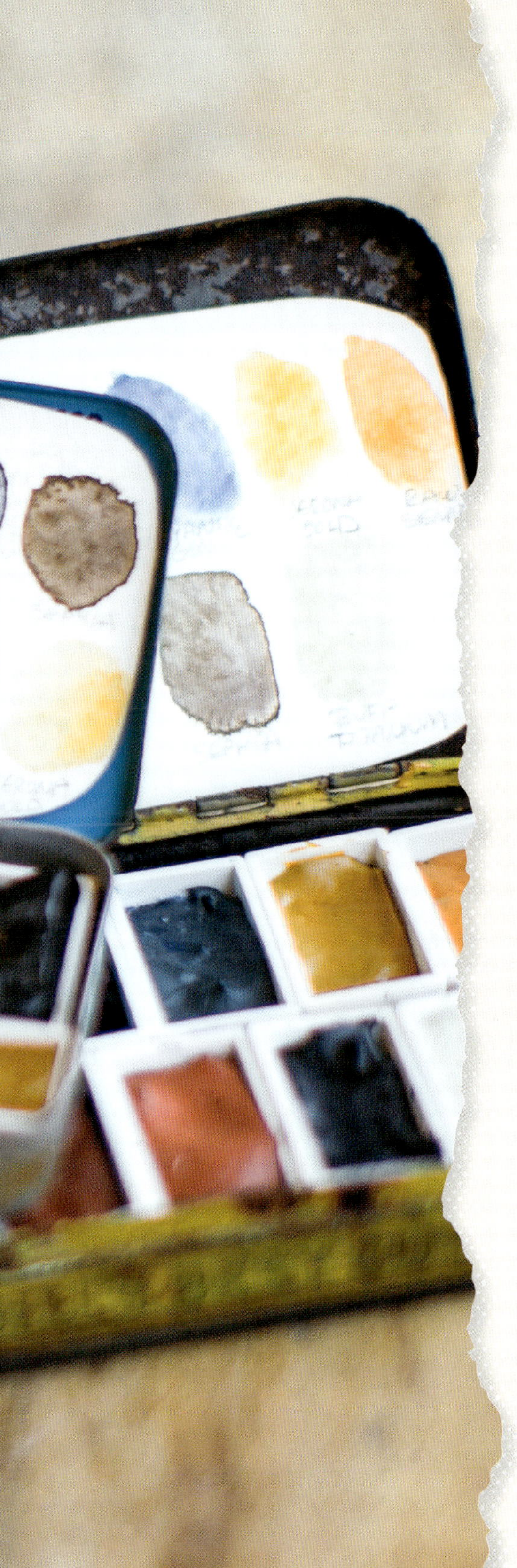

CHAPTER 6

Creating a Portable Studio

TELLING OUR STORIES THROUGH OUR ART DOES NOT need to happen only in our creative spaces. So often we forget that our creative space can be found on the front porch, at the local café, time in the car waiting and a thousand other alternative places where we can choose our art over our phones. The simple and intentional act of being prepared can make all of the difference in our day-to-day for practicing, gathering and storytelling.

So let's focus our supplies to find freedom in our art. Using a small bag, limited palette and only our most favorite tools, we will create a studio that can go with you anywhere. Get lost in the beauty of practice and watch your story and your art unfold.

Create a Portable Watercolor Palette

I am not a watercolor artist but I love to include watercolors in my art journaling because they are a portable and convenient medium. They allow me to include highly pigmented color anywhere I go. I do not like buying premade sets of nearly any medium, and this applies especially to watercolors. If you're like me, you may find that if you buy a set of paints put together by a manufacturer, many of the colors included are not in your personal palette, the colors you'll want to return to over and over. This leaves you with unused supplies and wasted money.

Using a vintage tin, tubes of watercolor and empty watercolor pans, let's create a watercolor set to go along with that palette you have just discovered.

If you don't yet know your palette, go to Project 7 first.

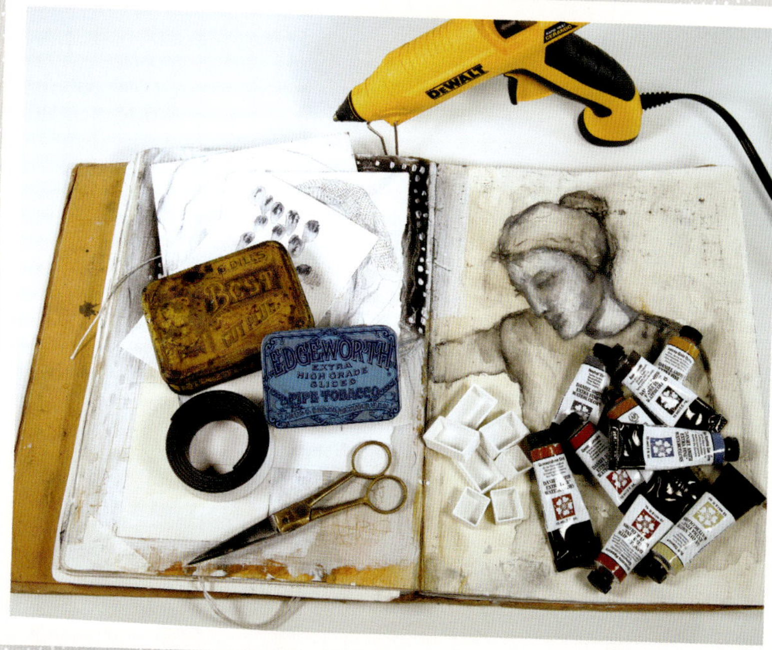

WHAT YOU NEED
- Glue gun
- Magnetic tape strip
- Mechanical pencil
- Scissors
- Vintage tin, small
- Water container
- Watercolor paintbrush
- Watercolor pans, individual small
- Watercolor paper cut to small pieces, approximately 1" × 1½" (3cm × 4cm)
- Watercolor tubes, colors in your personal palette

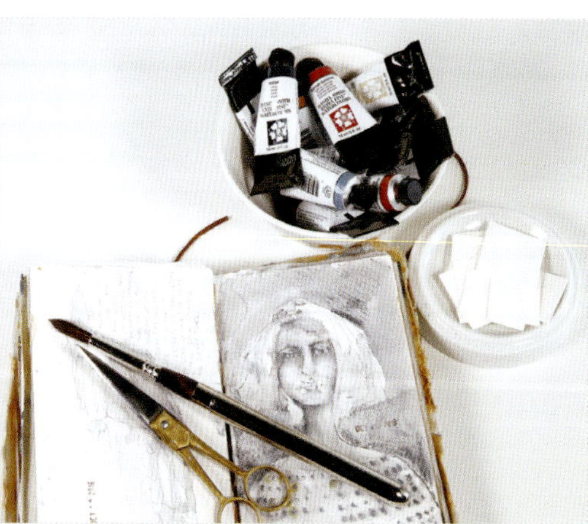

1 Gather your tube watercolors and watercolor paper pieces to sample the colors you have collected.

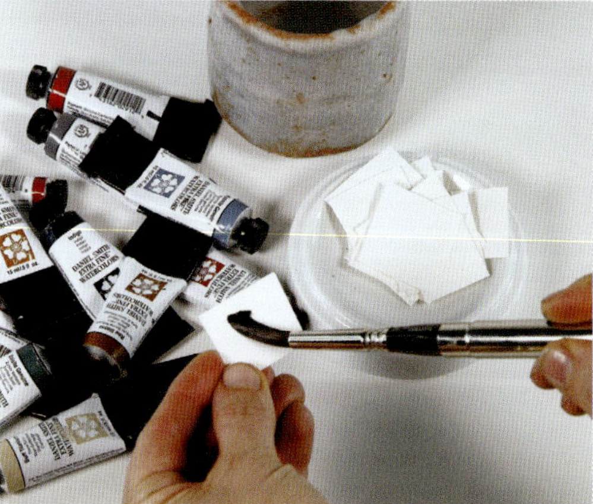

2 Paint a small amount of each color you're considering for your portable palette on a watercolor paper square. With a mechanical pencil write the name of the tube watercolor on the paper.

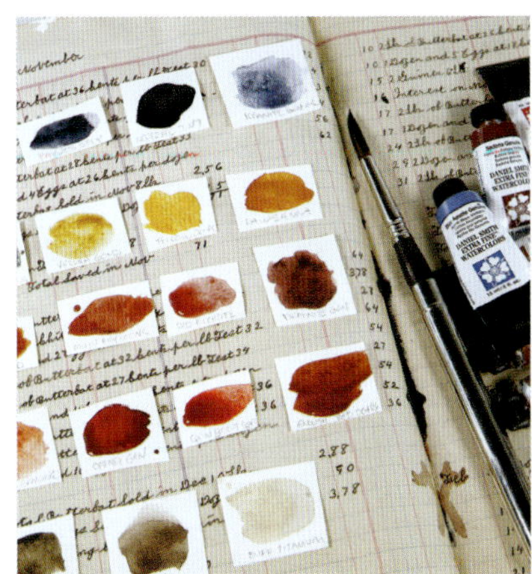

3 Lay out all of the watercolor squares to narrow down which colors will be added to your portable palette.

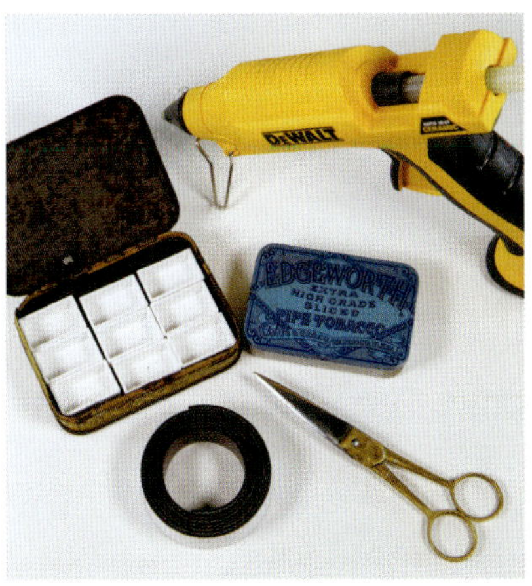

4 Gather your empty tin, empty watercolor pans, scissors, glue gun and magnetic strip. Be certain your pans fit into the vintage tin you have chosen.

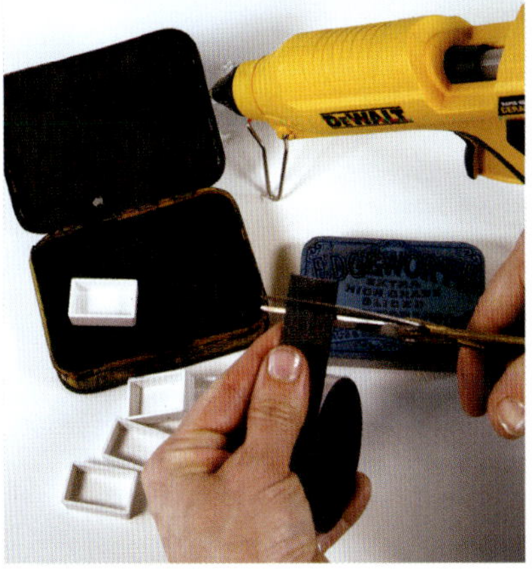

5 Magnetic self-adhesive tape allows you to move your paint colors around within the tin and also keeps them in place while you are out and about. If you later choose to replace a color, it makes doing so very simple. Cut a small piece of the magnetic tape for the bottom of each empty pan.

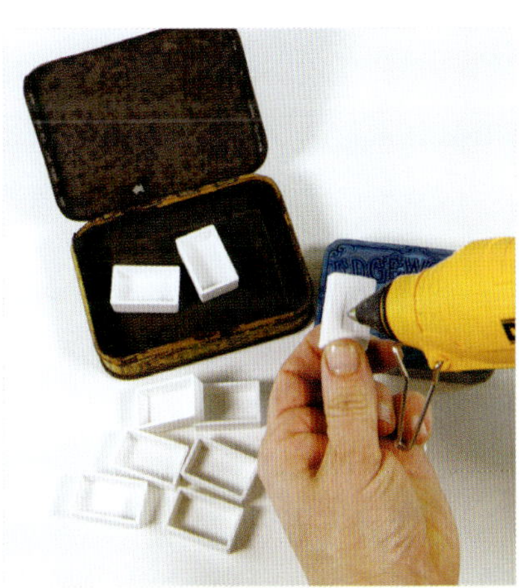

6 While the magnetic tape has adhesive on one side, it's good to reinforce things with a little hot glue because this will be a highly used tool. Adhere one small piece of magnetic tape to the underside of each pan.

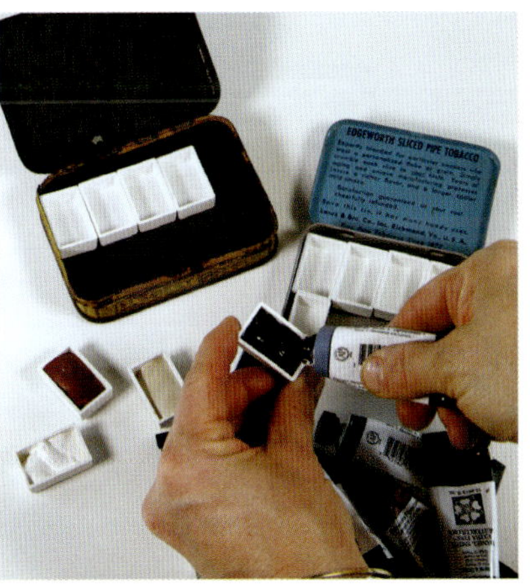

7 Fill the empty pans with your chosen watercolor paints. To do this, start squeezing paint into one corner and continue squeezing until the pan is full. Tap the pan on the table to help the paint to settle and then allow the paint to dry for 24–48 hours.

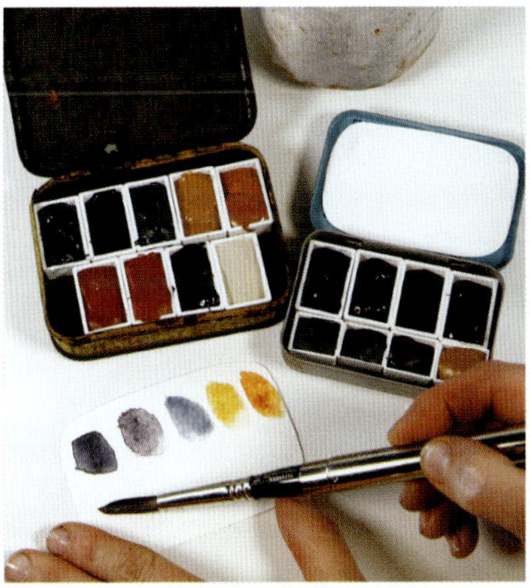

8 Because the dry paint looks different than it will when it's wet and applied to paper, it is handy to have a little palette cheat sheet. Cut out a piece of watercolor paper that fits into the lid of your palette, paint a sample of each color in order, and name each one of them.

Assemble a Tackle Box Studio

Always having a portable studio on hand has had one of the biggest impacts on my creative practice and growth as an artist. Selecting the right tools to fit into a small tackle box or makeup bag can keep you from overanalyzing where to start, gets you out of your head and brings you another step toward creative freedom.

When I started carrying a portable studio with me wherever I was going, it gave me permission to truly practice and to not be worried about the results. By putting together this portable studio, you too will gain more practice time, you will grow as an artist and you will collect more sketches and ideas for future works. Like me, you may find yourself doing mini studies and eventually having art journals full of stories you can't wait to expand upon.

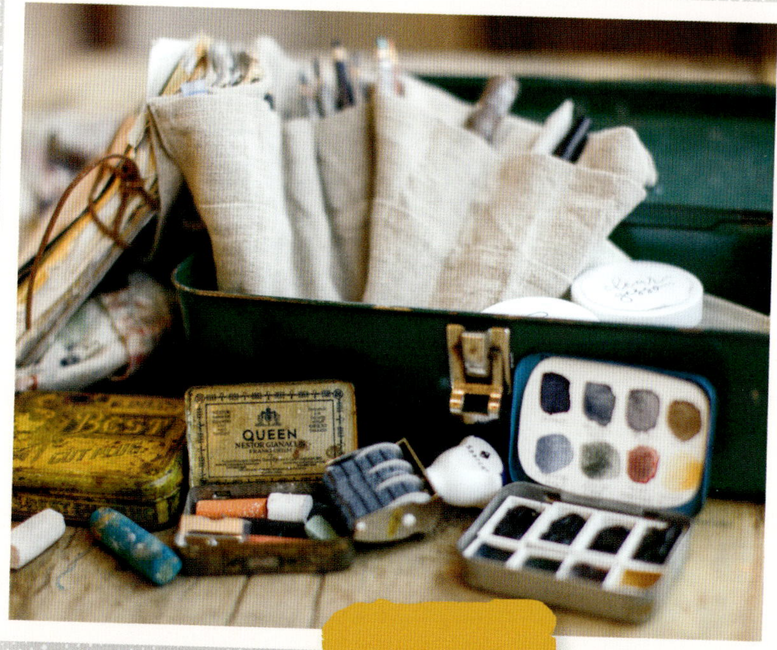

WHAT YOU NEED
- *Choose the supplies you use most often.*

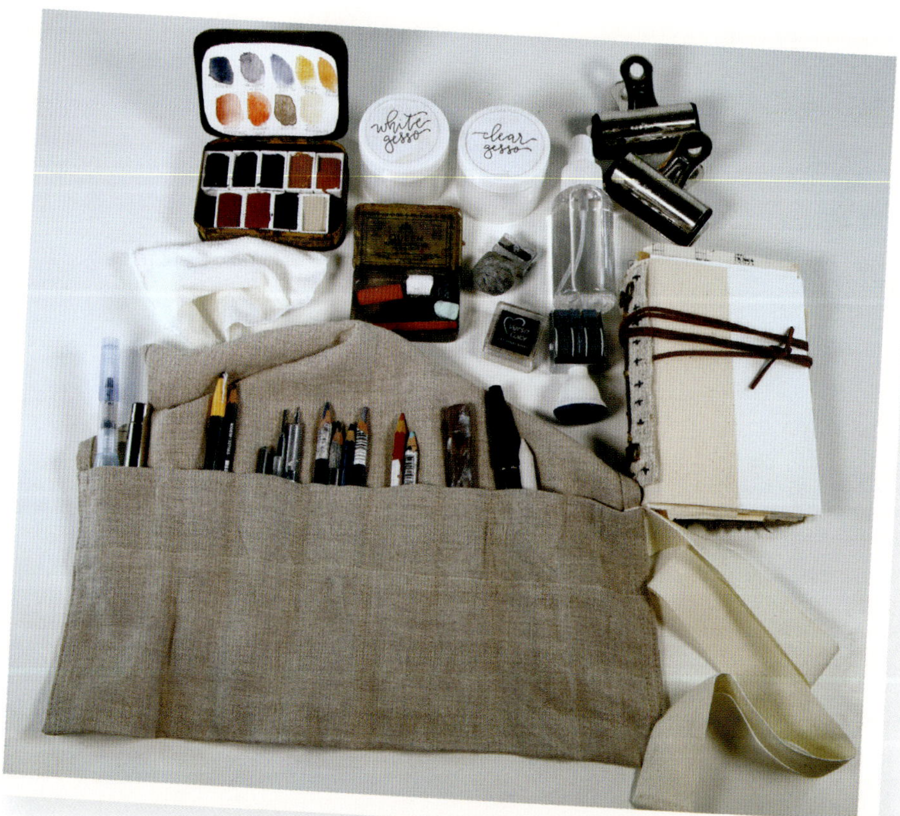

You may have a studio full of supplies, but you might never create on-the-go if you have to drag out all of your tools to create. A carefully edited portable studio encourages you to practice, collect and gather your story.

What's in My Portable Studio

- Binder clips
- Black pen, waterproof
- Charcoal pencil
- Craft knife
- Date stamp and ink
- Gesso, clear and white (go to the end of the book to find the link for the downloadable labels)
- Graphite: variety including a mechanical pencil
- Kneaded eraser
- Pencil sharpener
- Small journal
- Small tin of pastels, Conté Crayons, NeoColor II crayons
- Spray bottle
- Stabilo All pencil, black
- Water brush
- Watercolor palette
- Watercolor pencils

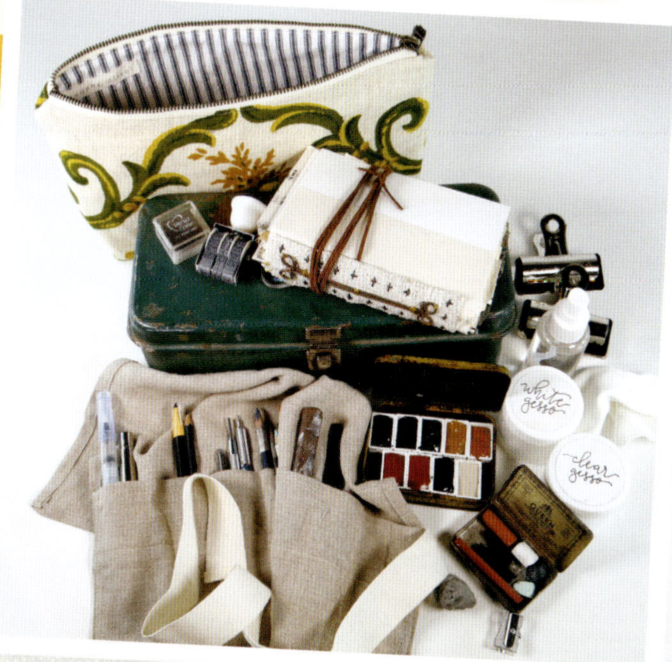

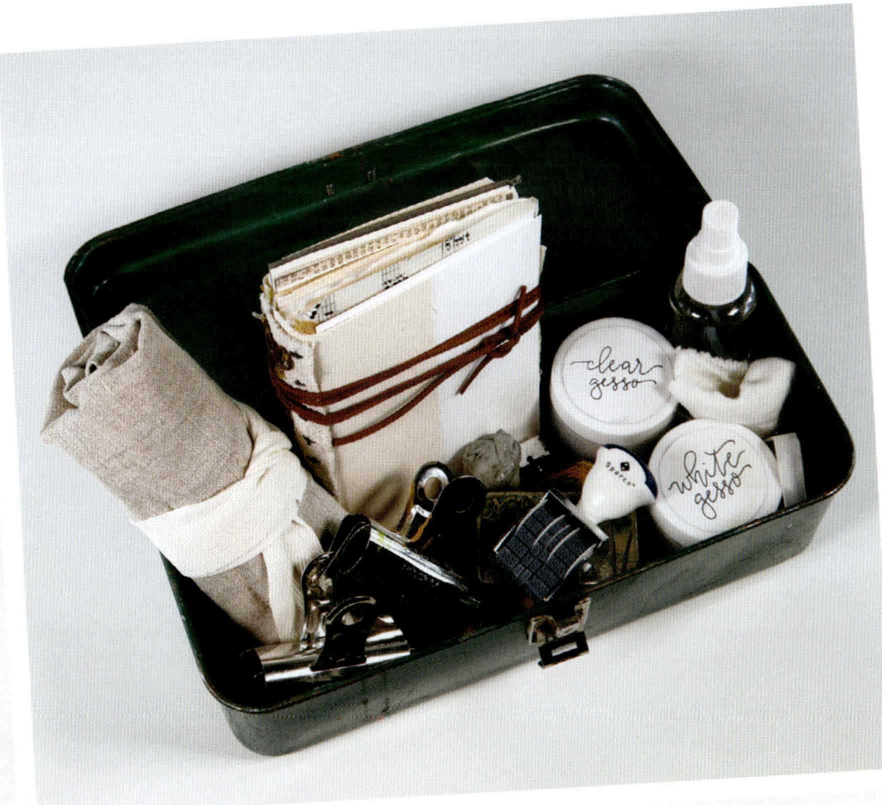

You don't need much to create a beautiful and usable portable studio. Your collection of tools will look different than mine, but I hope this shows you that you don't need as much as you may think to practice more and to engage in living a more creative life each day.

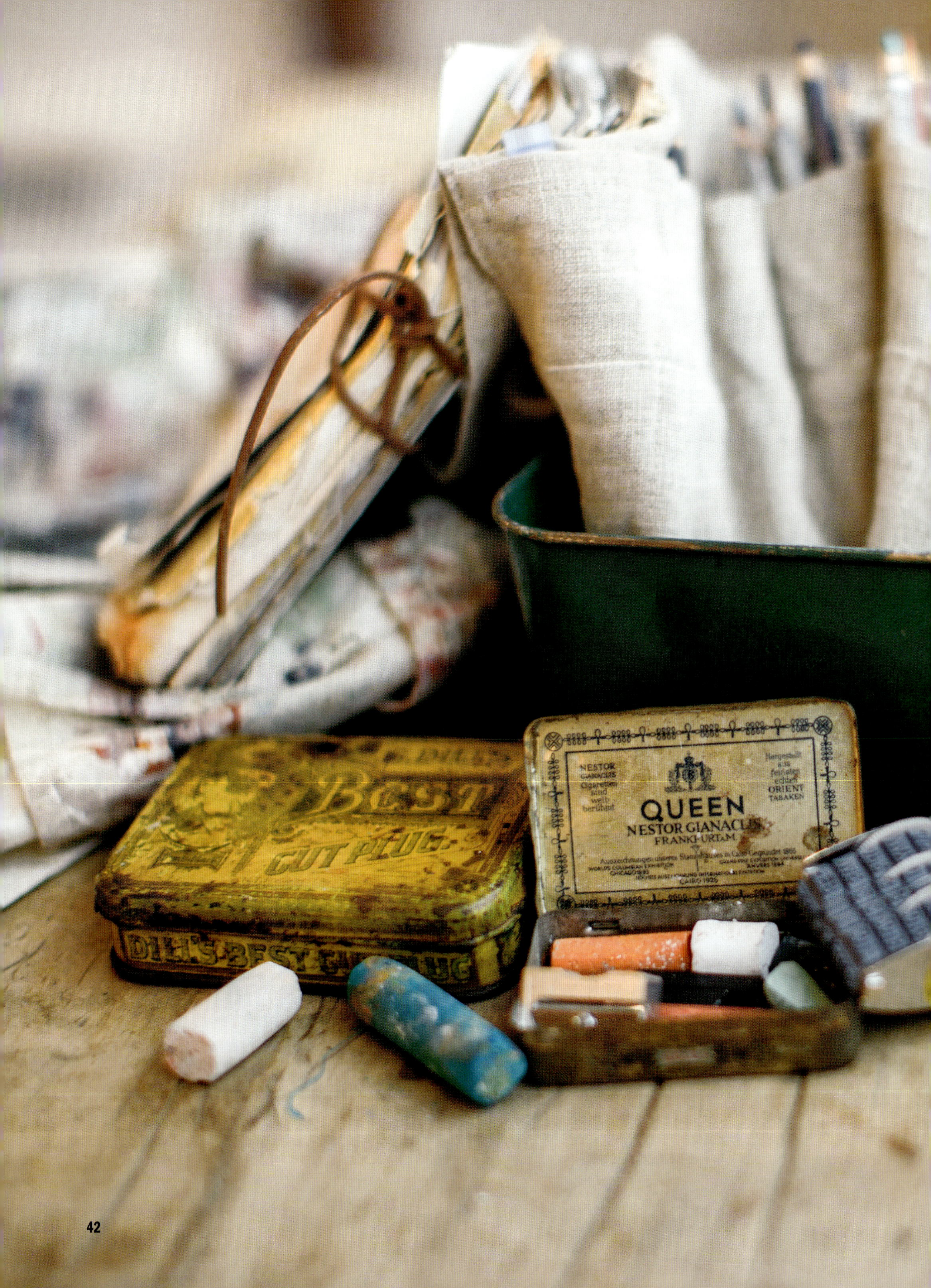

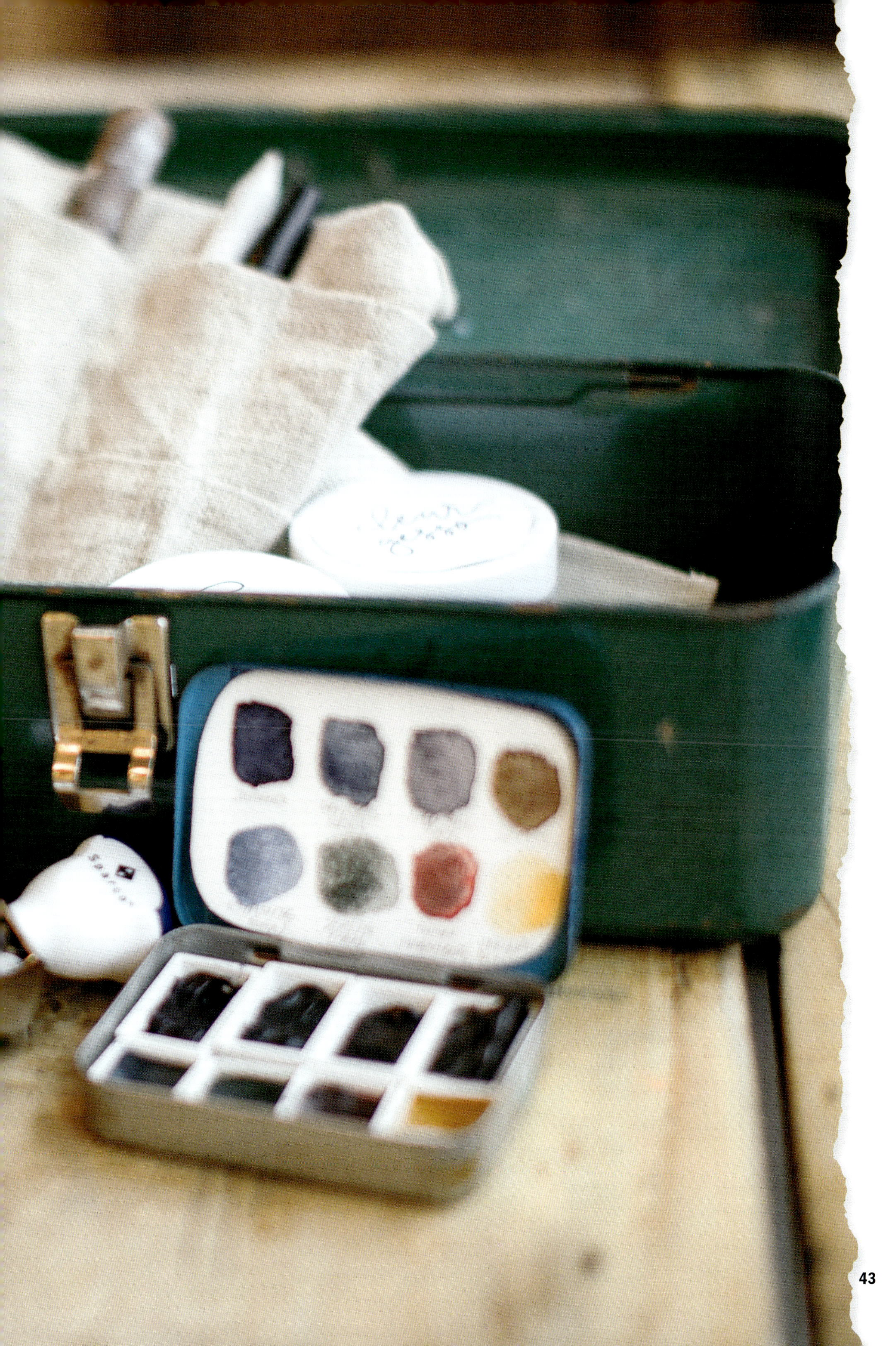

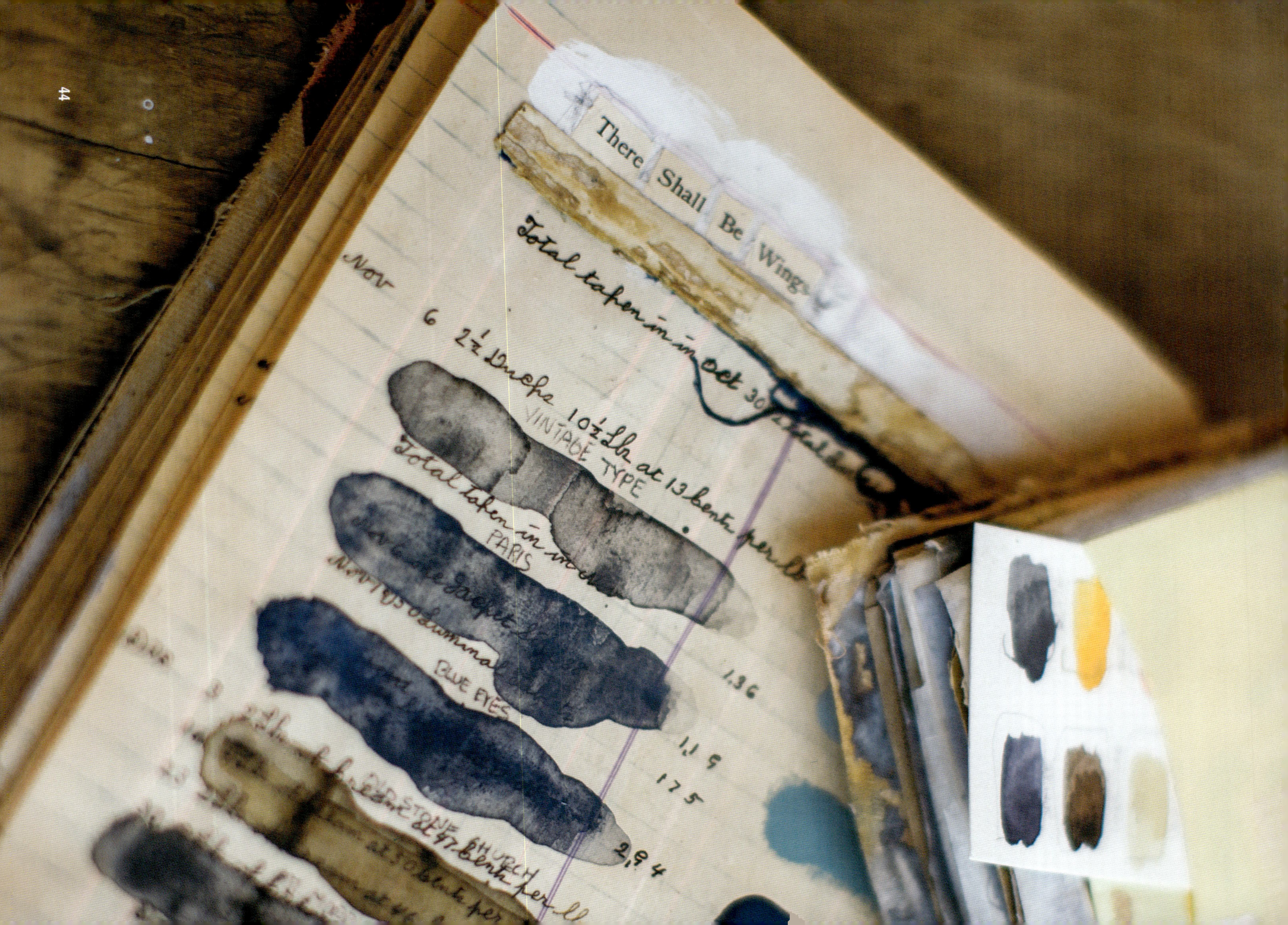
There Shall Be Wings
Total taken in in oct 30
Nov
6   2½ Bushels   10½Lh at 13 Benk per lb
VINTAGE TYPE
Total taken in in oct
PARIS
BLUE EYES
136
115
175
294

CHAPTER 7

Seeing Your Story in Color

HAVE YOU THOUGHT MUCH ABOUT WHY YOU MAY BE DRAWN TO a certain piece of art or the work of a specific artist? I believe that our first gut response to a piece has so much to do with color. When we can find our own color palette, it helps not only to narrow down our tools but to have freedom to create art that is authentic to our eye, our stories and our hand.

Creating your story's color palette is a beautiful exercise in looking for and connecting to the story you want to tell. This is an example of the fact that so often what you are looking for is already right in front of you. We will be referencing your storyboard to find your own authentic palette.

My storyboard is very broad and includes everything from photos, typography, sketches, childhood images and pieces from the present. You may find that your storyboard is very specific or that you created many storyboards for many parts of your life and/or interests. Whatever you have created is the perfect place to begin unraveling your own palette.

Creating Your Story's Color Palette

I believe that our gathering is a natural sieve to filter out the things that are the most pleasing, interesting and beautiful to our eye. Standing before your storyboard, start to pull out the colors that you see repeated again and again. Start with a basic color palette, and then look again and find subtle splashes of colors that are hidden throughout.

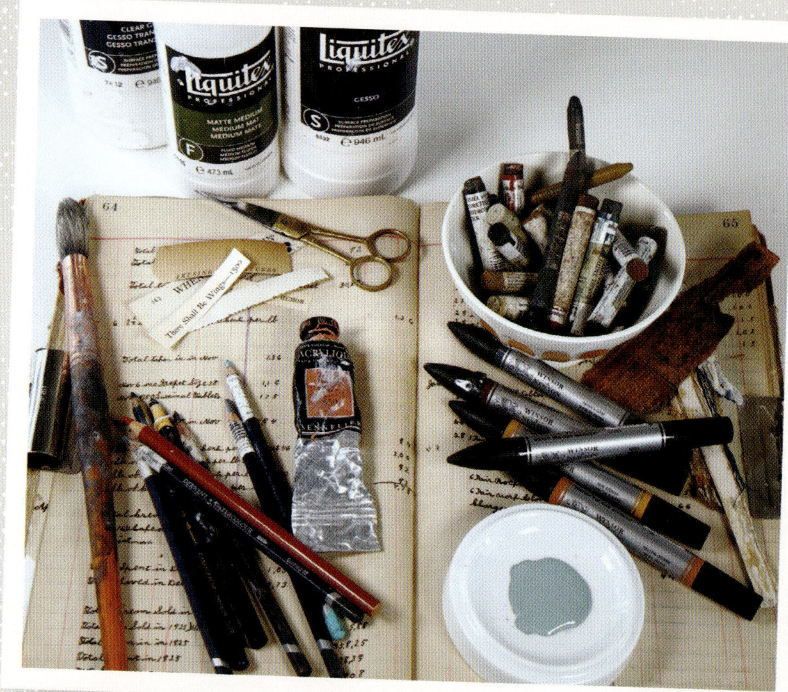

WHAT YOU NEED

– *Coloring mediums of your choice that you've selected to tell your story*

– *Gesso: white and clear*

– *Journal*

– *Matte medium*

– *Mechanical pencil*

– *Paintbrushes, assorted*

– *String or embroidery thread*

– *Words cut from newspapers or magazines*

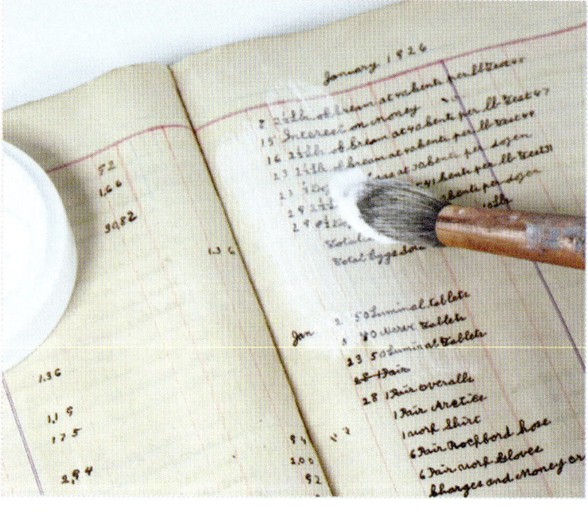

1 Apply a thin layer of clear gesso to your journal page.

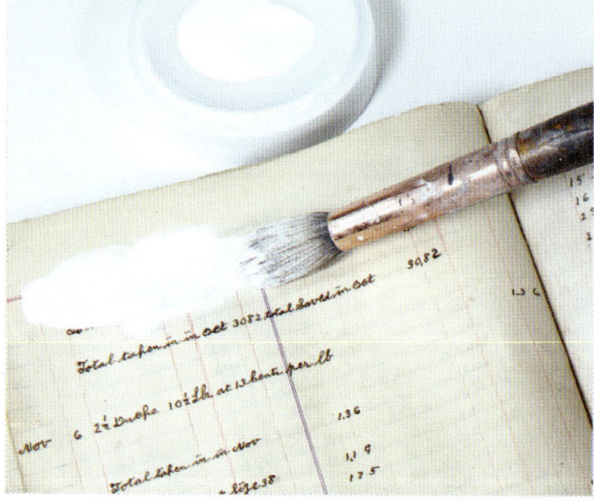

2 Apply a small swoosh of white paint or gesso to the top of your page.

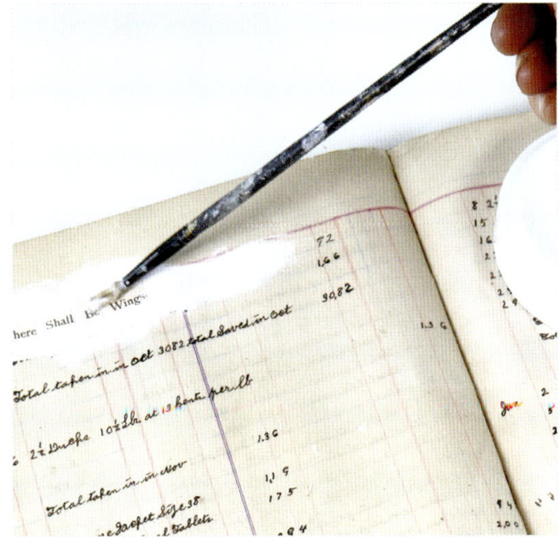

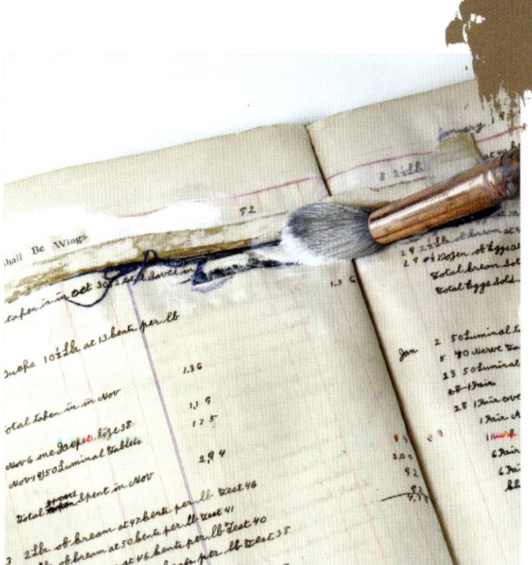

3 I love to collect words from magazines, books and newspapers. I gather the words and then have them on hand for future projects. Find some words that reflect this new journey of discovering your story. Apply a thin layer of matte medium over the white gesso, apply your cutout paper words and then apply a thin layer of matte medium to the top of the words. Allow to dry.

4 Take a piece of string, paper or vintage ephemera and layer it under your words. Apply a thin layer of matte medium to the journal page, lay the paper on the medium, press down and then cover with another thin layer of the medium. Allow to dry.

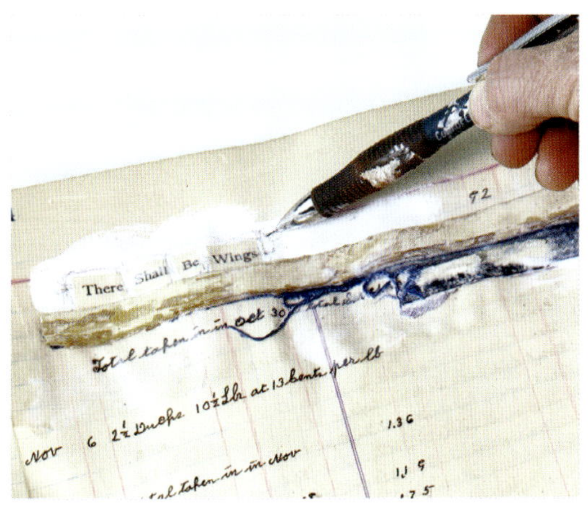

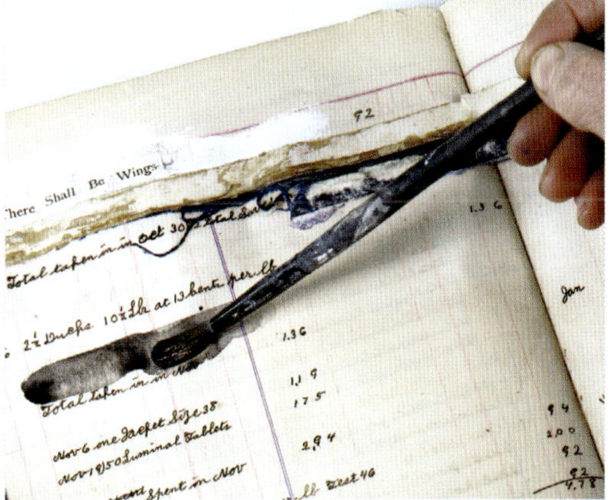

5 Use a mechanical pencil to create borders or designs around the words to help them stand out.

6 Now it is time to start collecting the colors that you have found in your storyboard. You may want to mix your own colors or apply straight from the tube. You can use pastels, colored pencils, paints or a mix of whatever supplies you have on hand.

This is for you, and my hope is that it becomes a reference for you of what you naturally gathered. If you don't want to start applying straight to your journal, you can always go through your supplies looking for the right colors, apply them to a separate page or loose piece of paper, and then when you have chosen the colors that most represent your storyboard, apply them to your journal. Have fun with this!

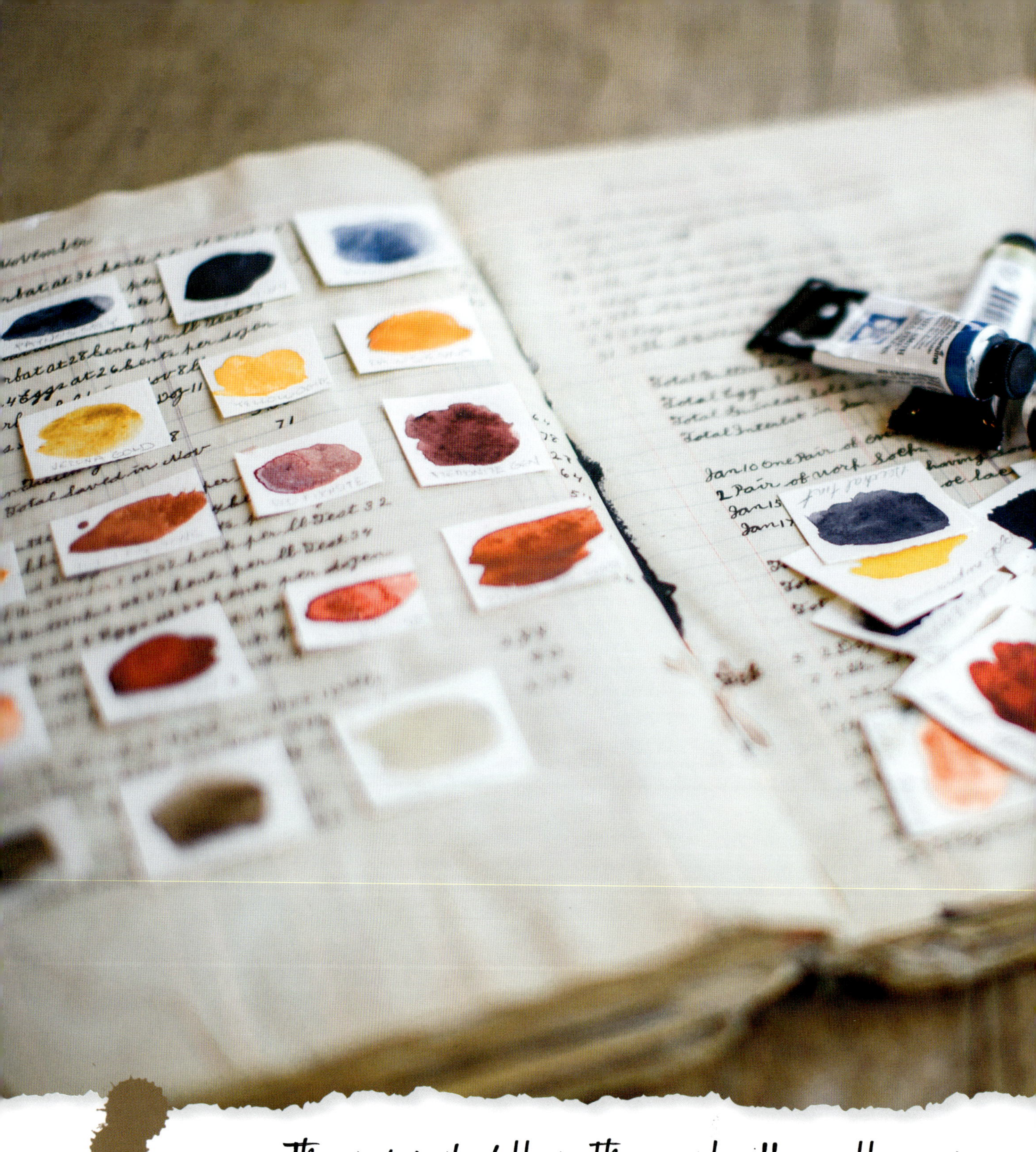

The woman who follows the crowd will usually go no further than the crowd. The woman who walks alone is likely to find herself in places no one has ever been.

—UNKNOWN

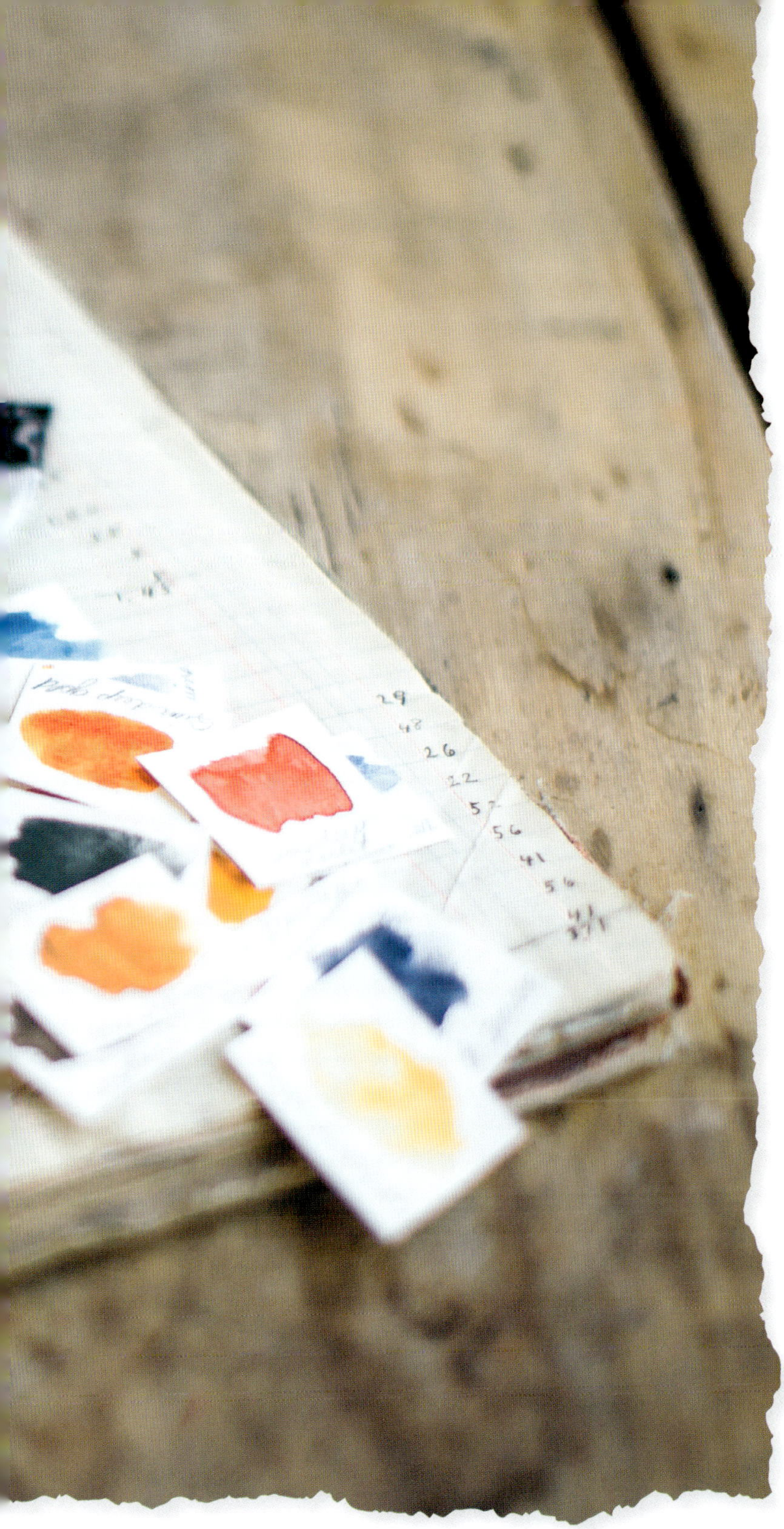

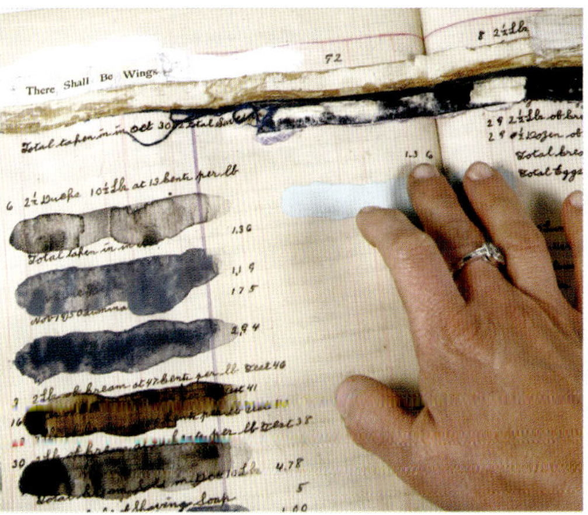

7 Now that you have gathered your colors, forget the names that were given to those colors and make up new ones based on your storyboard. Take your journal over to your storyboard; as you find those colors again, what names do they represent to you? Many of my names were about places I have been, architectural elements of cities, sweet memories of home and even a feeling I have when I look at my storyboard and my gathered colors. Why say "Yellow Ochre" when you can say "Swaying Cornfields!"

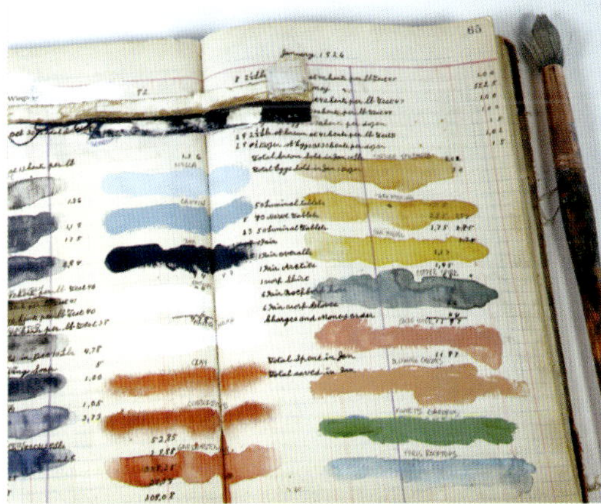

8 As you can tell I jumped around in the color wheel and just put colors down as I saw them. I could go back to my storyboard and create a color palette just for France or just for my time growing up in rural Illinois. There is so much freedom in this, and each time you create a palette you will learn more about yourself and the colors you want to use within your story.

CHAPTER 8

Mark Making + Symbolism

THE MORE WE PRACTICE CREATING AND FIGURING OUT WHAT OUR authentic marks are within our art, the more we will use the same marks again and again. Not only will you have freedom, ease and comfort using these marks, but when others see your work they will recognize it as yours. I have been aware of my marks for quite a while now, but when I started wanting to include my own symbolism in my work, I dove into the rich history of symbolism within art. It was eye opening and also fun to come up with my own symbolism and create new meanings for marks we see every day.

If you wonder what I mean when I say marks, I am referring to the intentional stroke of a medium onto your substrate. Your marks may be with words, graphite, paint or paper. Your marks may even be the absence of a medium and allow the raw substrate to show below. It is the design choices, lines and repetition that feel most natural to you. This can take time to develop and only comes with practice. Take a moment to look at many works of art by some of your favorite artists and find their common design choices, storytelling, lines and repetition. It is sometimes easier to see these common threads in the works of others at first and then see them in our own work.

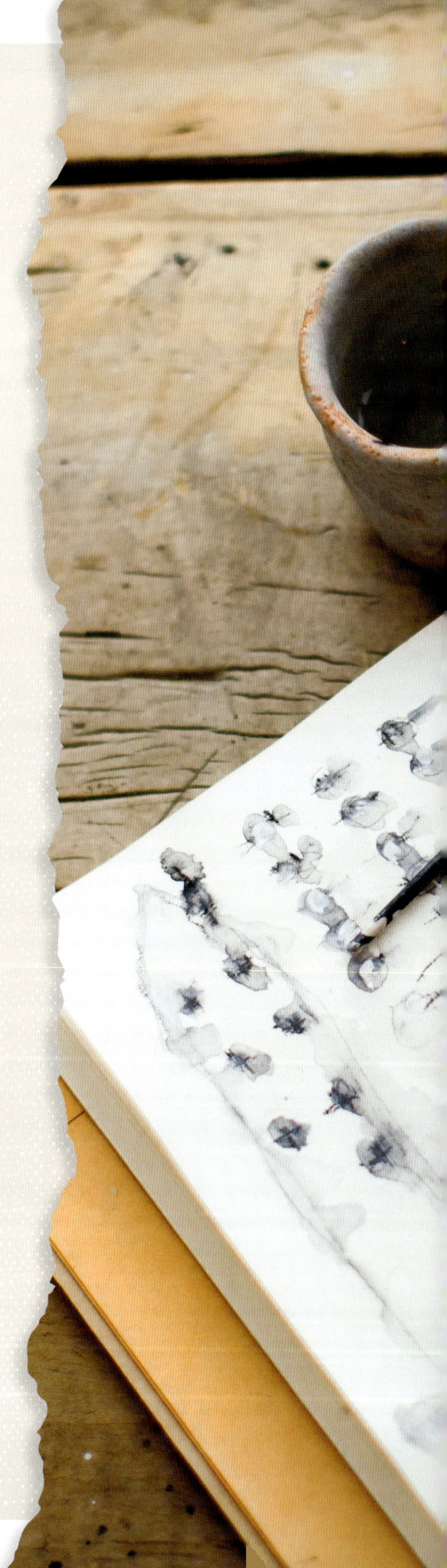

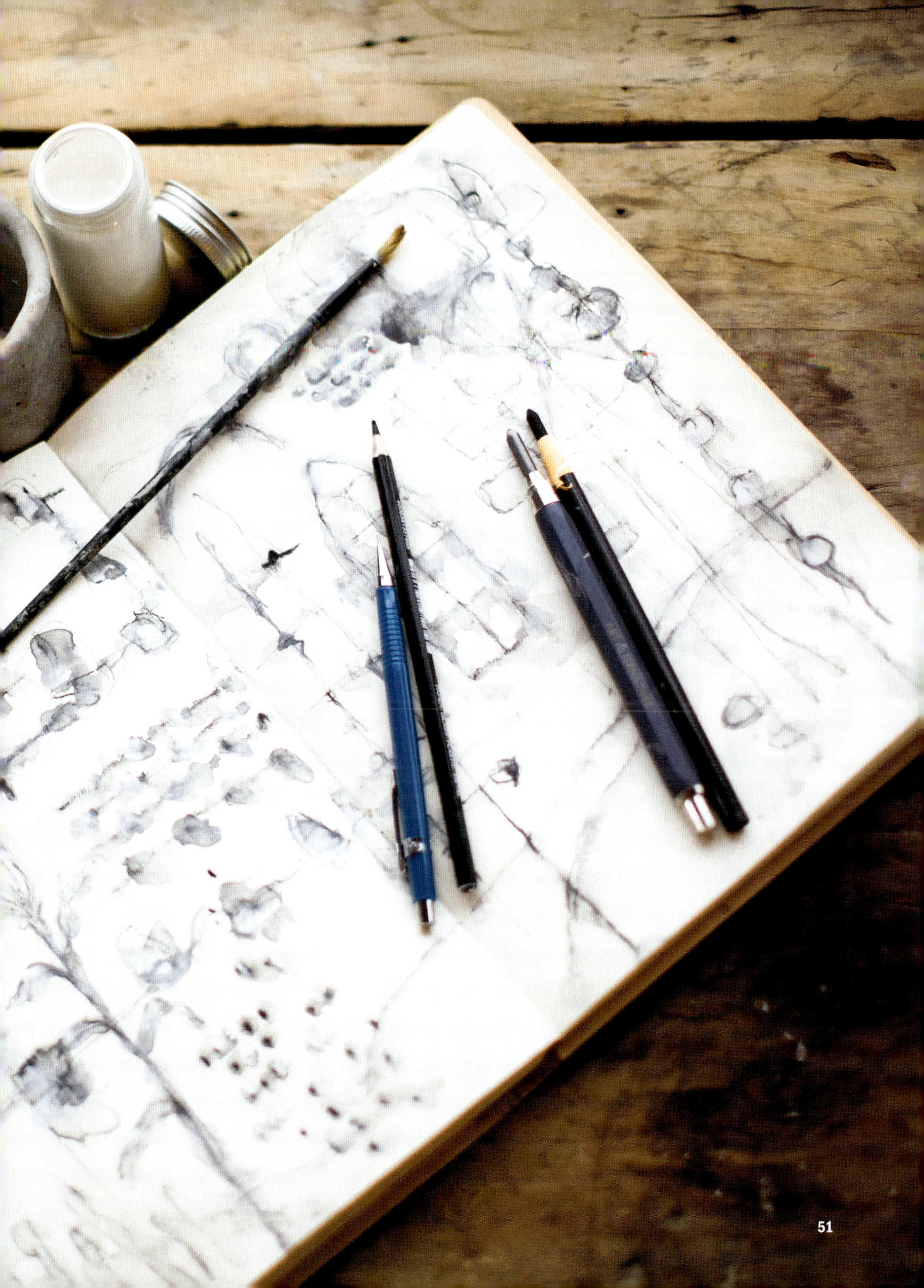

Finding Your Marks

While you are looking at your storyboard and brainstorming aspects of your story, try to come up with a list of patterns, marks and objects that you can include in your mark making and symbolism. Put the timer on and write and sketch until the buzzer goes off. Don't overthink it but allow as many ideas to flow as possible. Use your list for this next project. The ideas you are collecting will just be your jumping off point.

You may find that historically in art that a finch could represent a soul returning to heaven, a sparrow could represent a soul recently deceased or a crow could foreshadow wickedness. A single scallop represented shelter, and a cluster of circles symbolizes family for the aborigines. A ladder may tell the story of a journey. What do these symbols mean to you and can you make up your own?

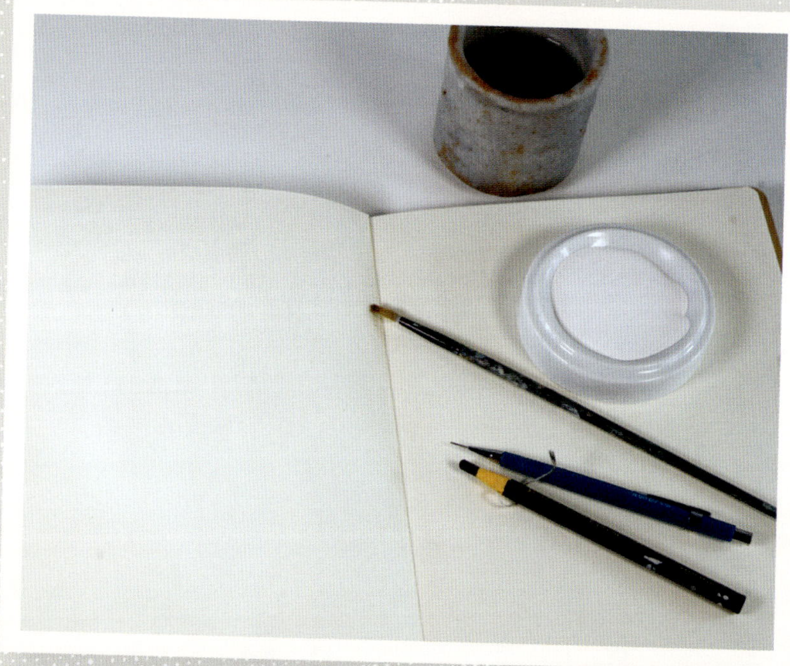

WHAT YOU NEED
- Art journal
- Charcoal pencil
- Mechanical pencil
- No. 4 long-handled brush
- Water
- White gesso

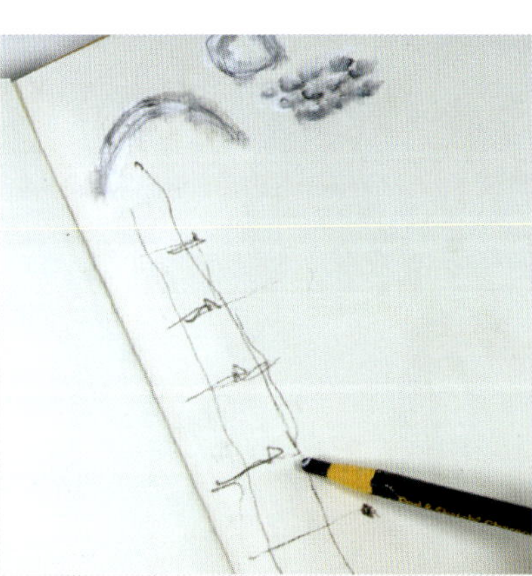

1 Using a charcoal pencil, begin to loosely sketch a scallop (shelter), a cluster of circles (family) and then a ladder (journey). Place your hand near the end of the charcoal pencil to encourage yourself to always be loose with your sketches.

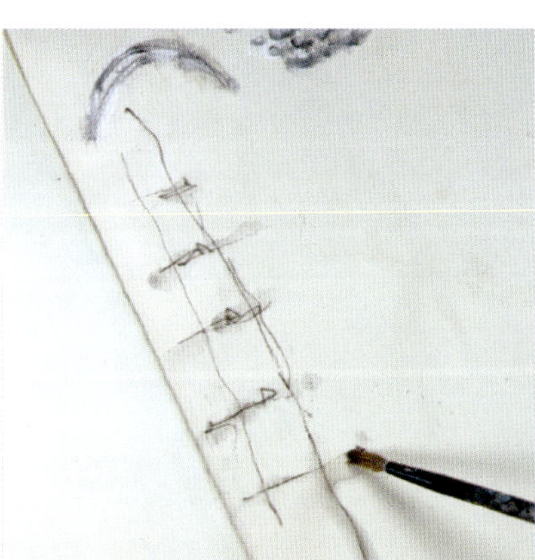

2 Charcoal is such a versatile medium because of how it moves with water and other mediums. After you have sketched with charcoal, move it around a bit with water to continue bringing the sketch to life. Use a no. 4 long-handled brush to lightly pull the charcoal away from your sketch with the water. This whole process is about exploring, so don't get bogged down in perfection. Do not add water to all of the charcoal; leave some of the charcoal dry.

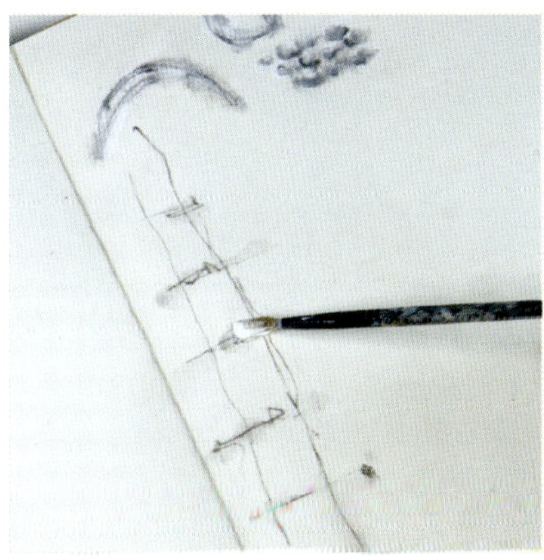 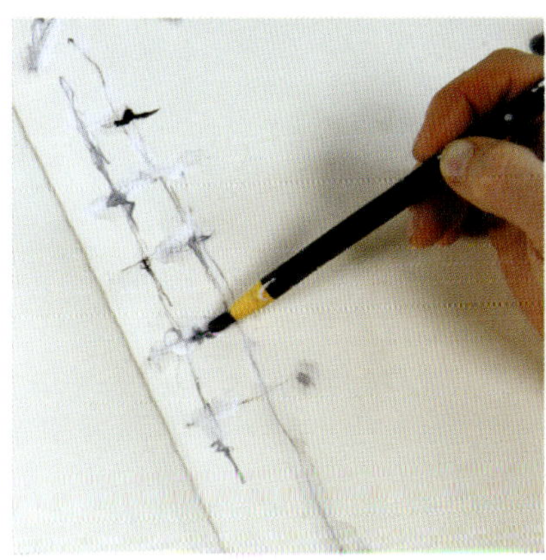 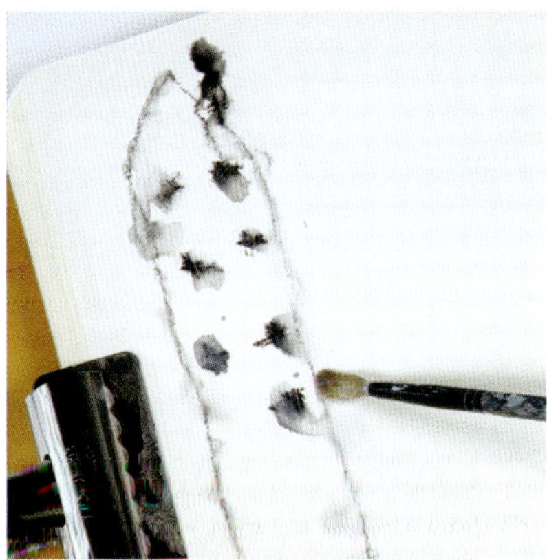

3 Using a small amount of white gesso, start to create values within your sketch. You will create your darkest areas, mid grays and then highlights or whites using just your charcoal pencil, water and white gesso. This technique allows you to "paint" with minimal tools and to practice creating sketches with depth in a short period of time. Just as above, add the white gesso on only some of the areas. I like the interest it gives to my sketches to leave some of the charcoal dry, some with just the water and then some with the values created by the white gesso.

4 Going back in with your charcoal pencil, add your darkest values. With the wet mediums you may find that the charcoal becomes a rich and vibrant black when applied. Once again, add it intentionally to your sketch.

5 With your list of ideas, symbols and objects next to you, fill as many pages as you want with these sketches and mini paintings. Roads and paths can represent a journey, windows can be about possibility and a source of light, figuratively and physically. Buildings and homes can become whatever you want them to be. For some they will represent roots and for others something completely different. The symbolism only has to mean something to you.

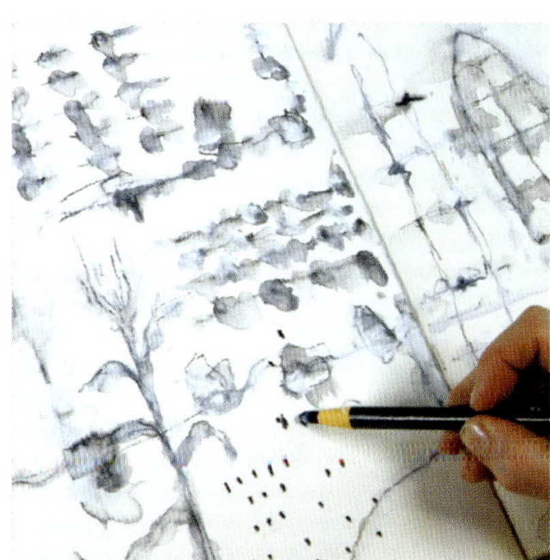 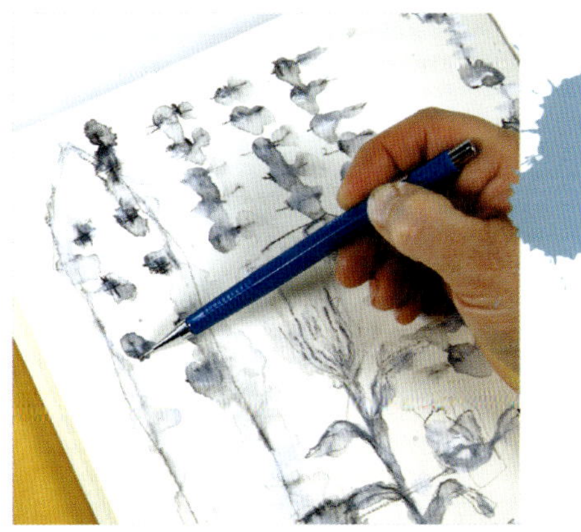

6 Once you find the marks that you are drawn to, try creating groups and collections of these marks to create drama and interest in your work. Simple marks that are repeated can become powerful focal points.

7 The combination of charcoal, water and white gesso creates a flowing mark with wide and loose strokes. At this point I bring in a mechanical pencil. You can create more definition with the mechanical pencil, but because of the thin graphite it does not overwhelm your mark making. Create small tick marks, long extended lines, scribbles and circles around your favorite parts of the previous marks.

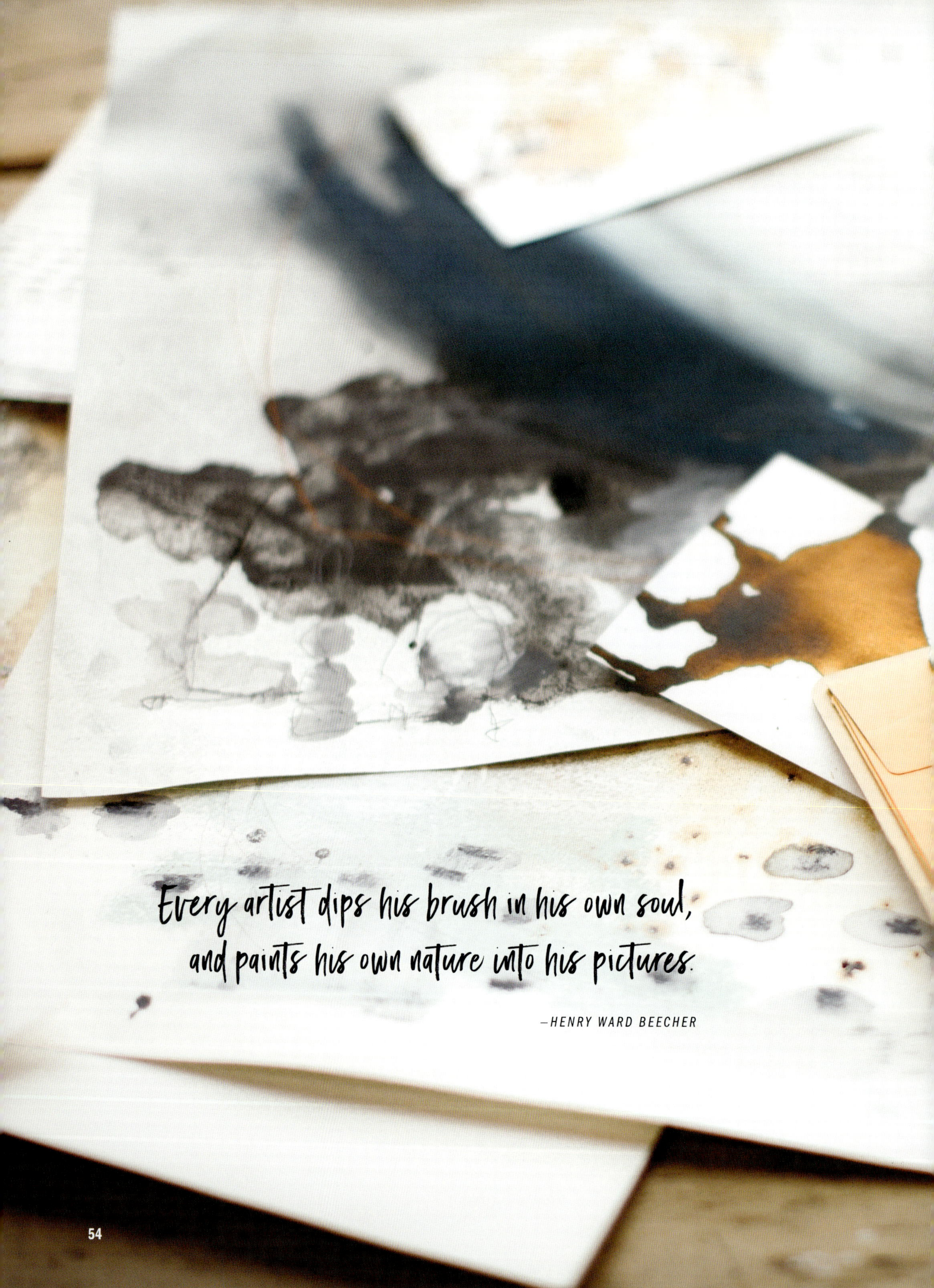
Every artist dips his brush in his own soul,
and paints his own nature into his pictures.

—HENRY WARD BEECHER

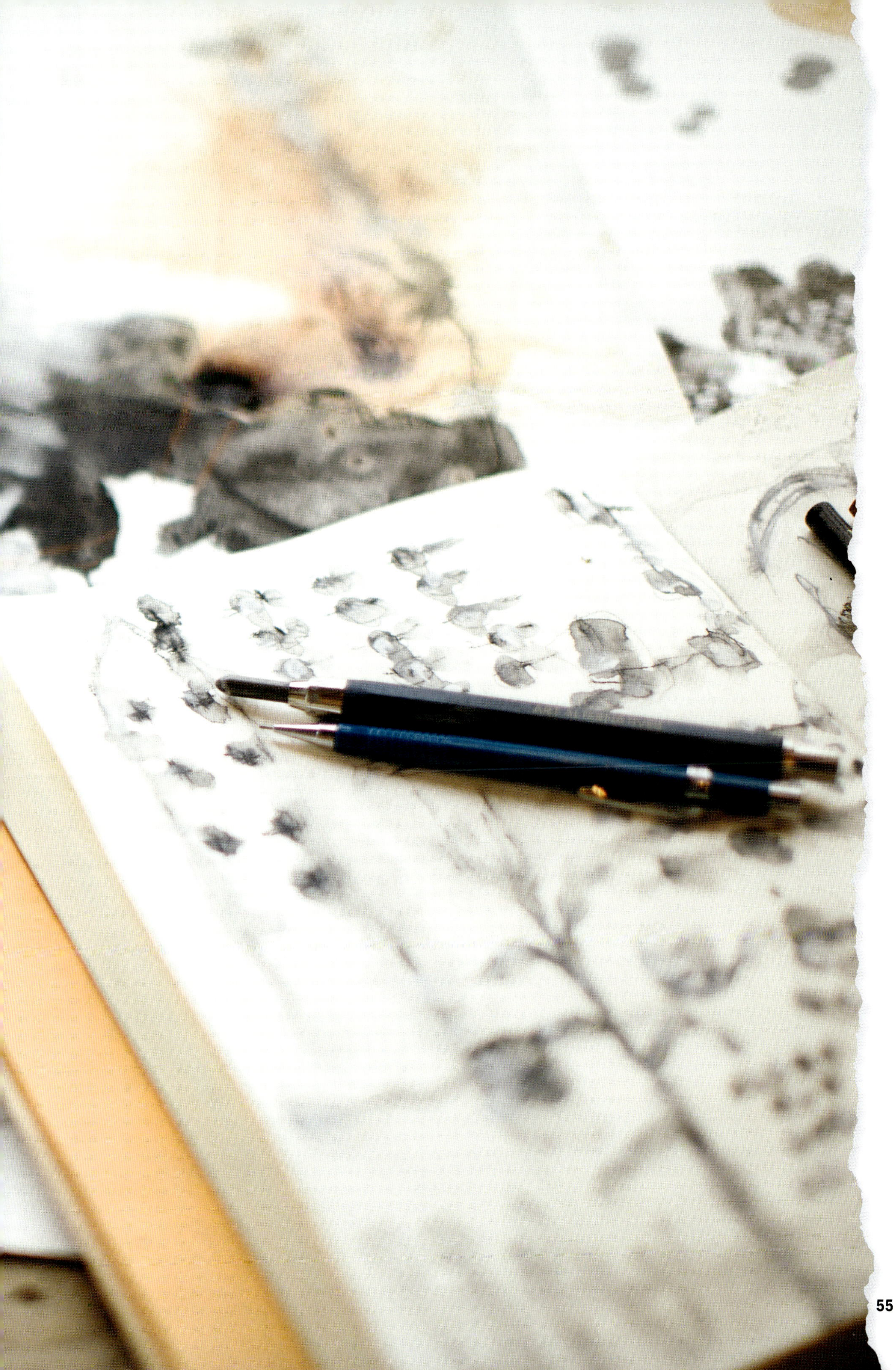

Alternative Mark Making

Some of my favorite ways to make marks have nothing to do with typical tools; it is with experimenting and adventuring that you find new ways to make new marks. This gets kind of addicting, so be prepared to start using almost anything in your art!

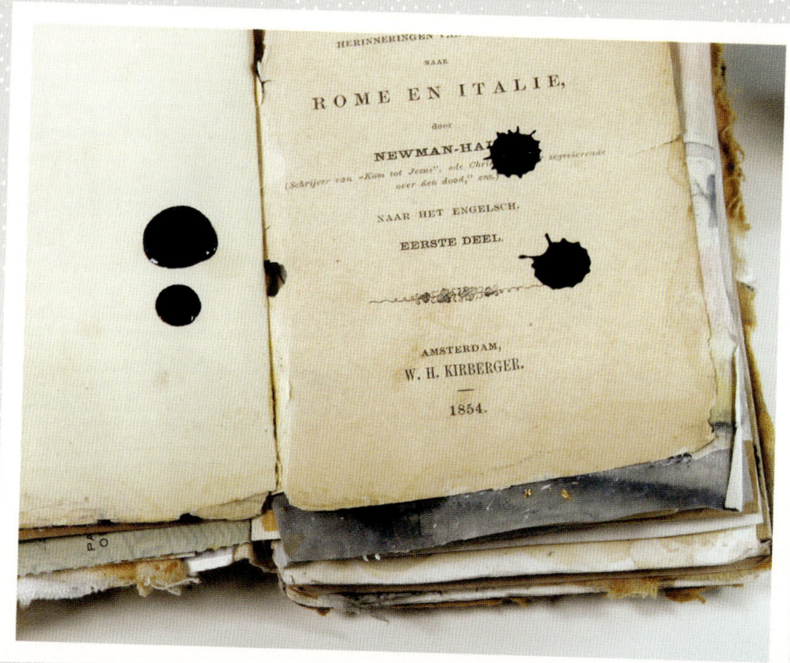

WHAT YOU NEED

- Art journal
- Camera
- Cotton cloth, cheesecloth or muslin
- Golden gel matte medium
- Hole punch
- India ink
- Ink dropper
- Instant coffee crystals
- Laser copy image, and your art
- matte medium
- Mod Podge photo transfer medium
- Natural elements
- Old cloth
- Old hotel key card or brayer
- Paintbrush
- Rusty objects
- Scissors
- Twine
- Water mister
- Watercolor paper
- White gesso
- White vinegar
- Workable fixative

#1 INK

Whether as a focal point in my art or as a subtle addition to the background, marks that appear random and without control or thought are very attractive to me. Even though there is a certain amount of the unexpected in how some mediums will react, flow or pool, there is definite thought behind their placement and intention behind why I chose it. Ink and India ink specifically make some of the most bold and powerful marks. This medium is worthy of much practice and experimentation to see how you will use it.

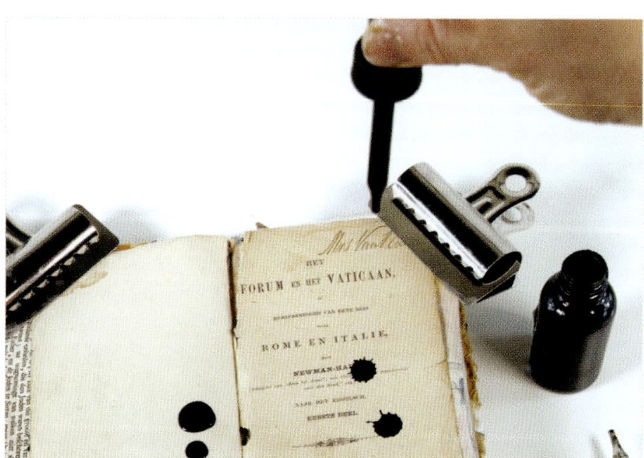

1 We will use ink in different ways during our journey together of finding and creating our stories. India ink is a favorite for how fluid it is and all of the different ways you can create marks with it. Here I am simply using a small dropper to add drips on the page. The closer I am with the dropper to the substrate, the more controlled and precise my drip will be. The higher up I drop the ink, the more unpredictable, splattered and loose the mark will be.

#2 COFFEE CRYSTALS

How can you say no to mark making that not only gives gorgeous interest to your art but smells incredible? I enjoy the color of aged paper and rust-stained anything, so when I discovered the ease, beauty and unexpected marks of including instant coffee crystals to my pages I was hooked. Maybe you will be too!

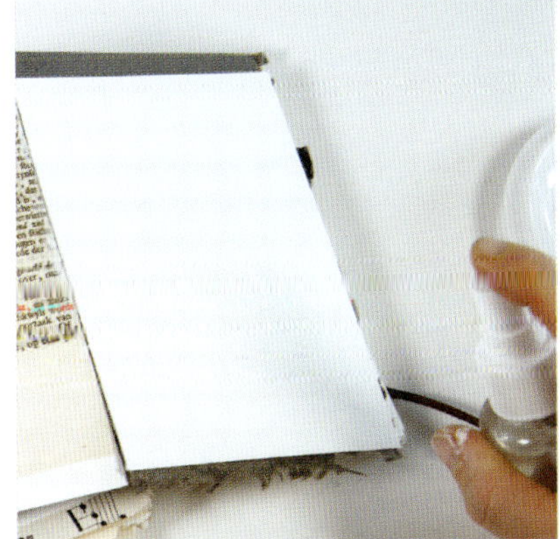

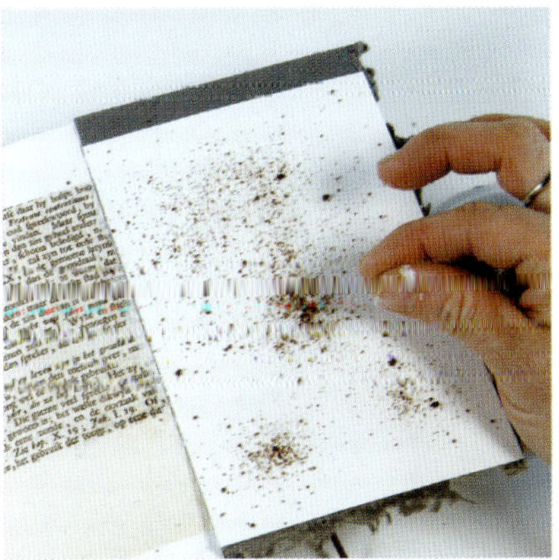

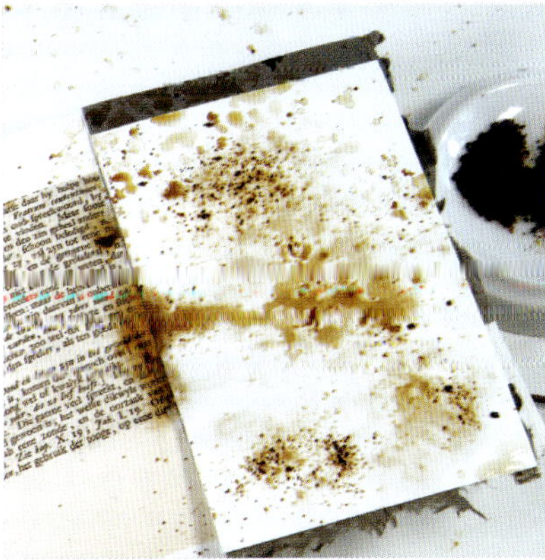

1 Lightly spray your surface with water. If you don't have a squirt bottle, dip your fingers in a cup of water and sprinkle over the paper. Don't worry if the whole surface isn't covered evenly. The more imperfect you are in the process, the more interesting your results and marks will be. I promise.

2 Sprinkle instant coffee crystals over your surface. Different brands will give different results, so just play with them. Allow your crystals to pool, and also lightly dust the surface.

3 Lightly spray your surface again and then allow the crystals to absorb the water. Barely spray some areas and saturate other areas to see what marks you are more drawn to. I like the lack of control in this form of mark making. This is the perfect mark making to do if a blank canvas feels overwhelming. Once you get these marks down, it is easier to bring in your other mediums.

#3 NATURAL ELEMENTS

I don't know if the foraging for alternative mark-making tools or actually using them is more fun. I went out on our land to find dried grasses and other finds in the woods to use as paintbrushes. I gathered pinecones, acorns, grasses, dried flowers, branches and pine needles. If you are able to gather many smaller grasses, you may find that binding them together with twine will give another option in your mark marking. You will have different treasures out your front door, too. Have fun with it and experiment with the different marks they each make.

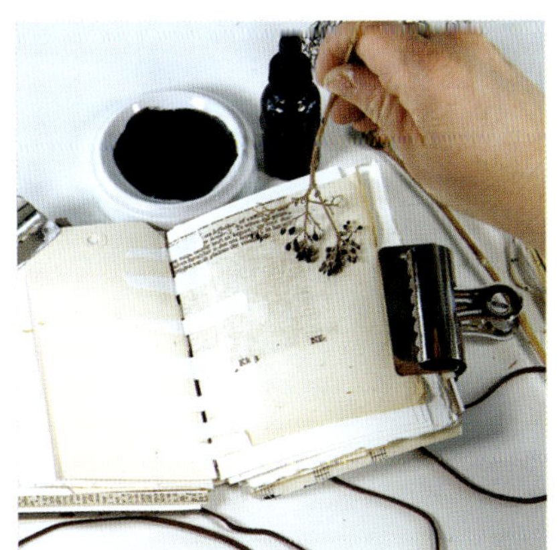

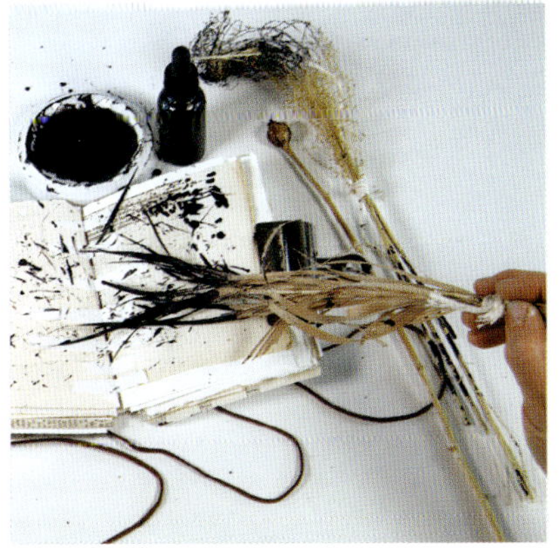

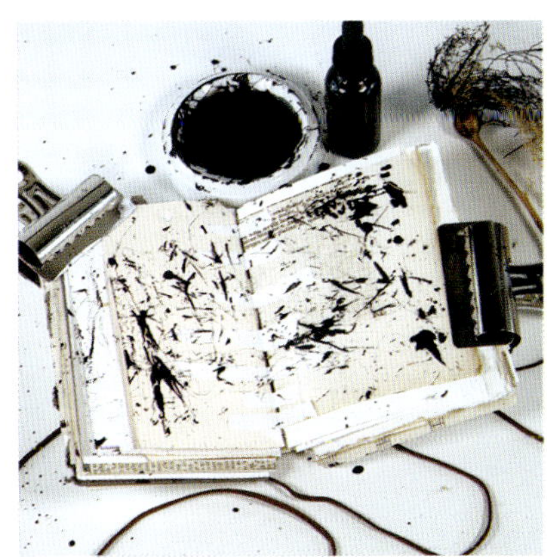

1 Take whatever element from nature that you have collected, dip it into the India ink and create marks on your surface by smudging, dragging or simply touching the surface. It won't take long for you to decide which tools bring the best marks for you.

2 Experiment with different tools, pressure, strokes and even inks or mediums.

#4 REPRODUCTIONS

Oftentimes we think we need to reinvent the wheel when it comes to our art when really the perfect material for creating layers and interest in your work is one of your previous sketches or paintings. I suggest looking at what you are doing already that you love and keeping your eyes open to where else you can incorporate those marks, images and compositions.

Using your cell phone camera or DSLR camera, take a photo of your art and print it out on your laser or ink-jet printer. If you are using an ink-jet print, test a small corner to see if the ink will bleed with medium. You may need to spray with a workable fixative before adding medium.

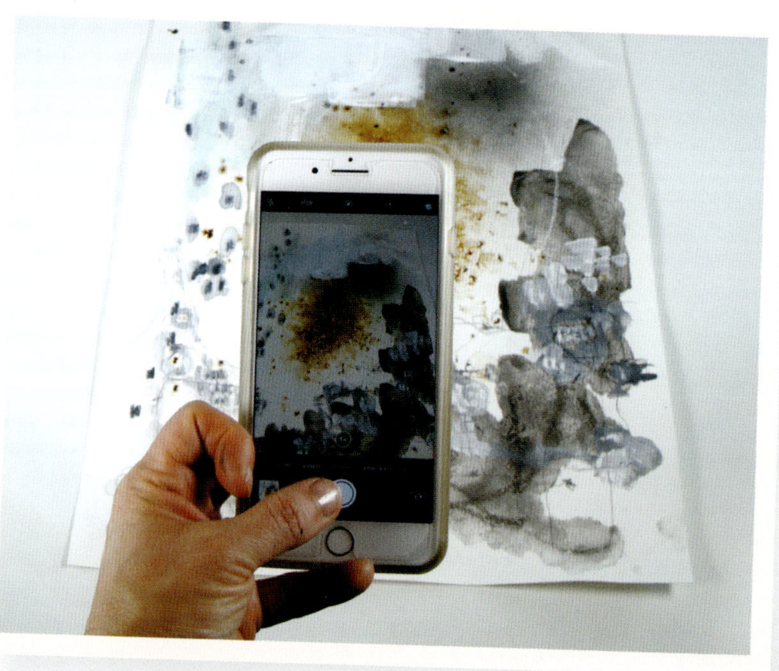

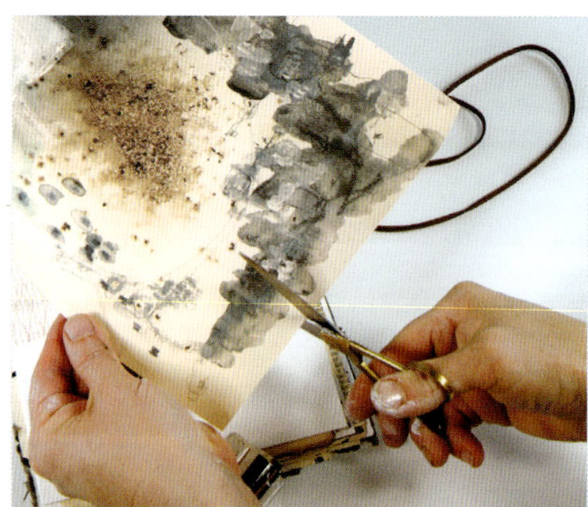

1 Using an ink-jet print on copier paper of a previous work, I cut out elements I am drawn to and want to use to create a new piece.

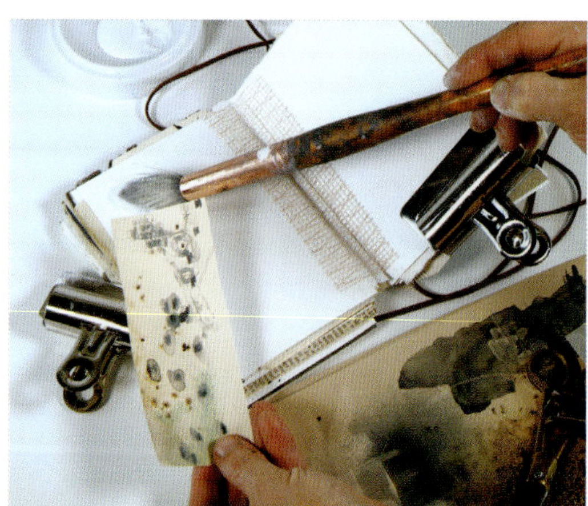

2 Apply a thin layer of matte medium to act as the glue on your substrate. Place the copy on the matte medium, and then apply a final coat over the copy.

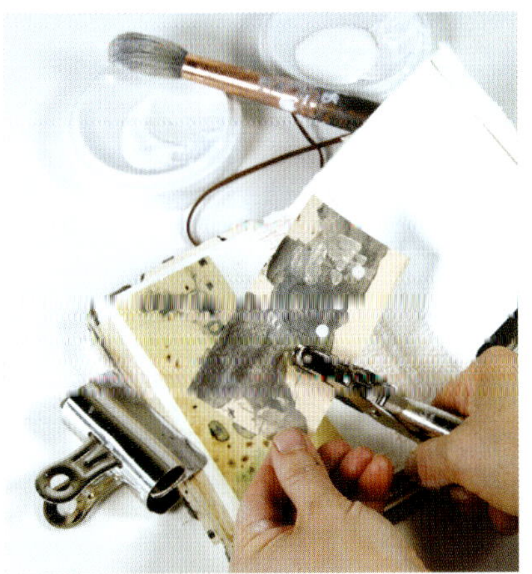

3 To add some whimsy and unexpected layers, use a hole punch not only to create a design within the paper but also to use the punched out circles as texture.

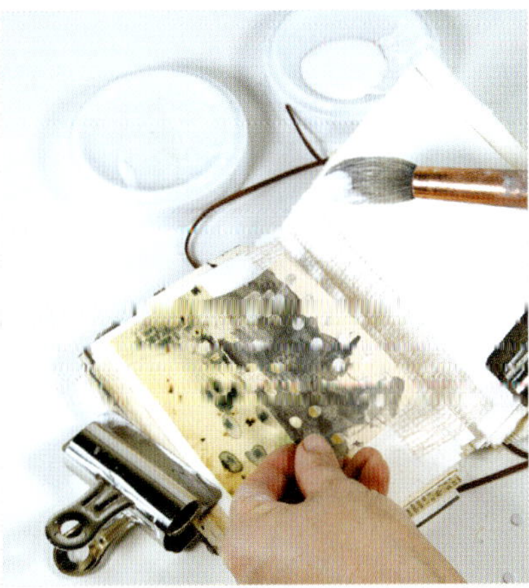

4 Using matte medium again, add more layers into the composition.

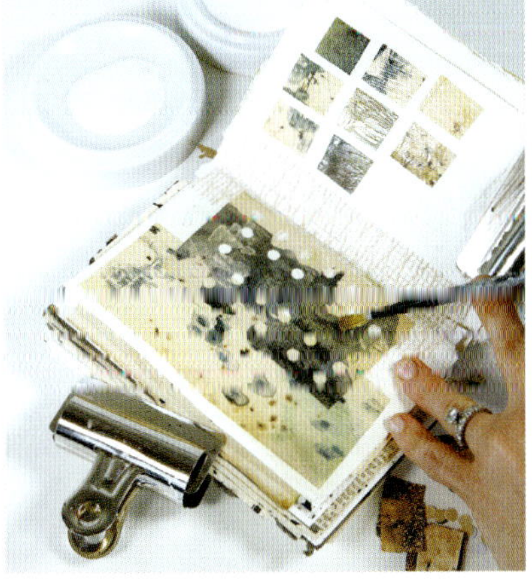

5 Randomly apply matte medium onto the collage in a thin layer.

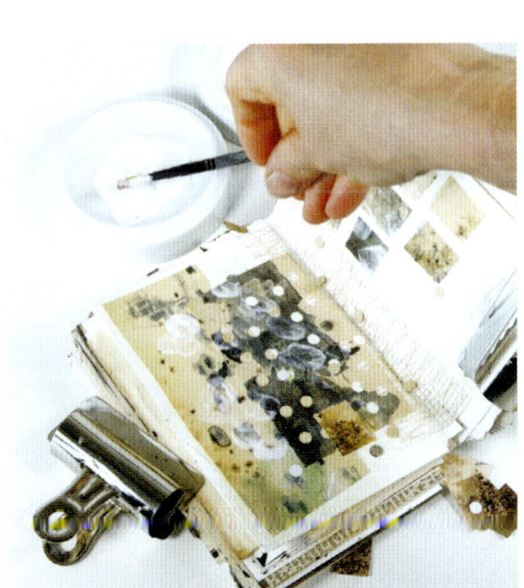

6 Sprinkle the cutout circles over the collage.

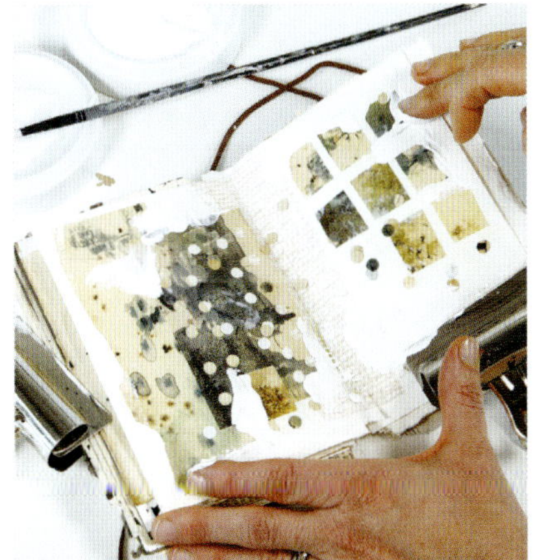

7 To soften the sharp edges of the collage and to create texture and layers, apply white gesso with your fingers.

When you cut up a previous work, you instantly have a new perspective on your work and also create more mini works of art. This is a wonderful way to get new ideas for larger works, and it is all based upon your own marks, ideas and palette.

#5 IMAGE TRANSFERS

You may find that you want to incorporate copies of previous works of art, old family photos, architecture from your favorite trip or copyright-free images into your art. Image transfers are a fun and easy way to add a different creative element into your story.

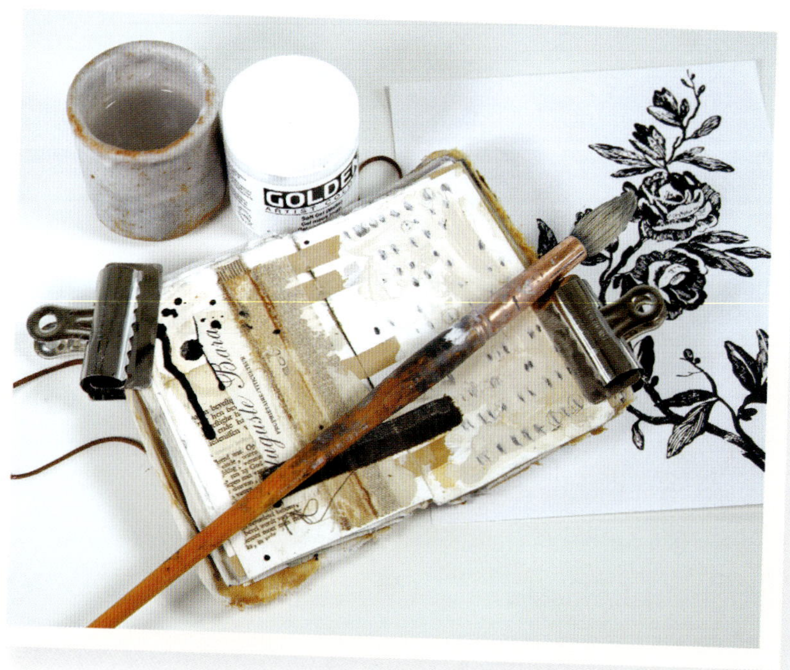

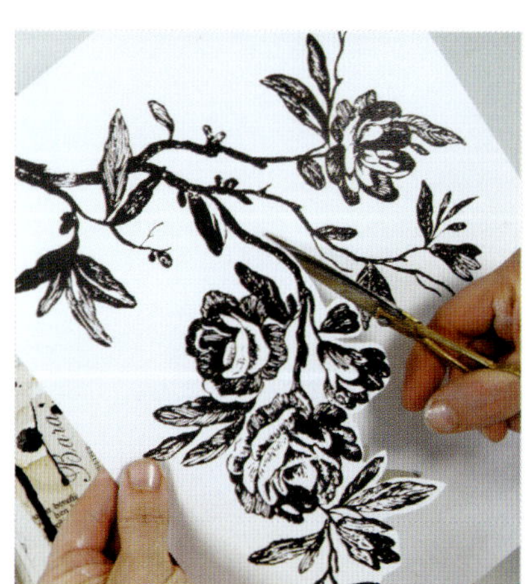

1 Start with a laser print image and cut around the image trying not to leave too much white space.

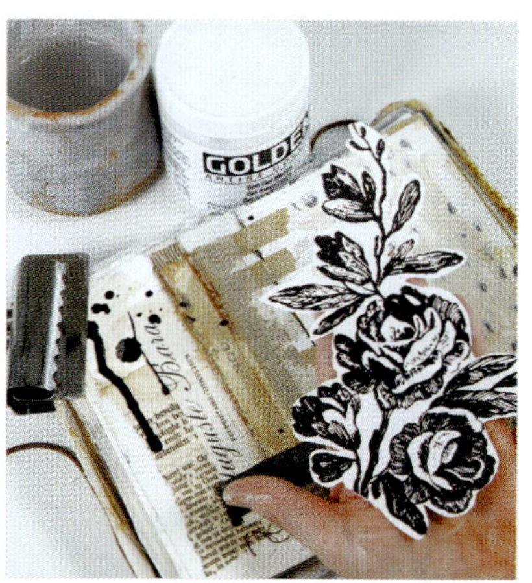

2 You do not need to be precise, but too much white paper around the image will mean more work for you later. I suggest laser prints over ink-jet because they do not bleed and you are more likely to have a successful transfer.

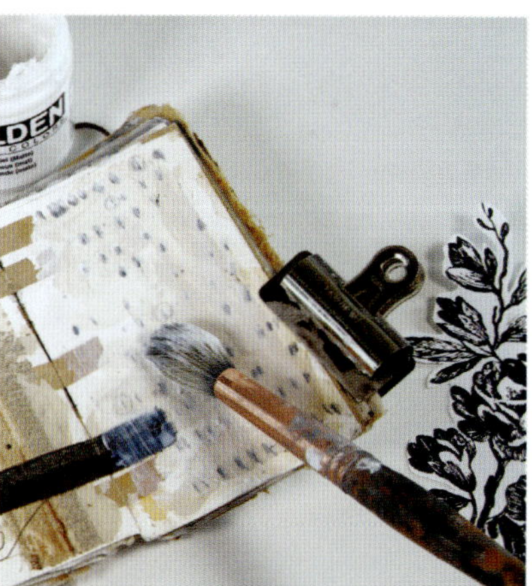

3 Apply a thin layer of Golden gel matte medium on the substrate where you want to transfer your image. This is my transfer medium of choice, but experiment with other adhesives you have on hand.

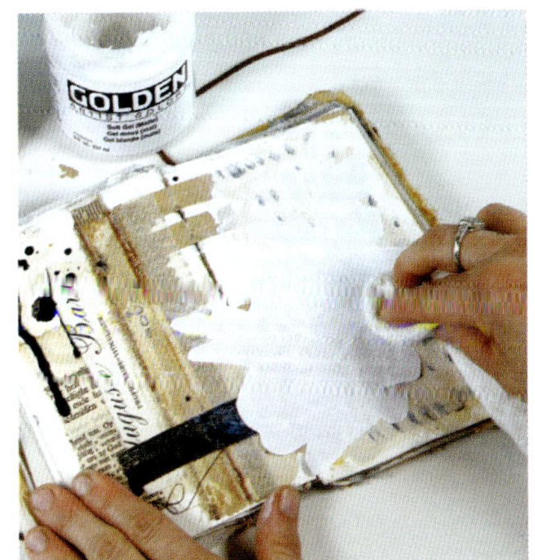

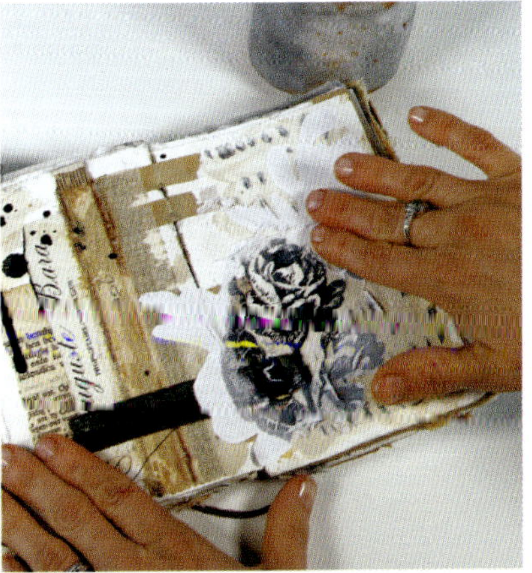

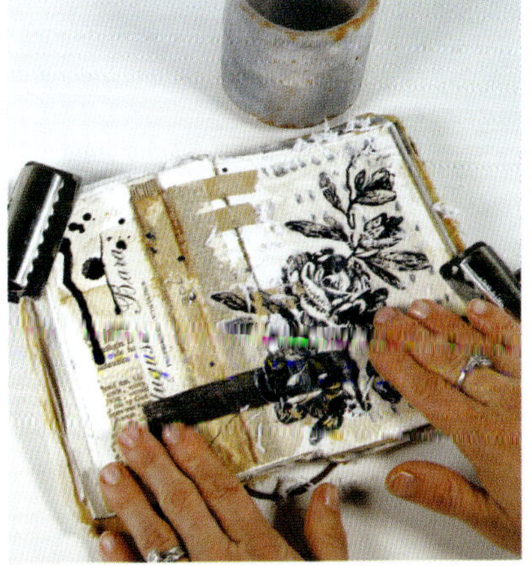

4 Place your image facedown onto the gel medium and smooth out all bubbles with a cloth, your hand or an old credit card. You just want to gently make sure your image is firmly in place. When I have the time I like to allow the image to dry overnight, but that is not always possible. I have rarely been disappointed with a transfer even when it has dried for only a short time.

5 Once the gel medium has had a chance to dry (you can always speed up the process with a drying tool), dip your fingers in clean water and start to gently rub away the back layer of the paper. I start with a circular motion and then use a gentle back-and-forth motion.

6 If you rub too hard you may pull up some of your image, but I think that can just add to your transfer, so do not stress over it. Imperfections make the best art!

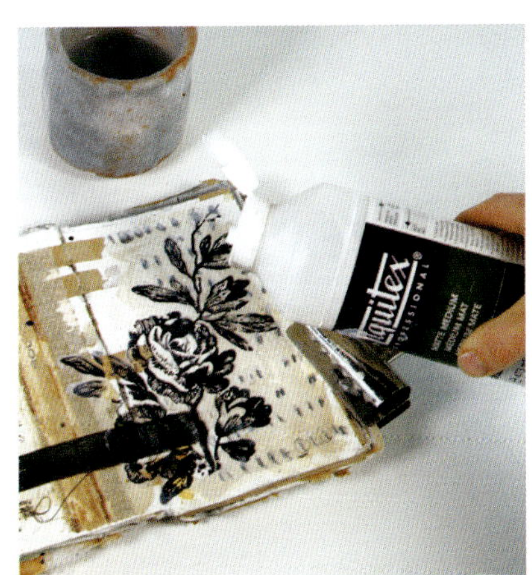

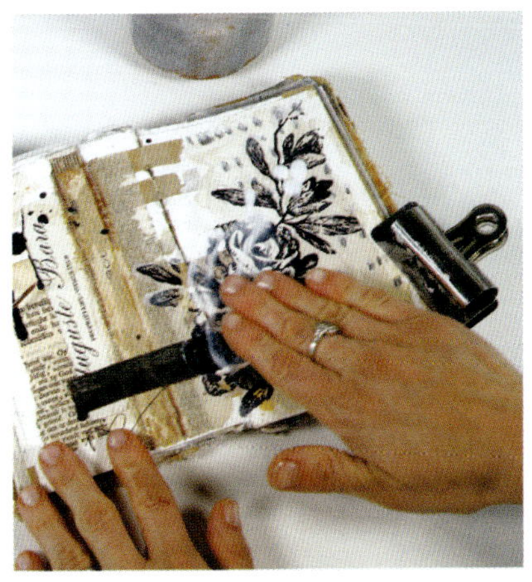

7 As your image transfer begins to dry, you may find that it becomes white and cloudy. If this happens, lightly dampen your fingers again and gently remove any of this excess paper. To prevent the image from fading again I like to apply a thin layer of Liquitex matte medium.

8 The matte medium will seal your image and keep it nice and dark.

#6 RUST TRANSFERS

Rust transfers are one of my favorite ways to create marks on my substrates and fabrics because they are unexpected and random. The colors they transfer are within my color palette, and the process has also opened my mind to be more creative with random objects, plants and spices that can bring color transfers into my art.

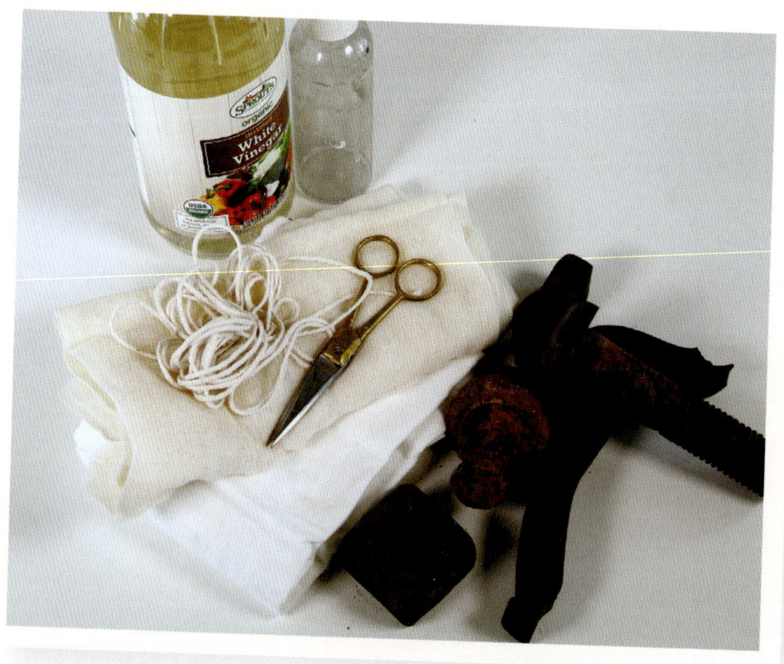

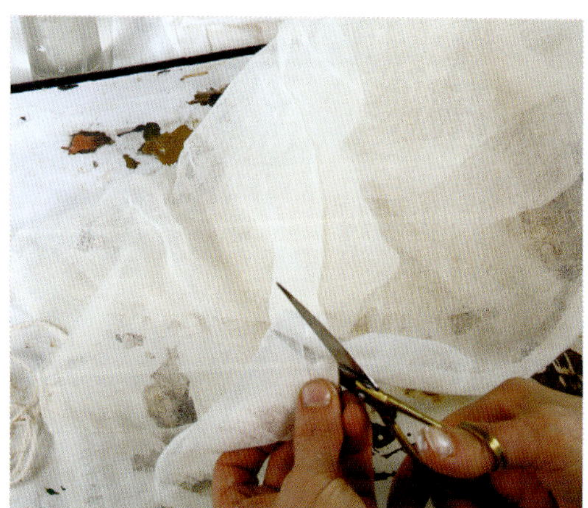

1 I prefer more natural fibers for my fabric. I have found that cotton flour cloth, muslin and cheesecloth are wonderful receptors for the rust. Once you have chosen your fabric you will need to cut a large enough piece to completely cover whatever rusty object you were able to find.

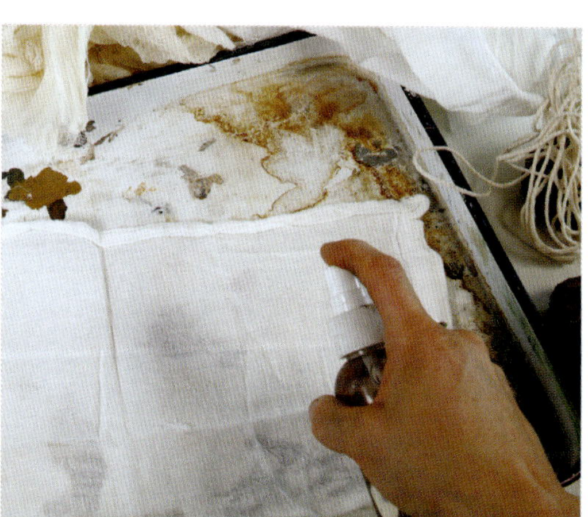

2 Using a mixture of one part water to one part white vinegar, spray the fabric until it is damp.

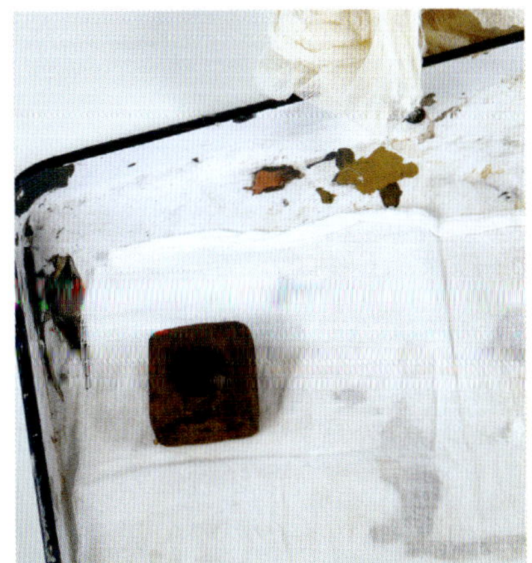

3 Place your rusty object on the damp fabric and begin to wrap the object. The more you twist, turn, bunch and wrap the object, the more interesting your transfer will be.

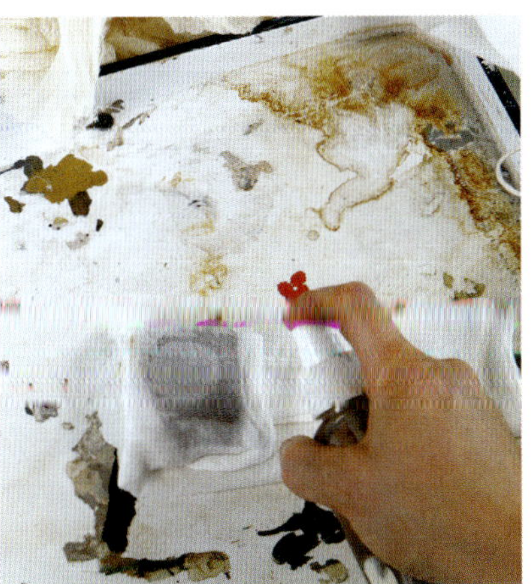

4 Spray the water/vinegar mixture as you are wrapping to make sure the fabric is well saturated. This will guarantee you have the best transfer.

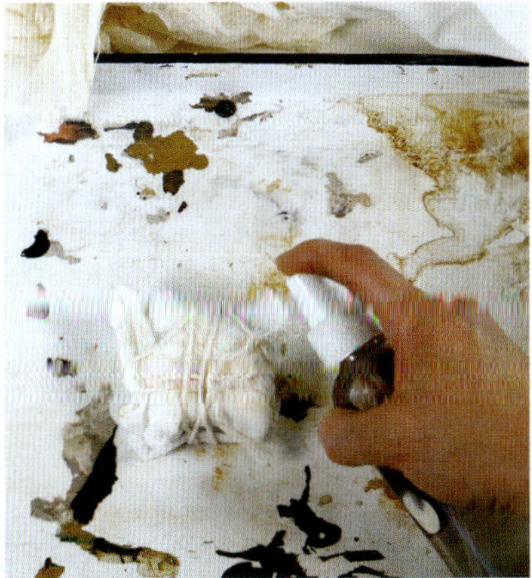

5 Once the object is completely wrapped up, tie it up with twine. This will ensure that everything stays intact while the fabric is dyeing, and you will also be able to use the rust-dyed twine in your work.

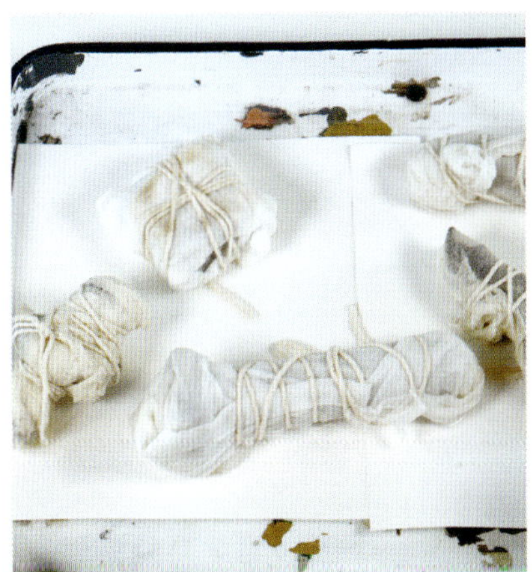

6 Repeat these steps with all of your rusty objects.

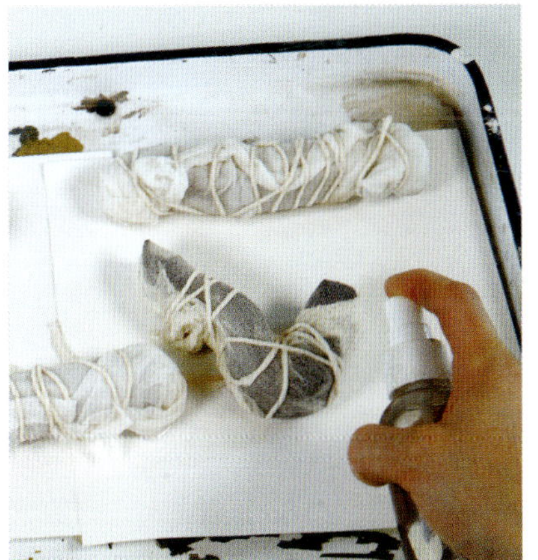

7 The transfer does not need to be only on the fabric. Before I set my wraps to dry, I like to place them all on a piece of watercolor paper and spray them again with the mixture. As the rust is transferring onto the fabric, it will also transfer onto the paper and it can often result in beautiful marks that could become a focal point of future work. Now, set your wraps aside to dry. If it is a sunny day, I highly recommend placing them outside.

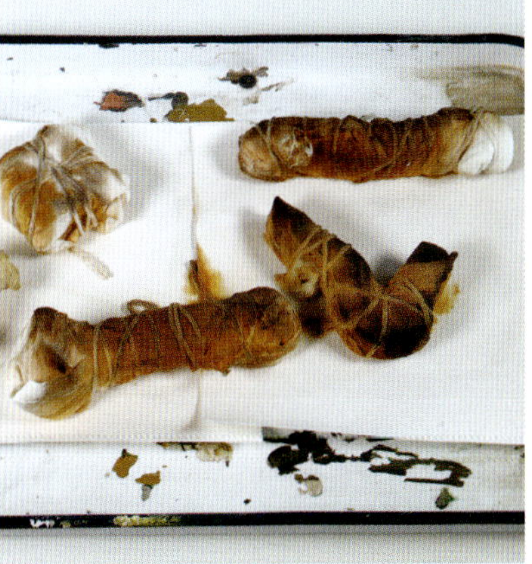

8 Based upon the amount of rust on your objects, this could be what your wraps look like after they have dried thoroughly. The drying time will vary depending on where you live and the season.

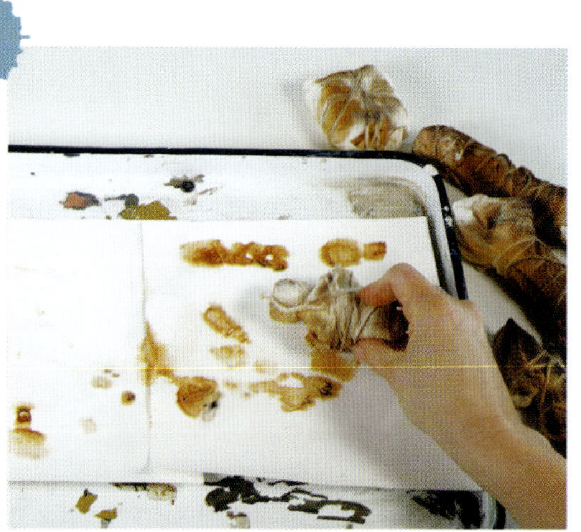

9 As I removed all of the wraps, you can see the fun and random transfers that have been left behind on the watercolor paper. Marks like these help me to see the shapes in new ways and give me fresh ideas of where to start in my work.

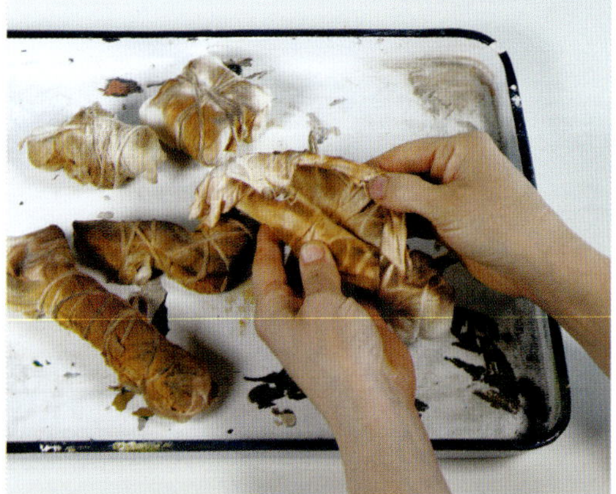

10 This is the fun part. You really don't know what you will get and what kind of transfer is waiting for you. Once your fabric is dry it is time to cut your twine and open up the wraps.

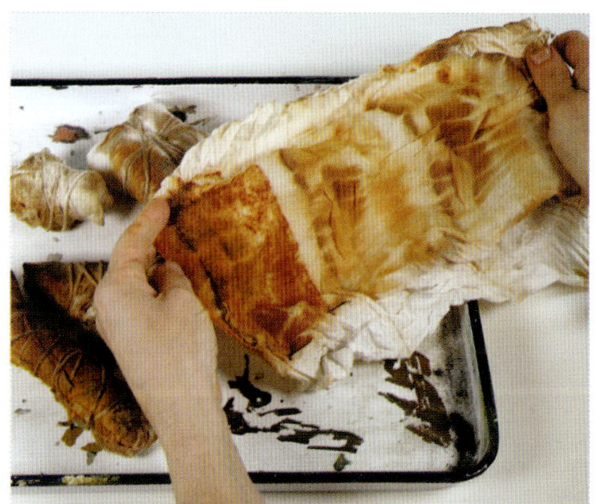

11 You may find that the fabric can be cut up into smaller pieces or that the piece will stay intact because it represents a landscape (or another image) and it is the jumping-off point for your next project.

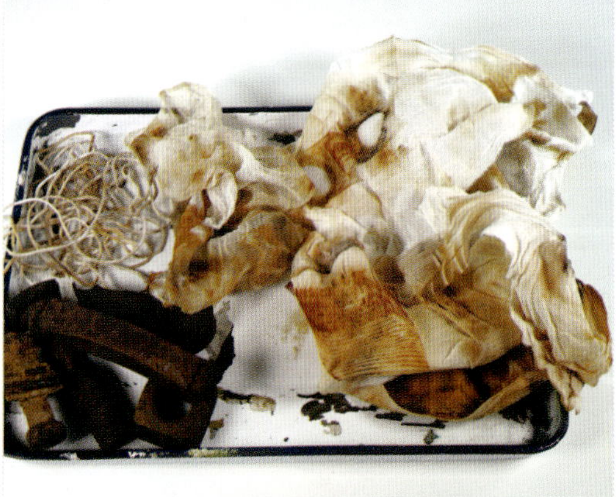

12 The uses are endless with the fabric. Include the fabric in your next journal, as an underlayer in your journal page, as a focal point in your work, or cut up or even stretched out if you are using cheesecloth.

#7 FABRIC TRANSFERS

After you have the beautiful rust transferred onto fabric, it is fun to add more layers and texture with an image transfer. Don't reserve your laser image transfers just for paper. Fabric and fabric transfers are the perfect mediums to cut, stitch, collage and more.

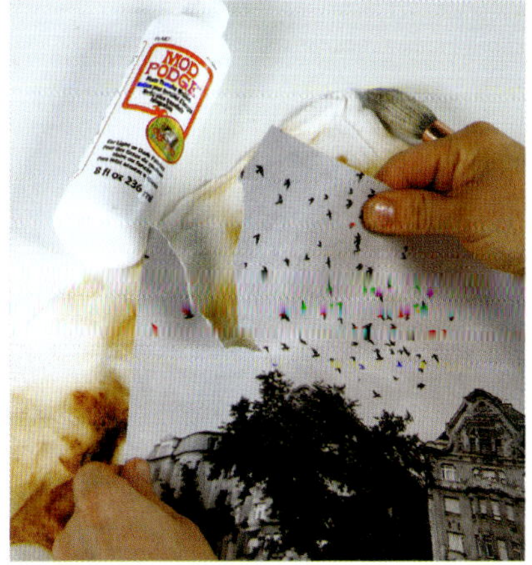

1 Using a laser print (I used an image I took while in Budapest), rip away the part of the image you want to transfer. A ripped edge is more organic and creates a more natural line in the transfer.

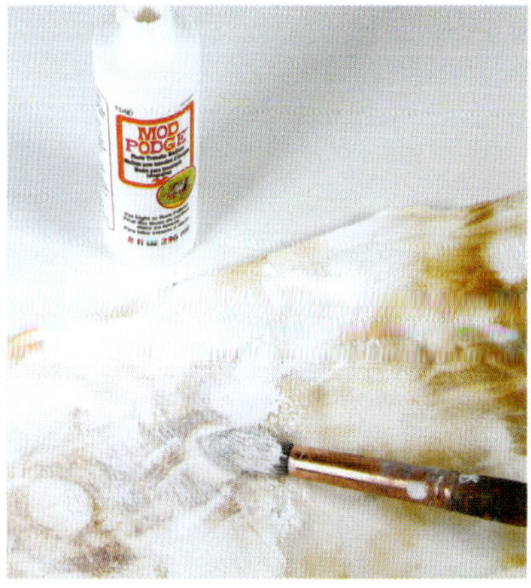

2 Apply a thin layer of Mod Podge photo transfer medium onto your fabric. Keep in mind what parts of your rust transfer you do not want to cover up.

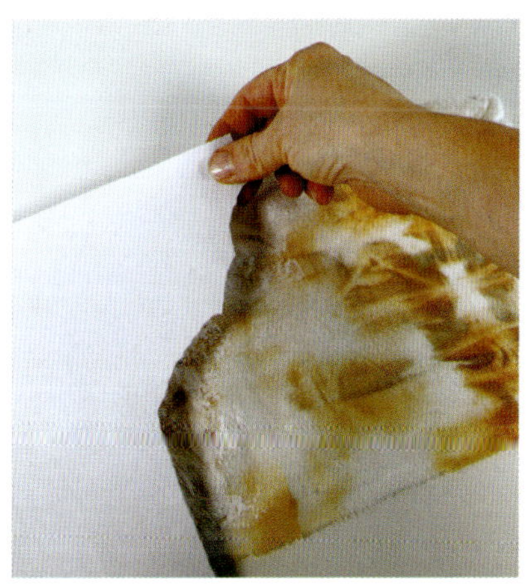

3 Place your laser print image face-down in the wet Mod Podge photo transfer medium. Using your hand, a cloth or an old credit card, smooth out any bubbles to make sure your image is firmly in place. Set aside to dry for up to 24 hours.

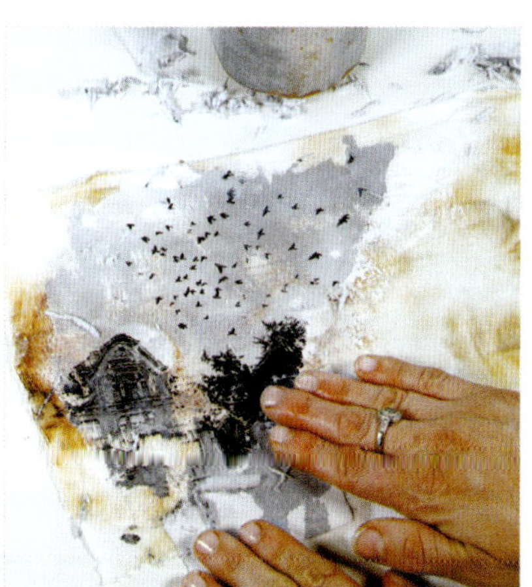

4 After your medium is dry, dip your fingers into a clean cup of water and gently rub in a circular or back-and-forth motion to remove the back layer of the paper. Repeat until the image is revealed.

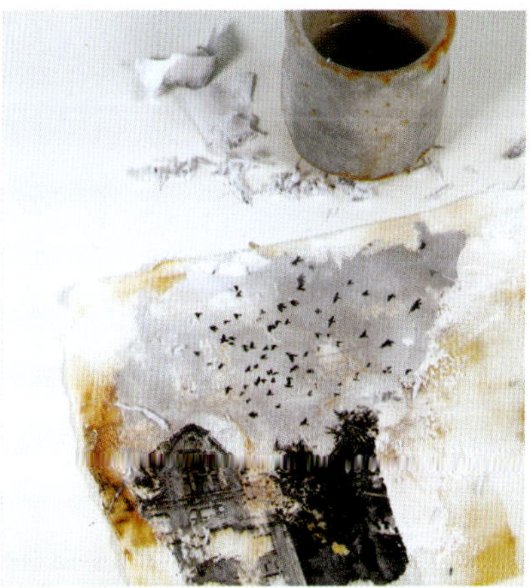

5 If you rub too hard, you may pull up some of your image, but that can add to the interest of your transfer. As your image transfer begins to dry, you may find that it becomes white and cloudy. If this happens, lightly dampen your fingers again and gently remove any of this excess paper. To prevent the image from fading again, I like to apply a thin layer of Liquitex matte medium.

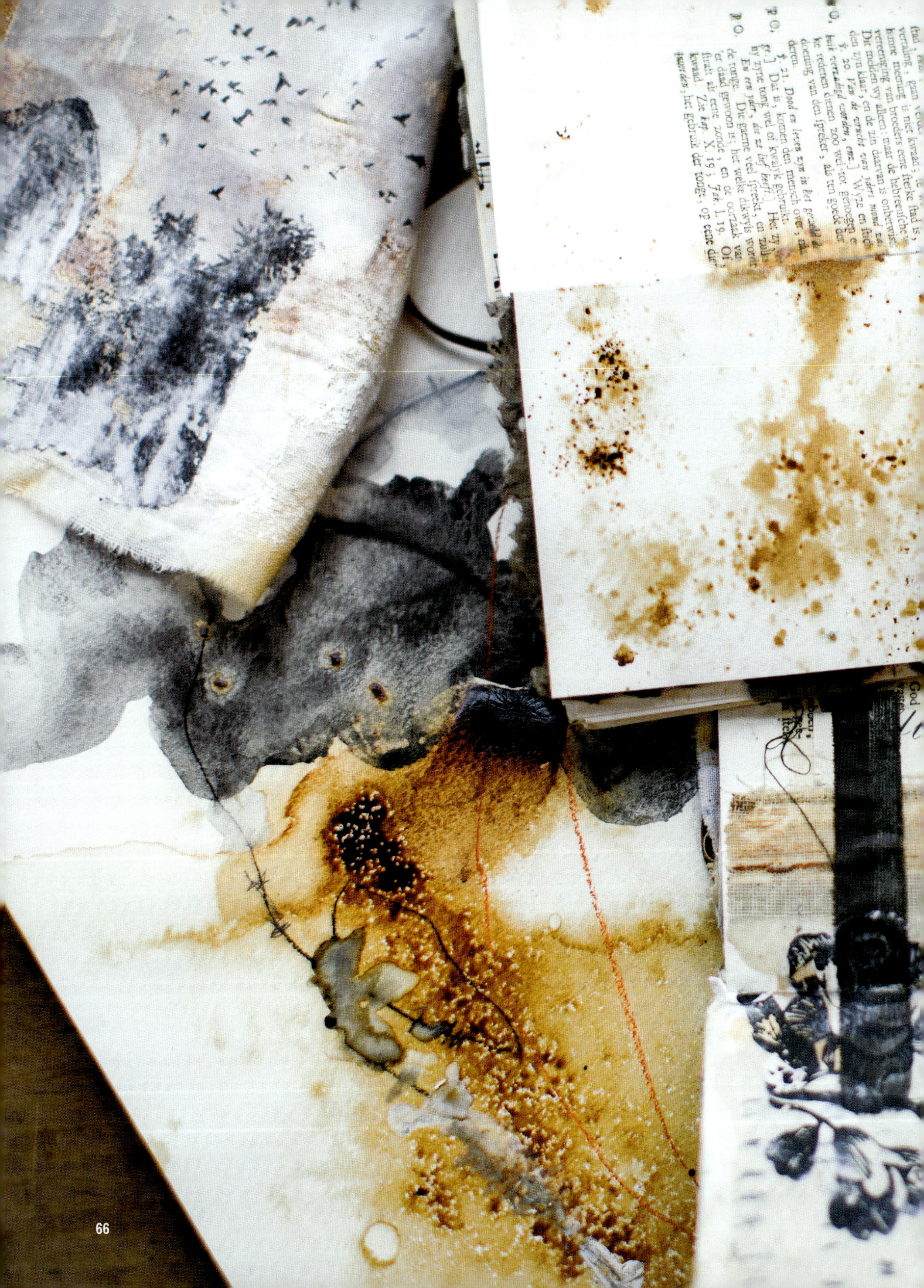

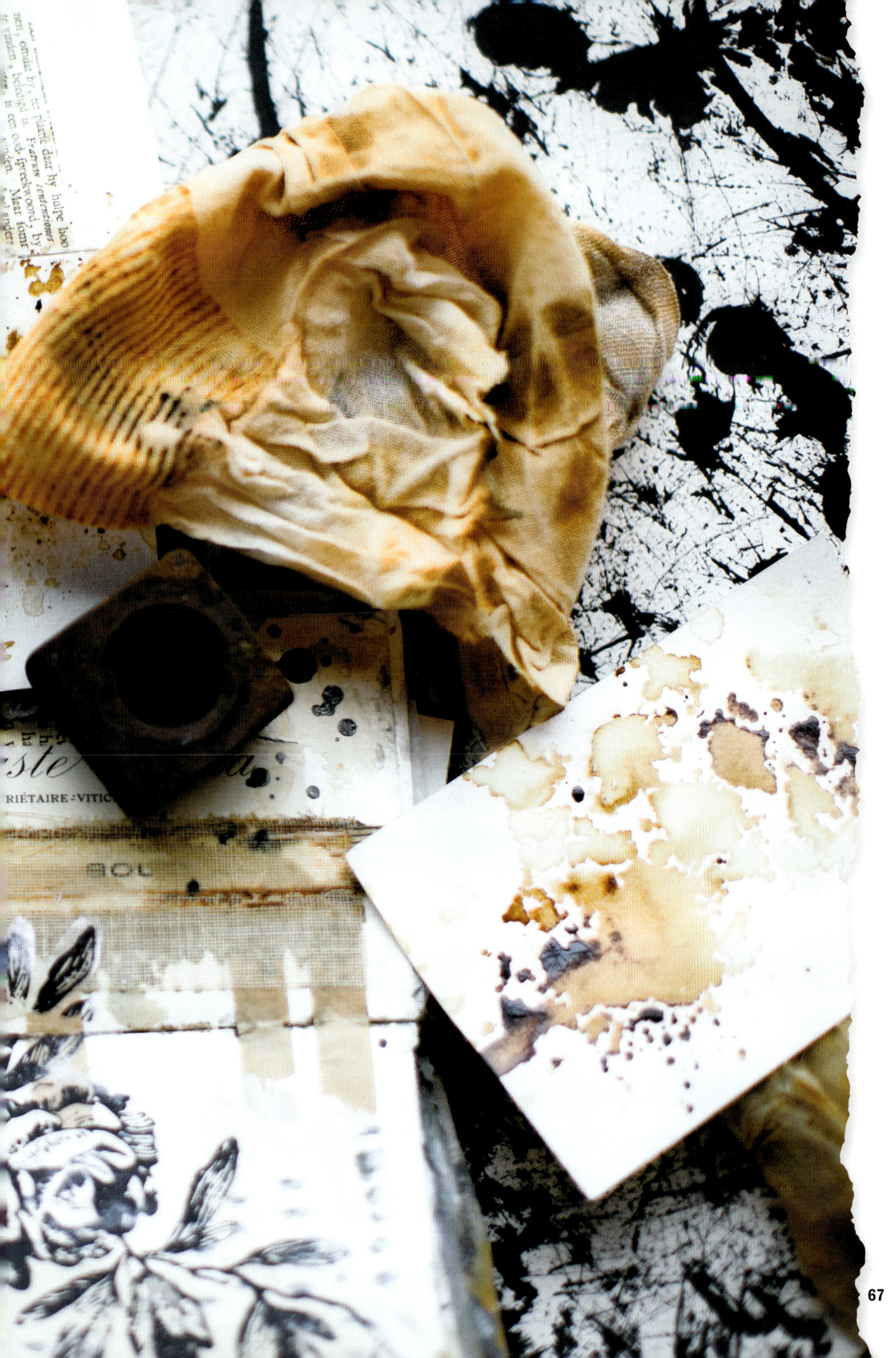

the heart

CHAPTER 9

Creating Your Timeline

AS I WAS ENVISIONING HOW I WANTED MY TIMELINE TO LOOK AND FEEL, I knew I didn't want a straight line. The idea of not knowing what would represent the beginning and the end, and how much of my story to include, felt daunting and intimidating. I also knew that taking the time to reflect a bit on my own history was the only way I could dig deeper into the art in front of me and the parts of my story that I had not yet uncovered or allowed to unfold. I decided that a circular timeline would allow me to explore my story in a manageable and edited version. The circular storytelling through the timeline also allowed me to see how each part was connected and built one upon another. Of any art I have ever created in my life, the timeline has been the most powerful to date in understanding myself.

The most beautiful part about telling your story through art is that it allows you to put your story out into the world. You know what each piece means, but you do not have to verbally share all of the details. It is the strange double story of sharing it all but holding back at the same time. It is for you, but just maybe someone else will find his or her own story in it, too.

Creating Your Timeline

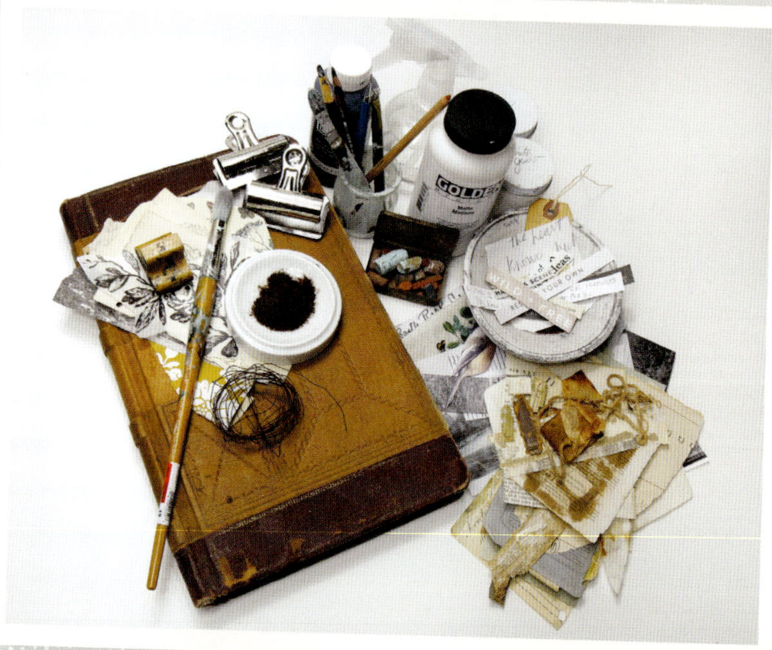

As you begin, enjoy the process of gathering, collecting your mark-making tools, symbolism, photos and color palette and brainstorming. This is an art-changing exercise if you want to understand yourself better and you want to tell your story though art in a whole new way.

This timeline is divided into eight segments to allow you to group events, people or time frames in an easier manner. My timeline is chronological, but please create this however you see fit. How you choose your eight segments is completely up to you, but I encourage you to allow segment one to be all about an event, person or circumstance that happened before your birth that has had an impact on your life directly or indirectly. Our stories do not just begin with our birth but with the stories of those in our lives before us. This segment is important to show how even things that happen before your life began can be significant in our own journey. I would also love to see you use segment eight for what is to come. Seeing your journey and creating something for yourself to visually connect with and seeing what you are working towards is a powerful part of your story . . . even if it hasn't happened yet.

WHAT YOU NEED

- Art journal
- Black Stabilo All pencil
- Charcoal pencil
- Cloth or rag
- Embroidery needle and thread
- Gesso: clear, black and white
- Large and small circles to trace
- Mark-making tools
- Matte medium
- Mechanical pencil
- No. 4 round, long-handled paintbrush
- Paintbrush
- Personal ephemera
- Ruler
- Rust-dyed twine
- Tape, thread or glue
- Thin jewelry wire
- Wire cutters
- Your personal color palette

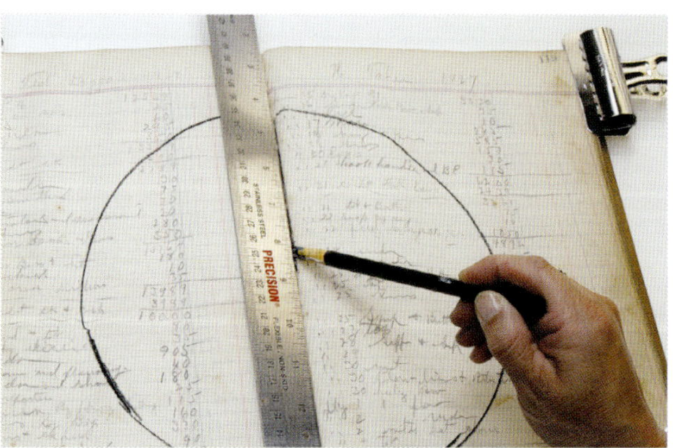

1 Apply a thin layer of clear gesso to your journal page. Using a large bowl as a template, turn it over on the rim and outline the bowl with charcoal. Using a ruler, divide your circle into eight even segments.

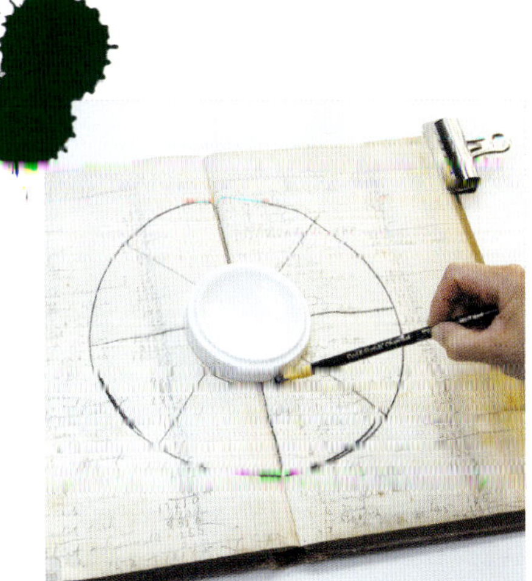

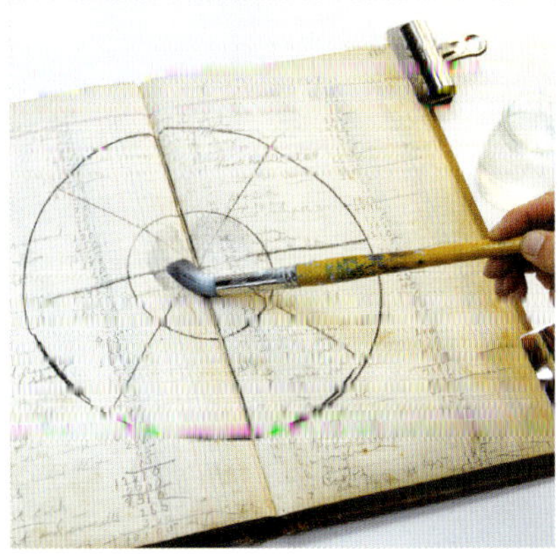

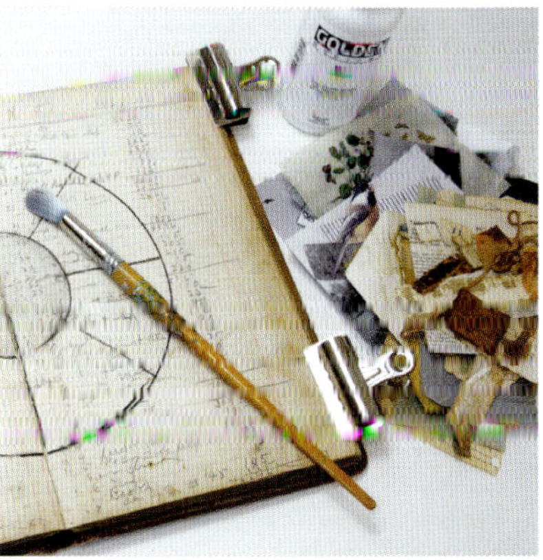

2 Using a smaller circular item, create another circle within the center of your timeline. This center section will represent your core values and what guides you in all other areas of your life.

3 All of those extra charcoal lines can now be washed away with a brush and water. This is why I also use charcoal so much in preliminary sketches. Charcoal allows me to make whatever marks I need while knowing they are not permanent.

4 This gathering stage is where you can refer to your color palette, storyboard, photos and vintage ephemera, and then bring those key elements together. This time of gathering also allows you to be open to the parts of your story you want to document.

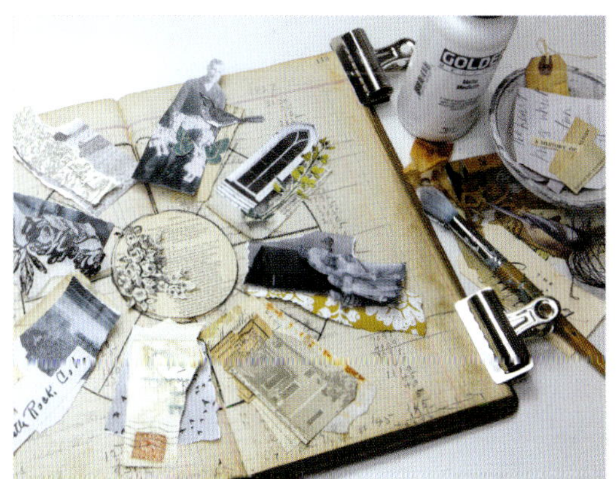

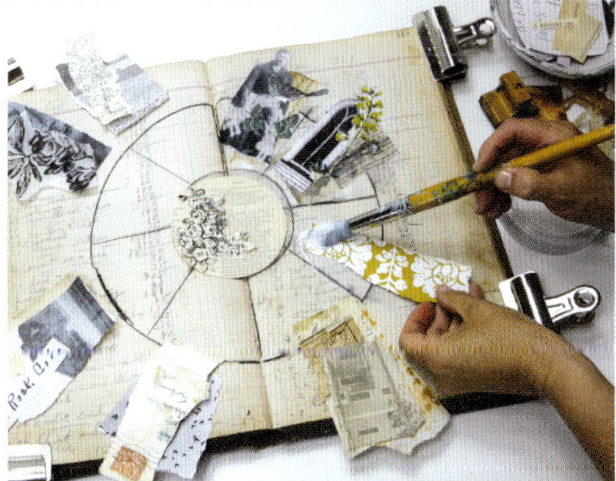

5 Start layering your different segments. I chose to use vintage papers, photocopies of photos, images from magazines, copies of my own artwork and the first layer of symbolism collected in Chapter 8.

6 Using matte medium, adhere your first layer of papers to your journal. Remember to use the matte medium not only to attach the papers to the journal but also to apply a thin coat on the top. This will seal your layers as you go.

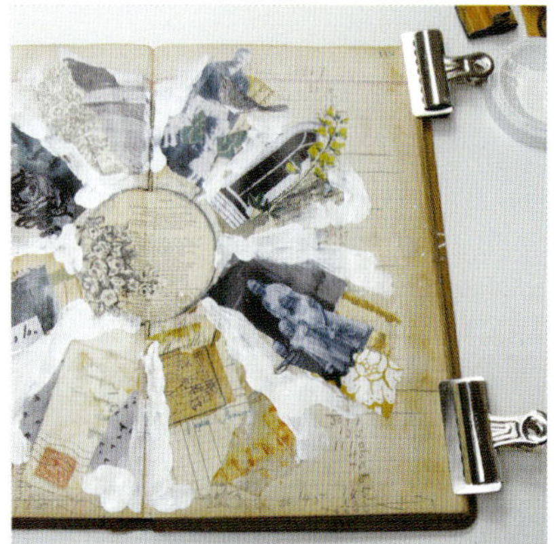

7 Using white gesso, soften the edges of your papers, which will also help to show division among the segments.

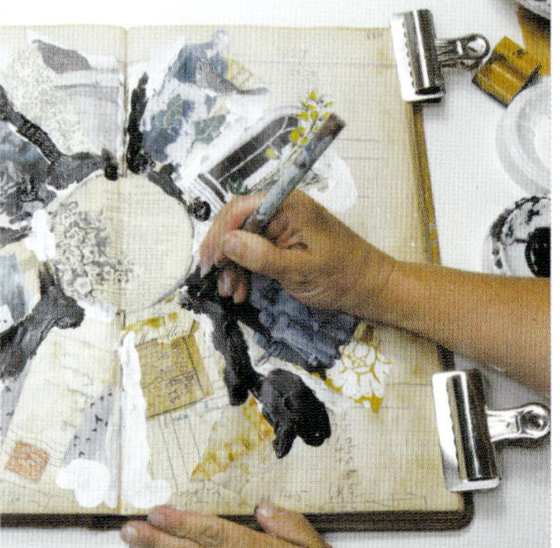

8 Bring in black gesso sparingly to ground a few spots in your timeline. While the gesso is still wet, use a mark-making tool to bring in repetitive marks, lines or symbolism. This initial layer and mark making will help to bring more depth and interest to your final piece. It can also be a powerful yet subtle story-telling technique. Refer to your journal page on mark making and symbolism if you get stuck.

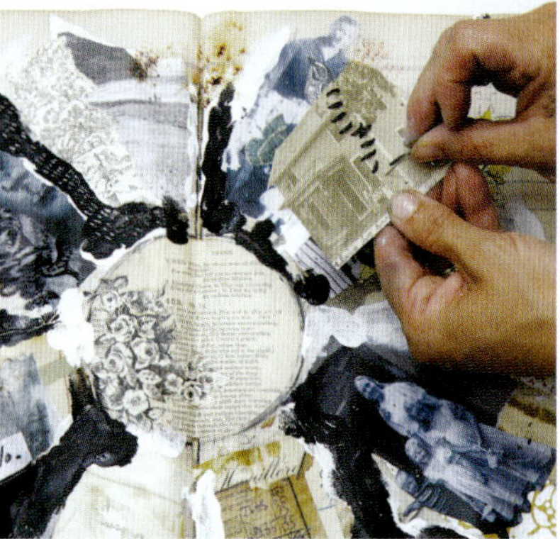

9 What images can you begin to add to your timeline to represent part of your story? I cut a vintage photo of a farmhouse into broken pieces and, using a needle and embroidery thread, I stitched it back together. Using your color palette as a reference, you can pick a more dominant or accent color in your palette and incorporate it in subtle ways through stitching or mark making. I used a Red Oxide thread in my timeline.

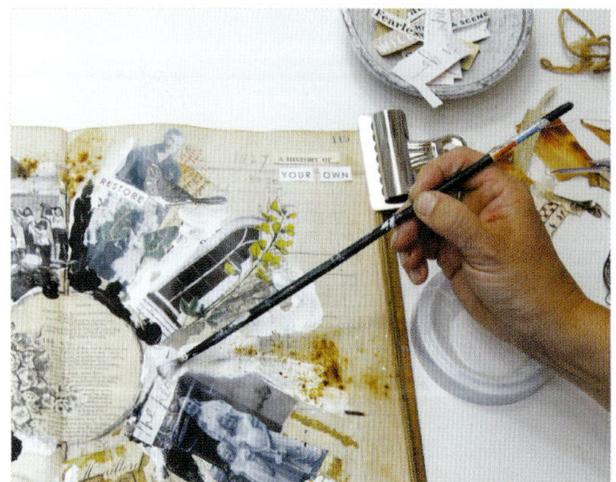

10 Cut out words from newspapers, magazines and old books that connect to your emotions and story, or even because you are drawn to the typography. I like to always have these on hand for my creating. You can also type up words and print them out if you do not have the resources above. Add handwritten, cutout, stamped or typed words to your timeline. This can be poetry, places, feelings or whatever you are trying to express.

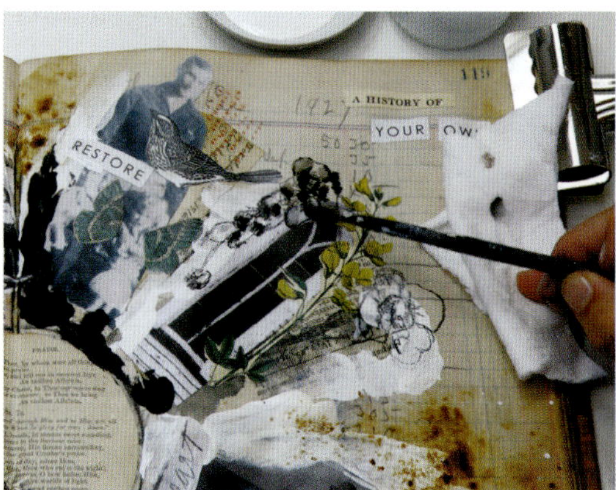

11 Using a black Stabilo pencil, loosely sketch flowers. I used flowers to symbolize beauty, growth and nurturing. If you choose to add flowers, you can attach any meaning you want to them. Dip a no. 4 round long-handled brush in water and gently wipe it on a cloth to prevent too much water from pooling on the paper. Once the Stabilo is activated with water it provides a very intense black, so I was light-handed with my sketching and also with how much water I used to activate it. Staying within the lines of the floral, draw the black into the floral. Make sure not to activate the entire sketch and to leave some of the lines dry. We are using the same techniques shared in Chapter 8.

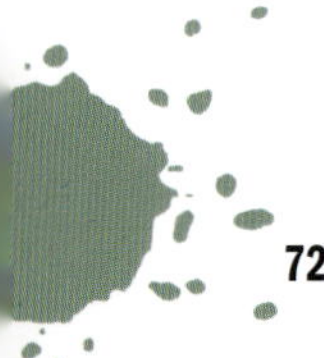

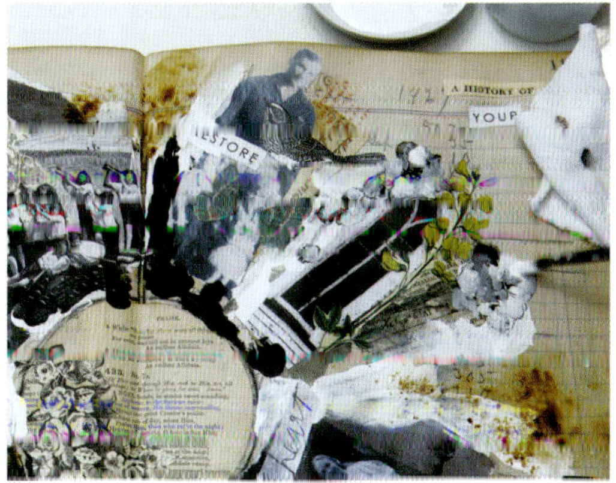 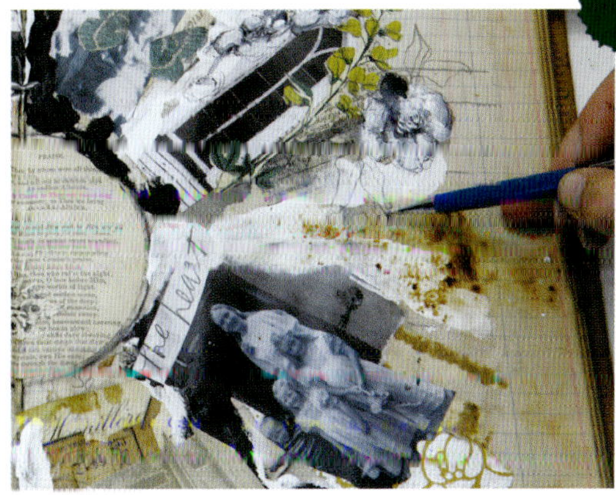

12 Using white gesso, add highlights and values to create a more dimensional floral. Adding white gesso to the Stabilo creates a permanent sketch (no longer water-soluble) once it dries. This also allows you to add more mediums as you layer without smudging your original sketch. You will add more black and white elements as you are creating your floral. If you find you do not have enough values, this may be because too much of the sketch is wet, or it is too white or too black. Try to be more random with your brushstrokes to create a looser floral with definite highlights and darker values. By not blending everything together you will create a floral with more interest and depth.

13 While your floral is still wet, use a mechanical pencil to add mark-making details into your floral. You can also add leaves, which don't need to have details added to them. I like the skeletal imagery of leaving them as just graphite sketches. The painted floral and the basic graphite sketches complement each other beautifully.

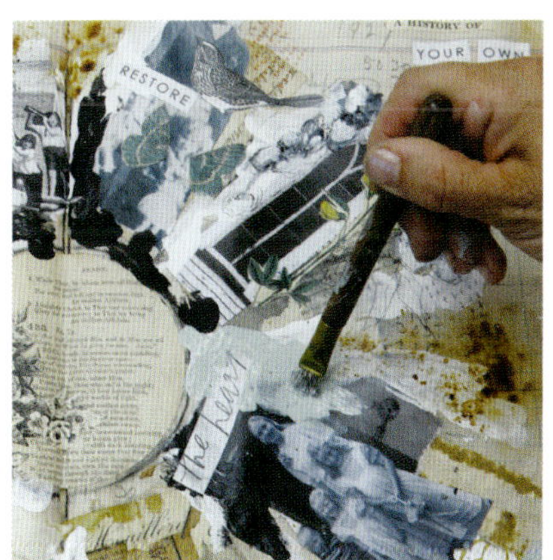 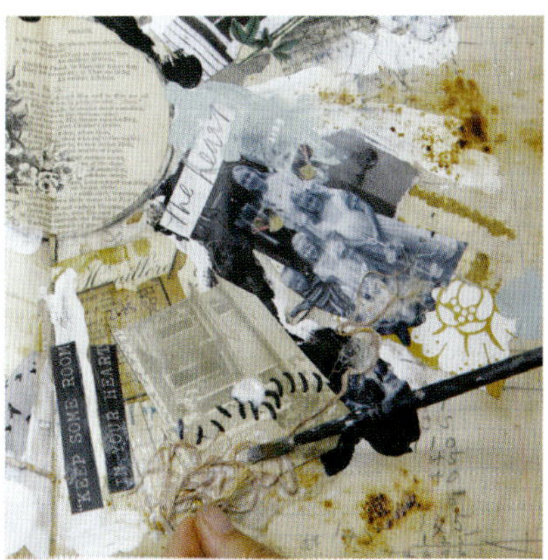 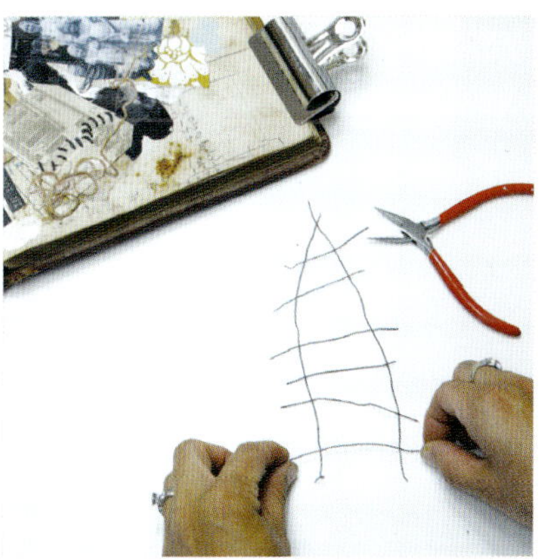

14 Using one of the main colors from your color palette, add color elements through any medium of your choice. If you are using a wet medium, this is also a good time to add more mark making.

15 Use your rust-dyed twine to create symbolism, words or shapes. You can adhere the twine with tape, stitching or glue. In this piece I used the twine to symbolize a complicated situation and then a breaking away. I used Liquitex matte medium as my glue.

16 Wire is a fun and easy way to make a big impact in your art and timeline. Using your journal pages of symbolism and mark making, find a shape to incorporate into your work. Jewelry wire is easy to manipulate and cut and is a perfect wire to use for this project. Loosely measure the size of the shape you want to make, cut the wire with jewelry cutters or an old pair of scissors, wrap the wires with your fingers and then cut off any remaining ends. I wanted to symbolize the journey I was on by using a ladder.

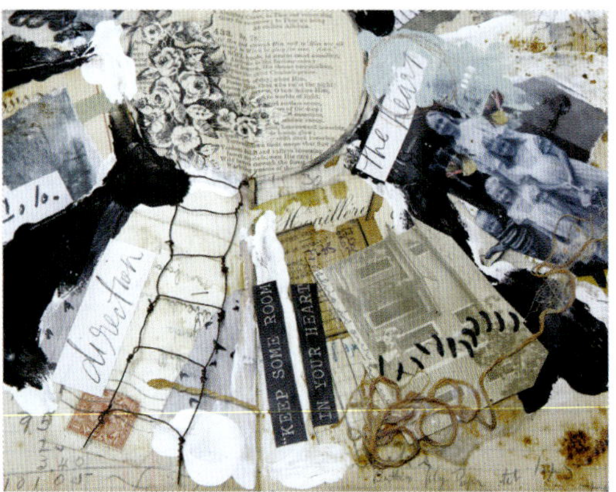

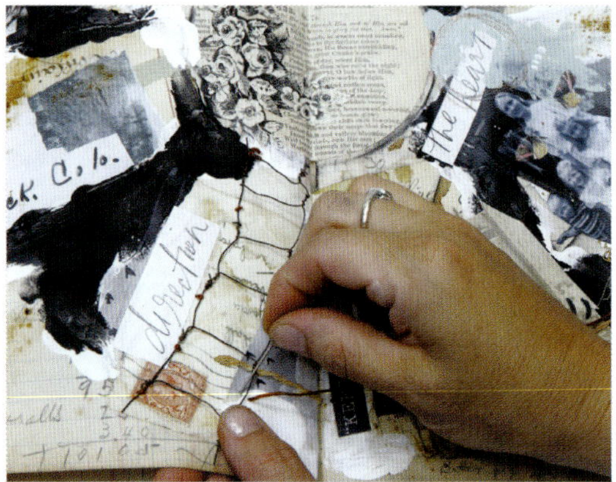

17 Once your wire form is completed you can attach it with tape, thread or glue. This is another opportunity to bring in another color from your palette. I chose to bring in Red Oxide embroidery thread to lightly tack it to my vintage paper.

18 The vintage journal I used is very easy to stitch through because of the age of the paper, but if you are using a thicker paper, you may need to create your holes with a needle or awl before you begin stitching. This will prevent your paper from ripping.

Do you have the courage to bring forth the treasures that are hidden within you?

Look, I don't know what's hidden within you. I have no way of knowing such a thing. You yourself may barely know, although I suspect you've caught glimpses. I don't know your capacities, your aspirations, your longings, your secret talents. But surely something wonderful is sheltered inside you. I say this with all confidence because I happen to believe we are all walking repositories of buried treasure. I believe this is one of the oldest and more generous tricks the universe plays on us human beings, both for its own amusement and for ours: The universe buries strange jewels deep within us all, and then stands back to see if we can find them.

—ELIZABETH GILBERT FROM BIG MAGIC

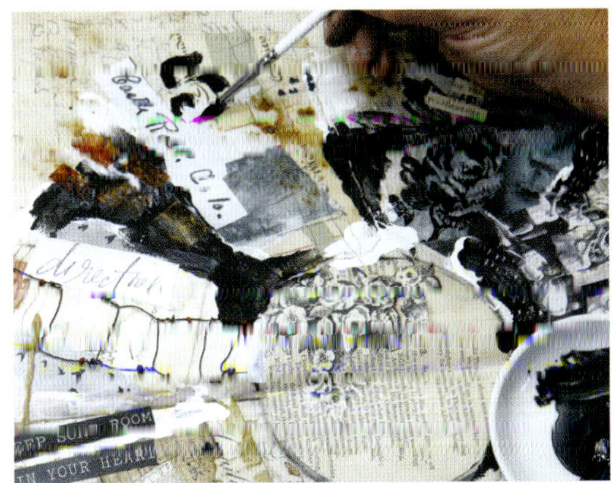 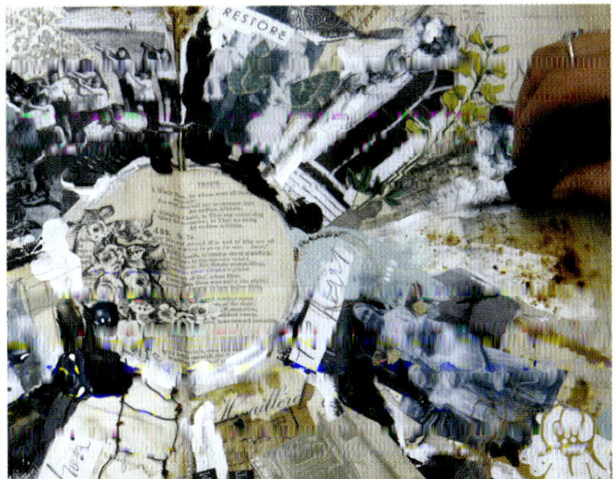

19 How can you represent your story on this top layer with collage, mark making, stamping or more? I used cut up old tea bags to represent the five members of my family, a vintage "5" stamp, mark making with paint, repetitive marks and graphite sketching repeating some of my marks and symbolism. Once you know your marks and symbolism you can repeat them again and again in different ways.

20 Once you are at a stopping point, many of your collage, paint and mark-making elements may have overlapped and your segments may not be as clear. If this has happened you can use charcoal or another medium of your choice to lightly divide the segments. I used charcoal and then lightly rubbed the lines with my hands to soften the division. This timeline is ultimately for you, and you can choose whether you share it or not. If you do choose to share the art and what each piece means, I can promise you from experience that it is such a thoughtful way to show the intimacy of your journey. As your story changes and grows, I hope you will also create more timelines and find new ways of sharing the journey you are on.

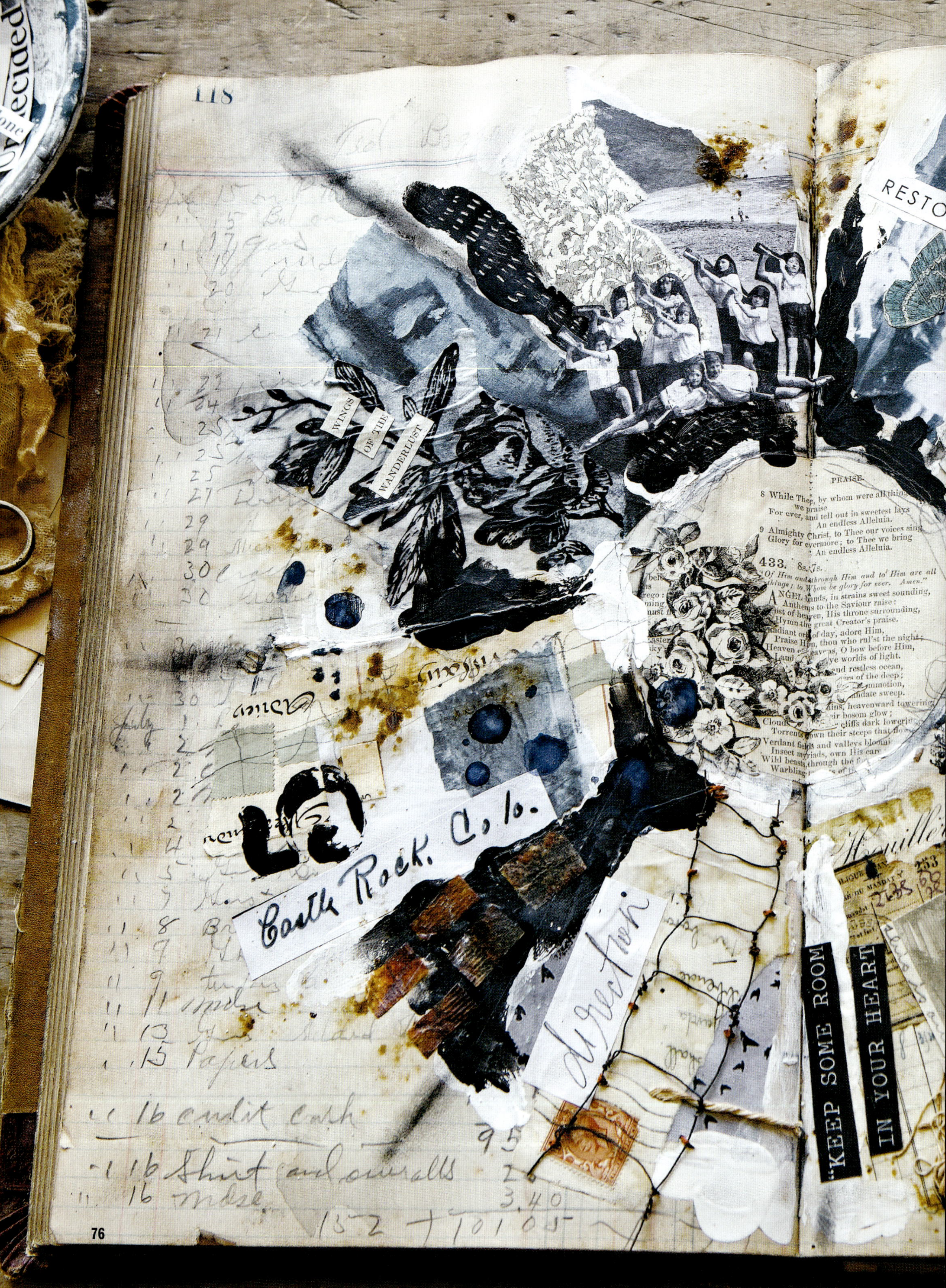
WINGS
OF THE
WANDERLUST
Castle Rock. Co. lo.
direction
"KEEP SOME ROOM
IN YOUR HEART"
RESTO
PRAISE
amen

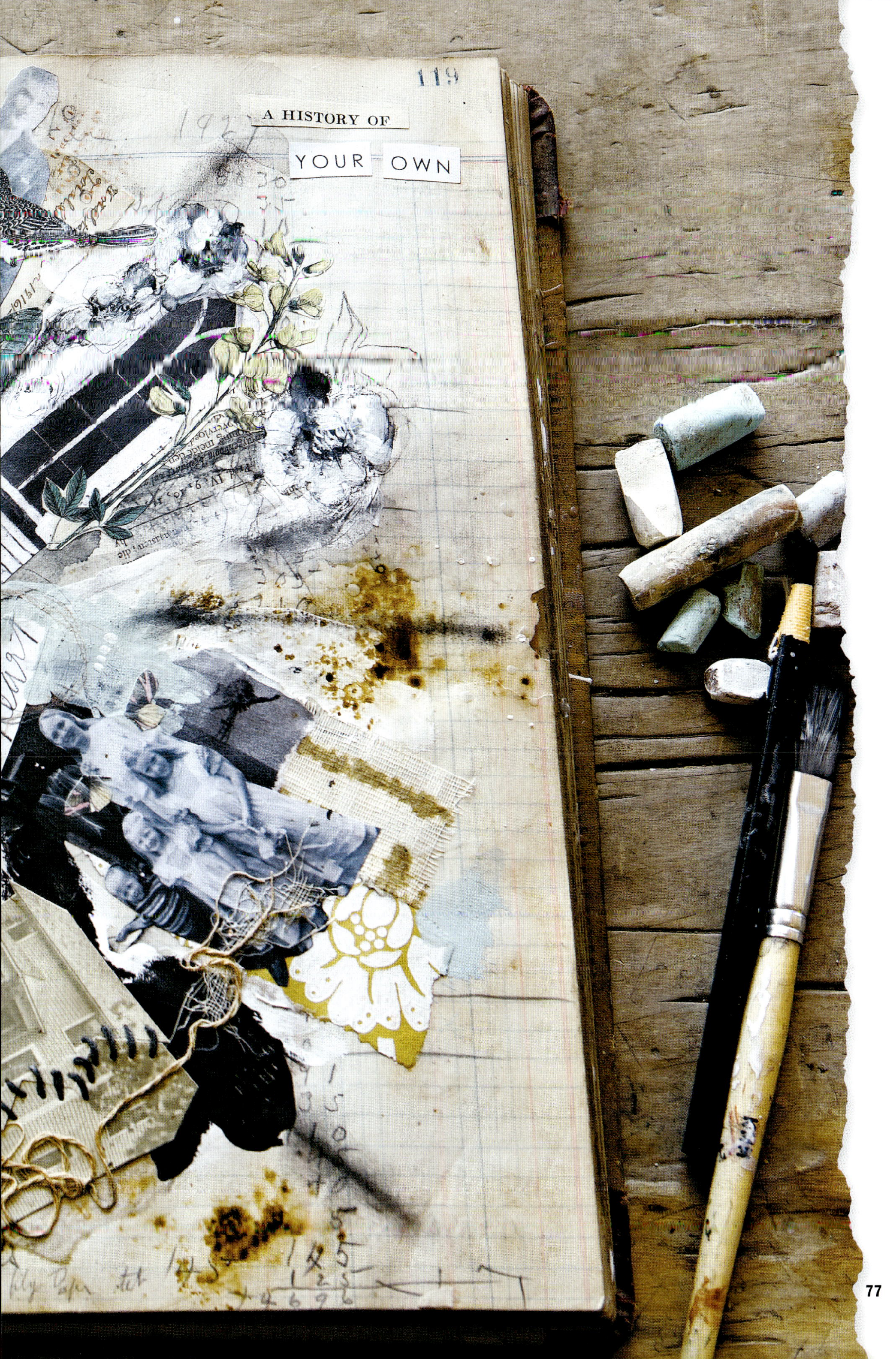

119
A HISTORY OF
YOUR OWN

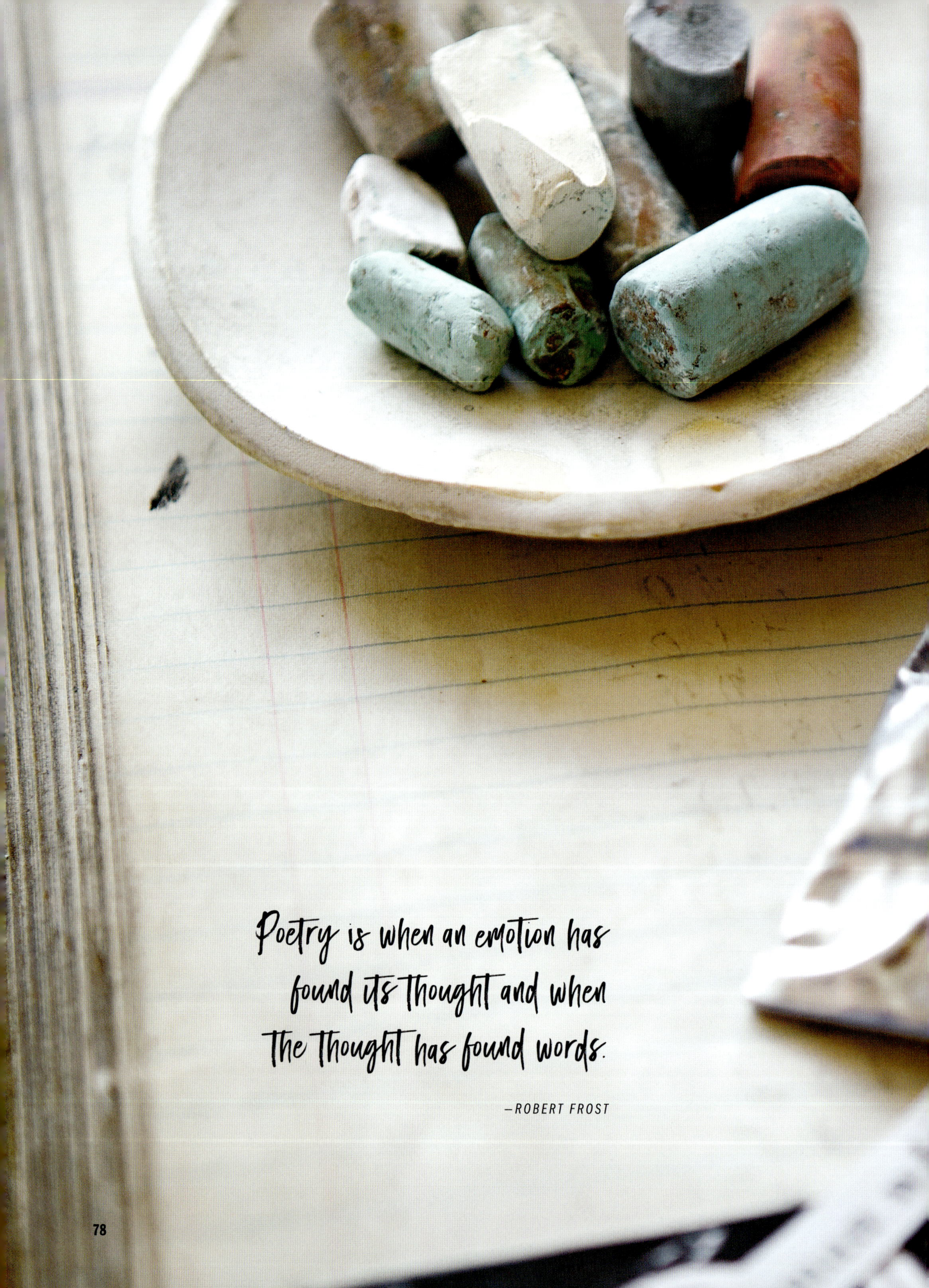

Poetry is when an emotion has
found its thought and when
the thought has found words.

—ROBERT FROST

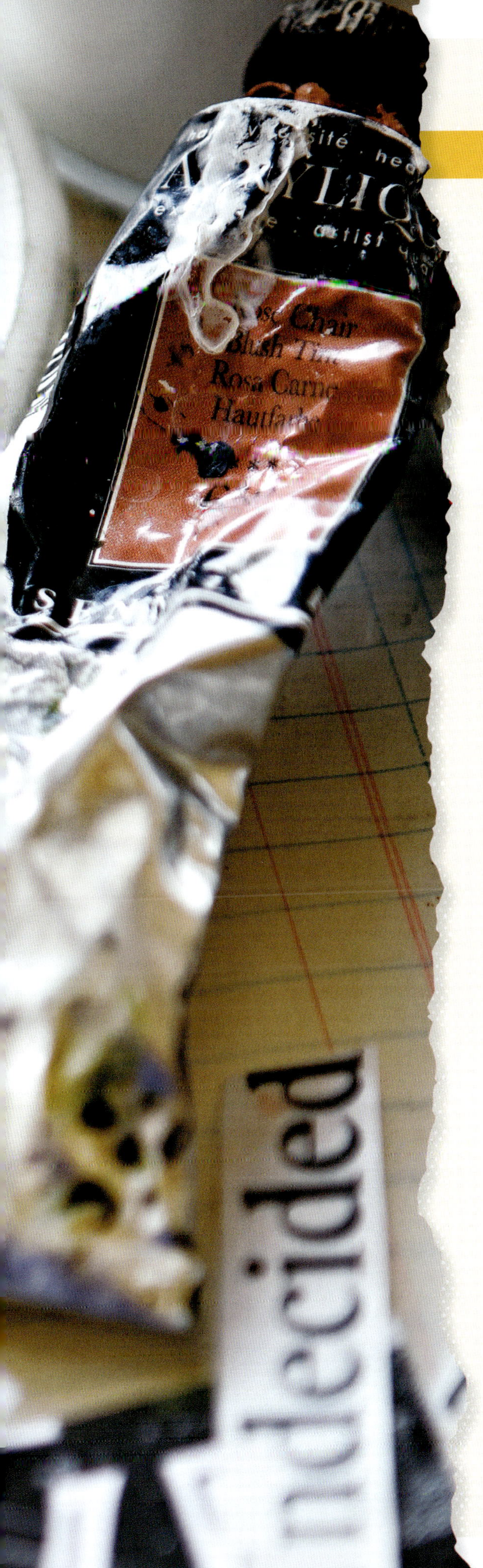

CHAPTER 10

Gathering a Poem

MANY PEOPLE FEEL THEY ARE NOT WRITERS, LET ALONE POETS. I think with some new tools that can change. As you gather words you are drawn to, watch what can happen when you pull words out based upon your current emotion. It seems like magic how lines come together, and before you know it—a poem, a verse, a story has been born.

You may find your words in old books, magazines, newspapers, flyers or vintage ephemera. With eyes open to the type and words around you, you can start your own collection. Give these collected words a special place to land in a vintage bowl, tin or special tray. They will be ready for you the next time inspiration strikes.

Gathering a Poem

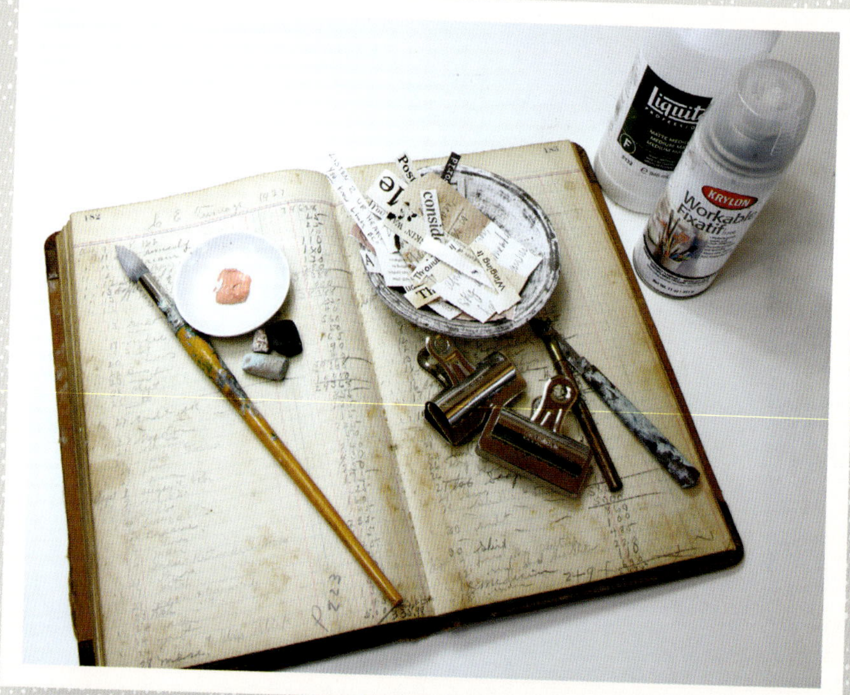

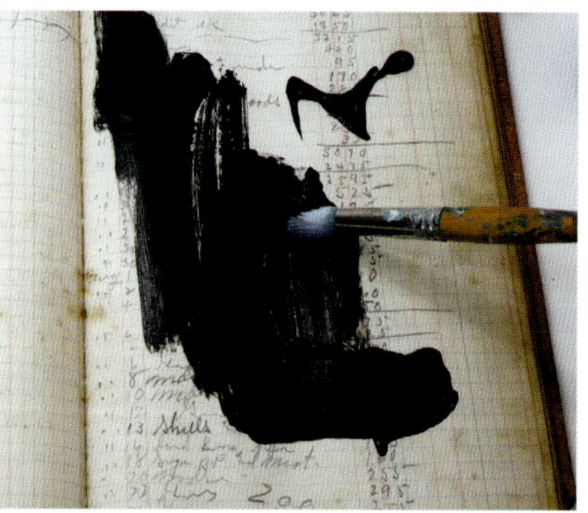

1 Using black gesso, cover both pages of your journal, leaving a border of the natural journal page around the edges. Allow to dry.

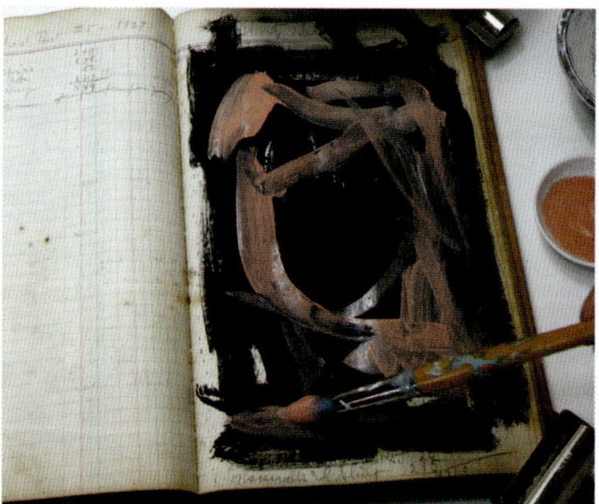

2 Using a color from your color palette, create some loose abstract designs and lines to be the backdrop for your poem. Do not overthink your marks.

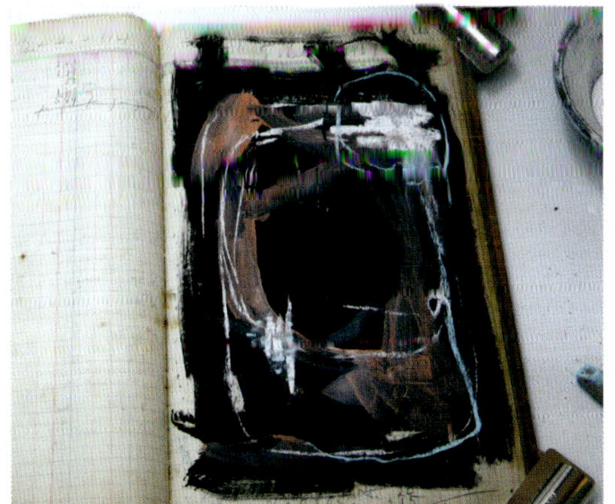

3 Bring in more mark making with pastels, charcoal, graphite or another medium of your choice. Remember, you are always encouraged to use what supplies you have and what you connect with versus what is shown.

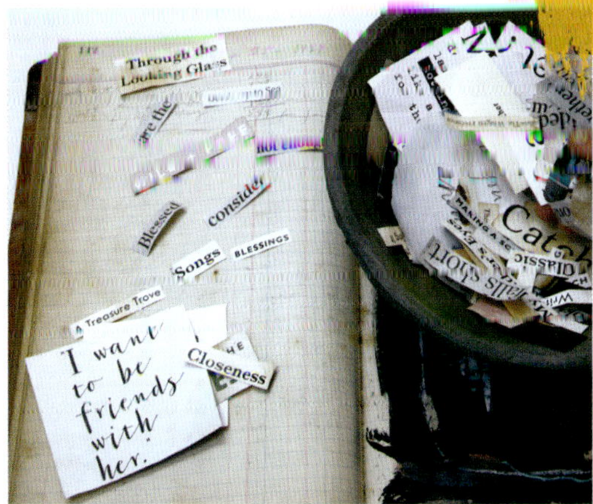

4 Using your collection of words that have been cut out, handwritten or printed, start to collect the words and phrases that connect with you right now. That is what is so fun about this exercise— the words you'll be drawn to will change based on where you are and what you are experiencing.

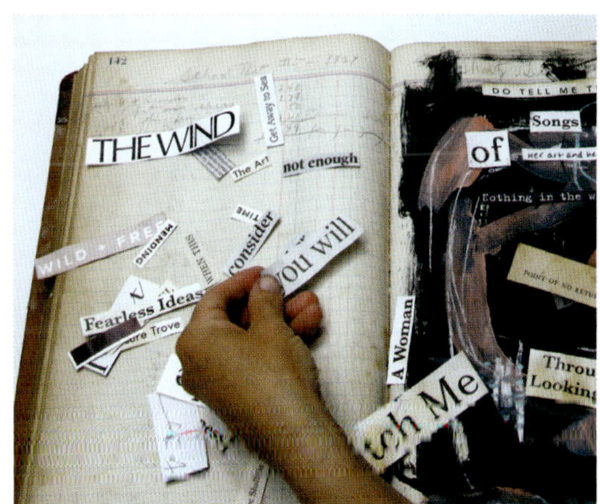

5 Enjoy this process of trying different arrangements of the words and phrases you have gathered.

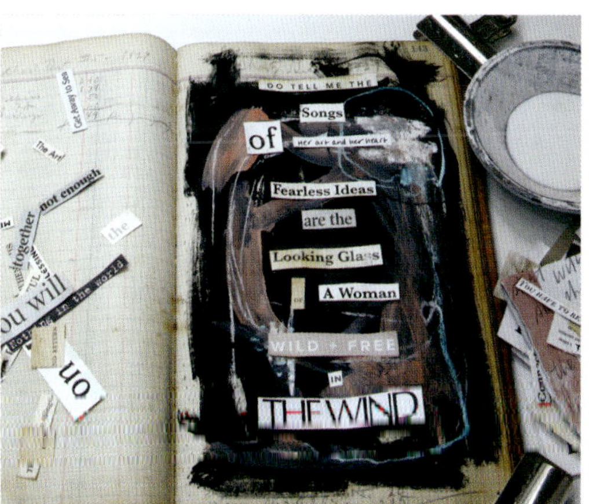

6 Once you have your poem in place, glue the words down with matte medium.

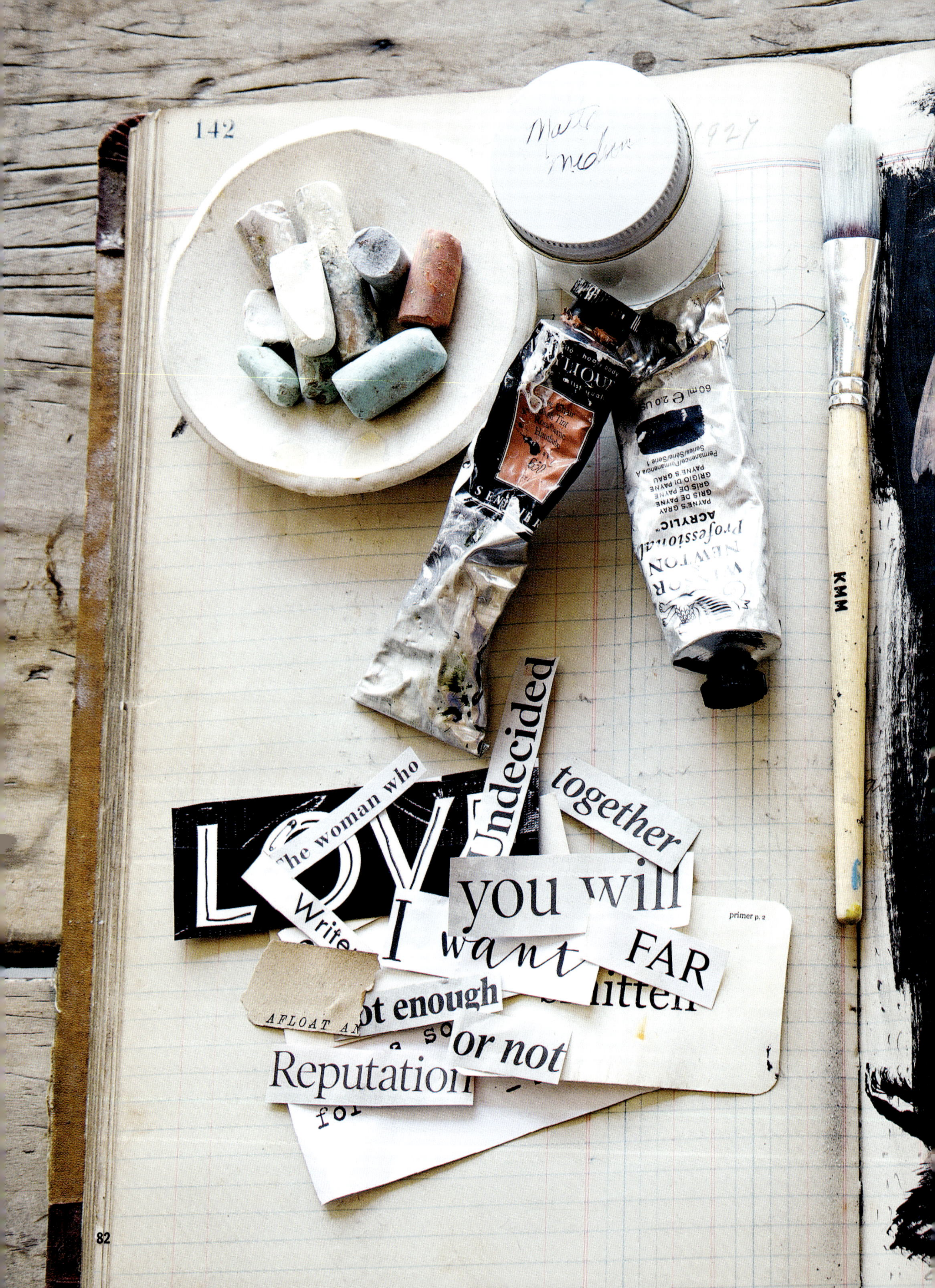

142
1927
primer p. 2
82

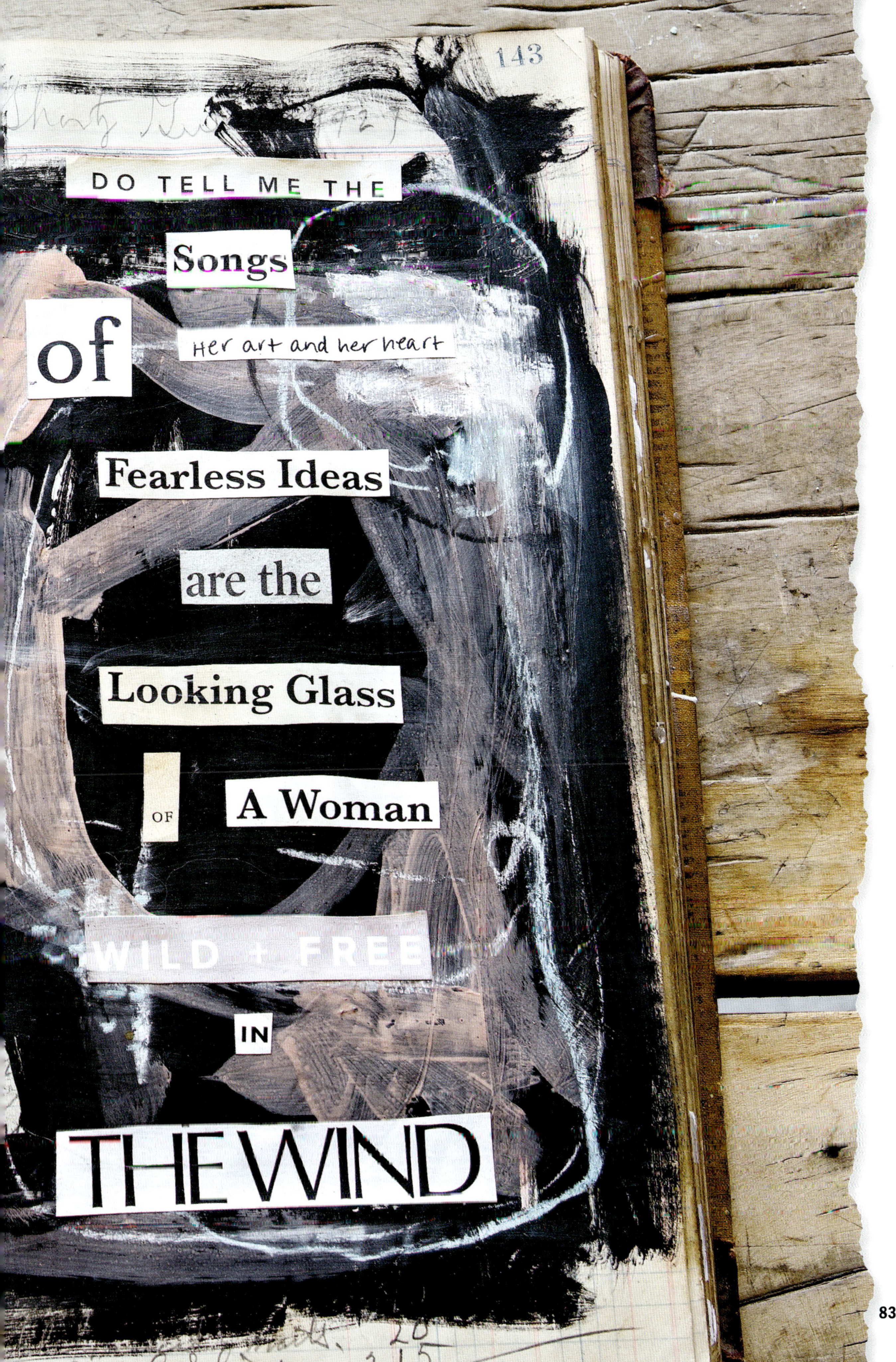
DO TELL ME THE
Songs
of
Her art and her heart
Fearless Ideas
are the
Looking Glass
OF A Woman
WILD + FREE
IN
THE WIND

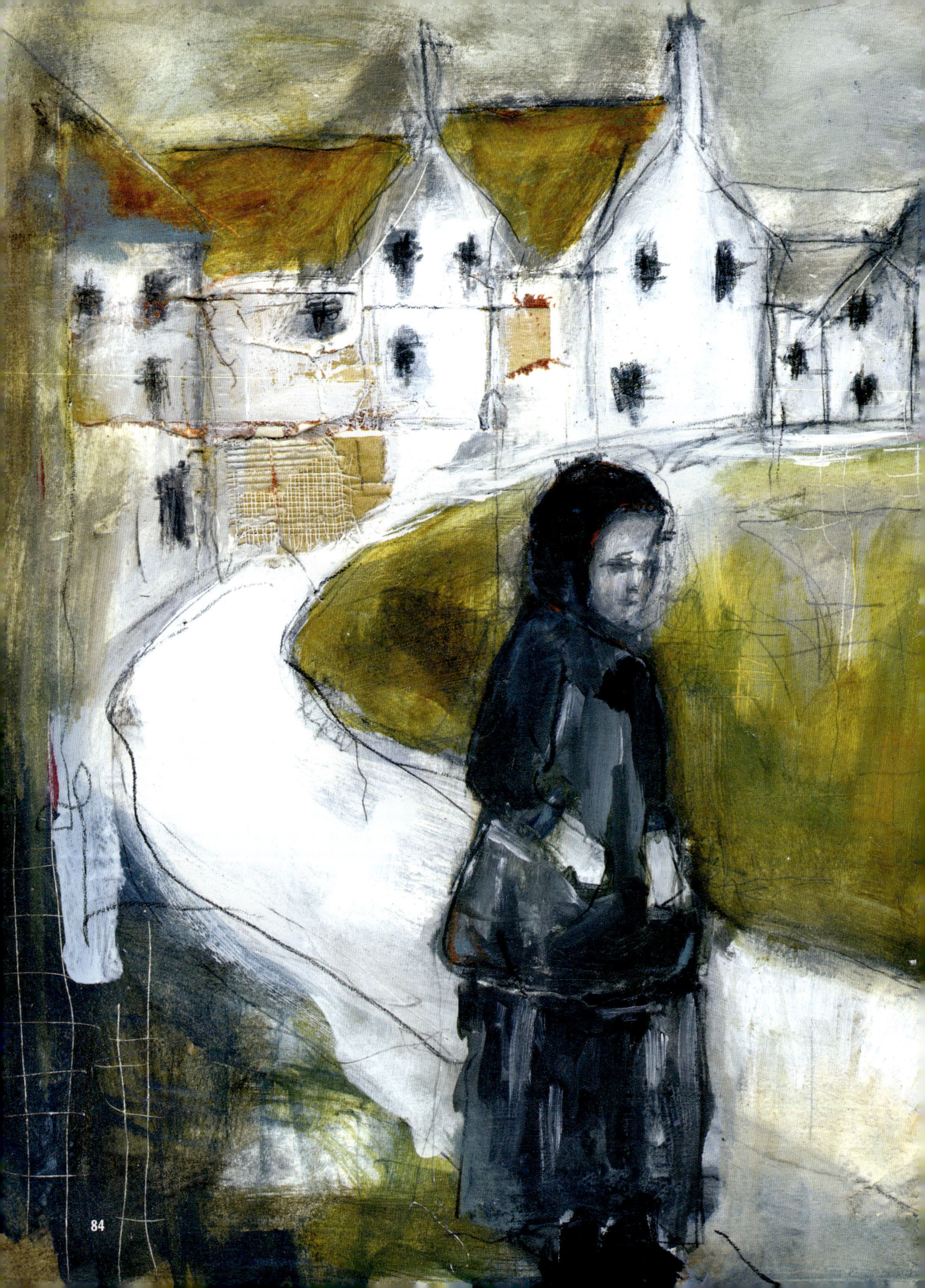

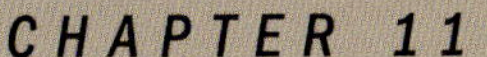

CHAPTER 11

Composition 101

WHEN YOU ARE FLIPPING THROUGH AN ART BOOK, strolling through an art museum or working on your own pieces, have you ever stopped to think about *why* you are so drawn to a piece? Is it the subject matter, elements of design, composition or maybe a combination of them all? When you study the basics of composition and the elements of design, it not only helps you to be aware of what can make a piece pleasing to the eye, but you can also understand the power you have as the artist to direct the piece and to direct the eye of the viewer.

Composition techniques and ideas can fill a book and I would never act like I am qualified to fill chapters with the subject, but I do think it is good for artists to be aware of basic principles of composition and design elements. These are all just suggestions and you are free to throw it all out the window if you don't connect with the techniques and ideas. Ultimately you are the boss of your work, and if art has taught us anything it is that there are no rules.

Composition 101 and Elements of Design

Have you ever stared at a blank canvas or journal page and felt stumped at where to begin? I think we have all been there. One of the basic principles of composition is the rule of thirds and just being aware of it can have a huge impact on your work. This rule (which you can embrace or throw out) can not only help give you a jumping-off point and make your composition more pleasing to the eye, but can also help give you control of the focal point of your piece.

In the painting above I have placed a grid over my work to talk about the rule of thirds in art. You will notice that the art has been divided horizontally and vertically. The rule of thirds is based upon the theory that any area of interest should fall along these lines and/or in the areas where the lines intersect. This means that

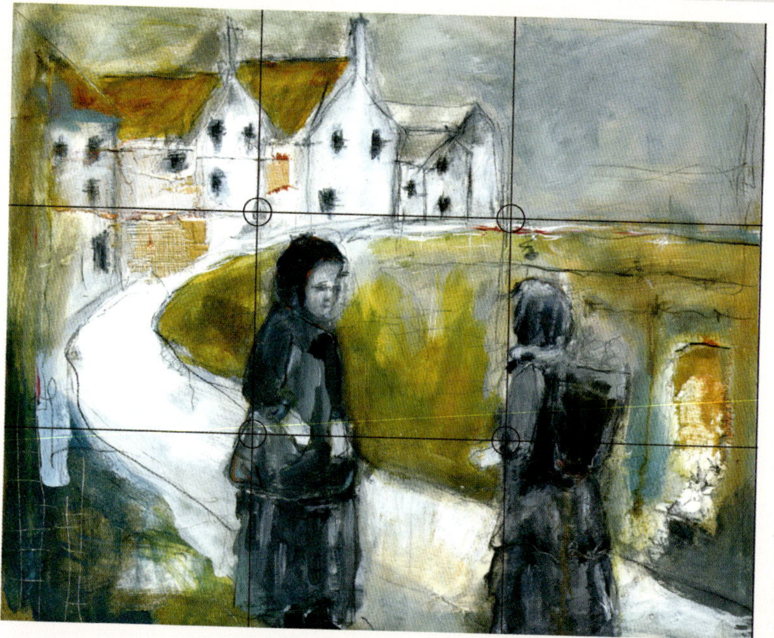

if you have the choice between having your portrait smack-dab in the middle of your substrate or off to a side, try moving it to the left or right for more interest. This will create negative space in your work and, in turn, create a more pleasing composition. Negative space is the resting place in your art that surrounds your areas of focus.

In the piece above you will notice that my horizon line and the homes falls close to the one-third line and both women fall along the lines vertically. You will also notice that this is not exact, but by being aware of the composition I was also cognizant of where I wanted the path to lead and how I wanted the negative space to enhance the women.

> *Whether you succeed or not is irrelevant, there is no such thing. Making your unknown known is the important thing.*
>
> —GEORGIA O'KEEFFE

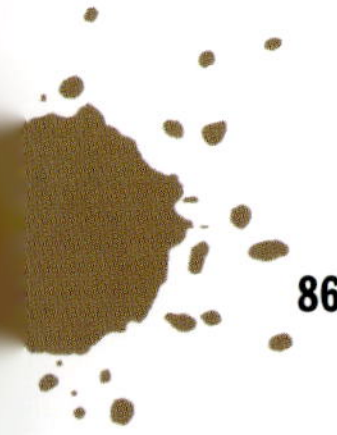

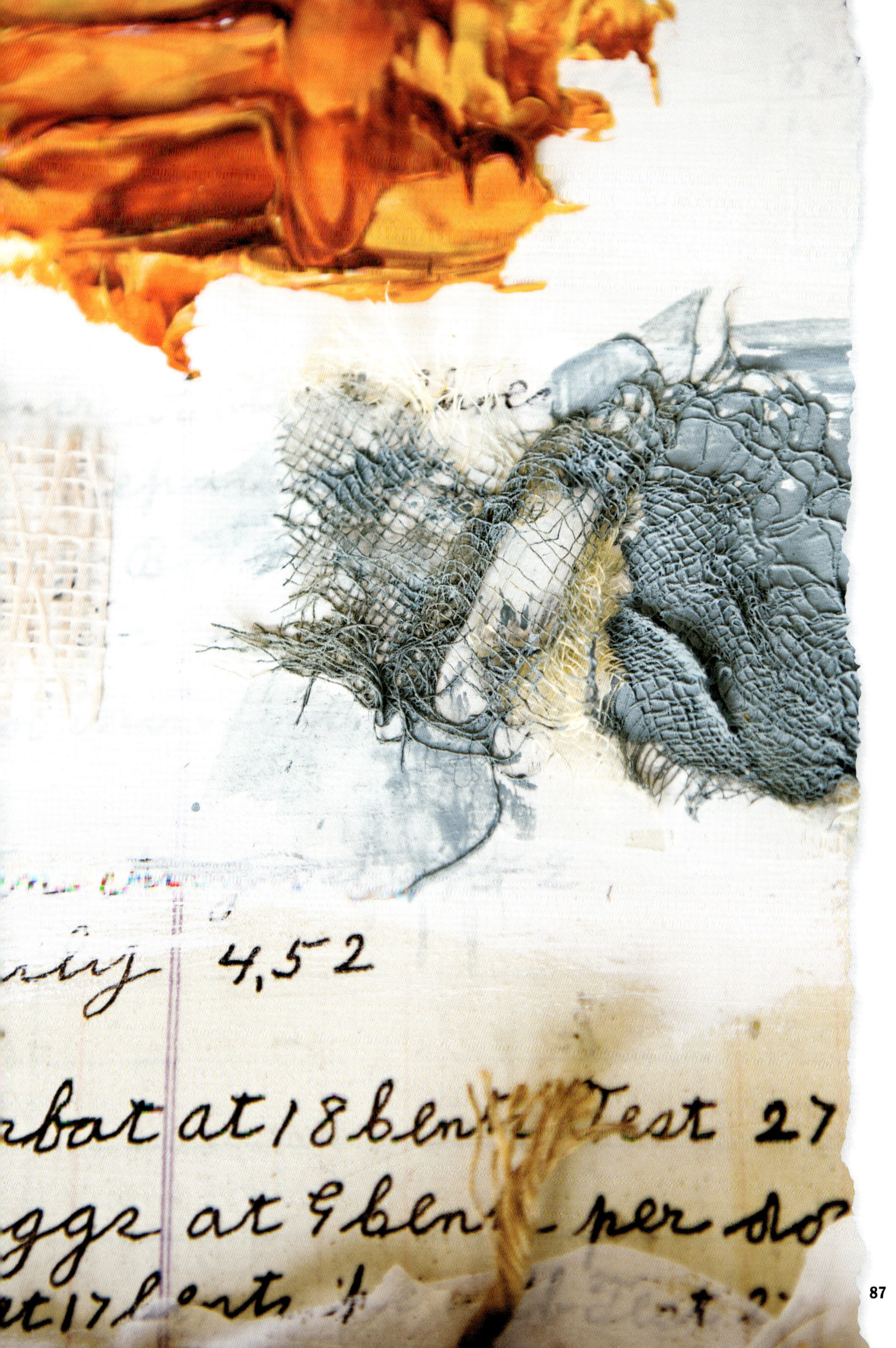

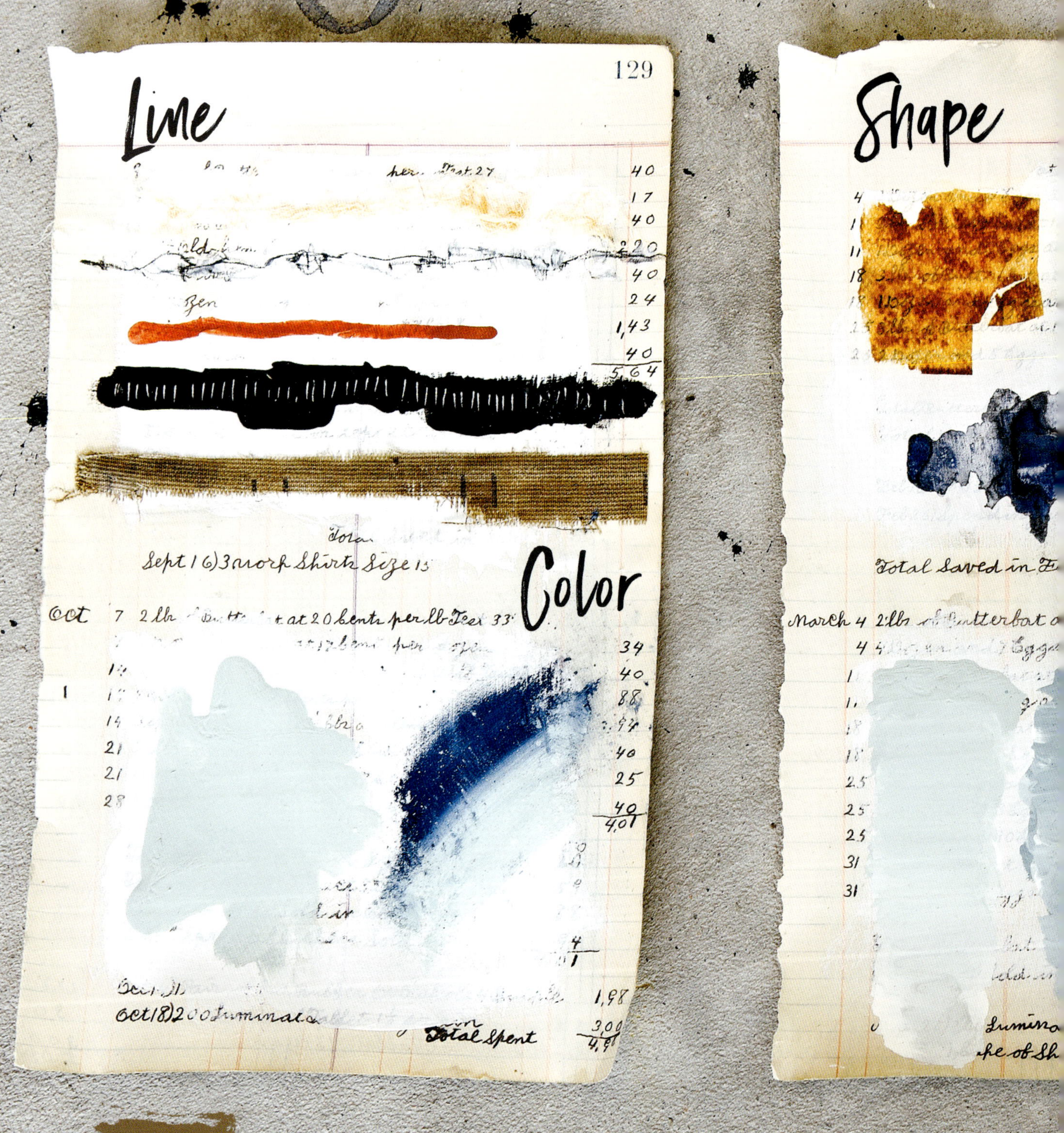

As you bring your composition together, it is always nice to remember there are more elements to design that we may not be thinking about. We are going to break down the basic six. I hope these elements will get you thinking outside the box and possibly bring some new elements into your work.

Line is a moving point and draws your attention in a direction. It can take the form of a straight line with a medium or it can take the form of a squiggly line, mark making in a repetitive direction, vintage paper, a drip of paint or even an arm extended within your work and so much more.

Color is the element that we all may naturally think of. It is created by light and is made up of hue, value and intensity.

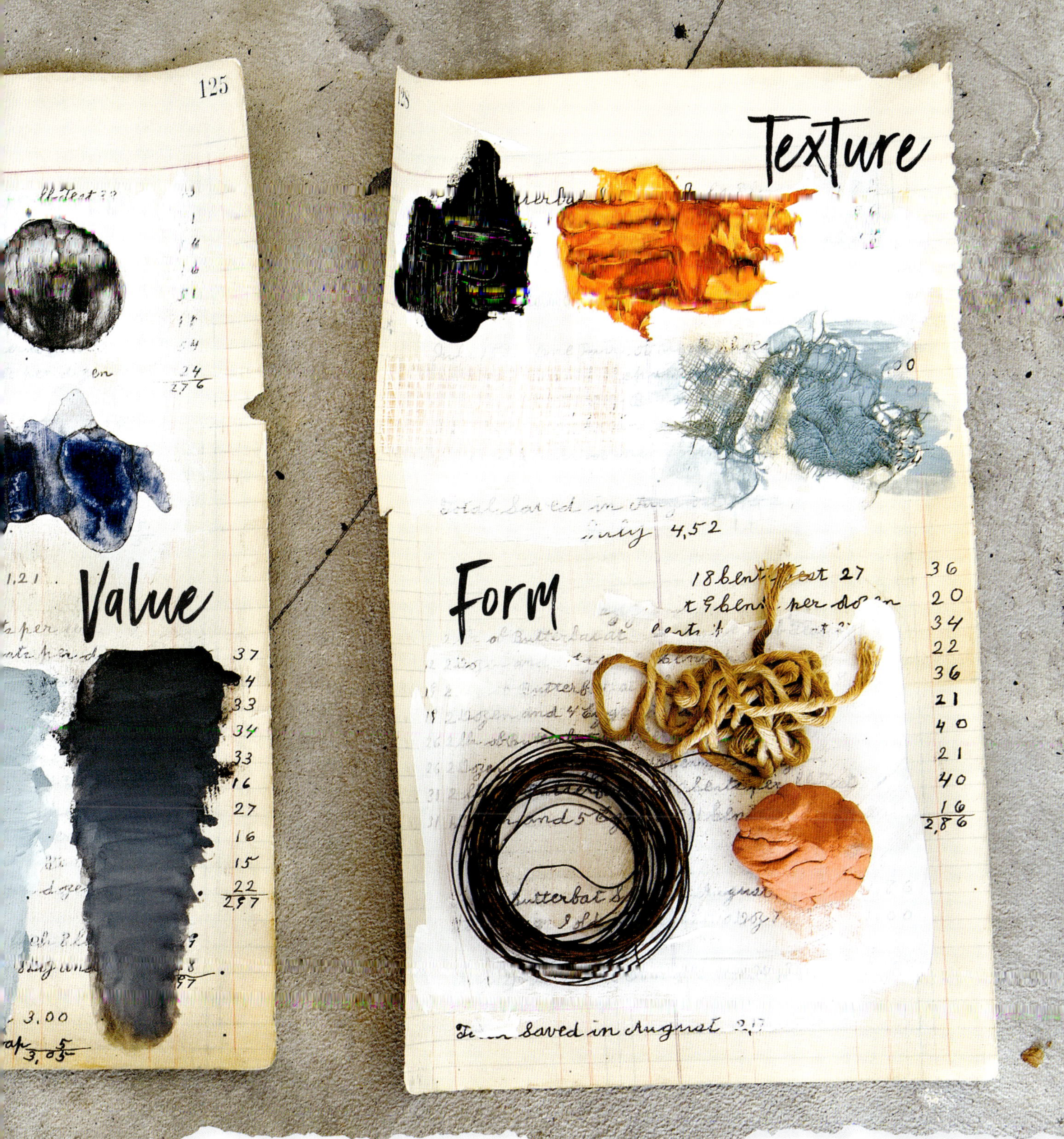

Shape is two dimensional with areas created by lines that are joined. These can be organic or geometric shapes.

Value is the lightness or darkness within a color.

Texture is the feel of a surface. This can be created by applying plaster, heavy body paints, string, fabric, wire, clay, etc.

Form is a three-dimensional object. A few examples of that would be sculpture made from wire or clay.

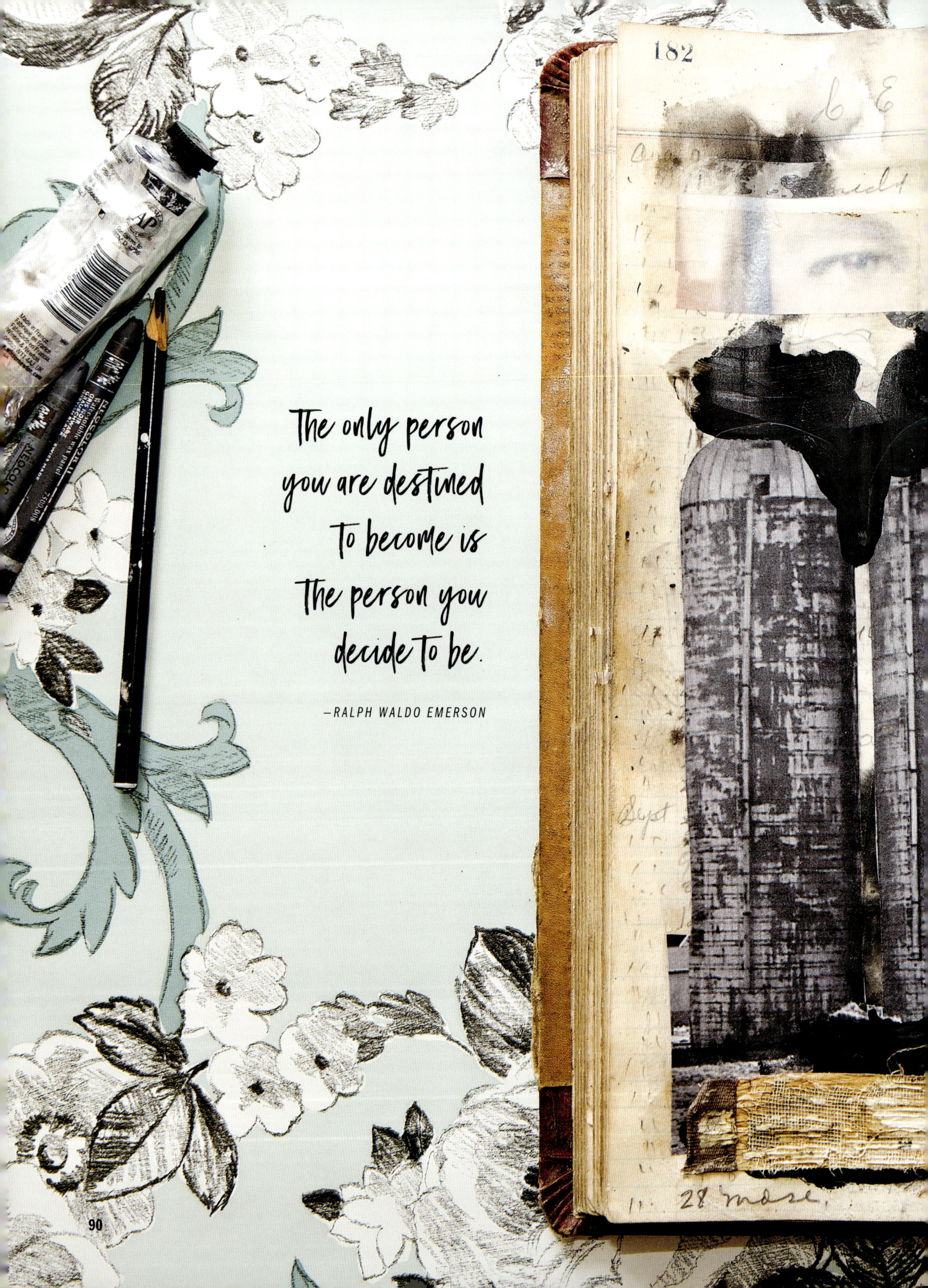

The only person you are destined to become is the person you decide to be.

–RALPH WALDO EMERSON

CHAPTER 12

Your DNA

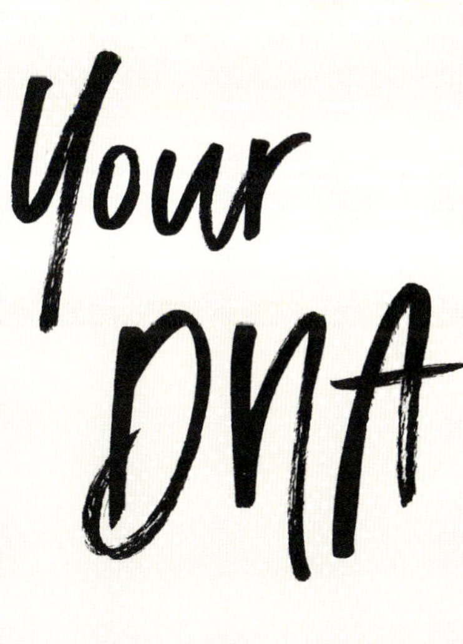

SINCE THIS STORY STARTS AND ENDS WITH YOU, I thought it was only appropriate that we highlight that and make you the focus of the next project. This collage and mixed-media piece focuses on where you came from. I chose to show that for myself by actually showing some of the people that make up my DNA, but you can use any part of your story to show who you are, where you come from or even where you want to go.

There are elements of our stories that we may not love or know how to share. That is common, and you are encouraged to share what you want in a way that you are comfortable with. This is *your* story. It is also OK on this creative journey to rewrite any part of your story through your art.

Your DNA

When you are starting to tell your story, you may not know where you are going with a piece. This is the most beautiful time for you to be receptive of what stays in the piece and what you want to tell. It is in this process that you discover the stories you may have forgotten. Step away from the things distracting you, limit your tools and show up in your own practice. This will do so much for your art and your creative journey.

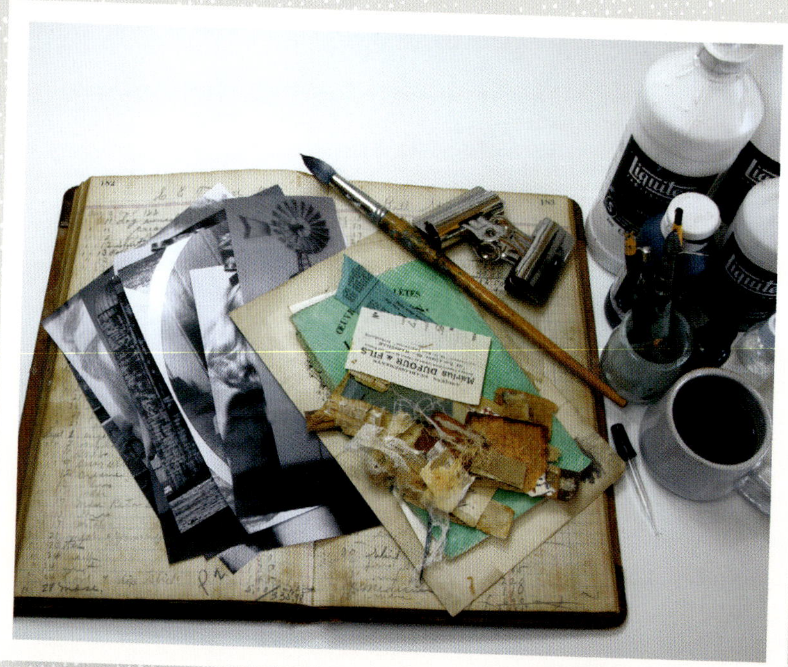

WHAT YOU NEED

- *Art journal*
- *Black India ink*
- *Black Stabilo All pencil*
- *Camera*
- *Charcoal pencil*
- *Cloth or rag*
- *Copies of photos on photo paper*
- *Espresso*
- *Gesso: clear, white and black*
- *Ink dropper*
- *Laser print of meaningful photos*
- *Mark-making tools*
- *Matte medium*
- *Paintbrushes*
- *Scissors*
- *Spray bottle*
- *Vintage ephemera*

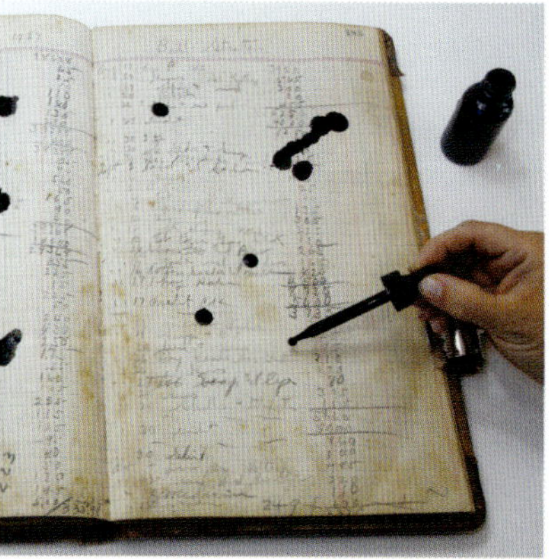

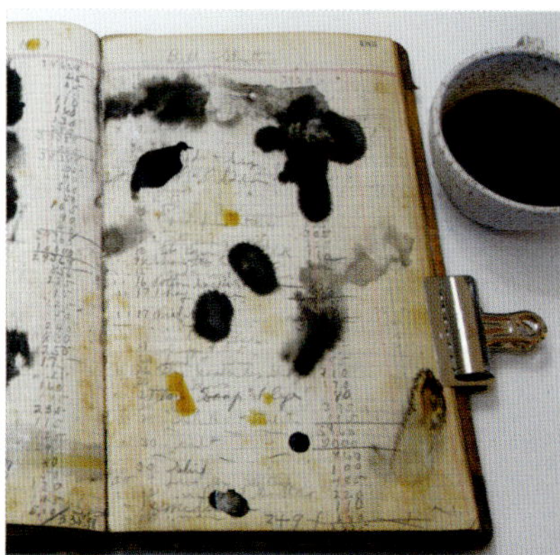

1 Apply a thin coat of clear gesso to your pages and allow to dry. Using a dropper, randomly apply some black ink to your pages. The higher up you release the ink, the larger the splatters will be. Using a spray bottle, move around some of the ink.

2 Using espresso, add some staining throughout your pages. You can use a dropper or dip the bottom of a coffee cup into the espresso and apply randomly to the page. Allow to dry.

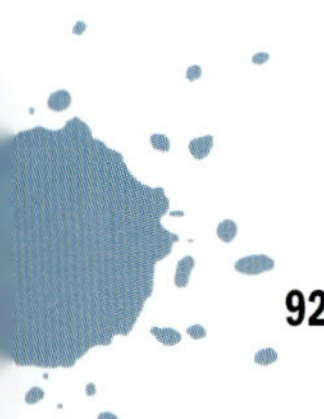

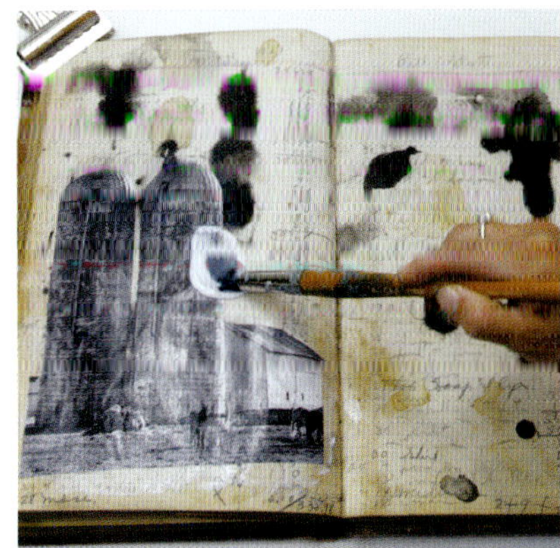

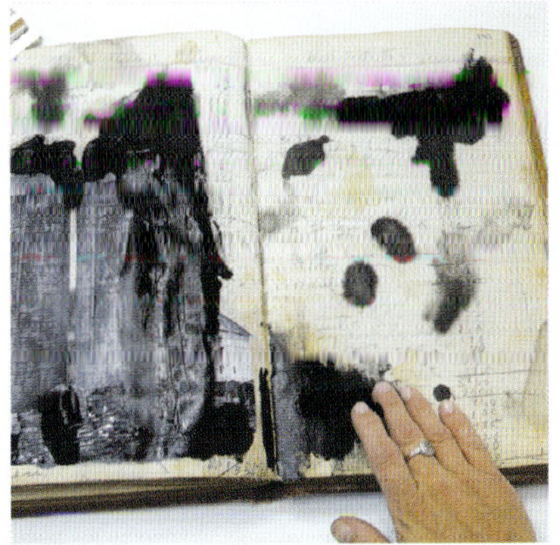

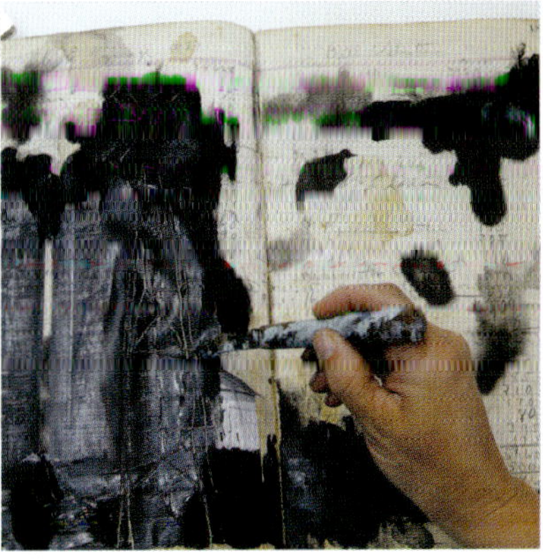

3 Choose an image that is a part of where you are from or an area you connect with. This can be a person, architecture, land, etc. Using a laser print on photocopy paper, glue that image down with matte medium.

I grew up in a small town in Northern Illinois, so silos, barns, windmills and gravel roads were a normal part of everyday life. The area I am from is just as much a part of my story as the people from which I come. This image is being used with permission by Illinois photographer Lance W. Young.

4 Using black gesso, add negative space around your image to use as a base for mark making. I often prefer to use my hands when applying paint and gesso to allow the medium to have a more organic look.

5 While the gesso is still wet, use your mark-making tool to bring in marks or to add an image. I added a windmill, which allowed me to add another architectural image to the composition without allowing the piece to become too busy.

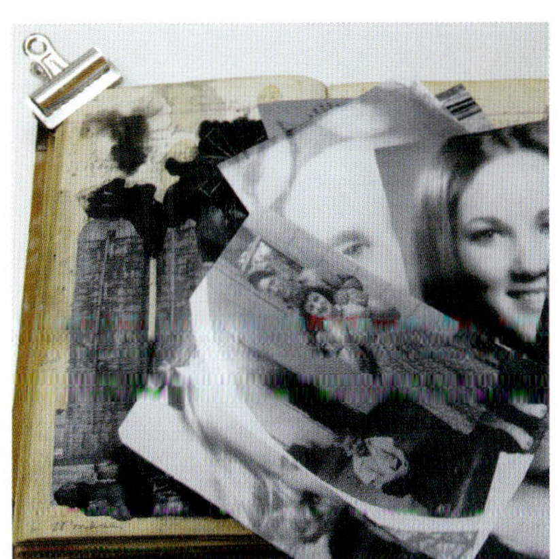

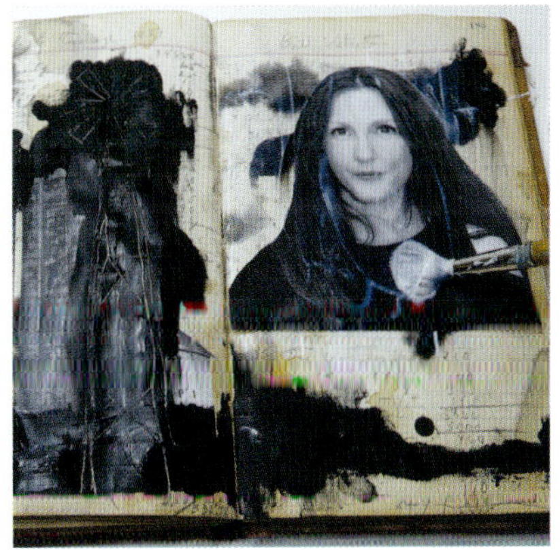

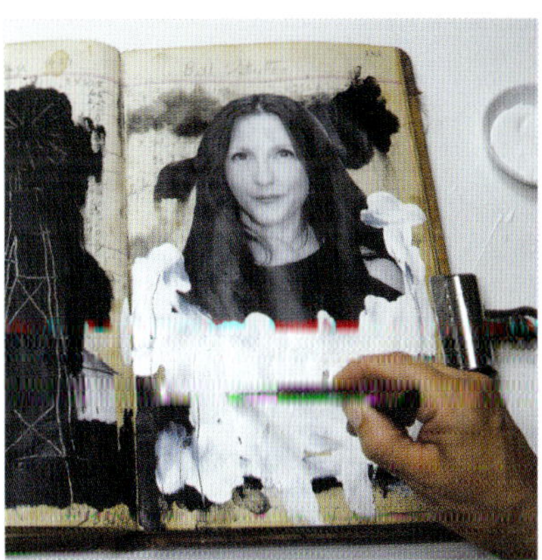

6 I gathered black and white laser prints on photocopy paper of my parents, grandparents and myself. You do not have to choose family members. You can gather images online of where you are from, elements from nature that you feel connected to, or women that have inspired you. This exercise could be created again and again using different elements about yourself.

7 Cut out and adhere another image using matte medium. Allow it to dry. I was already thinking about where the next elements might go. I knew I wanted to alter the area around the photo and was intentional about leaving that space.

8 Add white gesso to soften the edges of your image and allow another opportunity to bring in mark making and texture

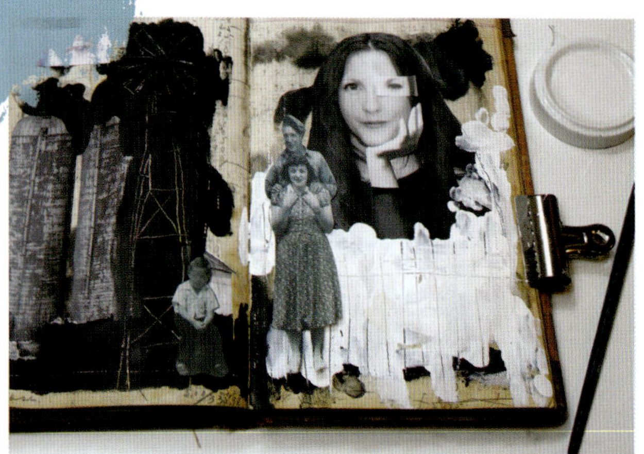

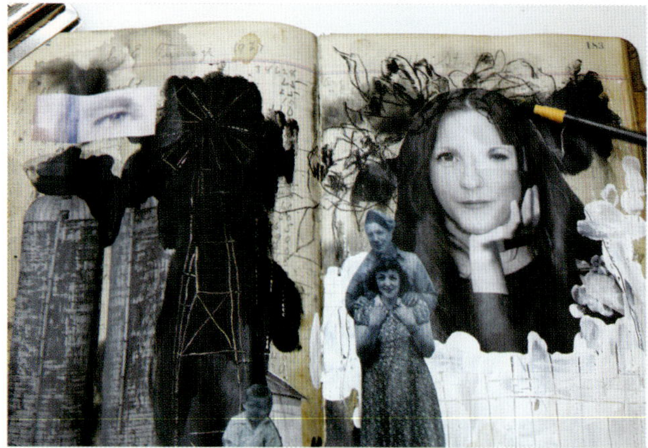

9 As you go through your images, look for pieces you can use from each image. Play around with different designs until you find the elements and composition that connect. After you have the composition you desire, glue each piece down with matte medium and allow to dry.

I used different elements from the photos of each person that make up my DNA. I played around with the design until I settled on this one. This arrangement became a perfect representation of each person and how I wanted to share them within my own story. I didn't know that until they were all on the page though.

10 Because my piece has a face as a focal point, I used a charcoal pencil to start to draw loose floral sketches around the face. I used the floral headdress to represent blooming that can happen at any age.

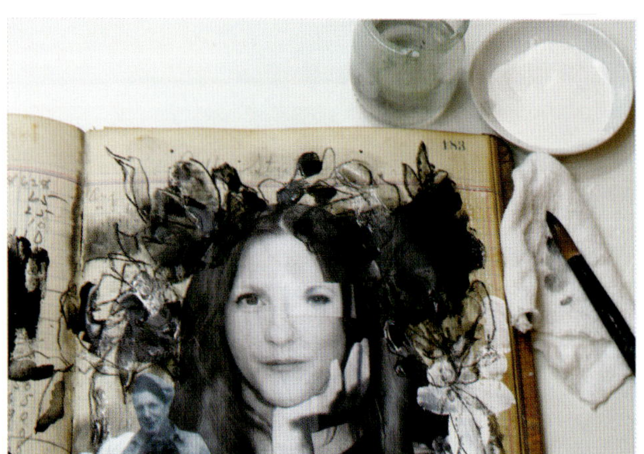

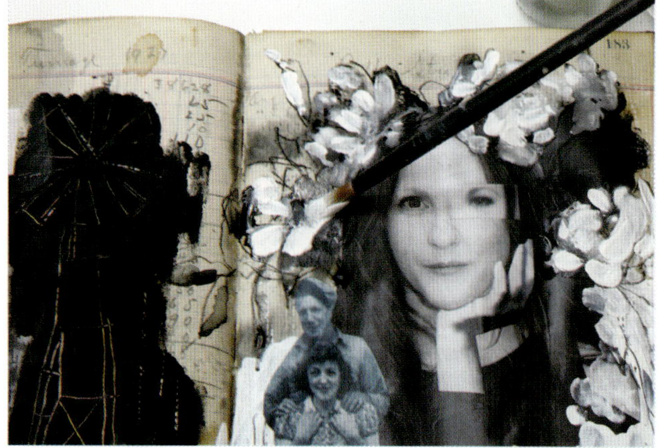

11 Dip a no. 4 round long-handled brush into water. Before applying it to the journal, gently wipe the brush on a cloth to prevent too much water from pooling on the paper. Staying within the lines of the floral design, pull the black charcoal pencil marks out into the floral elements. Be careful not to activate the entire sketch; leave some of the lines dry. You are using the same techniques shared in Chapter 8.

12 Using white gesso, add highlights and middle values to create a more dimensional floral design. Adding the white gesso to the charcoal creates a permanent sketch (no longer water-soluble) once it dries. This also allows you to add more mediums as you layer without smudging your original sketch. If you find you do not have enough values, this may be because too much of the sketch is wet, or it is too white or too black. Try to be random with your brushstrokes to create a looser floral element with definite highlights and darker values. Don't blend everything together. If you find you want to bring in a more intense black into your flowers, try adding the black Stabilo and following the steps above.

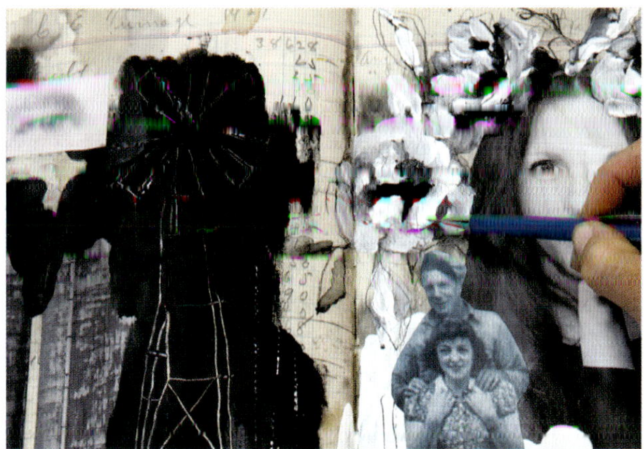

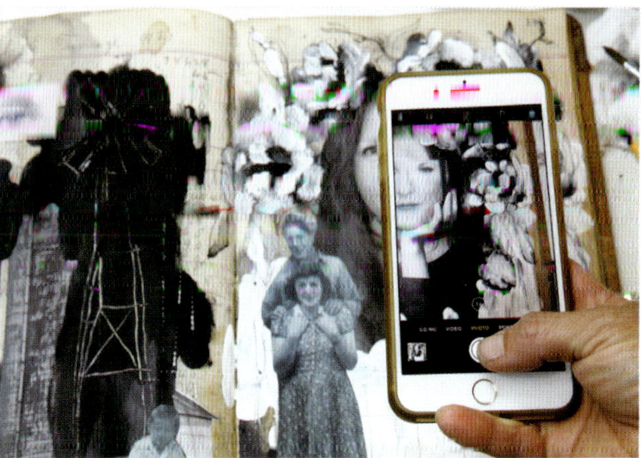

13 While your floral is still wet, come in with a mechanical pencil to add delicate details and to cut into the wet mediums. You can also sketch vines, leaves or add other floral elements, and allow them to just be the simple sketch of the graphite.

14 Don't forget to take progress photos with your camera phone if you have one. This is an invaluable tool for looking back to see your steps and the progress that your art is taking. It also will remind yourself that when a piece feels lost oftentimes you can turn it around and make something beautiful out of it. Another reason this step can be so helpful in your art is that oftentimes we know something is "off" or missing in our art but we can't put our finger on it. When you photograph it, it is amazing how you can clearly see your art through new eyes. When you have photos of your work in different stages you are also able to print them out and incorporate them into other bodies of work.

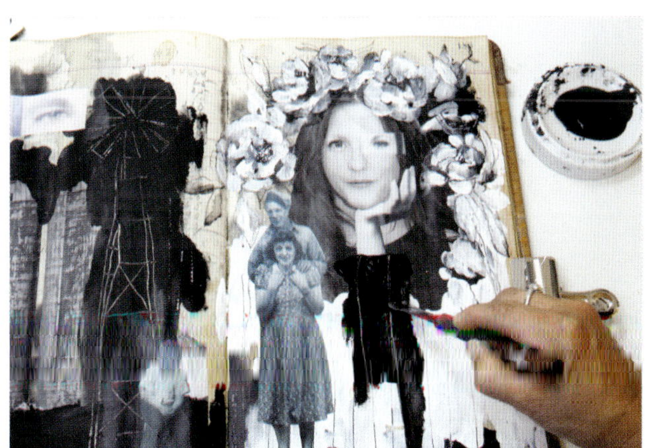

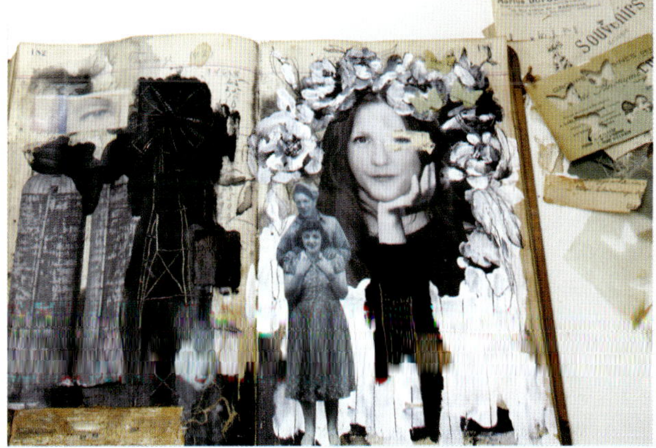

15 Bring in black gesso to create depth and drama within your piece. This is another area with the black gesso that, while it is wet, you can add interesting composition aspects to your piece with just a mark-making tool.

I added an arm and repetitive marks. By adding the arm I was also able to extend the lines of my photographs and to redirect the eyes. You no longer go first to the black gesso but to the lines created within it.

16 Using vintage ephemera, continue the lines of your photos and composition. Glue the papers down with matte medium. Extend the lines with papers, twine, stretched cheesecloth, etc.

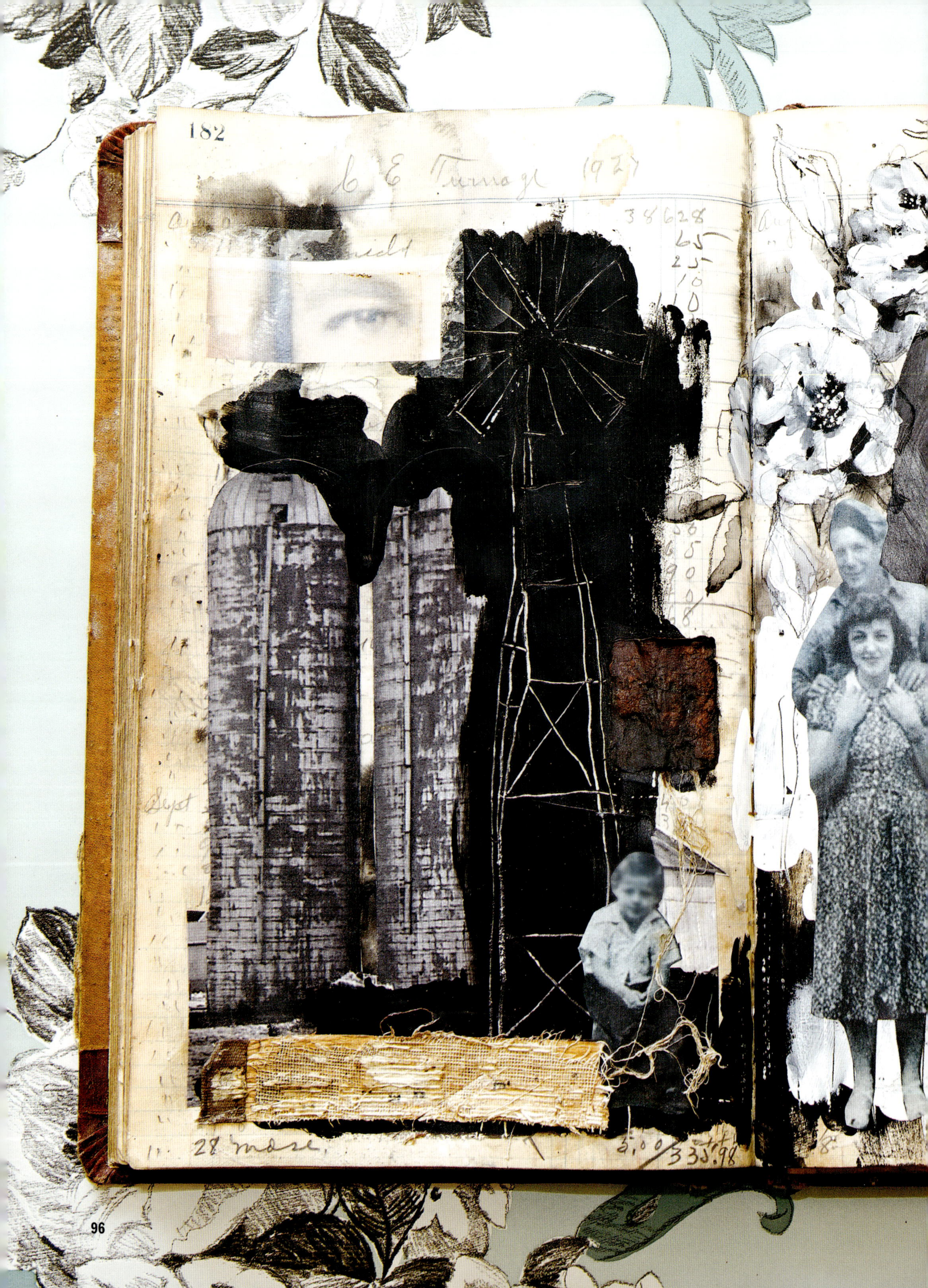

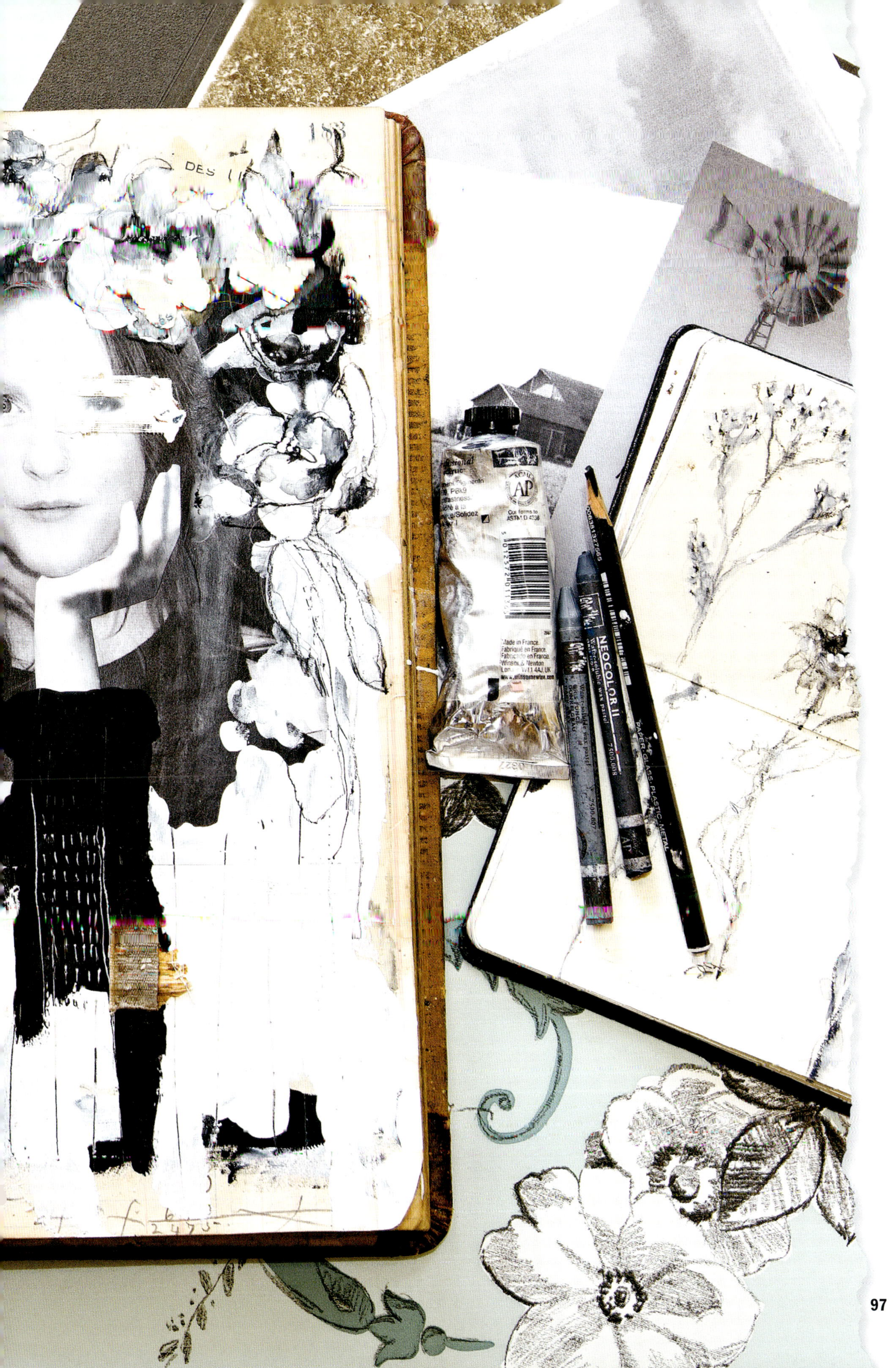

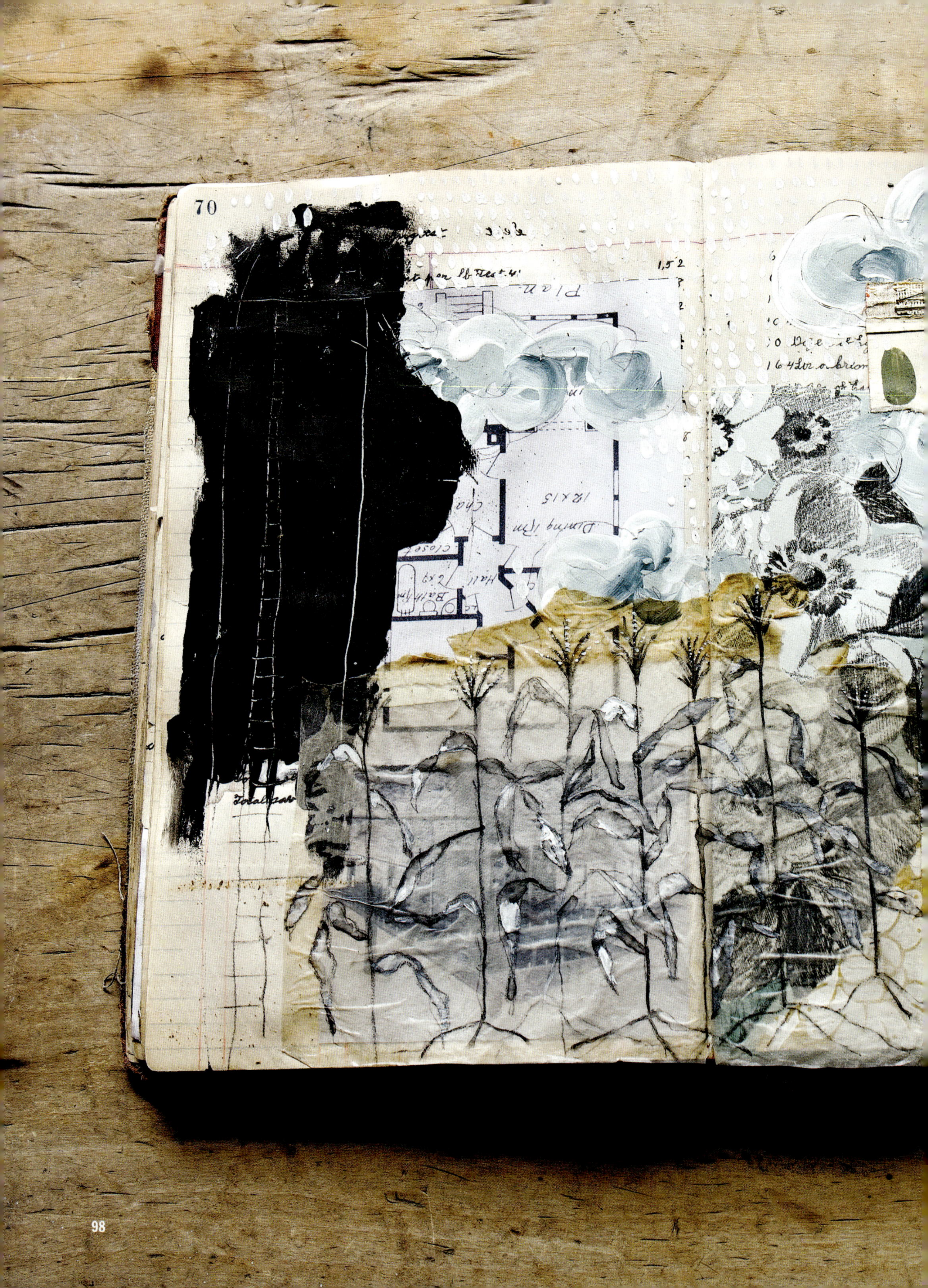

CHAPTER 13

Gathering Your Story

WE HAVE ALL COLLECTED STORIES FROM OUR PAST and the pasts of those who have crossed our path. Sometimes these stories make us laugh, cry or rethink a previously held truth. Recently my mom told me a story that she had never shared before. I guess we are all like that—we carry these stories around with us until something triggers it and we allow it to spill out. I am so glad I was around that day to catch this story and make it a part of my own to tell.

My mom was sixteen and her parents were getting a divorce. Her dad would stay behind in the small town in Illinois, and her mom with the kids would move back to Nashville. The day was quickly approaching when my grandma and all of the kids would leave. My mom didn't know how to say goodbye to her dad or even express how sad and sorry she was to leave. How could she share her love and grief with him? She worked at a local farm picking the harvest each season, and something she and her dad had in common was their deep love of fried green tomatoes (a love I also share). The farmer told her she could take home as many green tomatoes as she could carry, so she filled a basket that overflowed. Those green tomatoes represented more than a shared food but unspoken words, emotions and sad goodbyes. As a child what do you give and what do you do when you don't want to go and your words fall short?

Gathering a Story

This next project is a glimpse into how I break down a story and bring it to life in my work. Many times the stories I tell in my art journal are spilled out and that is the only place I tell them. Other times, the story I begin to unfold in my journal becomes the jumping-off point for larger works of art. I wanted to share the creative process of taking a story and then finding ways to tell it through photos, color and imagery. My hope was that this will get you thinking about your stories and new ways you can express them.

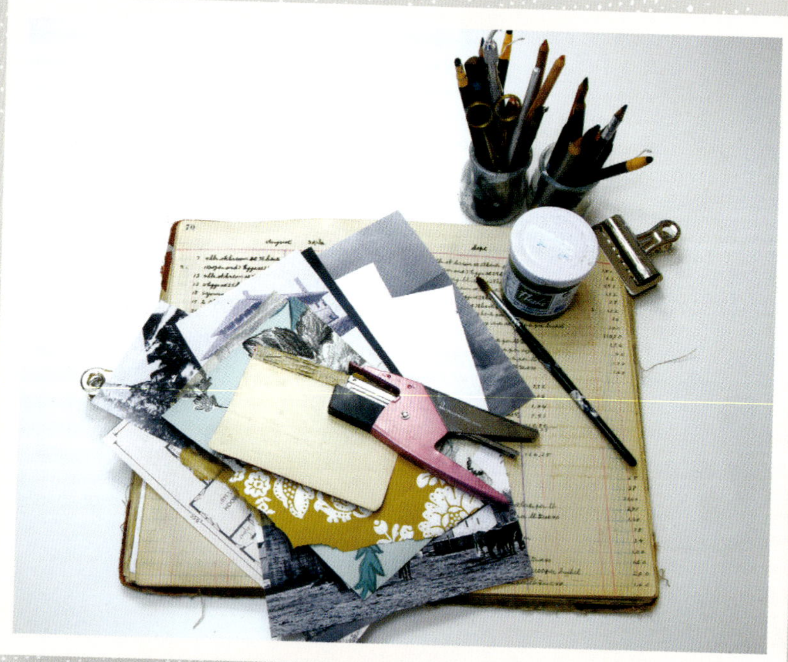

WHAT YOU NEED

- Art journal

- Black Stabilo All pencil

- Gesso: clear, white and black

- Images of your choosing

- Laser copy of a photo

- Mark-making tools

- Matte medium

- Mechanical pencil

- Paintbrush

- Scissors

- Stapler

- Vintage ephemera

- Your color palette

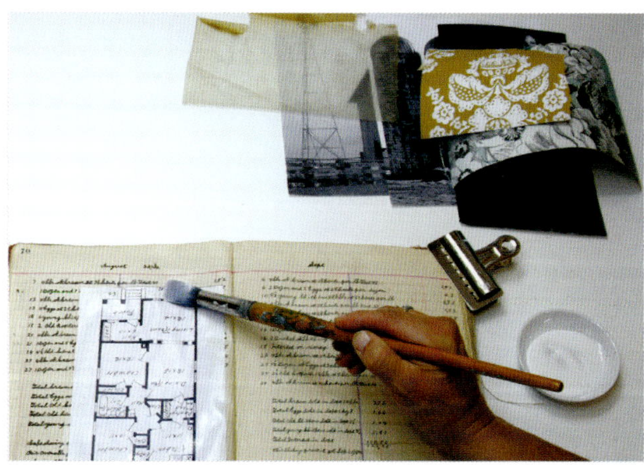

1 I wanted to represent a family home that had been turned upside down. I found a copyright free image of an old house and blueprint. This image was adhered with matte medium on a page that had already been primed with clear gesso.

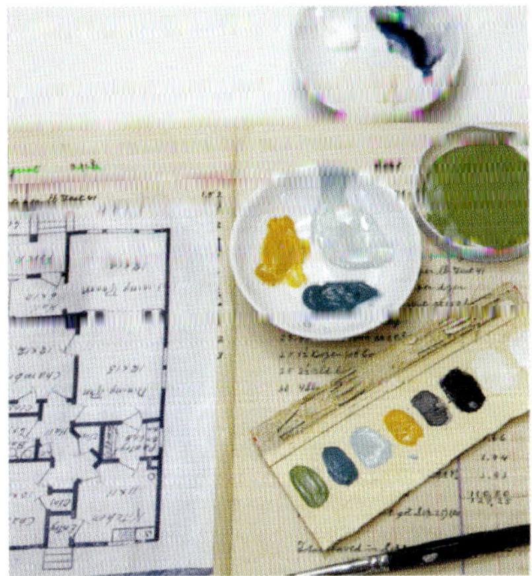

2 Sometimes I know where I want to start but have no idea what direction it will go in. While the previous step was drying, I starting gathering colors, keeping in mind Illinois cornfields, late summer skies, green tomatoes and what represented youth to me. Using a vintage piece of book spine and cover, I put down my collected color palette for this piece.

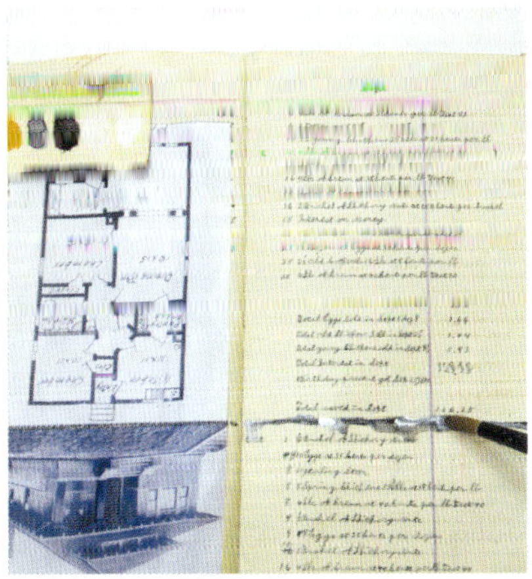

3 Using the rule of thirds (Chapter 11), I decided to use the two-thirds mark for my horizon line, which set the composition for the rest of the piece.

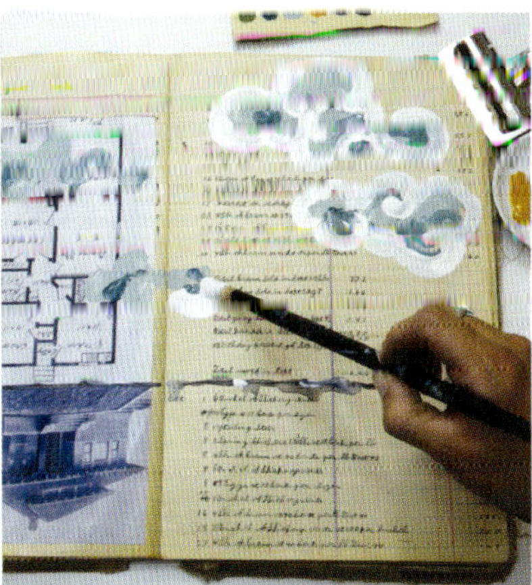

4 Using an image of an Illinois cornfield and sky, I started creating whimsical clouds using colors from my chosen palette. I started with a lighter color, and while the paint was wet, I used a darker color to lightly blend together. I then surrounded the clouds with loose layers of white. The light and airy colors represent the kind heart of a child.

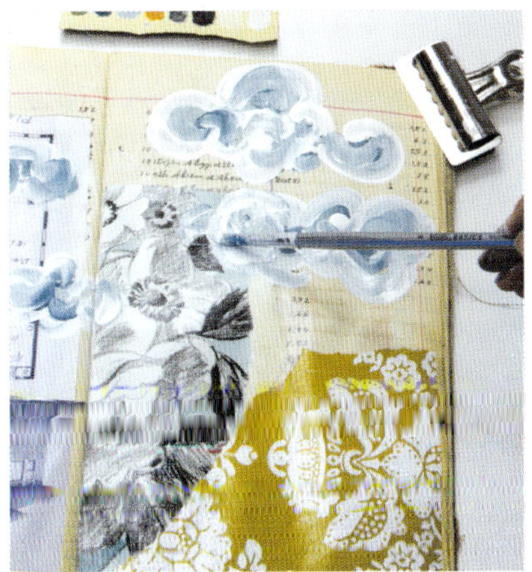

5 Growing up in Illinois and always living in older homes, I perceive all homes within that time period as having wallpaper. I gathered pieces of wallpaper that fit within my color palette and then extended the clouds over them where needed.

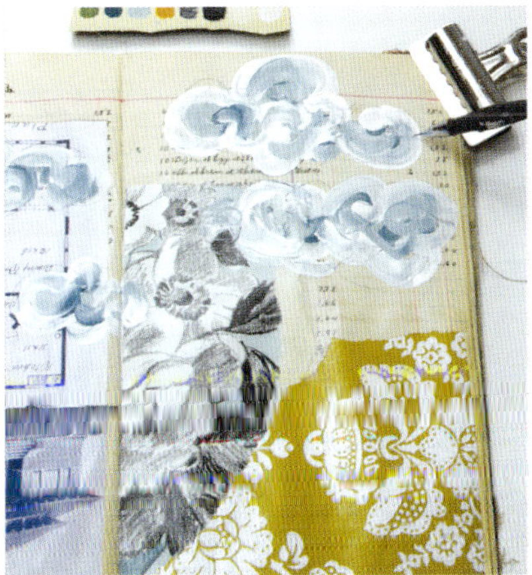

6 While the paint in the clouds was still wet, I came in with a mechanical pencil to create marks and also to extend the lines.

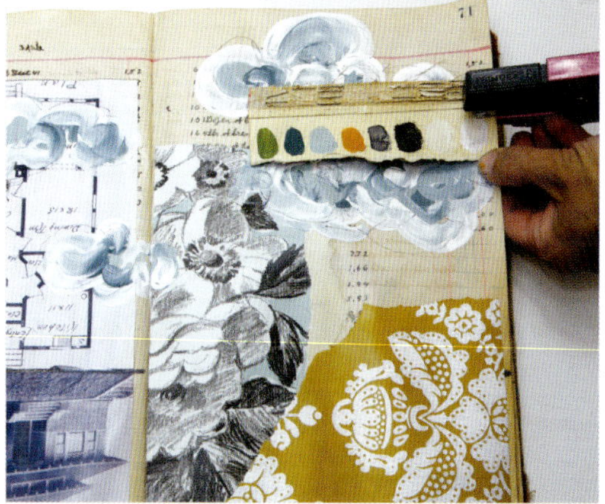

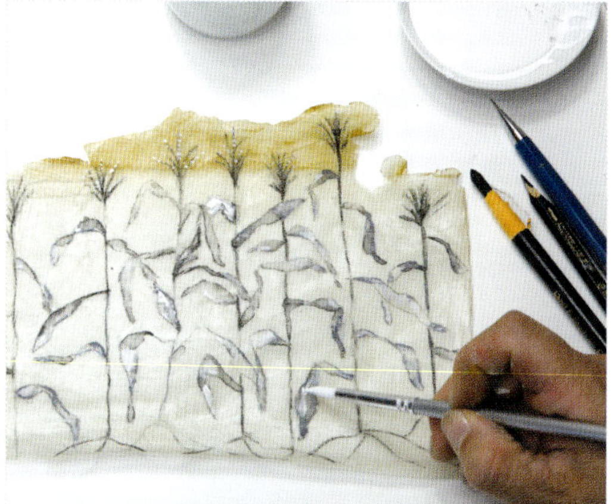

7 Using my fingers, I brought in black gesso. While the gesso was wet, I sketched a silo with a ladder with my mark-making tool. Because this is a loose study to be used for a more detailed work later, I have stapled the color palette directly into the piece. It also worked as a design element.

8 I was looking for a way to represent the gravel roads and cornfields of home. In my stash of vintage ephemera I was able to find some vintage patina vellum to represent gravel roads. I applied a thin layer of clear gesso to allow the vellum to become an instant substrate. Once the gesso was dry, I loosely sketched some cornstalks with a Stabilo All pencil, charcoal, white gesso and mechanical pencil to represent the cornfields that surrounded this small town. See Chapter 9 for more techniques regarding Stabilo, charcoal and white gesso.

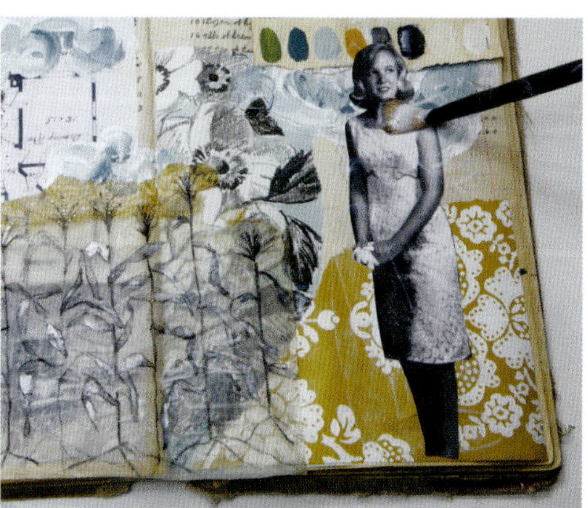

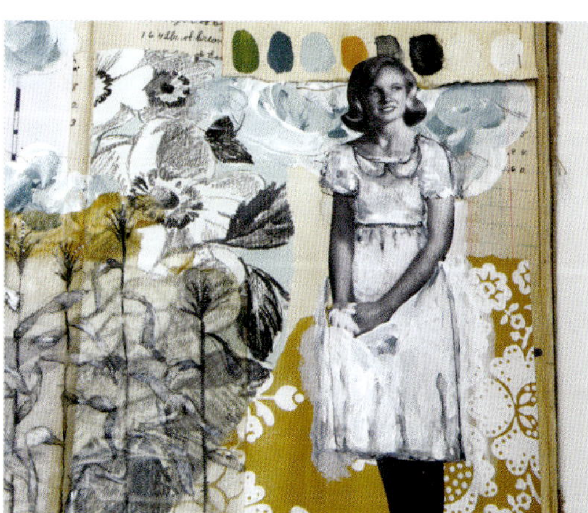

9 Using a black-and-white laser photo on printer paper, I cut out the image of my mom as a young girl around the time of the story. The image was adhered and sealed with matte medium. Her placement is based upon the rule of thirds.

10 Using a black Stabilo pencil and white gesso, I altered her dress to look more fitting for my story.

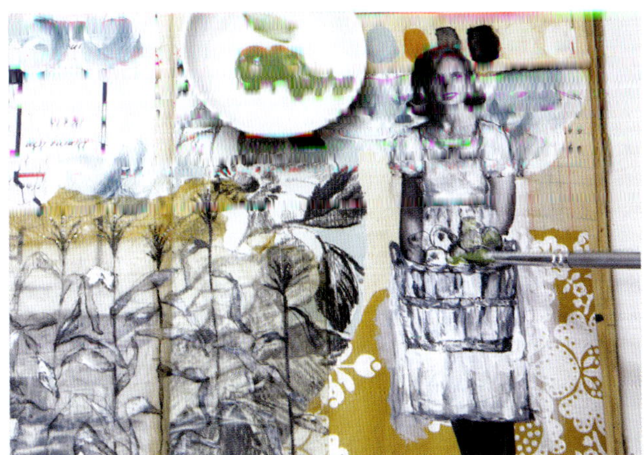

11 Using a black Stabilo and white gesso, I loosely sketched a basket of tomatoes. Using the green from my palette, I added the final touches.

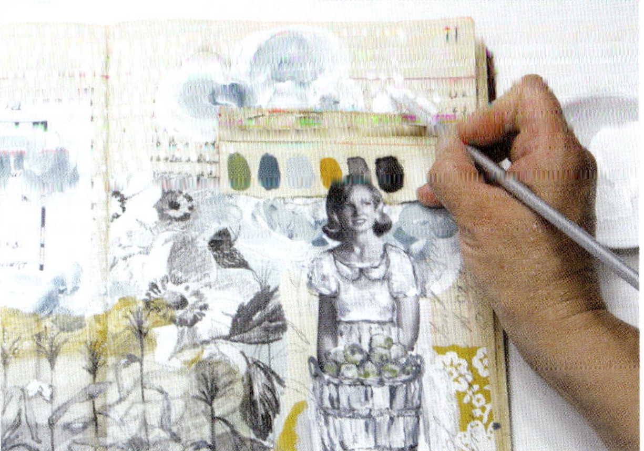

12 With a mechanical pencil I wrote parts of the story along the side of the page, and then using white gesso created repetitive marks to represent the tears and sorrow.

You have these little stories, too. These sweet and sad moments. Times of triumph and defeat that have purpose and deserve to be told and heard. Your stories will be different from mine, of course, but this exercise shows how a casually told story has life. How can you collect a story and find imagery to share it?

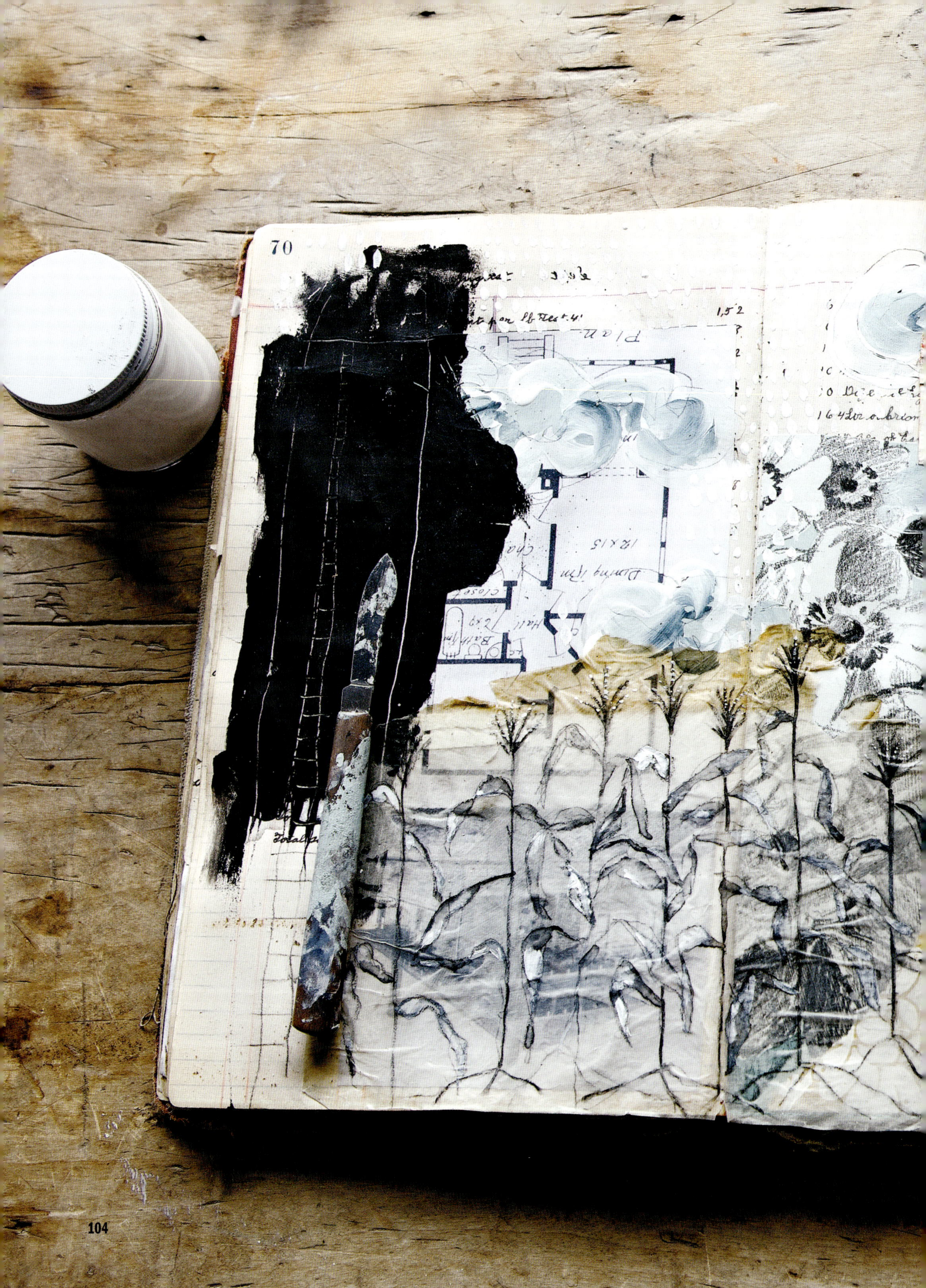

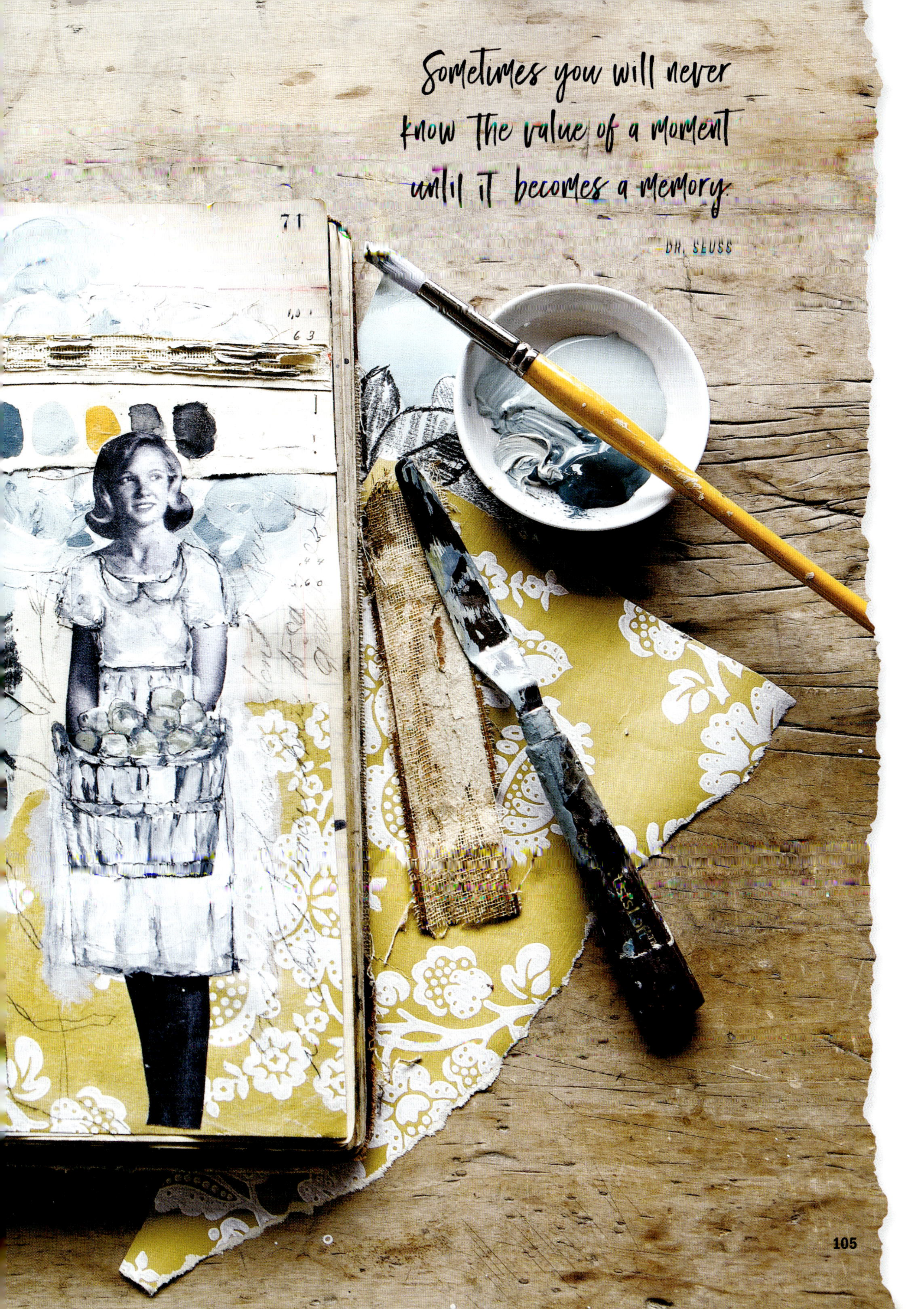

Sometimes you will never know the value of a moment until it becomes a memory.
DR. SEUSS

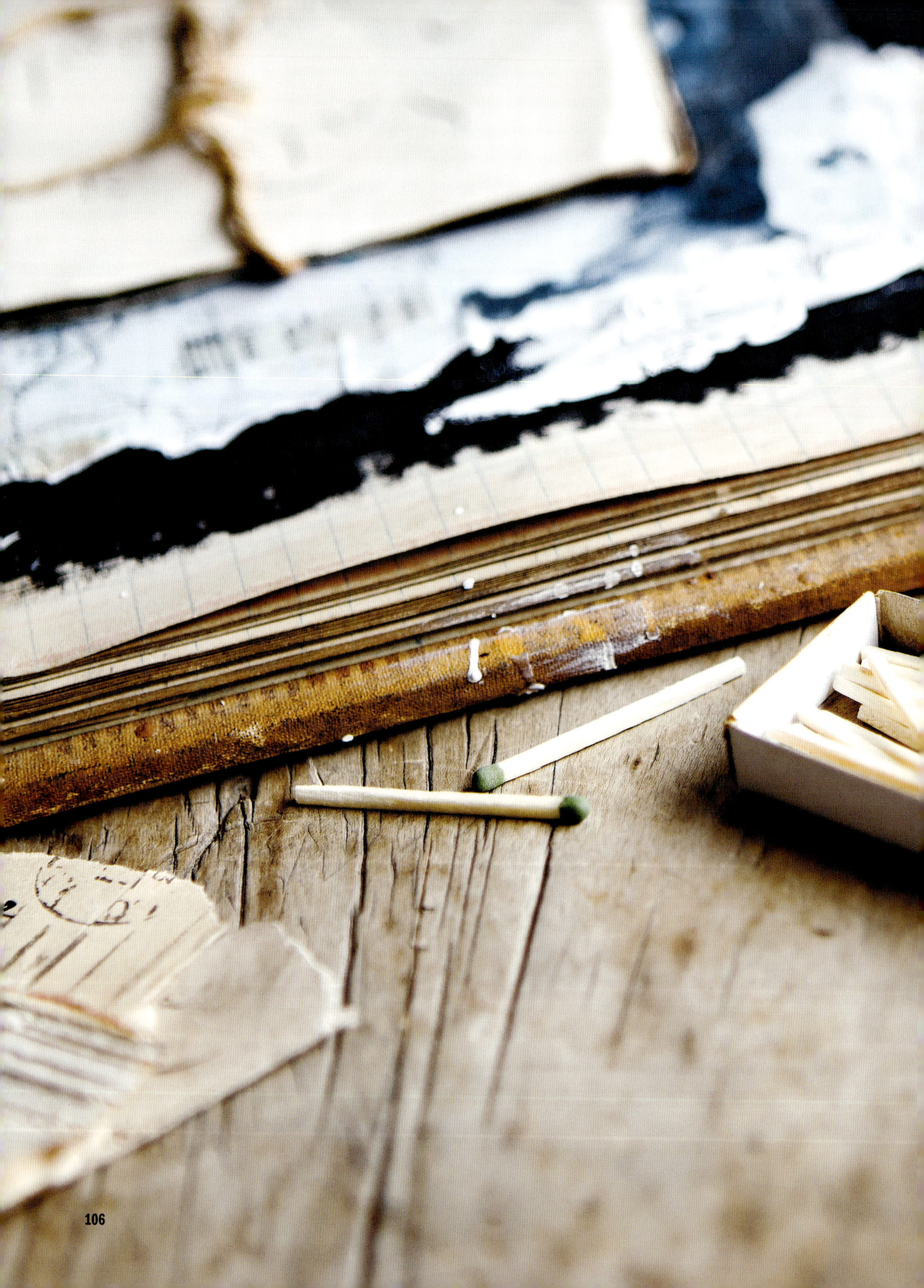

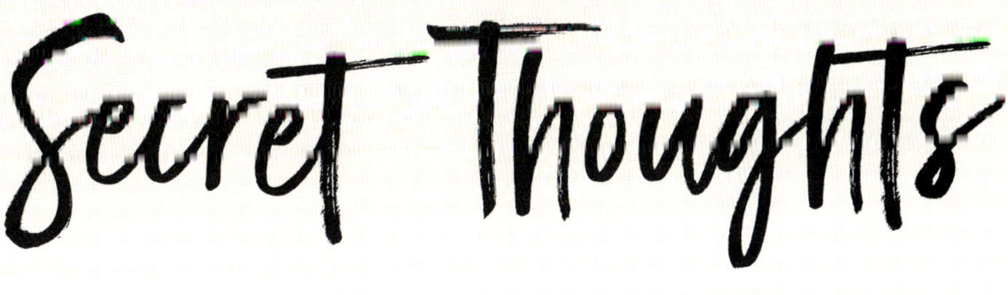

CHAPTER 14

Secret Thoughts

OFTENTIMES WE COME INTO OUR CREATIVE SPACE and think we have to start from scratch each time. We reinvent ourselves, our art, our stories when perhaps what is already unfolding is right where we are supposed to be at that moment. Maybe we just need to sit with it a bit longer. I think I have learned the most about these kinds of art processes and the ebb and flow of being a creative (and living a creative life) by studying the masters.

Have you ever thought sketching was a waste of time and you just wanted to get on to the main show in your mind, which may be painting, collaging, sculpting, etc.? I know there were years I felt that way until I intensely studied the life and works of Vincent van Gogh. He sketched with graphite, ink and charcoal for *years* before he ever picked up his paintbrush. Those brushstrokes that make me swoon and his authentic marks were developed and created in his practice. In fact, his style was born out of sketching the people and places all around him all of the time. He was constantly looking at his world and wanting to capture it. Those studies later became the works for which he is known. Nothing was wasted.

I have often created one piece of work that I loved and then felt the pressure to make the next great thing for myself. But then I studied Henri Matisse and saw how he used the same model for years, painted the same piece over, and over making adjustments each time and often using the same props but rearranging them. He actually studied his own works and improved upon them. Maybe staying put for a while and learning from your own work isn't a bad place to be.

Secret Thoughts

Let's take a look at the art that you already made and love, and use it to make something new! Using copies of your own work and some words that are just for your eyes, we will create a layout that shows new ways to use old work.

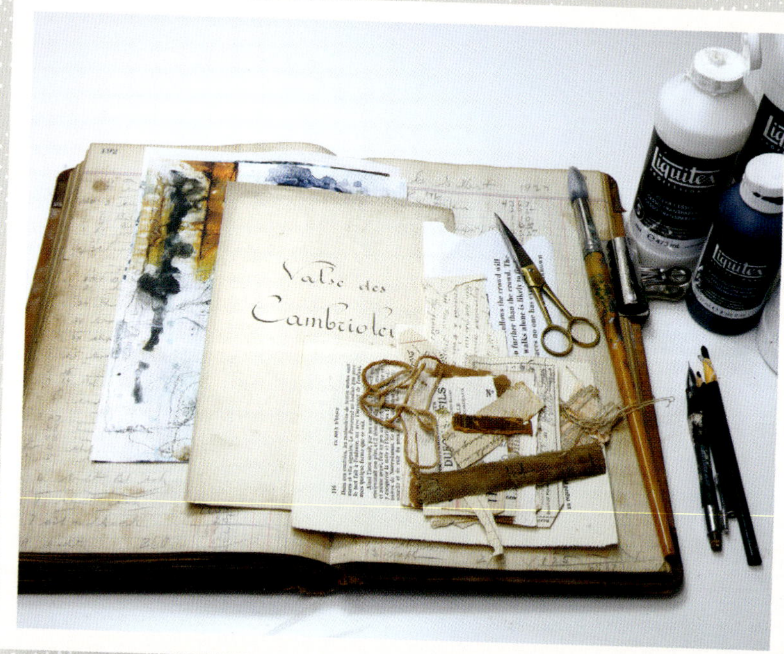

WHAT YOU NEED
- *Art journal*
- *Gesso: clear, black and white*
- *Ink-jet printout of an existing journal page*
- *Large paintbrush*
- *Matte medium*
- *Match*
- *Mechanical pencil*
- *String*
- *Vintage book pages, paper and other collage material*
- *Workable fixative*

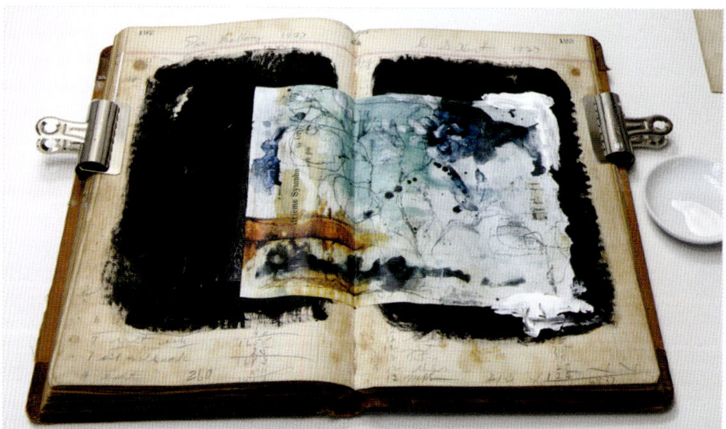

1 Apply a thin layer of clear gesso to a new journal spread and allow it to dry. Next, add black gesso with a large brush, leaving some areas where the journal page shows through. While this is drying, print out an image of your work on an ink-jet printer using photocopy paper. Spray the print with a workable fixative so you can add more mediums without smudging the ink. After the fixative has dried, adhere the print to your journal using matte medium. Add some white gesso to give the illusion that the piece is a part of the journal and to soften the sharp edges of the paper.

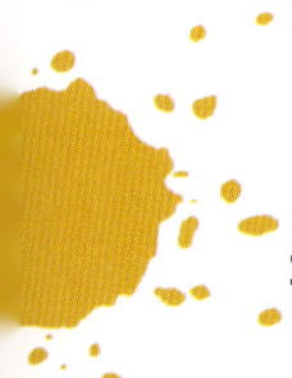

2 Take a small stack of vintage book pages and on each page write some part of your story that made you who you are today. After you have added your words, bind it up with string and lightly burn the edges with a match. Hold this bound stack of pages over a sink while you are burning the edges. Using matte medium, adhere your secret thoughts to the right-hand side of the your journal.

Make what you love. Use what you love.

Take note of what you are doing that you love. What marks do you make that feel natural? What symbolism do you want to repeat in different ways within your work? What piece have you recently created that you could study, paint again and make better or different? Where did we ever get the idea that each piece has to be so different from the piece before? Don't you want to know your brushstrokes, your palette, your subject matter? That comes with being comfortable in a creative space and letting it naturally unfold and grow.

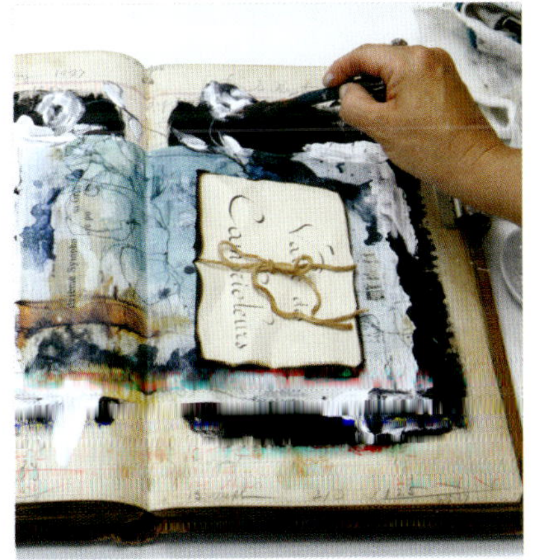

3 Extend design elements such as lines, shapes, color and values already within your reproduced art out onto the journal pages. In this piece I was able to extend the flowers and also some of the original sketch marks by mark making through wet gesso. To find the step-by-step instructions for making the flowers go to Chapter 9.

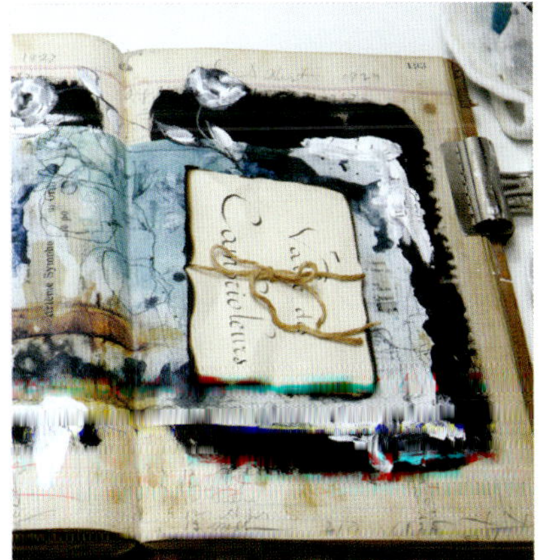

4 Using the lines already strong in the original work of art, I brought in vintage ephemera to continue the lines and also to bring a stronger design element to the new piece. This was accomplished using vintage papers and book spines adhered with matte medium.

Look for strong lines in your own reproduced art that can be extended by sketching, twine, vintage papers, paint or more.

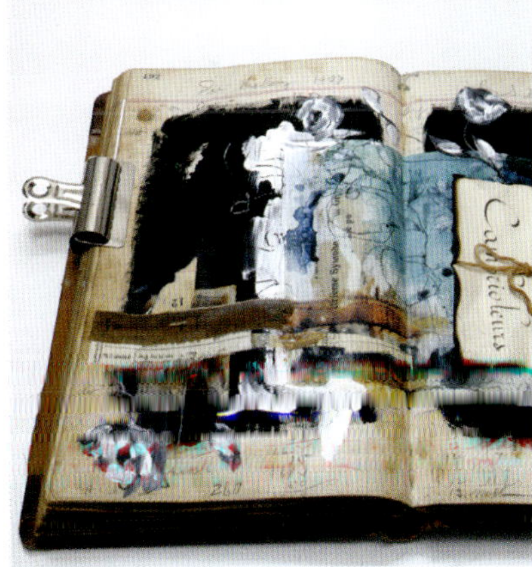

5 Using a mechanical pencil, create marks and natural scribbles that help connect the two pieces. If you get stuck, refer to your collected mark making and symbolism.

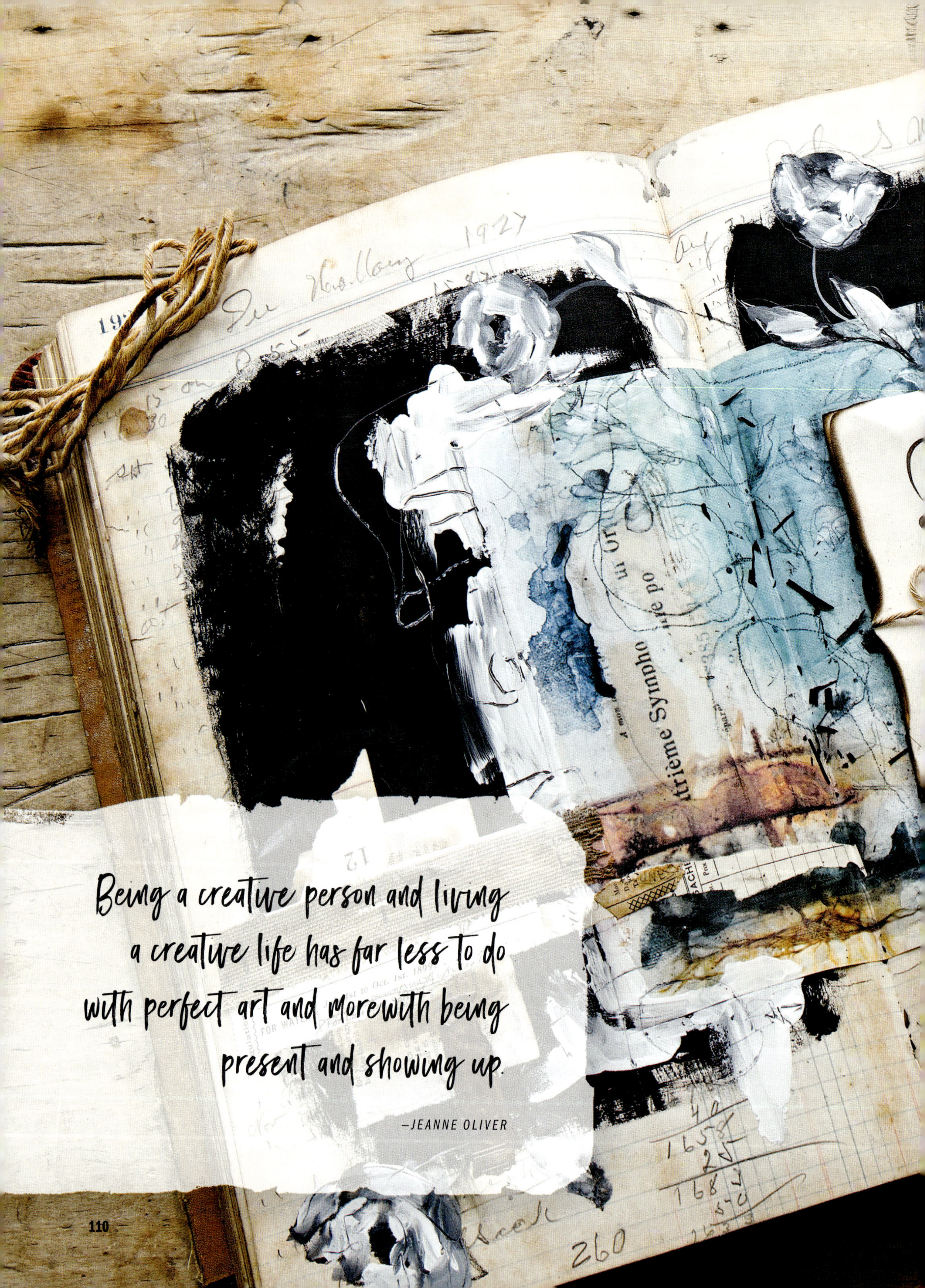
Being a creative person and living
a creative life has far less to do
with perfect art and morewith being
present and showing up.

—JEANNE OLIVER

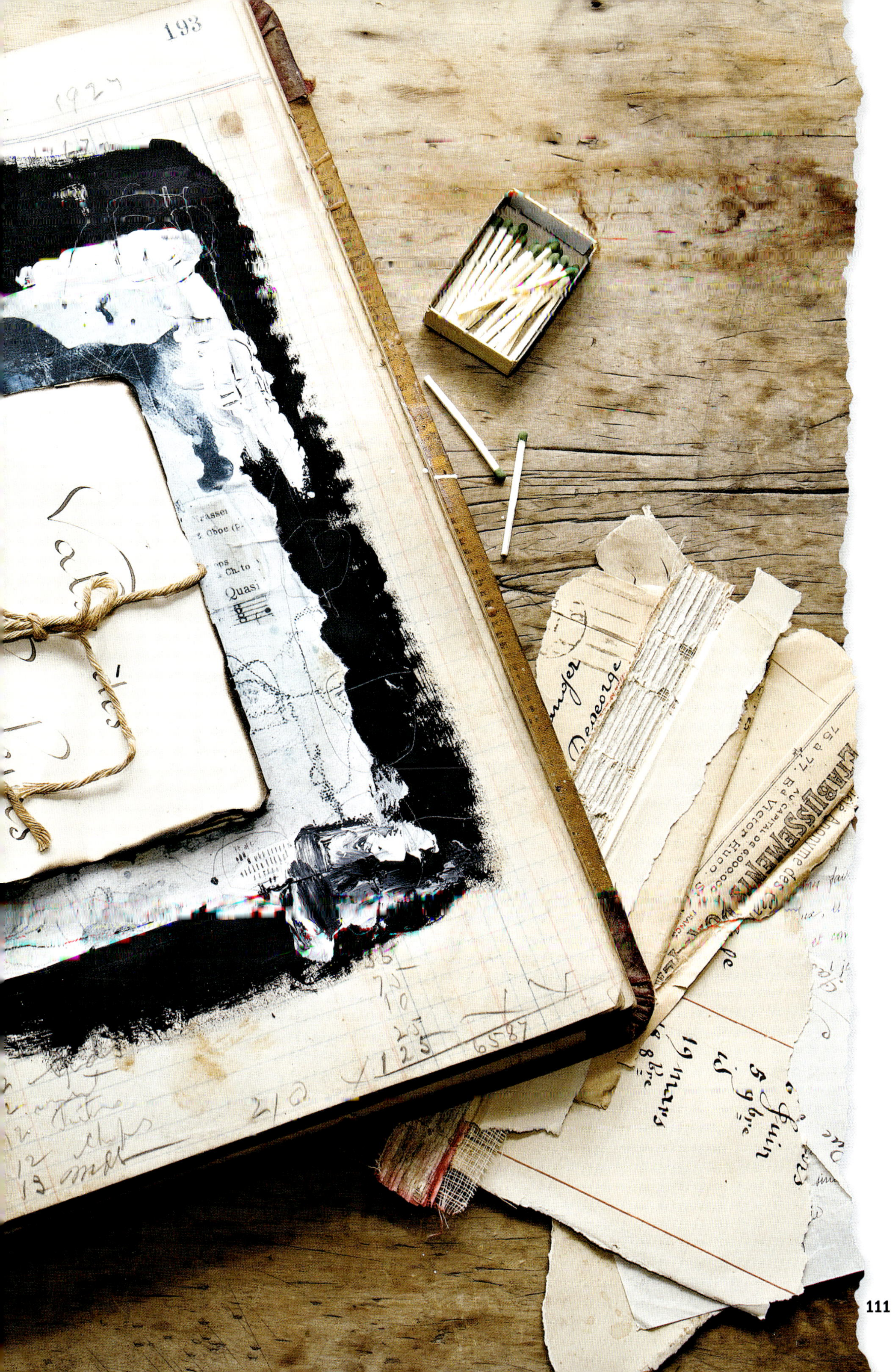

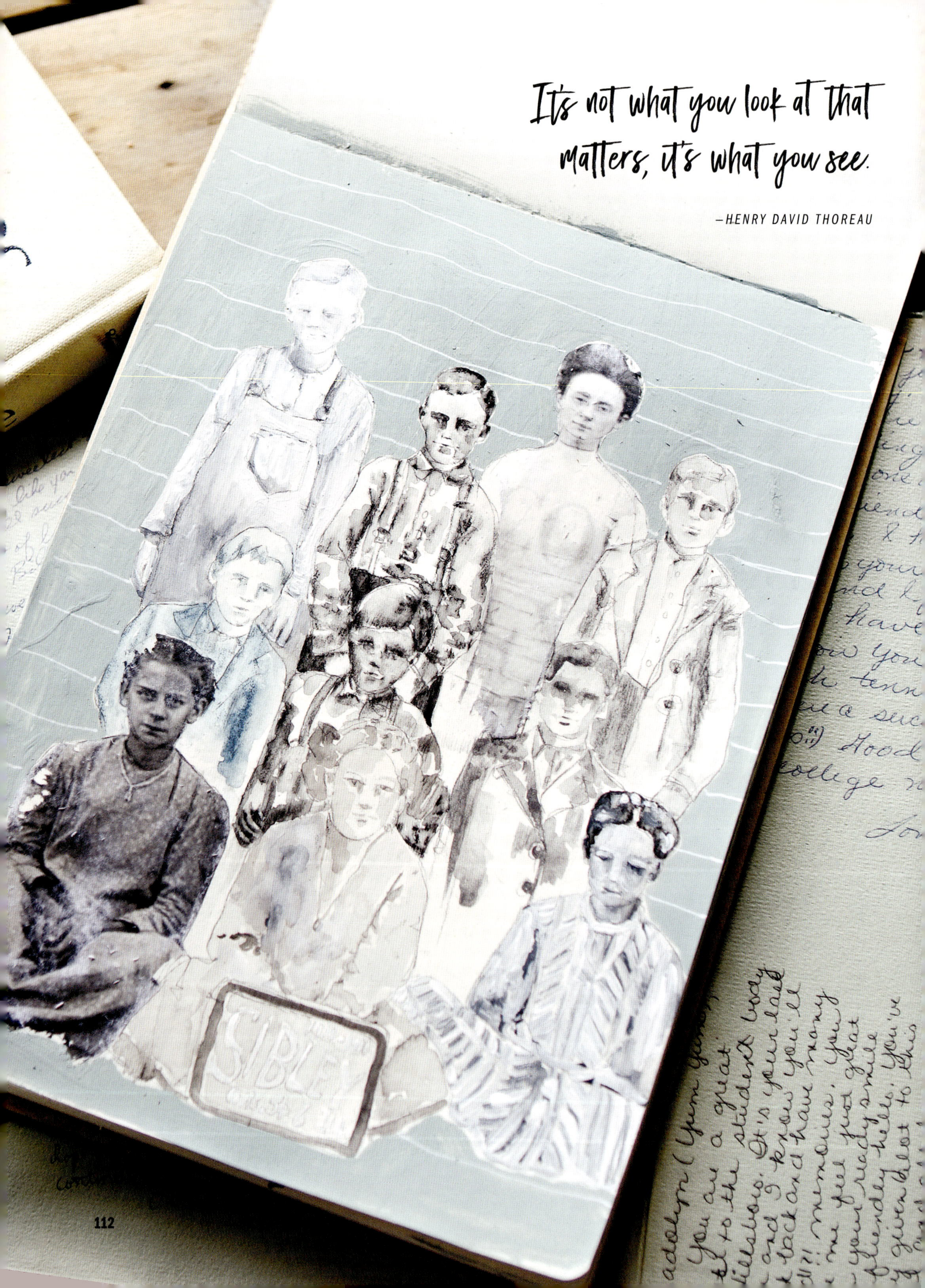

It's not what you look at that matters, it's what you see.

—HENRY DAVID THOREAU

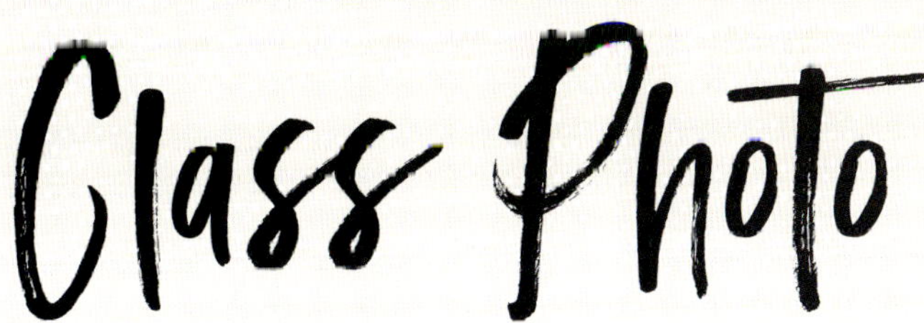

CHAPTER 15

Class Photo

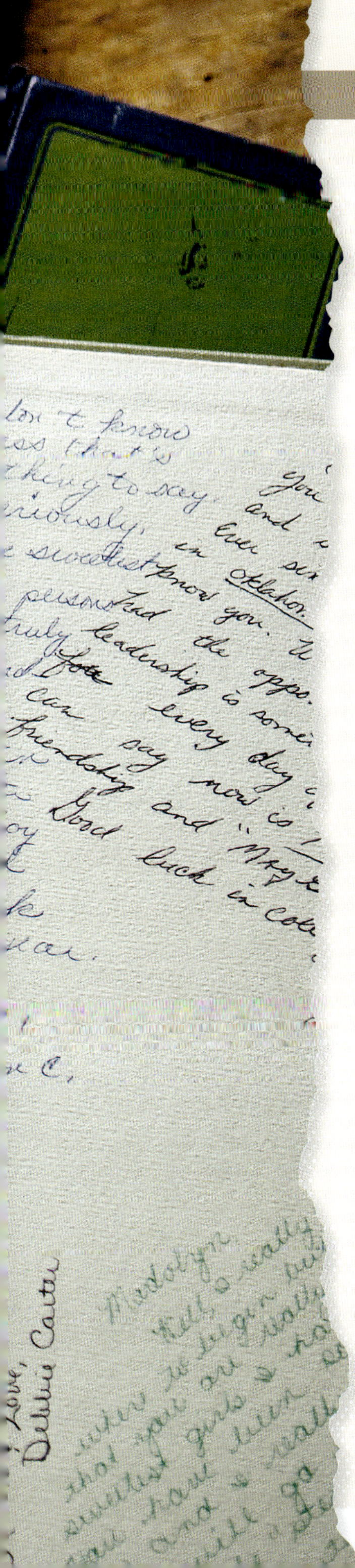

THIS BOOK CONCEPT BEGAN WITH A RANDOM VINTAGE PHOTO I FOUND a few years ago while antiquing with a friend. In the sepia photo there was an old farmhouse in the background surrounded by tall trees with an overflowing late summer garden in the foreground. In the midst of the garden was a posed woman standing next to an empty chair, a man seated off to the side and two more older gentlemen standing on the other side of the woman at a distance with one more empty chair. The photo was so random but completely staged. My friend and I joked that it looked like an album cover. I couldn't stop looking at it and was completely intrigued by the story I was making up in my mind. I spent way too much that day so the photo could be mine and I could continue to explore this untold story. Even now, looking at it again, I stare at them, make up stories, study them and then use them as inspiration. They are strangers to me but after so much time together I feel like I know them, or at least know what I tell myself about them.

Class Photo

I have been fascinated with vintage school and sports photos for years now. Maybe it is the serious faces or just the intimacy of many people squished together so one person blends into another. I do know for sure it is the untold stories. So, whether you have family photos on hand, or if you find something online or while antiquing, I hope this next project finds you making up new stories and being inspired by someone in the past.

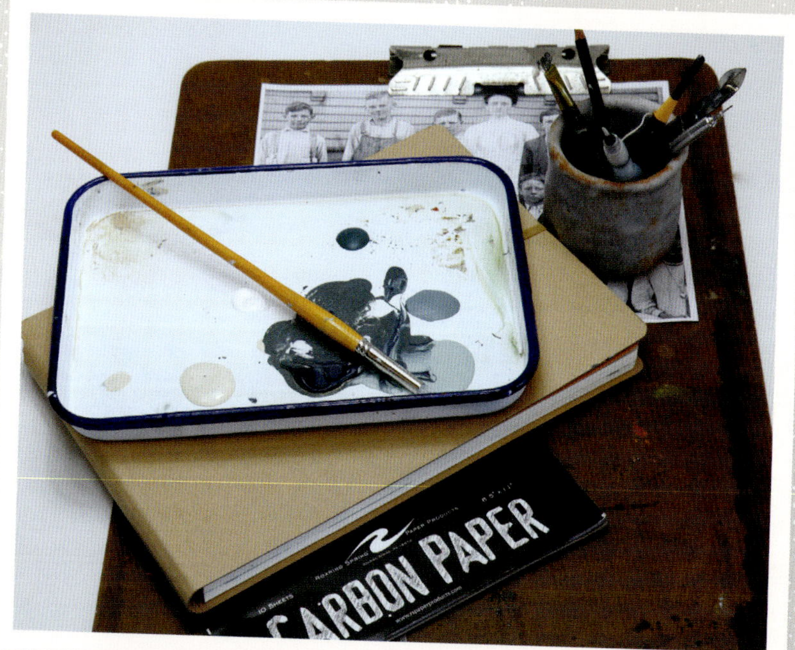

WHAT YOU NEED

- Art journal
- Black Stabilo All pencil
- Brayer or old plastic gift card
- Carbon paper
- Charcoal pencil
- Cloth or rag
- Gesso: clear and white
- Golden gel medium
- India ink
- Ink brush
- Laser print photocopy
- Mechanical pencil
- Scissors
- Water brush

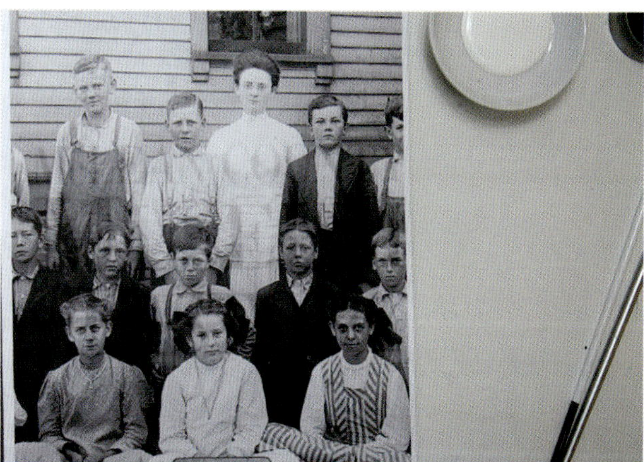

1 Apply a thin layer of clear gesso onto your journal page and allow to dry. After the gesso is dry take one piece of carbon paper and place it facedown onto your journal page. Next take a printed image of a class, sports team or family photo, place it face up and clip it to the sides of the journal to secure the image and carbon paper.

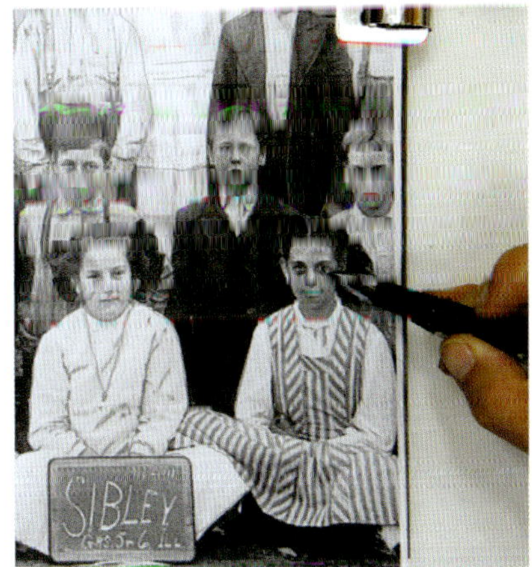

2 Using a mechanical pencil, go over the lines and shadows of the image. Lift your paper and carbon paper a few times to make sure your marks are strong enough to transfer the carbon onto your journal page. All rights were granted to use this class photo from McLean County Museum of History of Bloomington, Illinois.

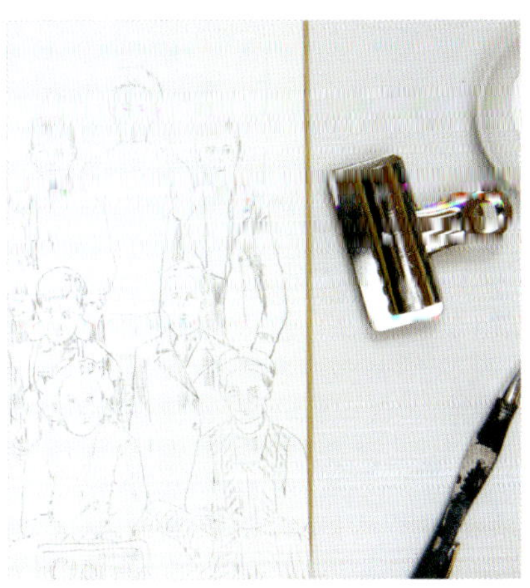

3 Once your image has transferred, add any elements you missed with a mechanical pencil.

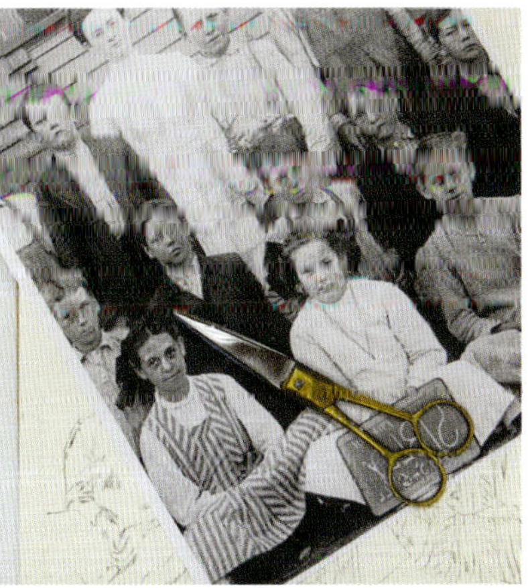

4 For the next step we will be creating an image transfer, so the original image will need to be flipped in the photo editing program of your choice (Photoshop, Illustrator, Picmonkey, etc.). I recommend this being a laser print photocopy.

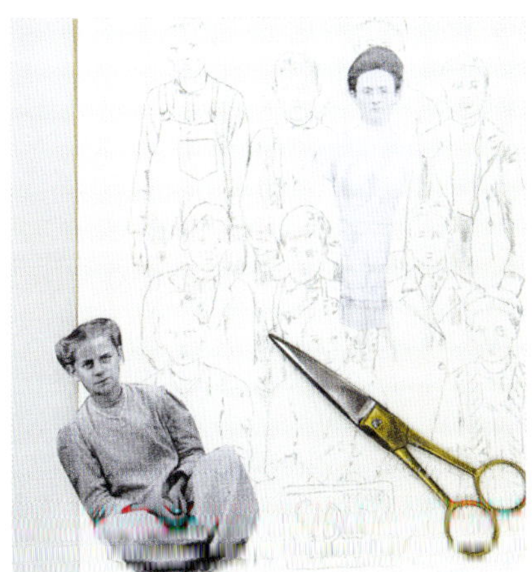

5 Cut out just a few of the images from the print. I suggest not having the images right next to each other to create more interest.

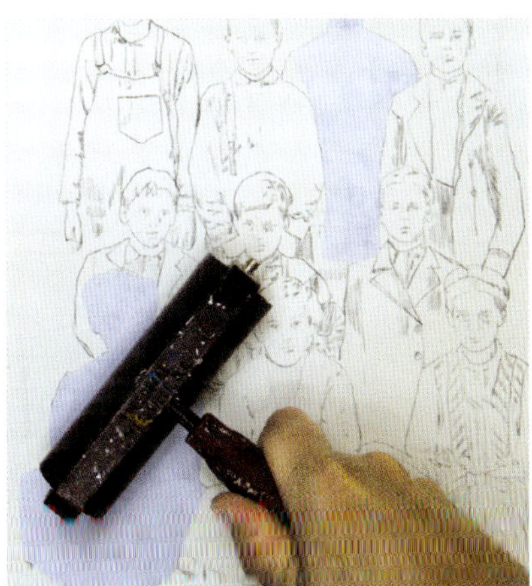

6 Apply a thin layer of Golden gel medium to the front of your image and adhere it face down to the matching spot in your sketch. Using a brayer or credit card, apply pressure to make sure the image is adhered and also to remove any air bubbles. Allow this image to dry.

In the following steps, we will use our original carbon paper transfer and simple tools to explore how to create values within the piece. At the end of the project you will have a sampling of simple "paintings" using Stabilo, charcoal, watercolor pencil, ink and graphite. You will have a side-by-side comparison to see with what technique you most connect.

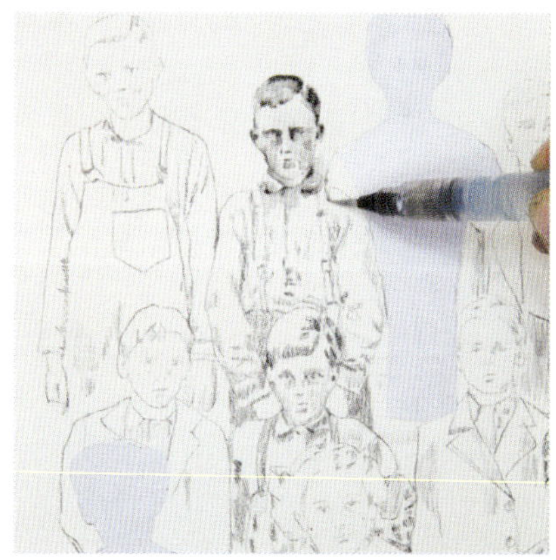

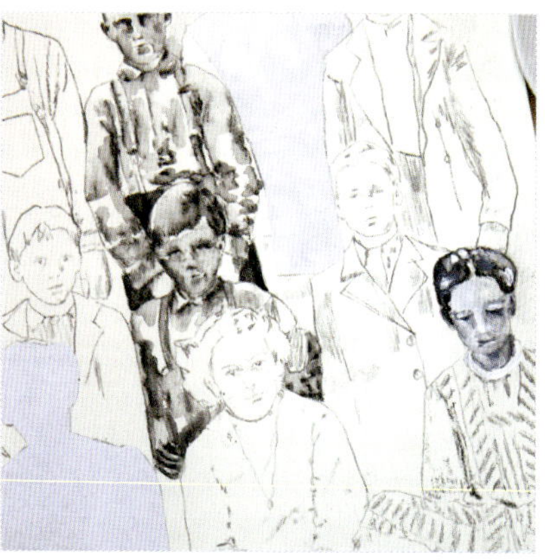

7 Lightly sketch in the darkest values with a Stabilo, using the original photo as a reference. Then start moving the Stabilo marks around with a water brush. Using the water brush over a paintbrush dipped in water gives you a constant source of water. This is a technique you can do anywhere. Have a small rag off to the side to wipe off excess medium or water. The Stabilo creates a beautiful watercolor effect when it is allowed to pool and dry. Have fun with this technique and medium. A black Stabilo is a staple in all of my creating because of how versatile and portable it is.

8 Next add some white gesso to at least one of your "paintings" with black Stabilo. The white gesso will allow you to create a wider range of values, and once the Stabilo mixes with the gesso it becomes permanent when dry. For more techniques using Stabilo, refer to Chapter 9.

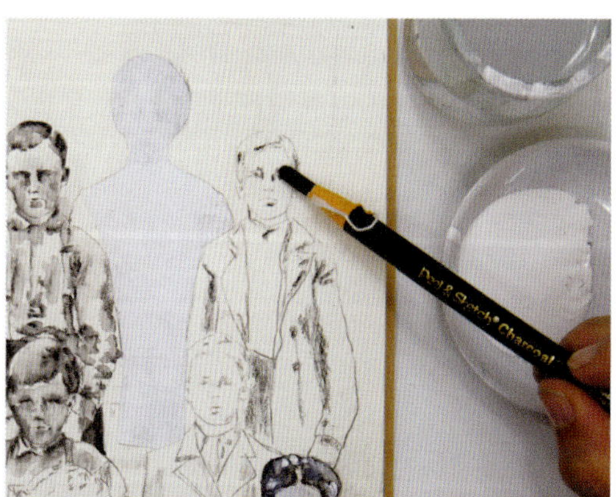

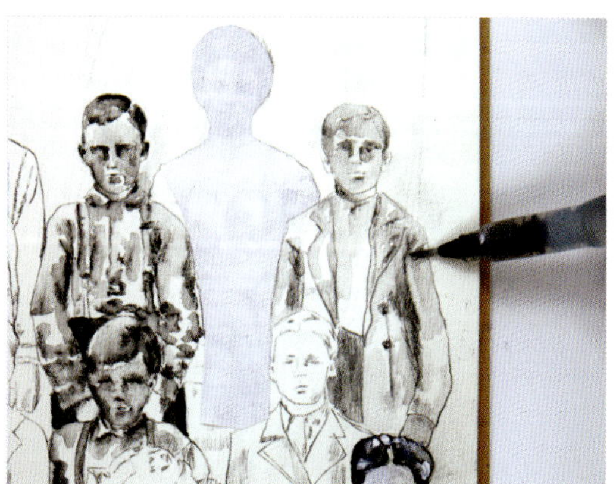

9 Repeat the above techniques but this time use charcoal. Charcoal and water create a softer black and is not as intense as the black Stabilo. Once again use the original image as your reference to see where the darkest values are in the picture and add extra charcoal to your sketch in these areas.

10 Using a water brush, move the charcoal around. For a lighter value, add more water. To keep your charcoal darker, add less.

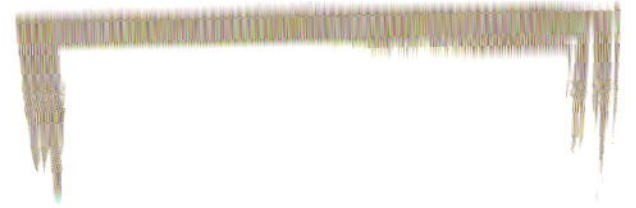

Remember that the black Stabilo pencil is an intense black once it is activated with water. I prefer to be light-handed when sketching with Stabilo and slowly add more where needed.

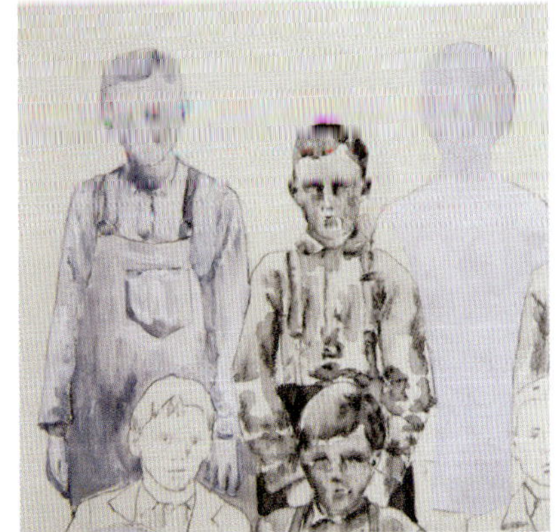

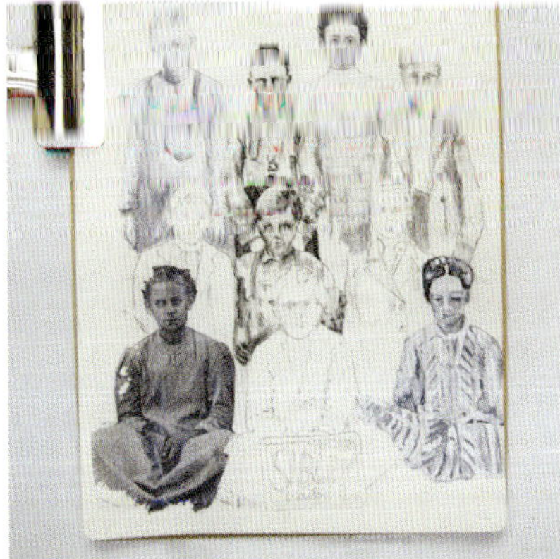

11 In the upper left-hand corner is an example of a charcoal sketch using white gesso to create more varied values. Compare this "painting" to the sketch using a Stabilo and white gesso. Do you have a favorite? Do you prefer a softer or more intense black or values within your work? Do you feel like you are better able to control and manipulate one medium over another?

12 Once your paper image transfer is dry, you can follow the steps shared in Chapter 9 to slowly reveal the image.

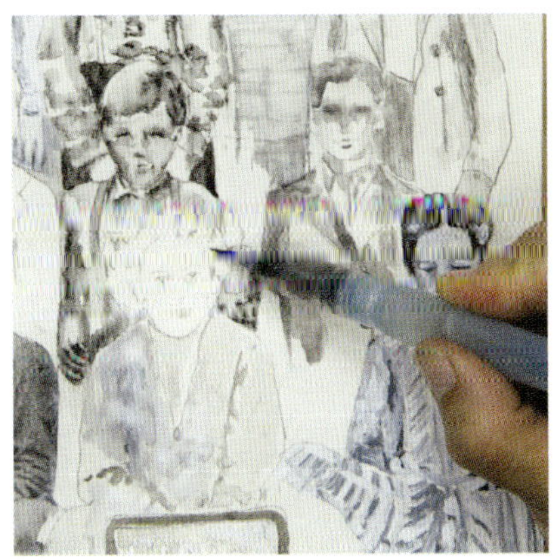

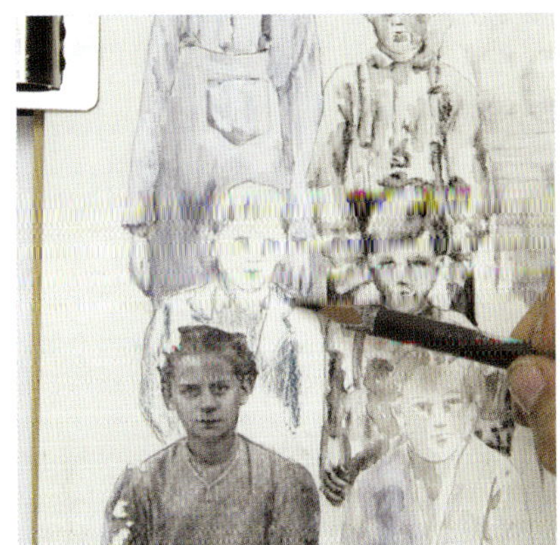

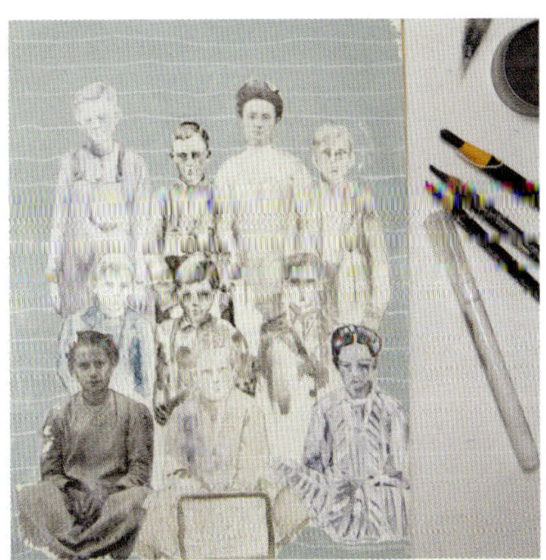

13 India ink brush pens can create beautiful and dramatic marks in your work. For this project I decided to add the ink into a small dish so I could use the medium diluted with water to allow for better control and a more subtle use of the ink. This piece also has areas where I included water-soluble graphite for interest.

14 You may not connect to the simplicity of the charcoal, Stabilo, water-soluble graphite or gray ink. This technique also works with a watercolor pencil. It will move around with water the same as all of the mediums above, but you can find these pencils in any color imaginable.

15 You have many different mediums before you, but we used almost the same techniques with many of them. Do you have a favorite?

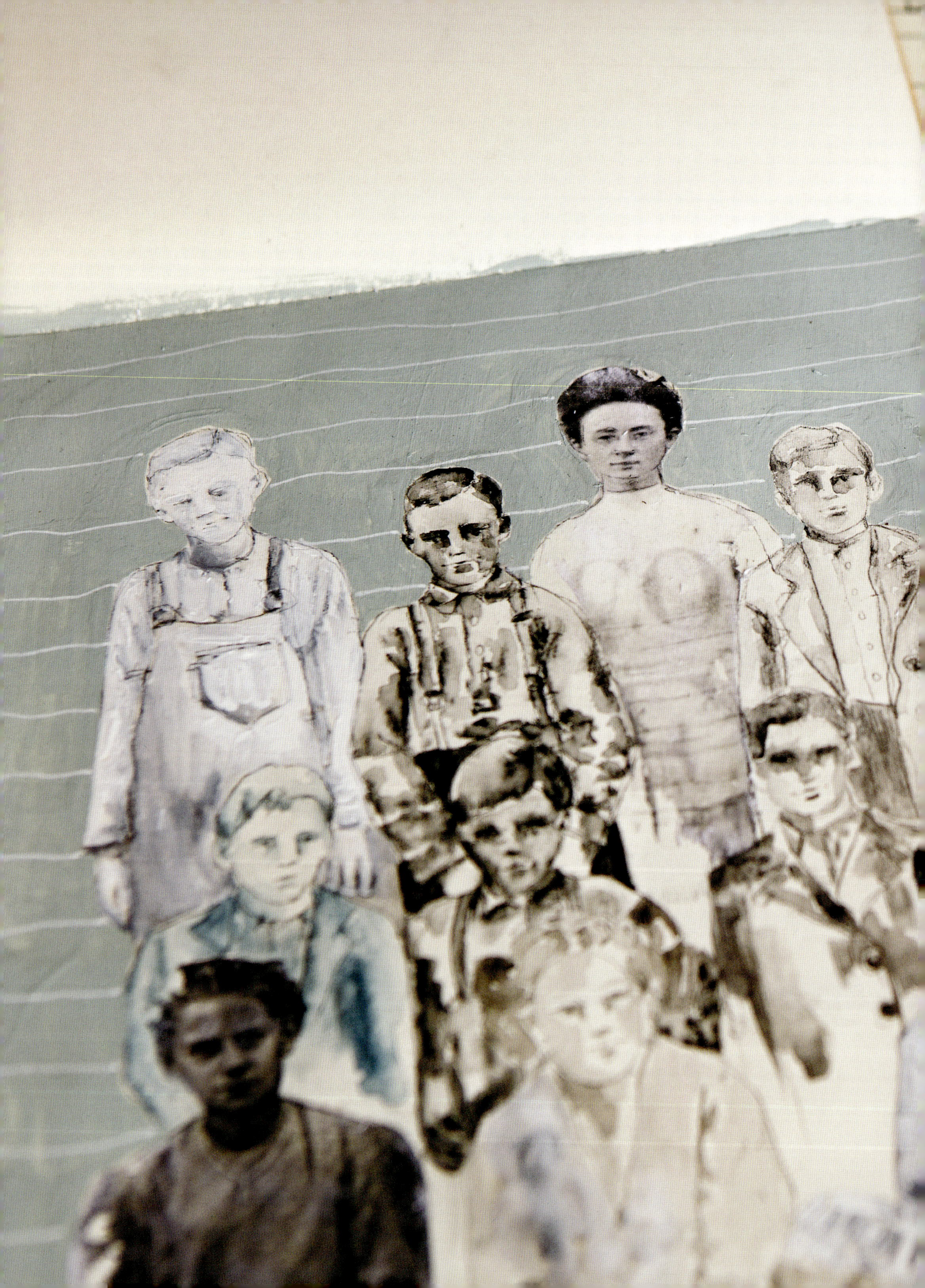

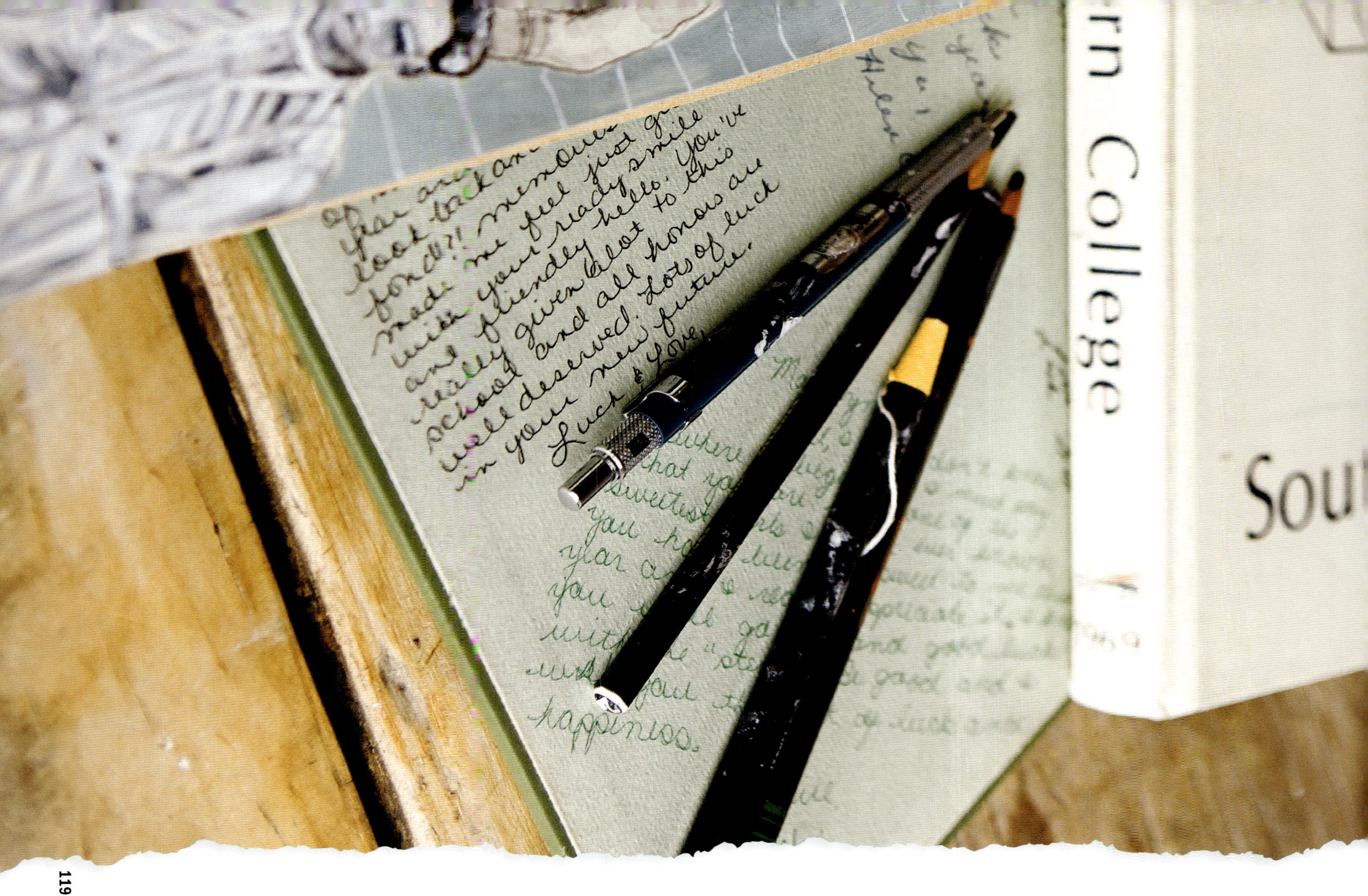

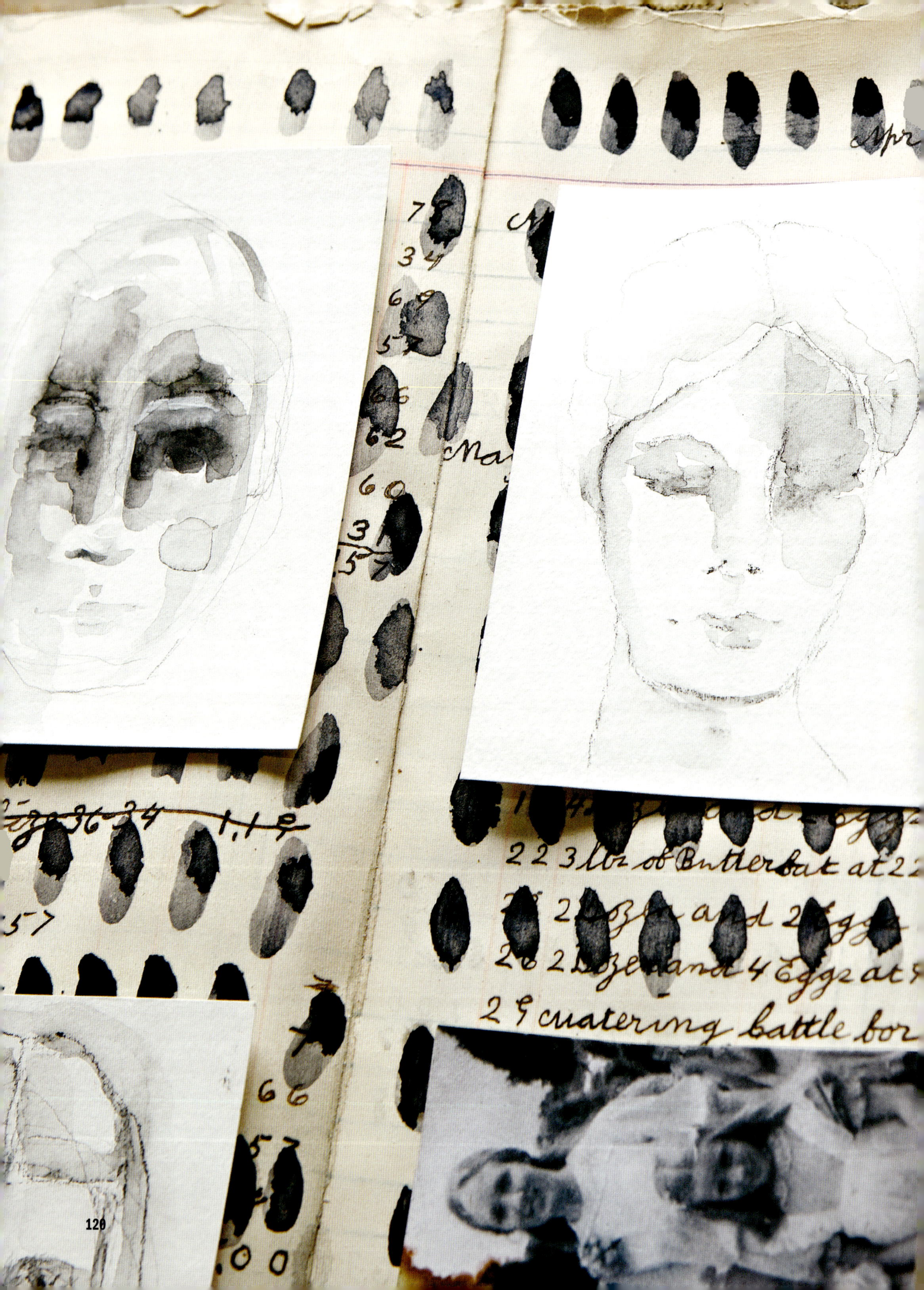

CHAPTER 16

Cast of Characters

IF YOUR LIFE WERE A PLAY, WHAT CHARACTERS would rise to the top and how would their stories intertwine with your own? Who would be the one who cheered you on? The villain? The love interest? There are those whose lives pass by ours for a short time, and those who are there for years and whose impact is life- or heart-changing for good or bad. There is no right or wrong cast of characters for your story. It just is. They are the places, animals, people or fill in the blank . . . that have played a part in who you are today.

Cast of Characters

Who is in your cast? Who will you gather on these pages to represent a part of your past, present or future? Using the techniques from Chapter 15, we will create our own cast of characters.

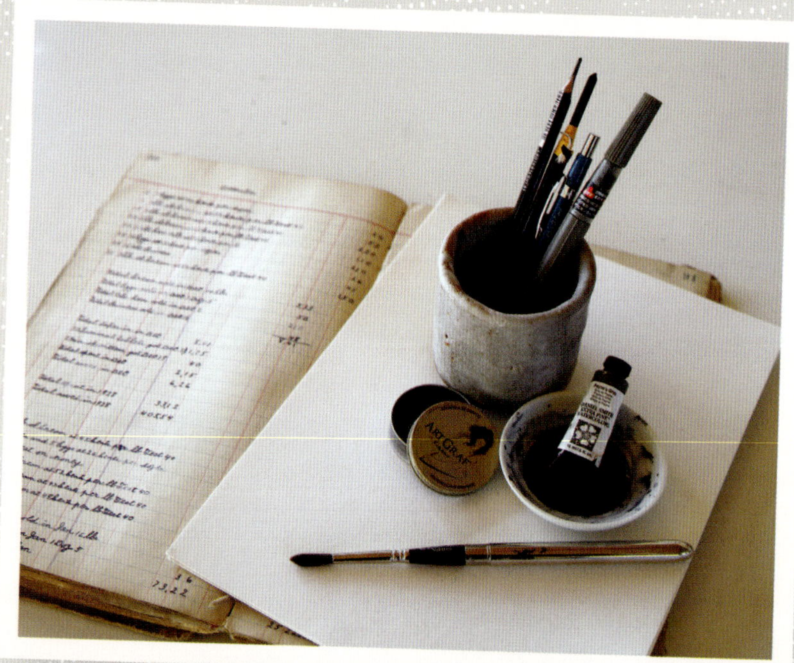

WHAT YOU NEED

- Art Journal
- Black Stabilo All pencil
- Brush ink pen
- Gesso: clear and white
- Glue stick, tape or matte medium
- Graphite
- Paintbrush
- Photos, online images, etc.
- Watercolor paint and brushes
- Watercolor paper cut into identical-sized squares

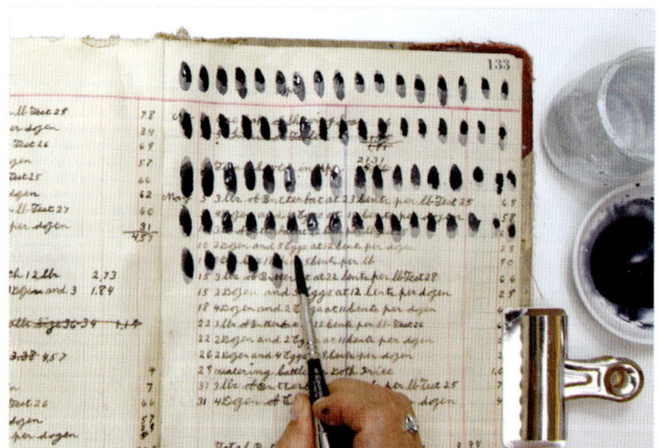

1 Apply a thin layer of clear gesso over your journal pages. Using a watercolor of your choice, create a repetitive mark over both pages. Allow to dry.

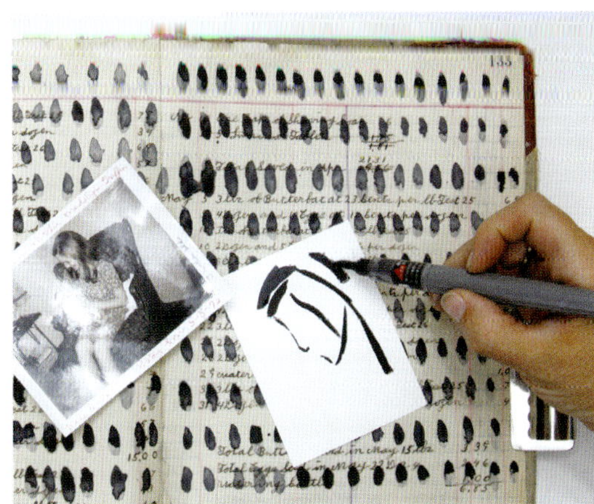

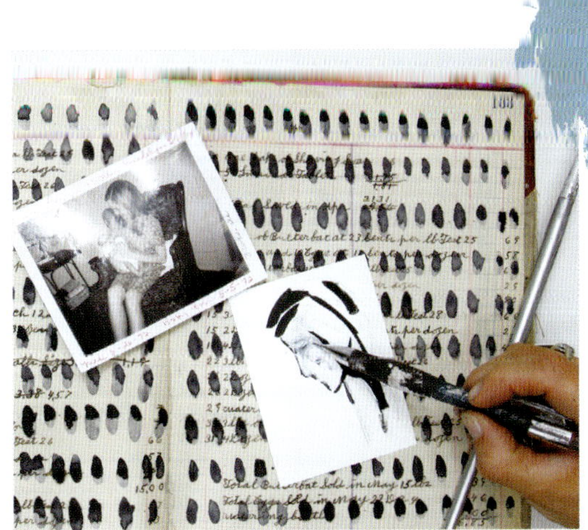

2 Cut out six to eight pieces of watercolor paper (hot-or cold-pressed paper) in identical sizes so they will fit onto your two-page journal spread. Using photos, online images or your imagination as reference, bring your cast to life.

3 In this example, I mixed broad-brush ink pen strokes with the softness created by combining white gesso, Stabilo and graphite.

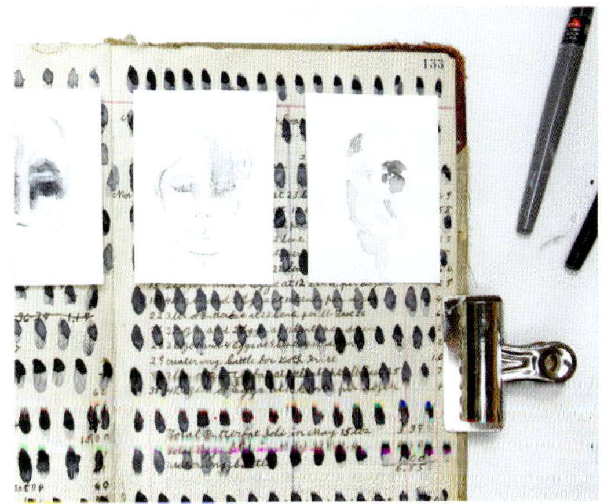

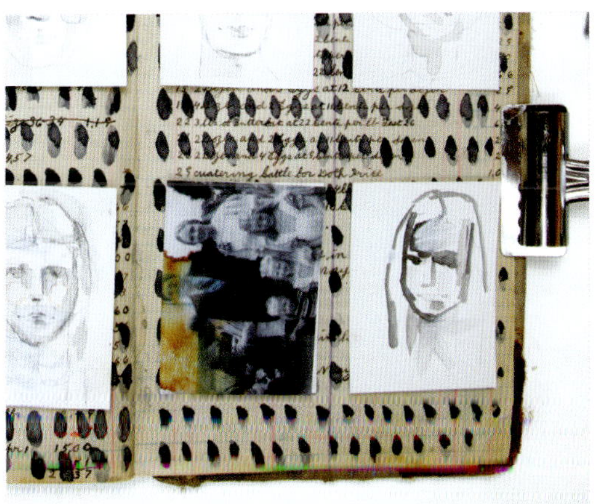

4 Try using different mediums and techniques for different subjects to see how a feeling can be created with a different combination of familiar tools.

5 I ended up using an ink-jet printed photo as a final member of my cast because it had gotten wet and I loved how the colors bled to create drama and feeling within the piece. You can then adhere each piece of watercolor paper to your journal with a glue stick, matte medium or tape.

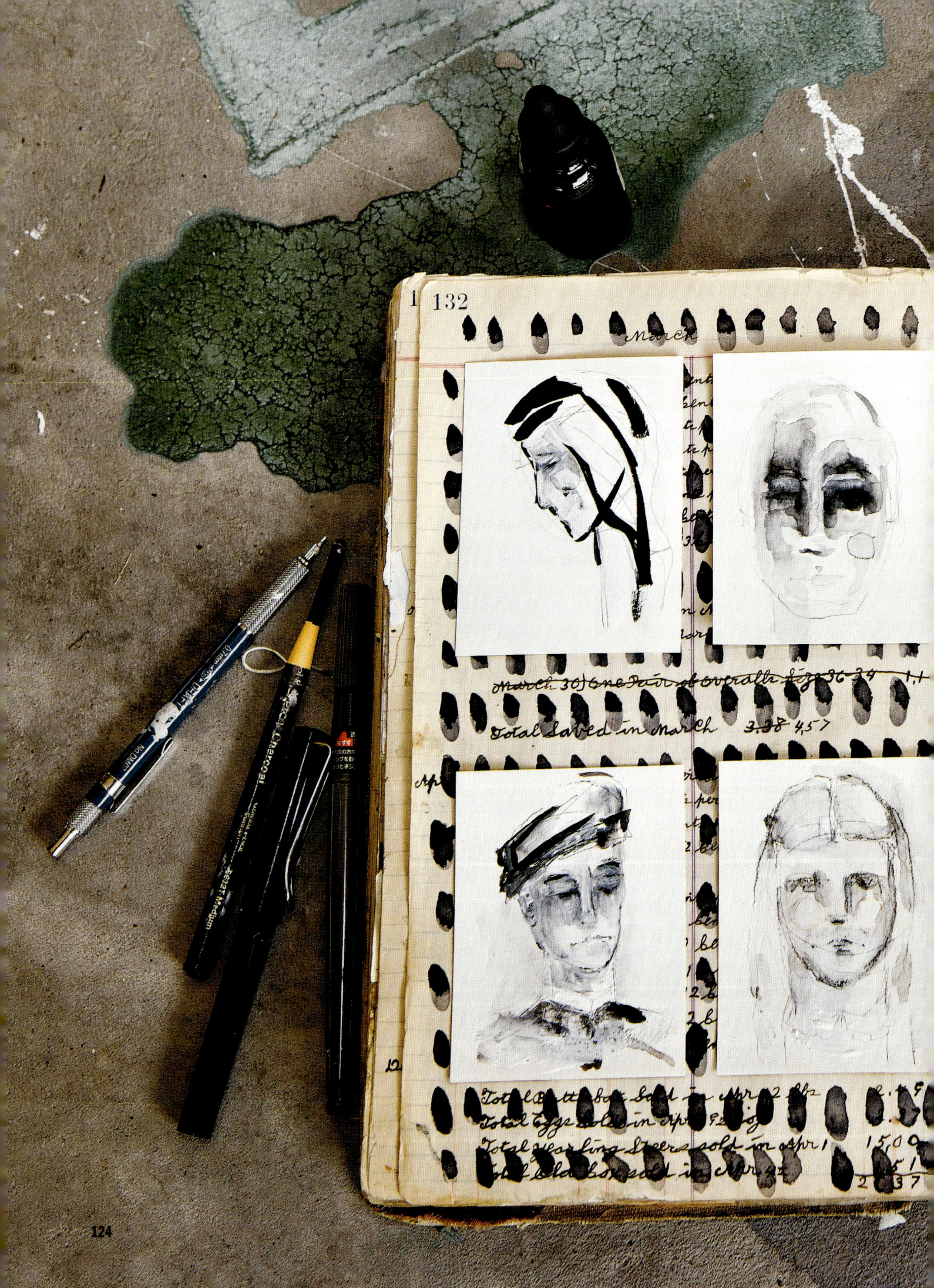

—JOHN STEINBECK

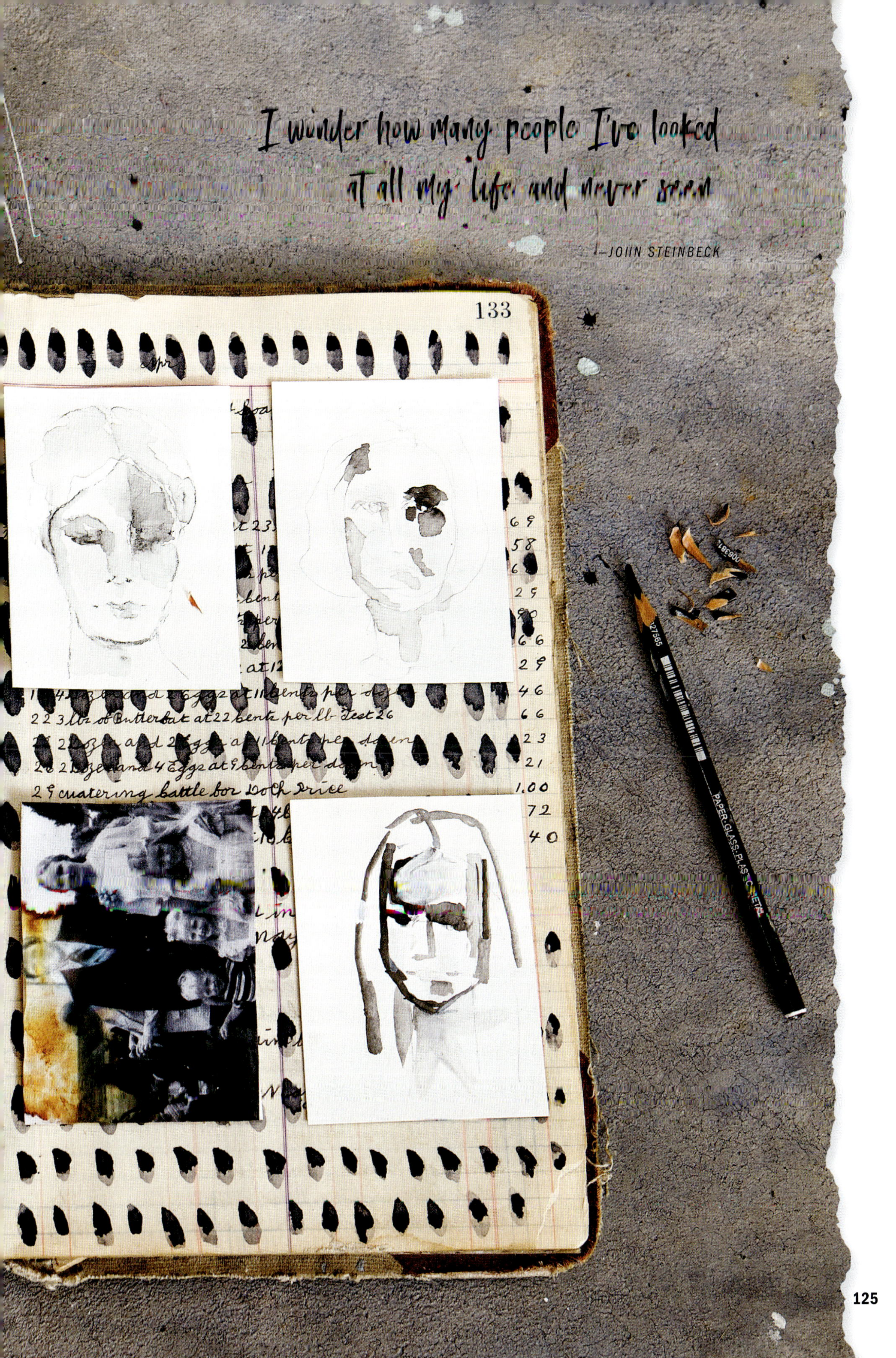

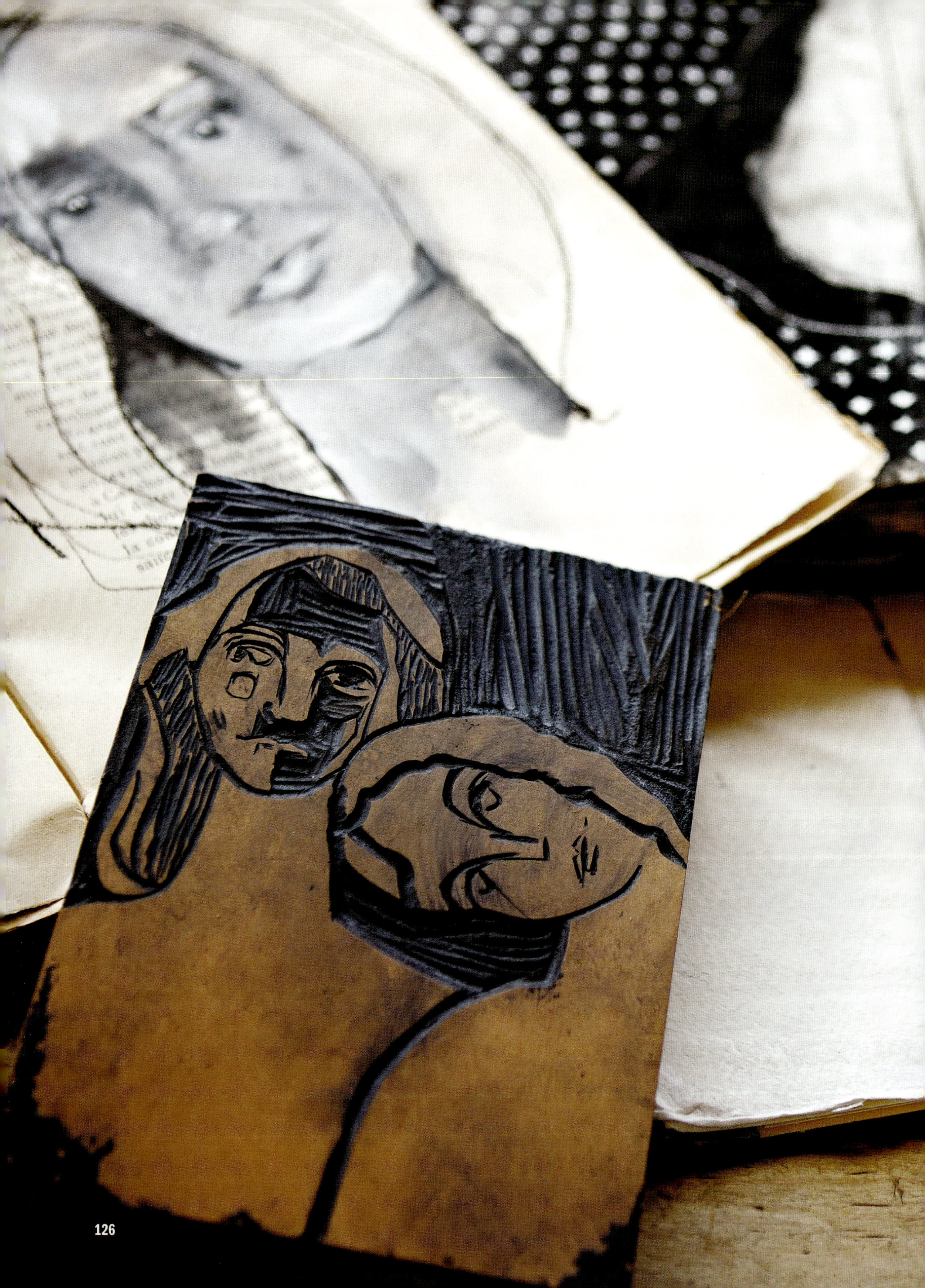

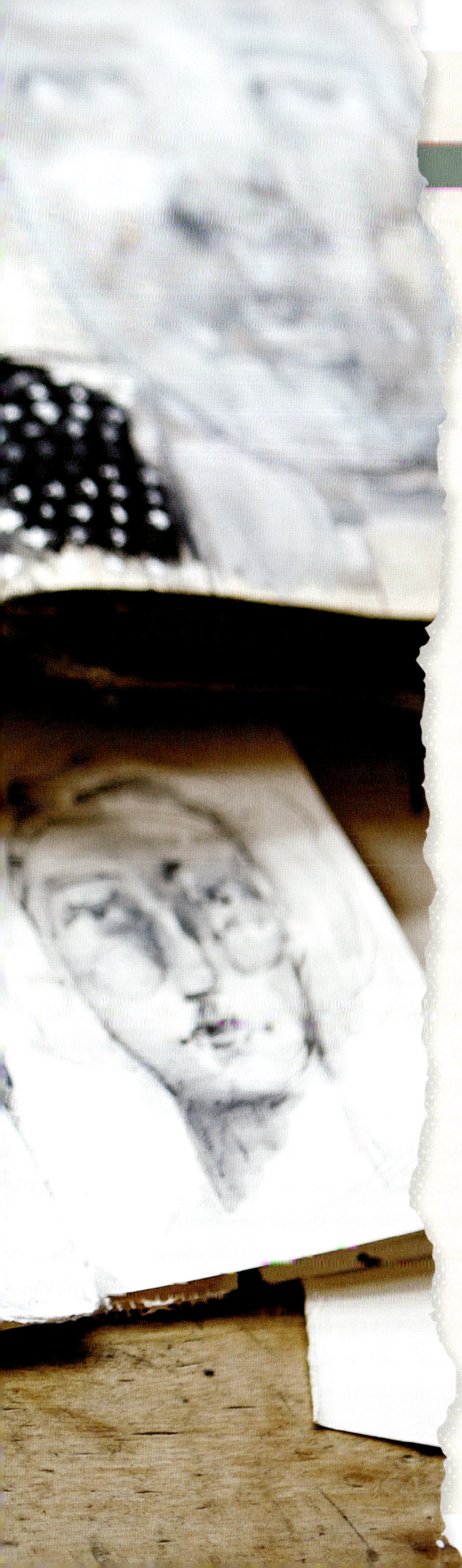

CHAPTER 17

Portraits

THE EYES, THE SHAPE OF THE FACE, THE AGE, THE MOVEMENT, the connection . . . the story. Portraits draw me in because of the beauty of connection, relationship and untold story. There are few things I gravitate towards creating as much as portraits, and they fill my sketchbooks and many of my canvases. They are in my mind and before my eyes.

This chapter is full of different techniques to share your story through portraits, hopefully in a way that makes portraits feel not so intimidating. It is very important to me to share techniques that will get many people out of their comfort zone and to give portraits a chance.

I can get lost in this portrait process, and each time I am surprised by what appears before me. Rarely what I end up creating is based upon what was before me, it's what is inside of me. Maybe you will find the same thing.

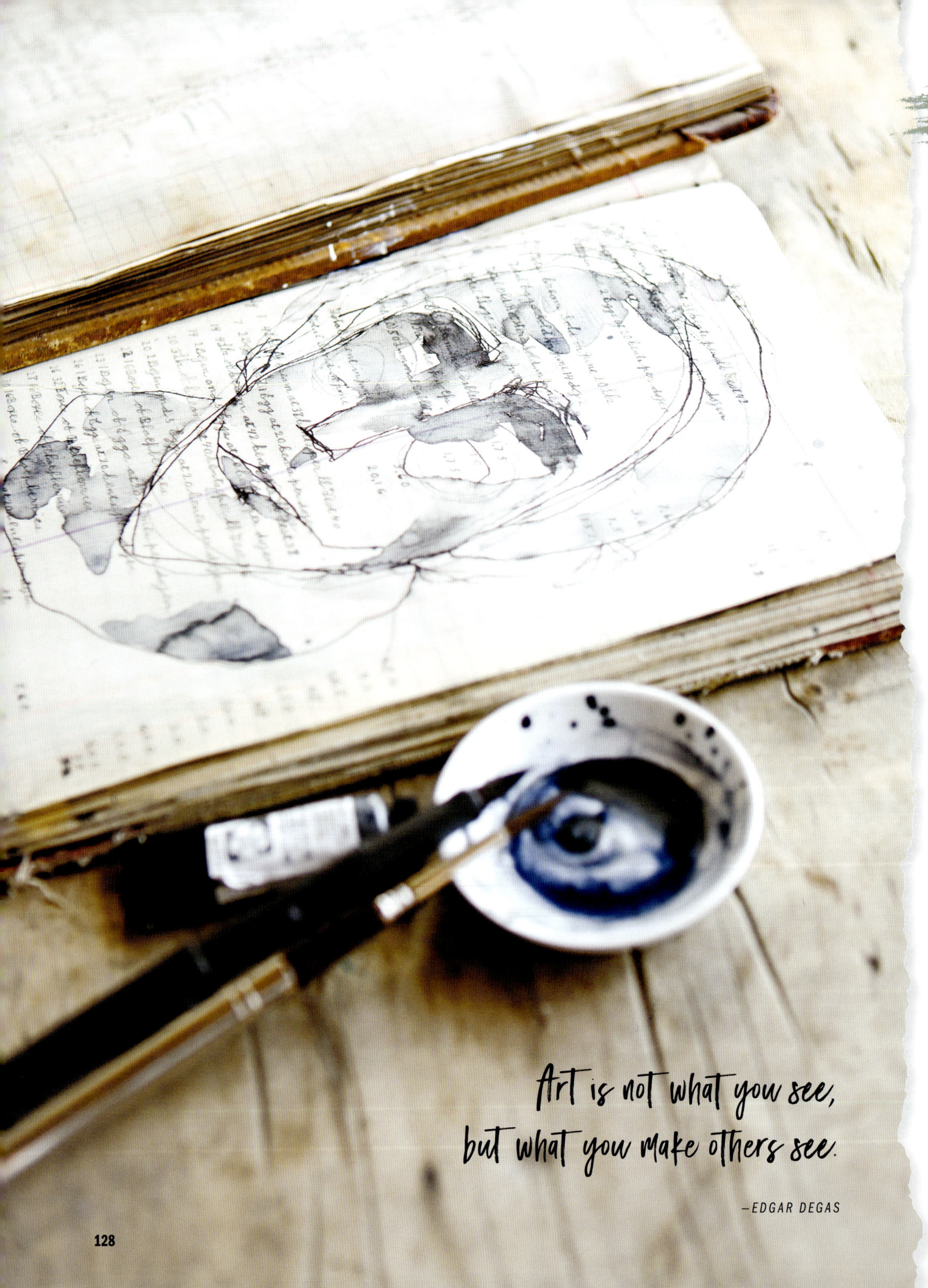

Art is not what you see,
but what you make others see.
—EDGAR DEGAS

Contour Sketch

Contour sketching is a sure way to get out of your head, comfort zone and to start practicing. It is a technique that can be done anywhere, and it allows you to let go of perfection and the end result. I often use this technique for portraits, but you can do this with furniture, architecture and even your own hand.

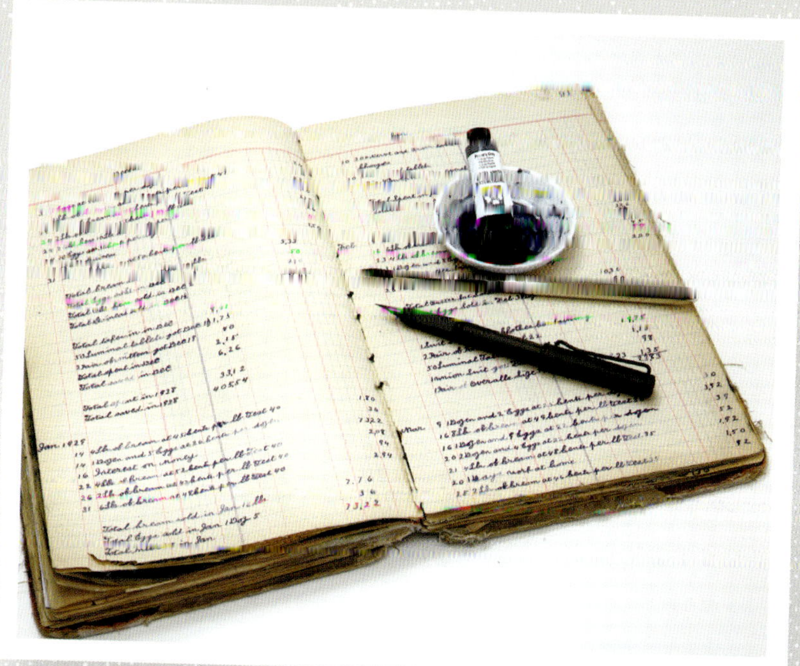

WHAT YOU NEED
– Ink pen

– Mechanical pencil

– Timer

– Watercolor paint and brush

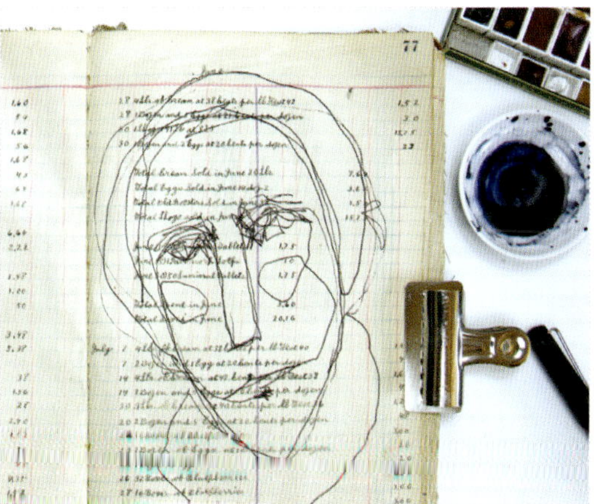

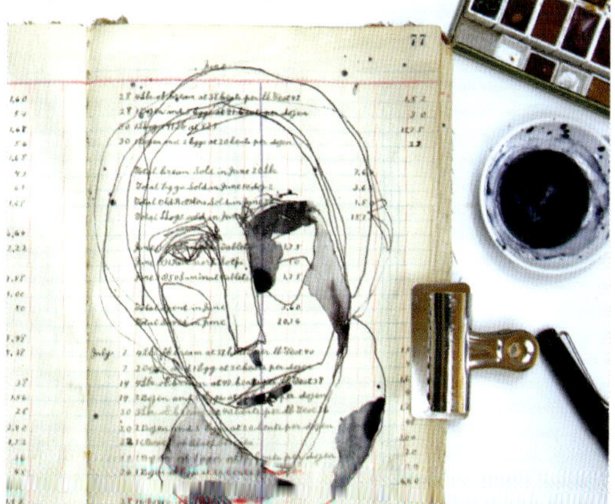

1 When I create a contour sketch I prefer to set a timer for 1-2 mintues so I don't look at the clock and am encouraged to work quickly. The point of the exercise is to really look at your reference image or an object in front of you. When you are creating a contour sketch, the technique is that you *do not* lift your medium the whole time you sketch. That's right! That means if you are doing a sketch with a pen, as I did here, the pen is never lifted off the page. This allows you to let go of perfectionism and end results and to truly be present and see the lines and shapes in front of you.

2 Contour sketches are a perfect way to warm up. Many times the contour sketch may be so interesting that it becomes the focal point of a painting.

After I did my contour sketch with ink, I brought in Payne's Gray watercolor and created varying values by adding more or less water to the pigment. Using a mechanical pencil, I created more elements through loose scribbles and small amounts of detail.

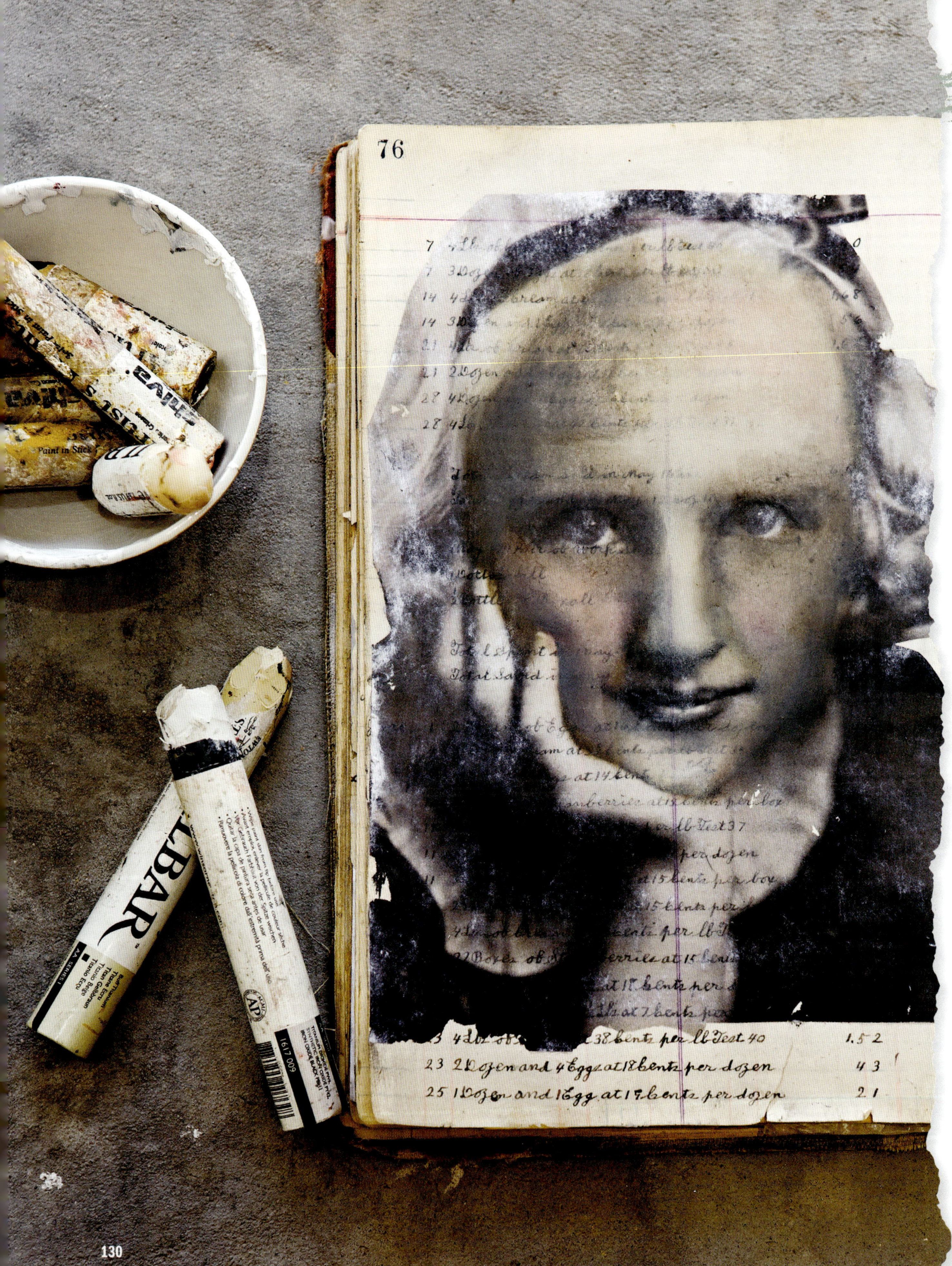

Oil Sticks and Image Transfers

Portraits can be intimidating for many. I hear this again and again from students and peers, so I wanted to include a project that would take away that fear and allow you to explore, create and know that in the end your piece will be a portrait you are proud of. You will also be surprised how much you will learn about values and color mixing.

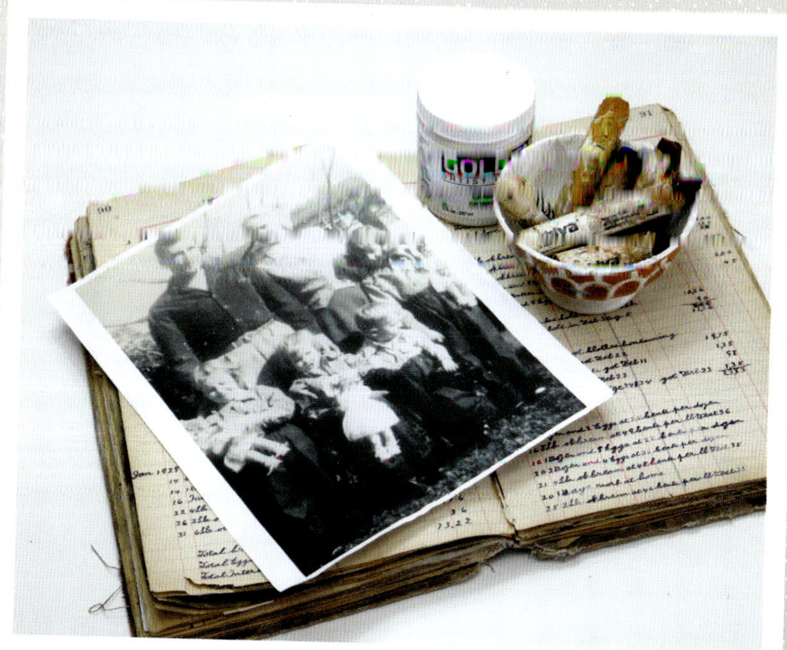

WHAT YOU NEED

- Art journal

- Gesso: clear

- Gloves

- Golden gel medium

- Laser printed photograph

- Liquitex matte medium

- Oil sticks: Raw Umber Titanium White, etc.

- Paintbrush

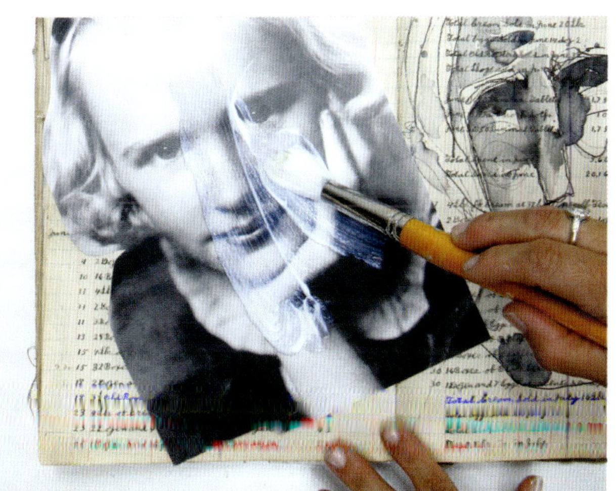

1 Using a laser print of a photograph, apply a thin layer of Golden gel medium onto the front of the image. Apply the image facedown onto your clear gessoed journal page and allow it to dry.

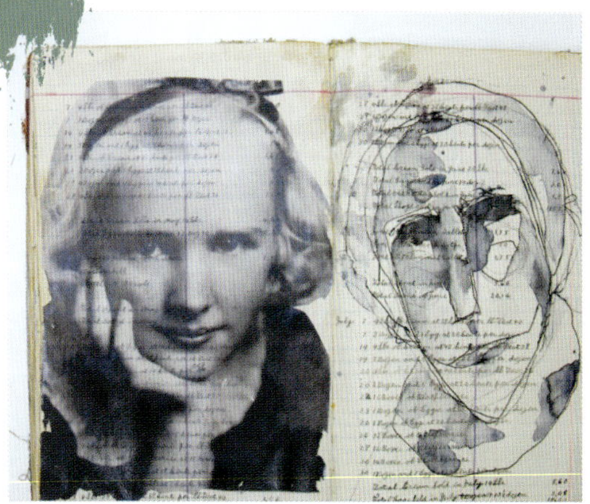

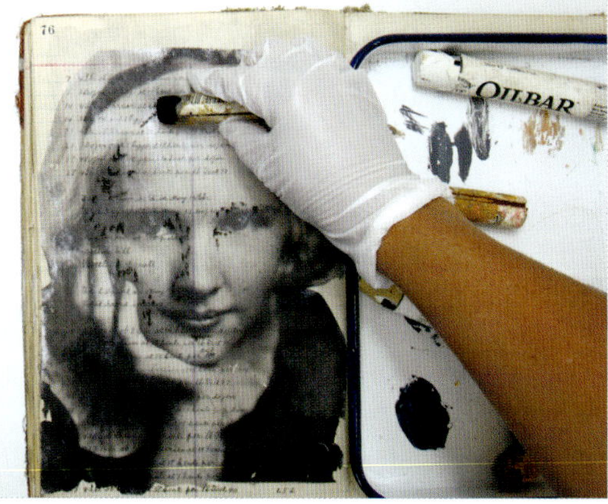

2 Once the gel medium is dry (you can always speed up the process with a drying tool), dip your fingers in clean water and start to gently rub away the back layer of the paper. I start off in a circular motion and then in a gentle back-and-forth motion. If you rub too hard you may pull up some of your image.

As your image transfer begins to dry, you may find that it becomes white and cloudy. If this happens, lightly dampen your fingers again and gently remove any of this excess paper. To prevent the image from fading again, I like to apply a thin layer of Liquitex matte medium.

3 Using your image transfer as your guide, apply Raw Umber oil stick directly onto your image where you see the darkest values. An oil stick is oil paint in stick form, so I always advise wearing gloves. Oil sticks blend like a dream, but if you ever need the oils to blend more, I suggest adding some clear oil stick to your painting and it will start blending again.

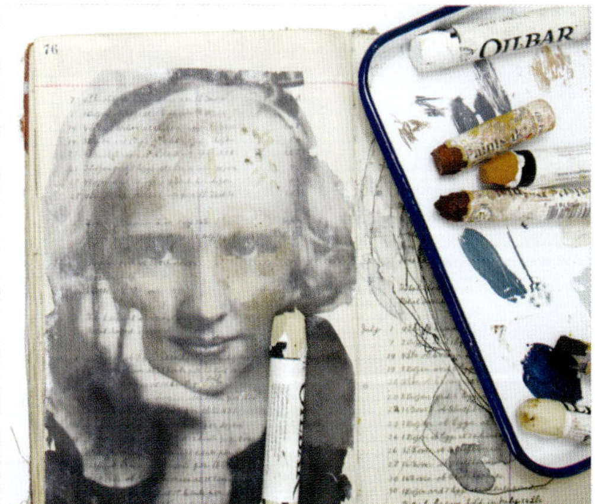

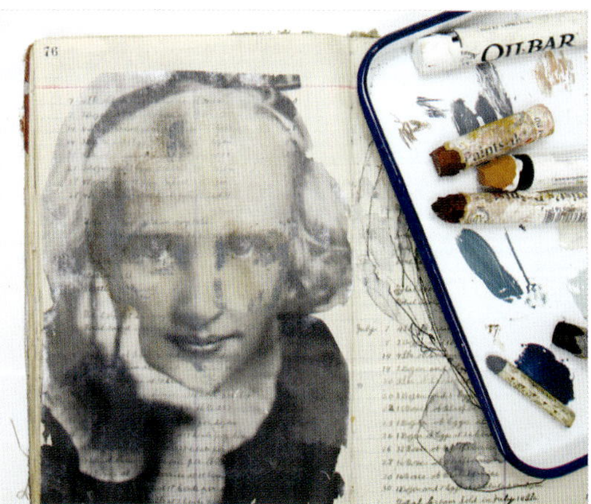

4 Next bring in an Ecru and lightly blend into the Raw Umber without losing the darkest values. You do not have to blend much.

5 Then I added a Payne's Gray oil stick, but you can use any darker color to create another layer of color. I added the Payne's Gray again where I saw the darkest values and lightly blended it into the piece.

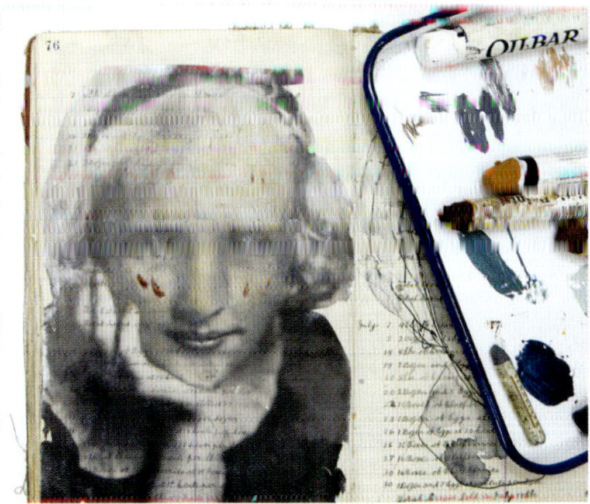

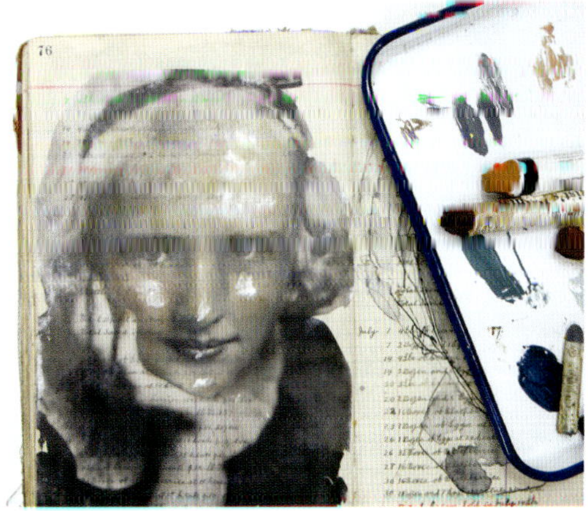

6 The skin tone was lacking yellow and pink undertones, so I started with a very small amount of crimson. A little goes a long way. This was then gently blended.

7 With so many different colors being added and blended, I was losing my highlights, so I came in with a Titanium White. Keep in mind, the highlights should not be overly blended.

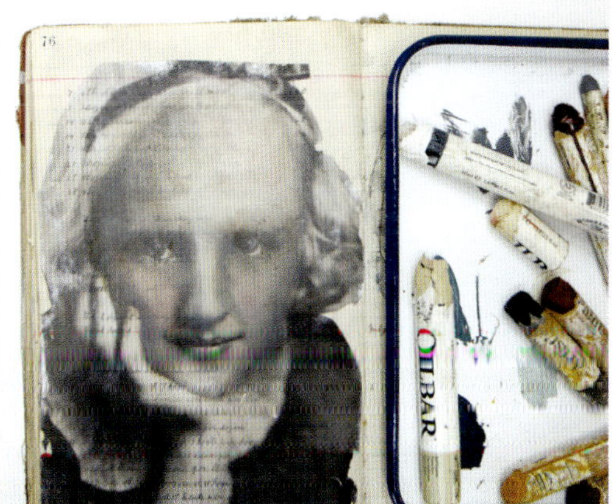

8 The final addition was little dabs of Yellow Ochre to warm up the skin and to blend it in. Oil sticks take longer to dry than an acrylic medium, which does not contain oil, so you will need to leave your journal page open. Or when you close it you can protect your portrait with a sheet of deli paper or wax paper.

Quick Tip

Oil sticks use the same pigment and drying oils that are used in tube oils. Oil sticks will dry with time, unlike oil pastels, which are made from a different oil and never fully dry.

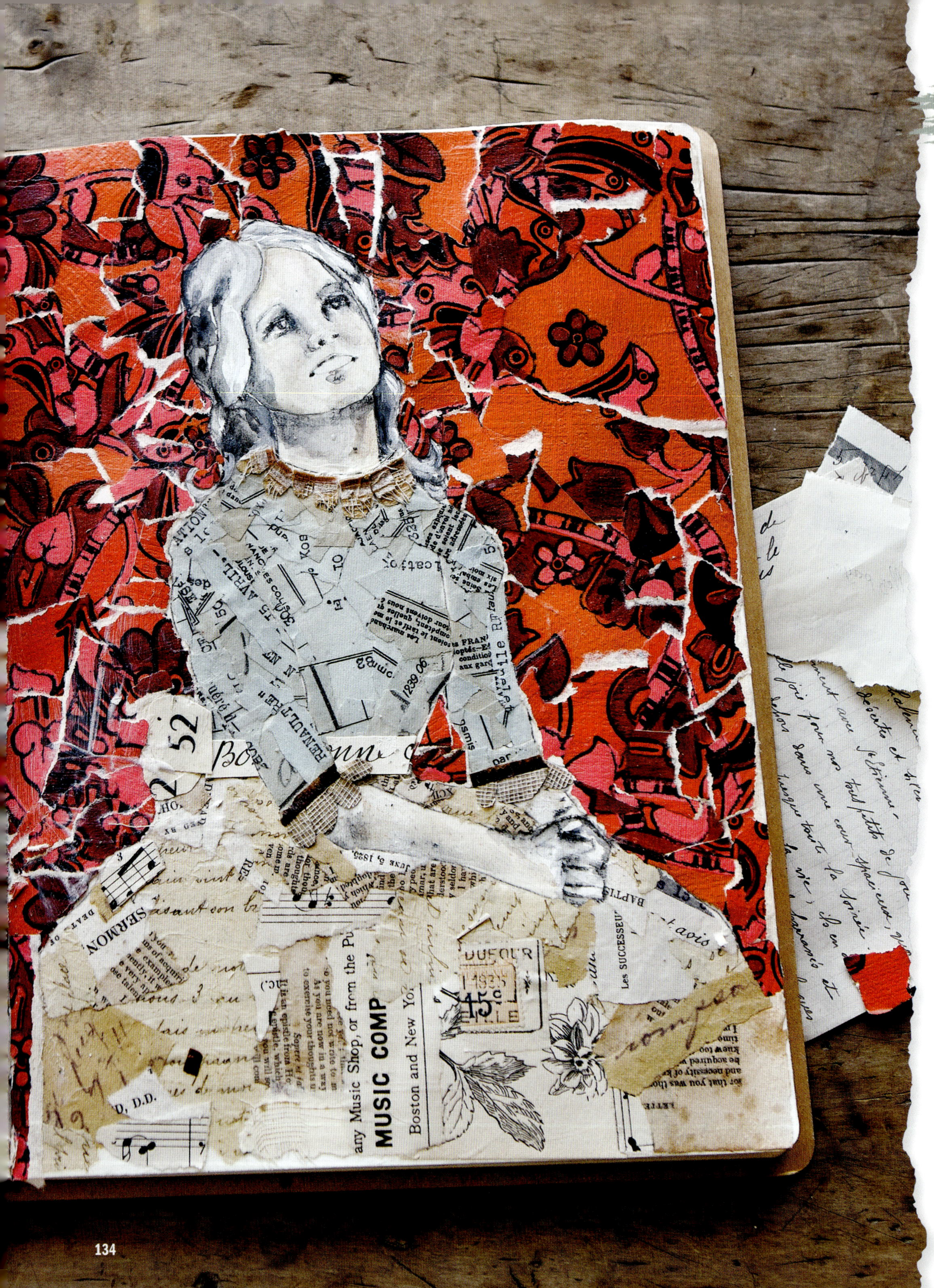

Collage

Collage can be created by using vintage ephemera, your own art, newspaper, found papers, wallpaper and even papers painted with tempera. There is no limit to the different papers you can incorporate into collage work. With a little glue and paper, you will be having fun like you did in kindergarten in no time! For this project I am using vintage ephemera because I am working in my journal, and vintage papers are usually thinner and more brittle, which work perfectly in collage. I find the process of collage relaxing and even therapeutic. So, turn on your favorite music and settle into your own groove as you create your collage.

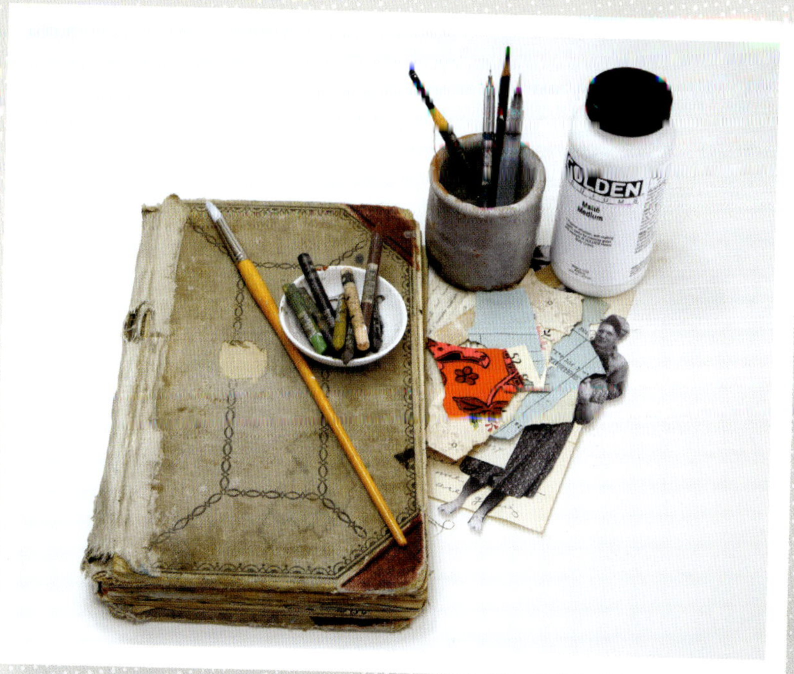

WHAT YOU NEED
- *Art journal*
- *Black Stabilo All pencil*
- *Carbon paper*
- *Collage papers*
- *Copy of a photo*
- *Matte medium*
- *Neocolor II crayon*
- *Waterbrush*
- *Workable fixative*

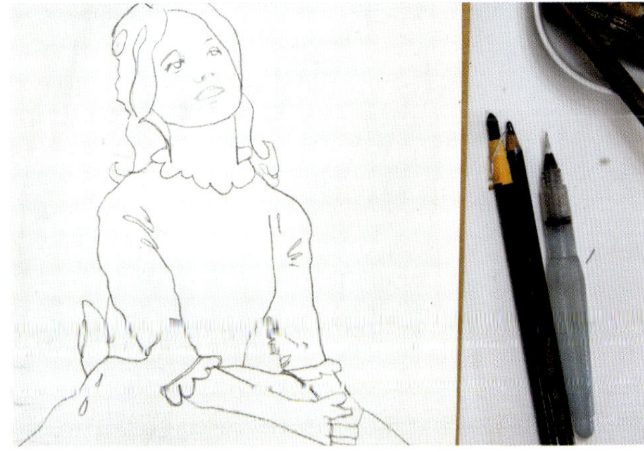

1 Using carbon paper and a photocopy of a photo, transfer the image using the techniques shared in Chapter 15.

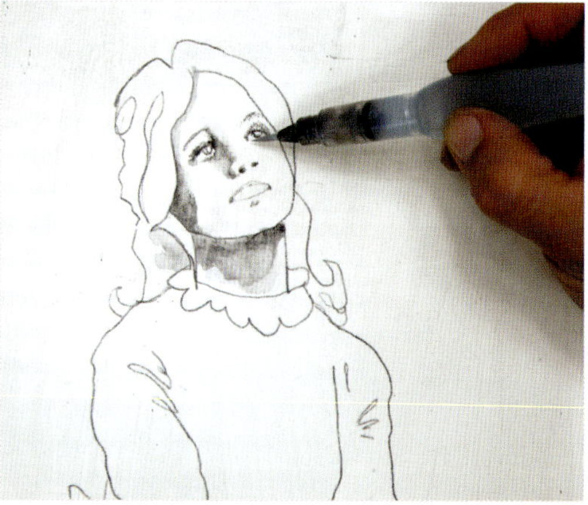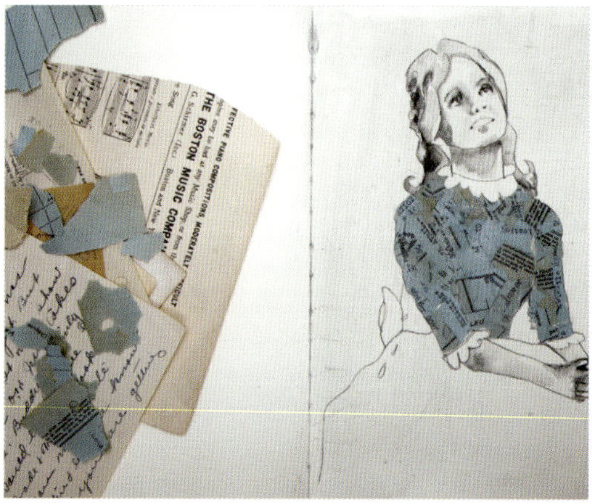

2 Using a Stabilo, lightly sketch some of the darker values and then pull the black out with a waterbrush. This technique is discussed in Chapter 9.

3 I used gathered ephemera to create the collaged dress. When you are using collage to tell your story, be on the lookout for papers that will be clues to the person, place or event you are creating. For this collage I used religious papers, sheet music and the favorite color of my subject. If you know these details of your subject, it is another way to bring a story to life. Otherwise, have fun making these details up. Adhere and seal each piece with matte medium.

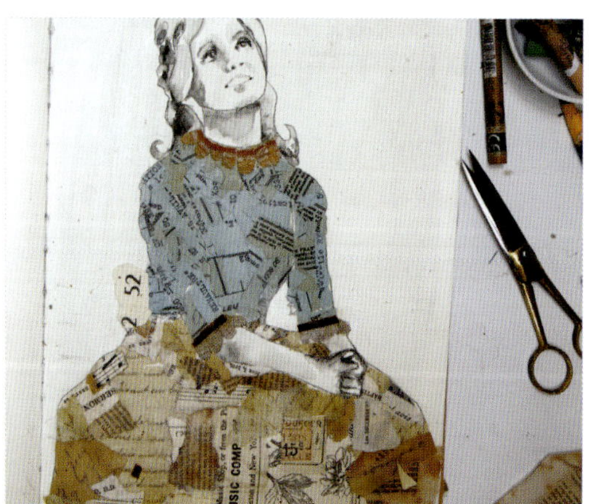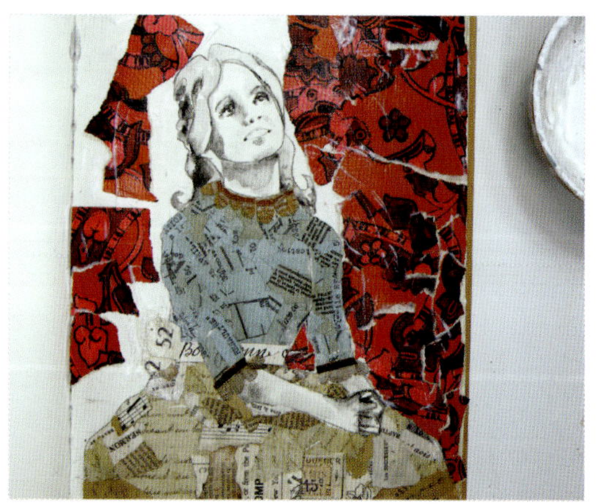

4 Get creative with your collage. The trim on this dress was collaged with vintage book binding.

5 Let color guide your piece! I was thrilled to find a perfect complement to the vintage blue papers with the red vintage wallpaper. Each piece was torn and then applied and sealed with matte medium.

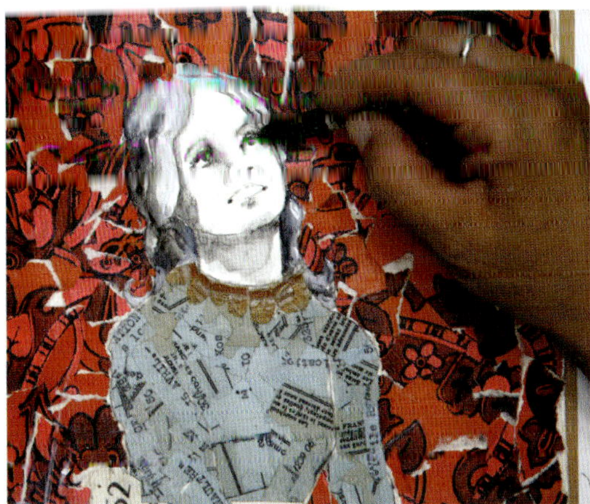 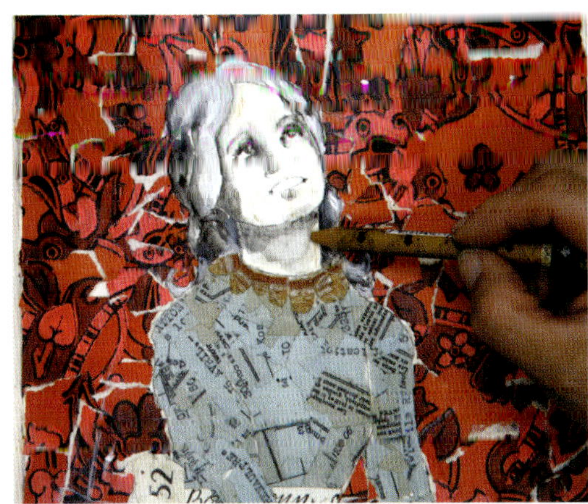

6 Using the same colors and techniques as with the oil sticks, use NeoColor II water-soluble crayons to get the soft coloring and blending for the skin. Use a Payne's Gray crayon followed by a Titanium White crayon. With your waterbrush, gently blend the colors while keeping the colors predominantly where you first applied them. The trick is to not overblend.

7 Add Yellow Ochre and blend with water. Then and just a touch of crimson on the cheeks, forehead, neck and arms.

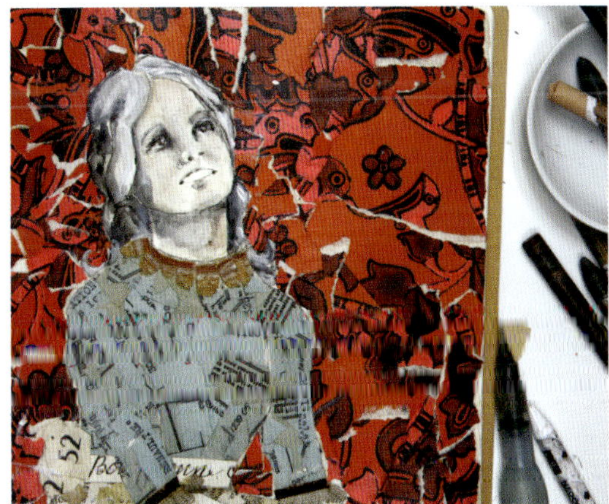

8 Using only a black Stabilo and water, create the values in the hair. The background and dress are full of color, and the simplicity of the Stabilo complements it nicely. Spray with a workable fixative.

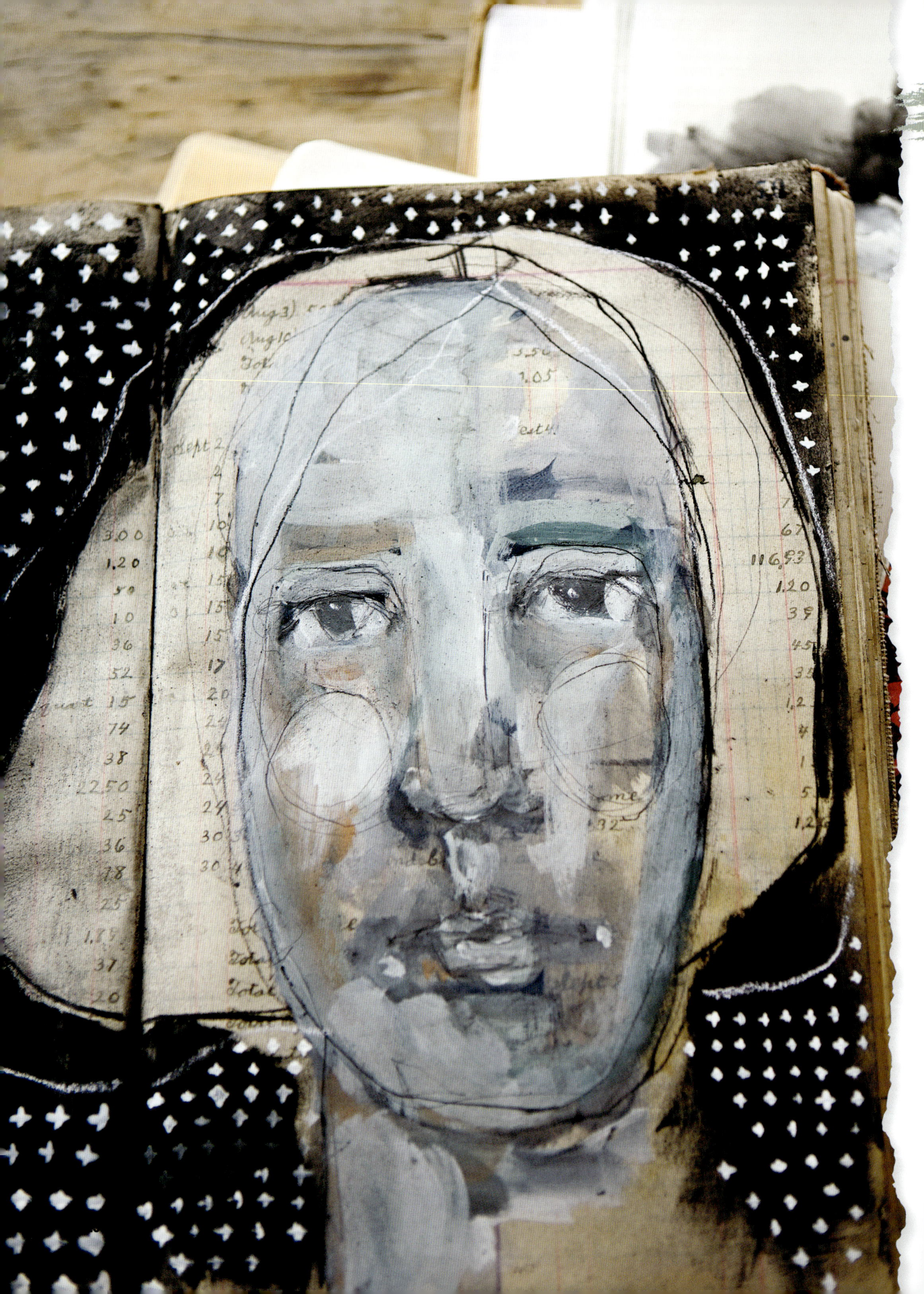

Painted Contour Sketch

Now that we are warmed up, let's take that contour sketch to the next level. Using whatever mediums you have on hand, allow the sketch to be your starting point for a more finished and colorful piece. Remember that it is not about the finished piece but about having fun and telling a story.

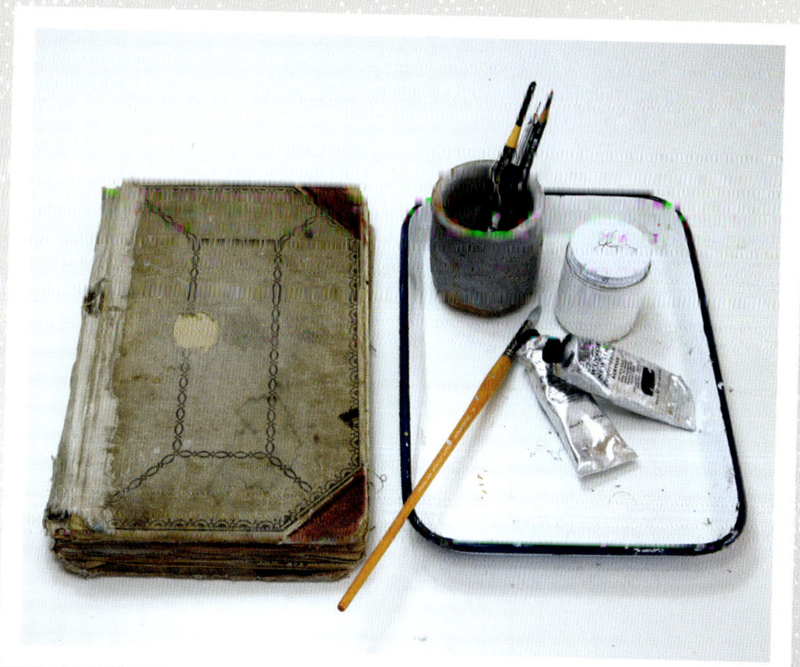

WHAT YOU NEED
- Art Journal
- Black Stabilo All pencil
- Charcoal pencil
- Gesso, clear and white
- Mechanical pencil
- Paintbrush
- Palette with your colors
- White pastel
- Workable fixative

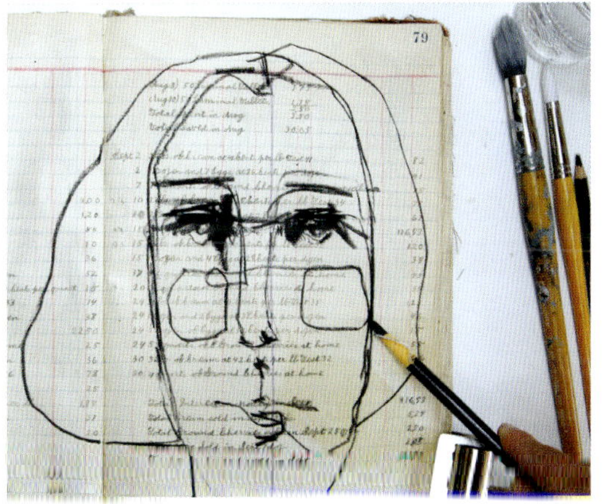

1 On a journal spread painted with clear gesso, draw a contour sketch with charcoal pencil. Remember to only allow yourself 1-2 minutes.

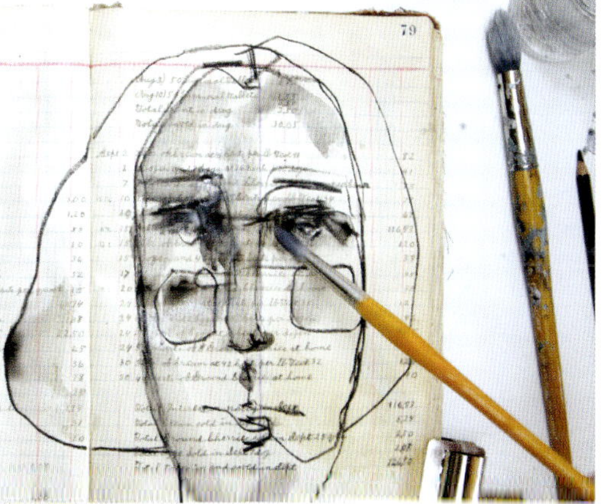

2 Use a brush and water to "erase" any marks that you do not want to keep. Charcoal blends away easily with water and allows you to make your marks as you create, but then you can take them away when they are no longed needed. As you are moving the charcoal and water around, you can start creating those first layers of values.

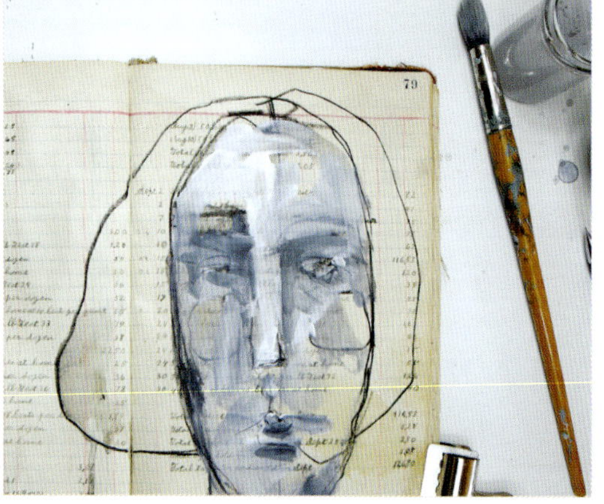

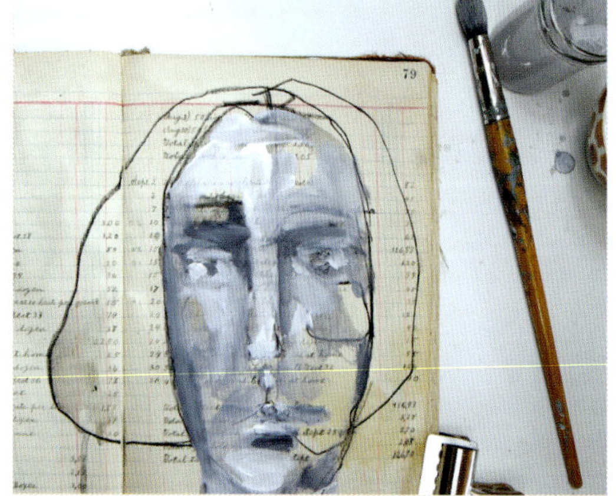

3 Notice I did not add water to all of the charcoal. There are many parts of the sketch that are dry. Overdoing a piece and overblending usually does not give us the results we are after.

Add white gesso and highlights based on the reference image. If you do not have a reference image, use a reflection of yourself to see the darkest and lightest values as you work.

4 This is a back-and-forth process of adding the darkest values and using the white gesso to highlight. Cut into the wet paint with a mechanical pencil and add an intense black with a Stabilo where needed. I can lose and find a piece many times while I am working.

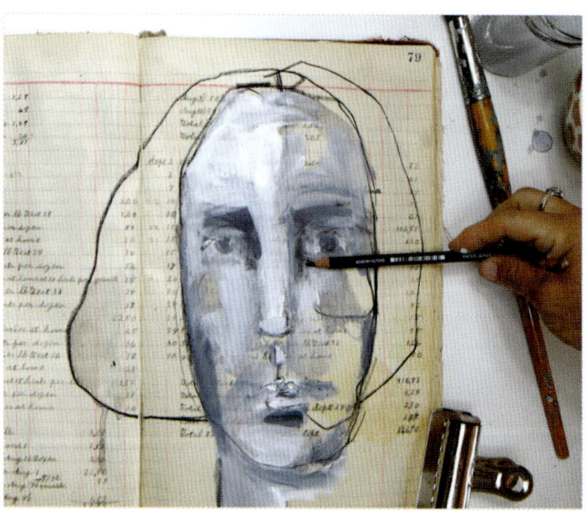

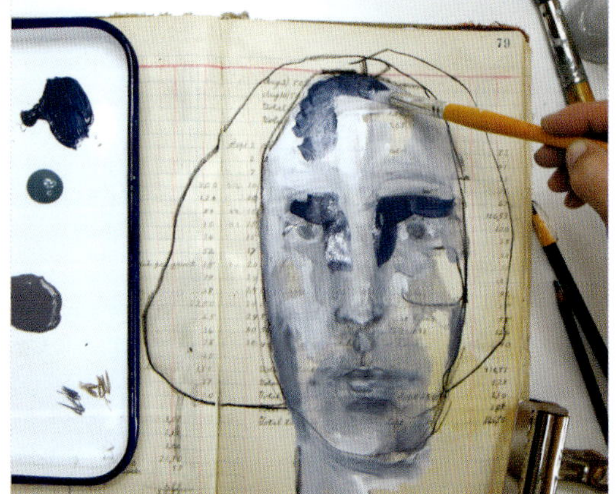

5 Use a mechanical pencil and Stabilo to bring back some details in the face that were lost in the layers.

6 Bring together some colors from your palette. Starting with the darkest color, start to add depth. This piece is whimsical and this can be exaggerated even more with the colors you use as the darkest and medium values. Based upon your reference image, where do you see the darkest values (or shadows)? Do not be intimidated about bringing in greens, blues, purples, etc. to these areas. You will love the results.

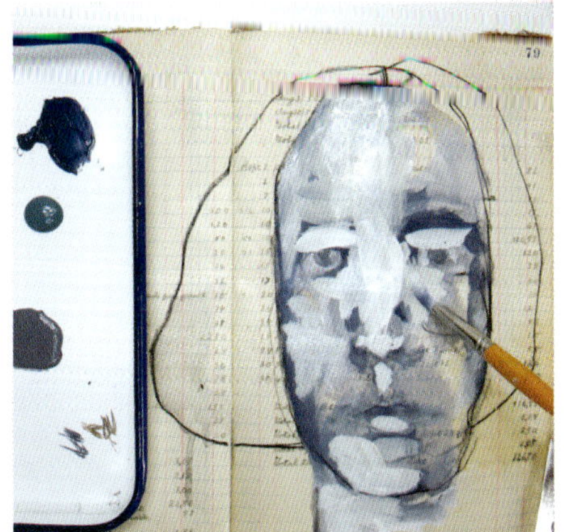

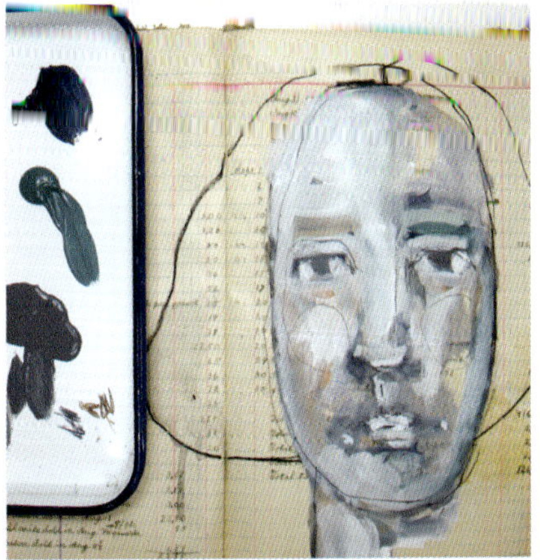

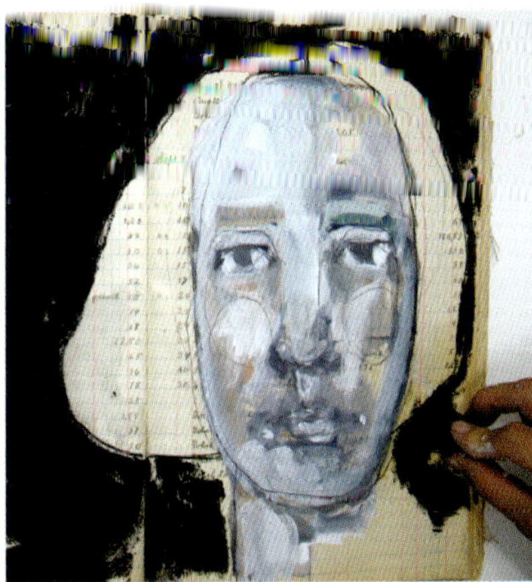

7 Then using a lighter color from your palette, bring in your highlights without overblending.

8 The face is coming together by layering and not overblending. This gives the face a raw and loose feel. Using a mechanical pencil and a Stabilo, bring the details back throughout the face. Turn your pencil in your hand as you work to create more organic marks.

9 Using a black Derwent charcoal, add charcoal around the whole piece and then slightly smudge it with your fingers. Spray the whole piece with a workable fixative and allow it to dry.

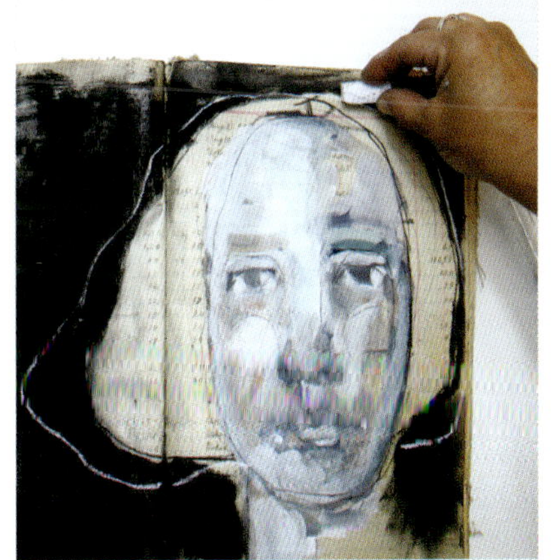

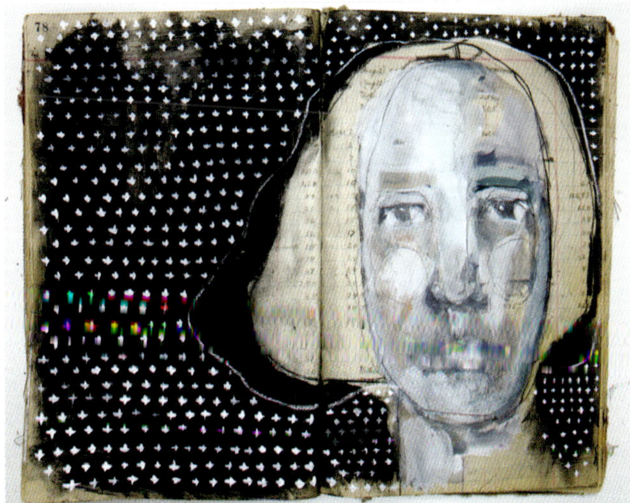

10 I felt that the hair should have come out farther with the composition, and so I used a white pastel to extend these lines and redirect the eye. You will also notice how the negative space of the woman's hair becomes a design element, too.

11 Using white gesso, I created repetitive mark making over all of the charcoal.

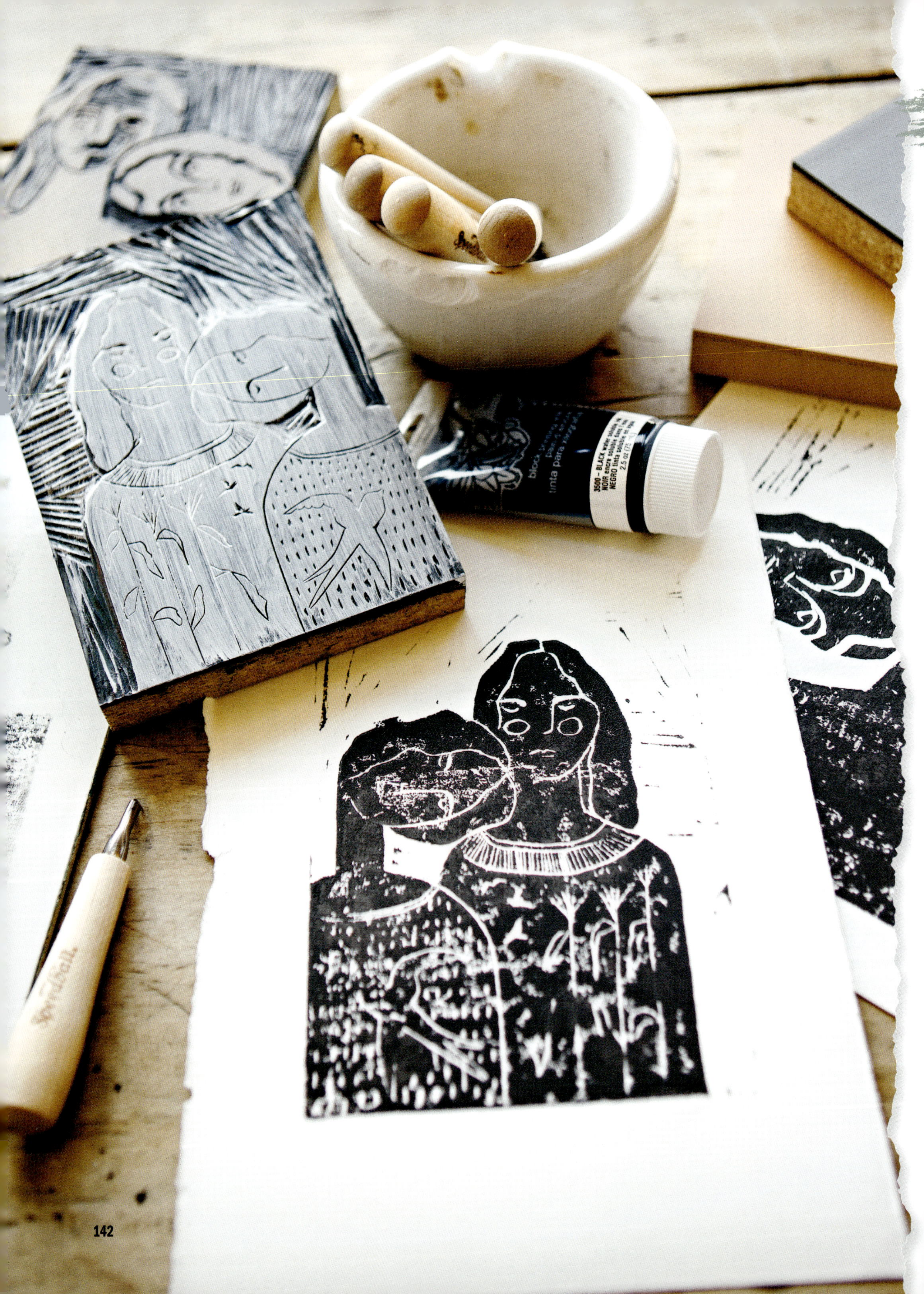

Linocuts

Next to my love of collage, Stabilo and charcoal, I have to add printmaking with linocuts. Cutting into linoleum to create a relief print is one of the most satisfying processes. It will get you thinking differently about what you want to keep and what you want to cut away to create your image. It is not very forgiving, but because of this the learning curve is fast. For this project I printed out one of my quick sketches and used it for inspiration.

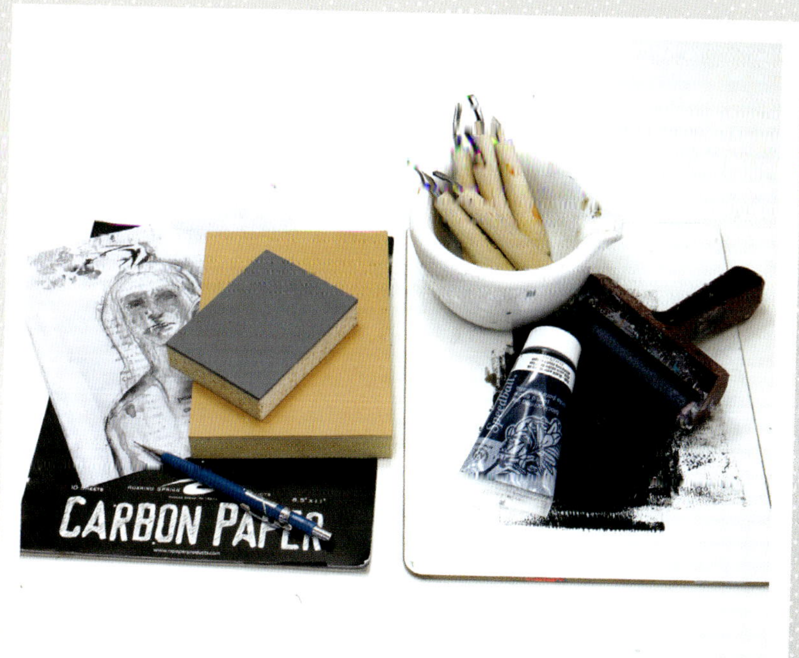

WHAT YOU NEED
- Blade/cutting tool (Speedball)
- Block printing ink
- Brayer
- Carbon paper
- Heat gun or hair dryer (optional)
- Linoleum block
- Reference sketch
- Watercolor paper

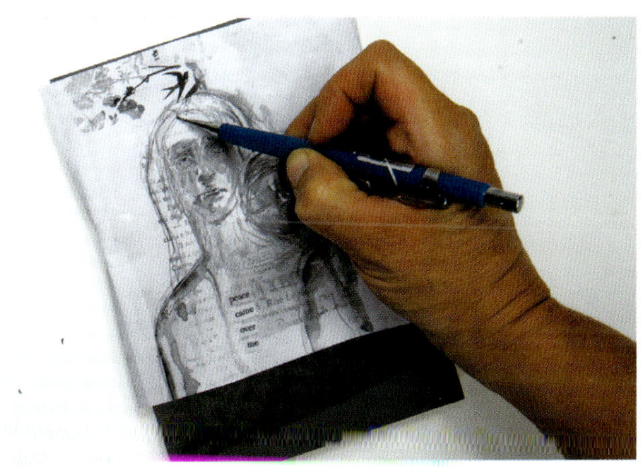

1 Using a copy of my sketch and carbon paper, I created an image transfer onto the linoleum block.

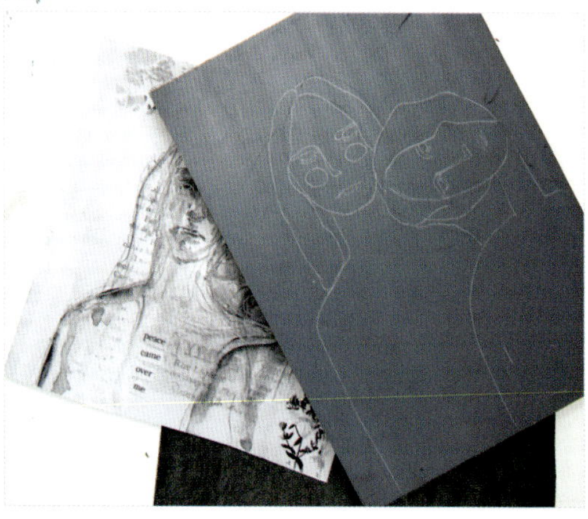

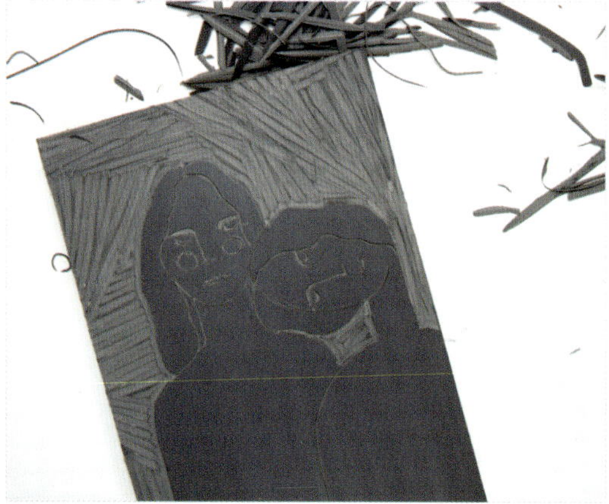

2 The linoleum can be easy or hard to cut depending on the brand. If you find that you have a harder block of linoleum, I recommend heating it briefly with a heat gun or a hair dryer. It can make a huge difference how well the linoleum takes to your cuts and designs.

3 The first step is to cut away from your image and leave the relief. This is the area that will touch the paper and transfer the ink. Because of the large surface to be cut away, you will want to use a higher number of blade (the lower the blade number, the smaller the blade). I usually start with a no. 6 in a set of carving blades from Speedball.

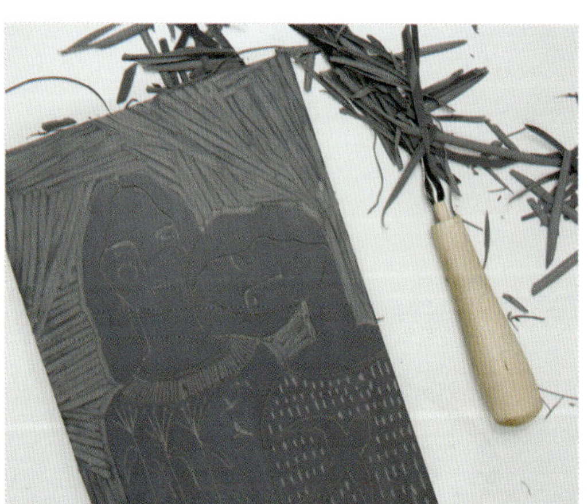

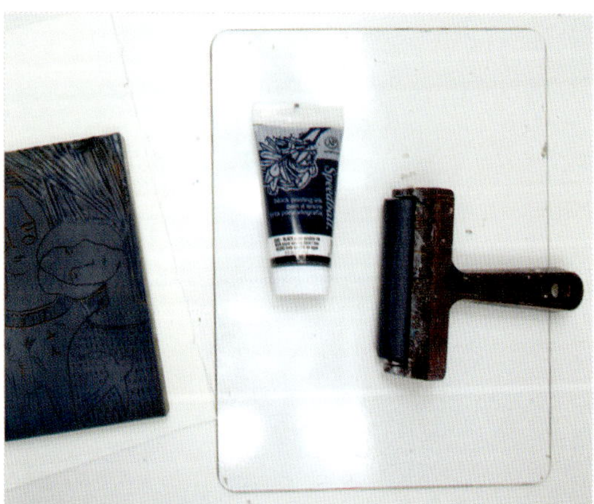

4 Once I cut away the area around my images, I used a smaller number blade to cut into the women. This piece represents my sister and me, and I used many elements of my gathered symbolism within the piece. You can see the cornstalks, birds and repetitive mark making within the body of each image. What marks and symbolism can you create within your linocut?

5 I have had the best results by using actual block printing ink over paint. Feel free to try what you have on hand, but if you are getting frustrated with how your image is printing, please do not give up before you find the correct ink.

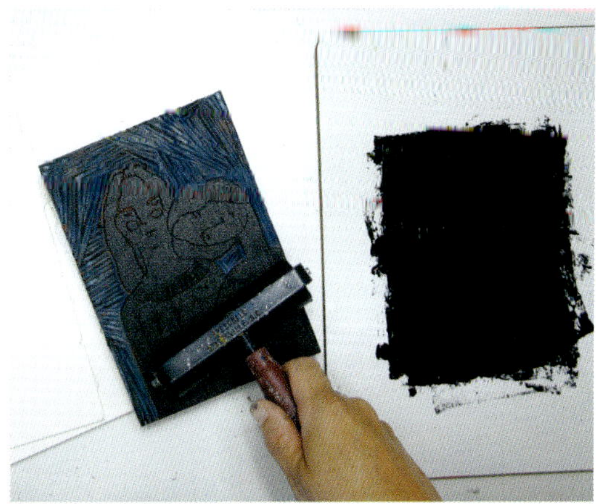

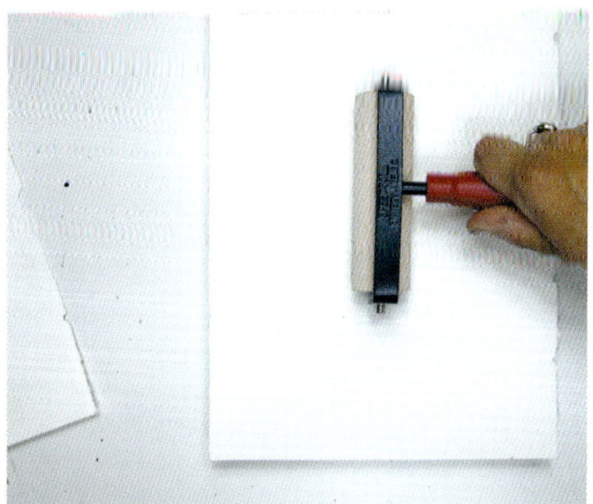

6 Roll the ink onto a smooth surface, and use your brayer to move the ink back and forth and then side to side to get out all air bubbles. With a nice layer of ink on your brayer, apply the ink to your linocut.

7 Apply your paper (I used both hot-and cold-pressed watercolor while creating these prints) on top of the block. Using a clean and dry brayer, roll back and forth over the image to make sure that the whole block has made contact with the paper.

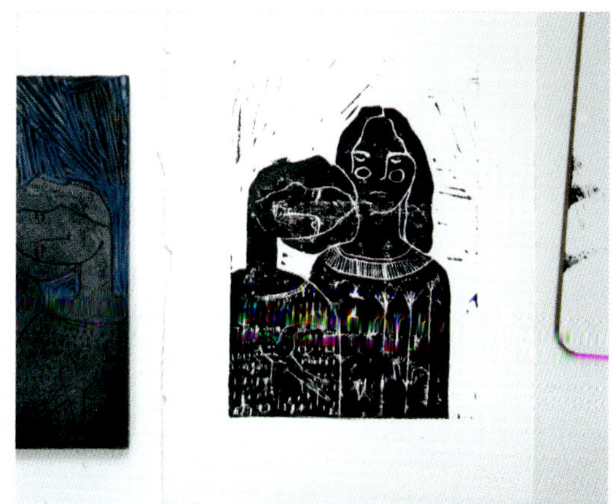

8 Pull back your paper and enjoy your print. I did not go back in and clear more of the linoleum around the images because I enjoy the extra marks that the cut marks can make. Sometimes it may even take several times of printing to get your cuts just right, but it is worth it!

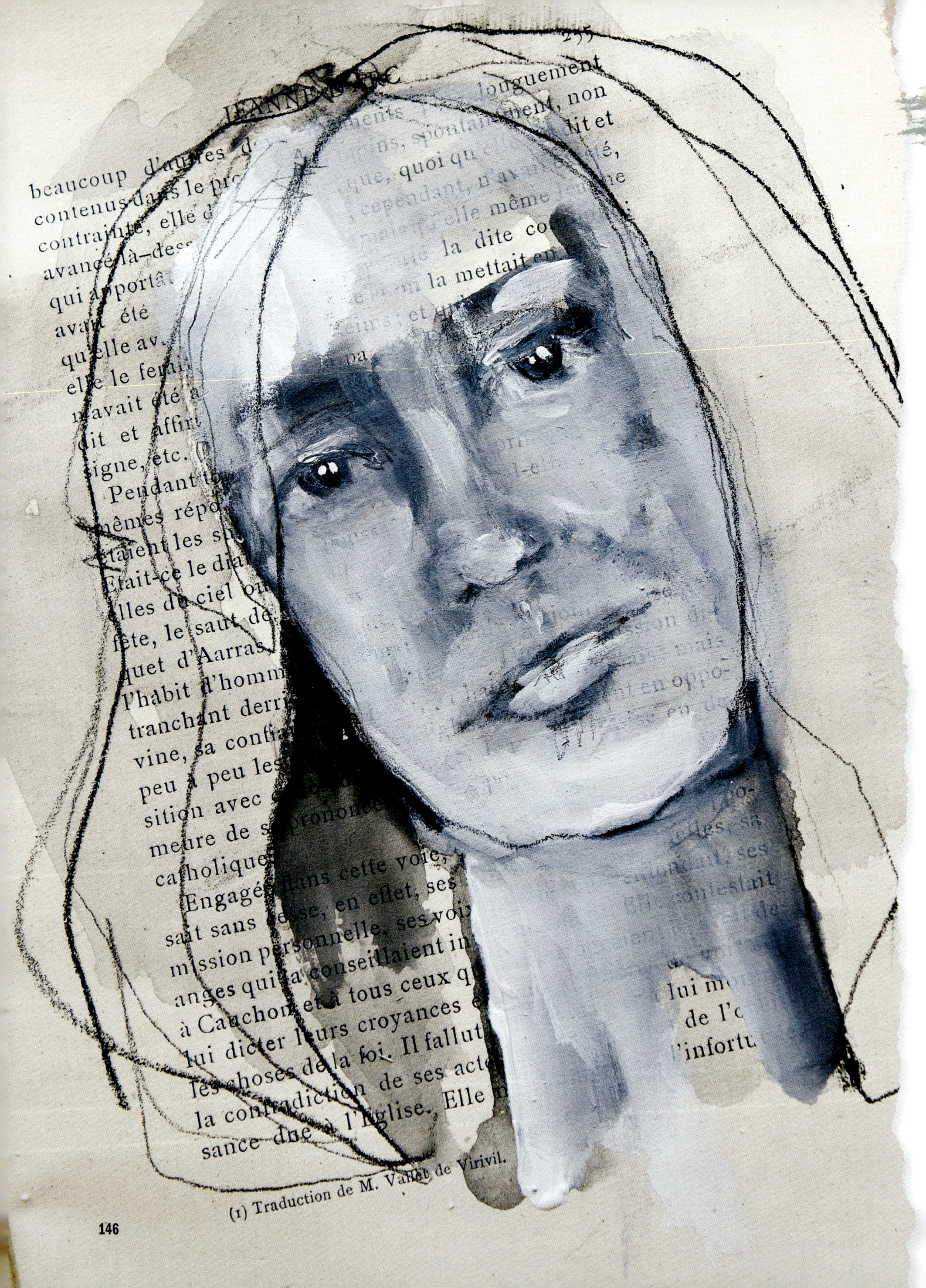

Breaking Down a Face

With all of the portrait practice that we have created together I wanted to end this chapter with some simple face measurement instructions that I hope will encourage you to capture faces wherever you go. Once you know some simple tips, you just may find yourself sketching a little more, and maybe portraits will become your favorite, too.

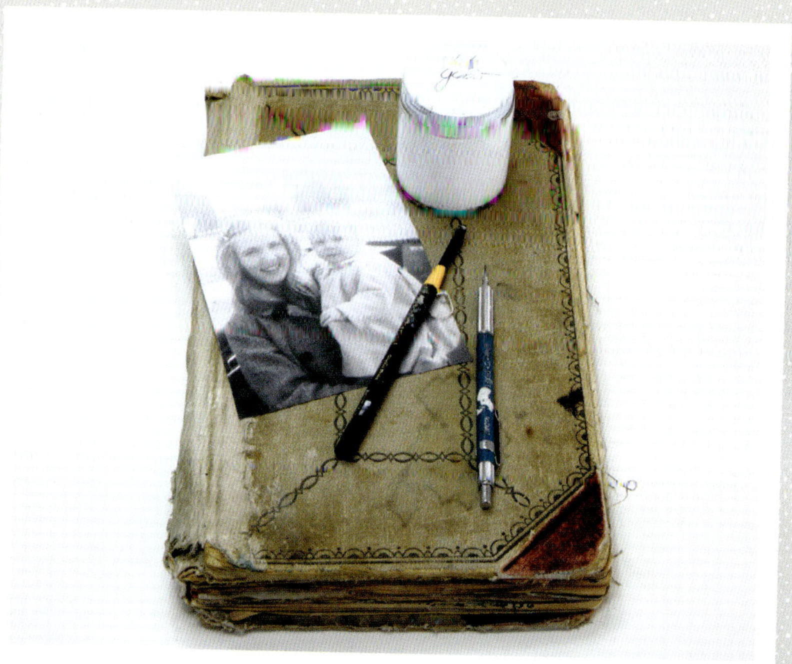

WHAT YOU NEED

– *Art journal*

– *Black Stabilo All pencil*

– *Charcoal pencil*

– *Gesso: white*

– *Mechanical pencil*

– *Paintbrush*

– *Reference photo*

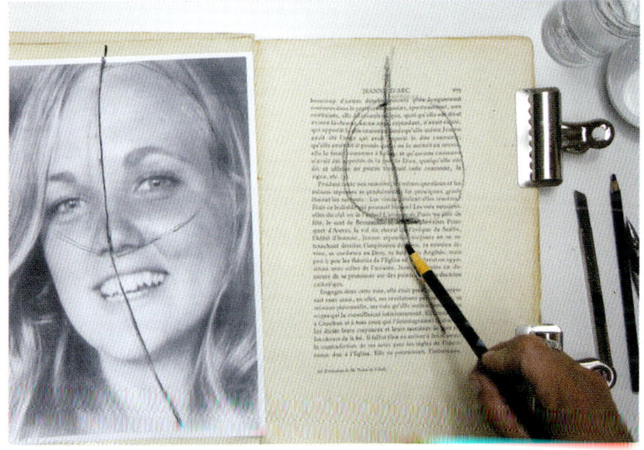

1 Add clear gesso to your journal and allow it to dry before beginning. When you are looking at an image or a live model, begin breaking down the face by drawing a circle from the top of the hairline to the bottom of the nose using a charcoal pencil. Then draw a line from the center of the hairline through the middle of the nose and down through the bottom of the chin. No matter what angle the face is positioned, this is the starting point.

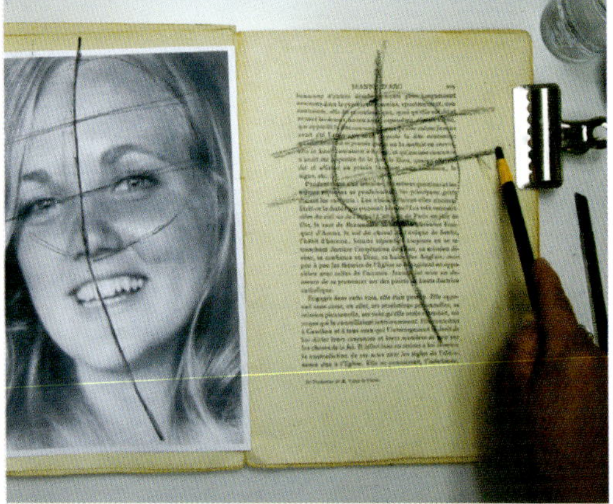

2 Draw a line across the circle horizontally at the one-third mark and again at the two-third mark. The two-third mark is around where the eyes should be placed. The eyes are typically one eye-width apart.

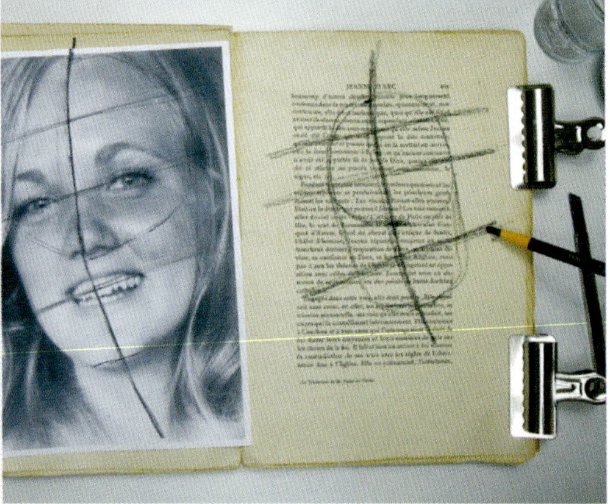

3 From the lower part of the circle extend the lines down to create a jawbone and chin. Draw another line horizontally halfway between the bottom of the nose and the bottom of the chin. This is where the lips will go.

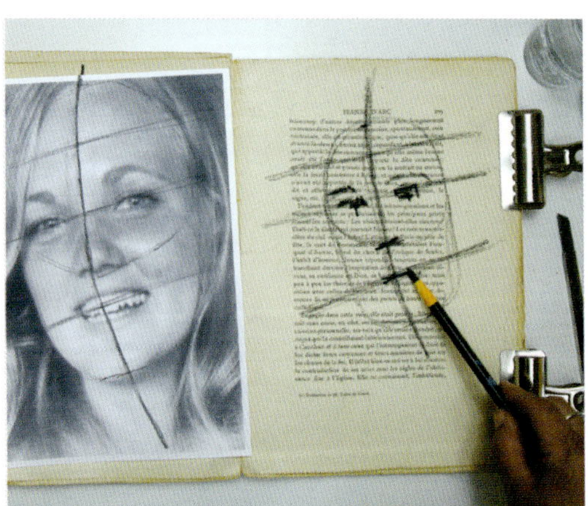

4 Using your charcoal or Stabilo, mark the eyes, the bottom of the nose and the lips. You have loosely begun putting your portrait together.

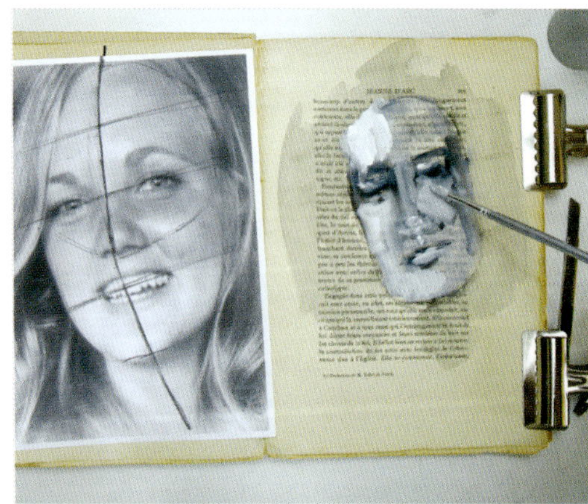

5 Using a wet paintbrush, "erase" away any of the marks and lines that you no longer need. After you have removed the excess charcoal or Stabilo, paint white gesso where you see highlights. If you add too much white, go back in with the Stabilo or charcoal. This is a back-and-forth process to create a face with depth. Keep in mind this is a quick painting sketch and is about the process and not the final result.

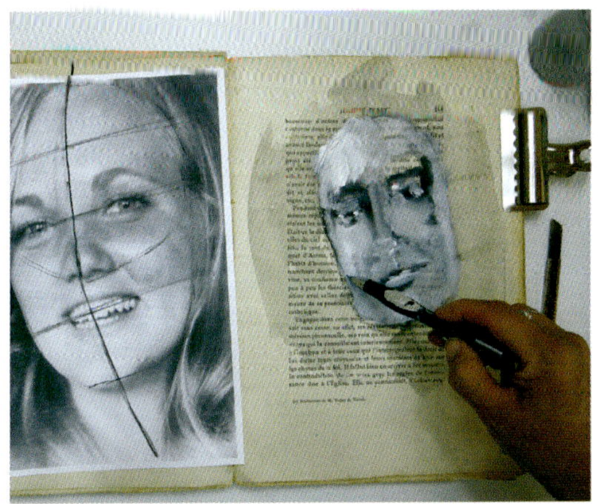

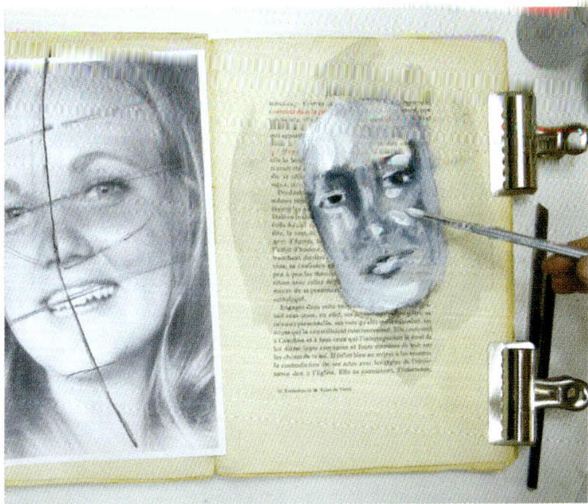

6 With your mechanical pencil, etch into the paint while it is wet and change the lines of the face, if necessary. Bring back the details in the eyes, nose and mouth. Continue to add darker values and highlights. Don't be afraid to use more water if you do not feel like you are able to quickly blend your mediums.

7 Extend the neck at this time and begin to use your charcoal, Stabilo and mechanical pencil to create values and detail.

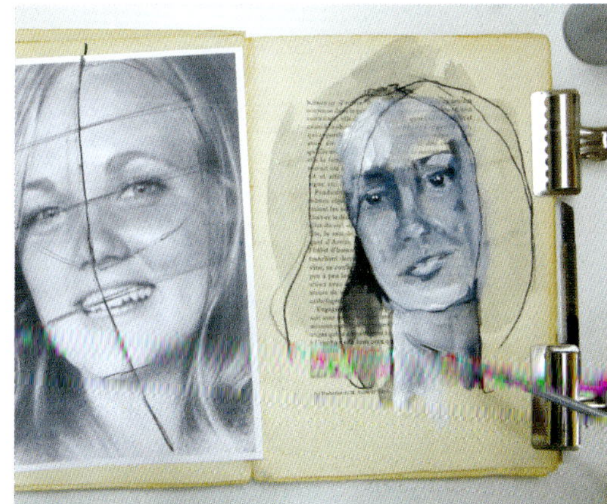

8 The last element to add is hair. Hair should never be added to a portrait before the facial features because it changes the dimensions and then changes the feature placement. If you've ever made a portrait that feels off, this might be why. This is another project in which taking photos along the way will help you understand your process better.

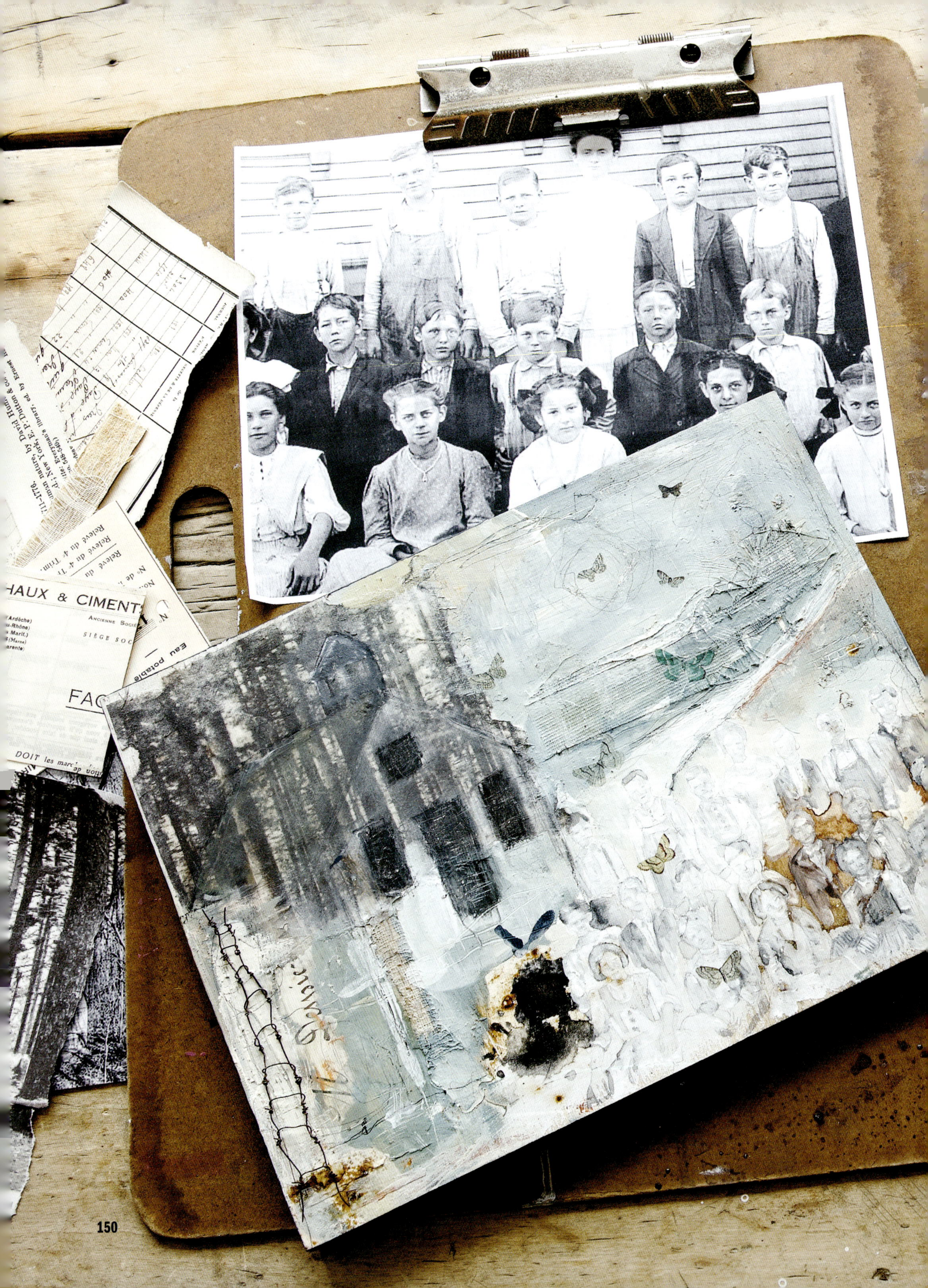

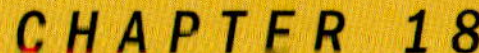

CHAPTER 18

Beyond The Journal

MY ARTIST'S JOURNALS AND SKETCHBOOKS ARE FULL OF TRYING NEW TECHNIQUES, ideas, quotes, compositions, color combinations, quick sketches, more detailed studies, beautiful layouts and quick works that I will never come back to. These art journals are a safe place to practice and grow as an artist, and they are a body of work that is just for me. They are filled with practice. I am the only person who could have pulled that off, and I am the only one who can show up for myself and in my art.

As a little girl, when I was sick my mom would sit with me, rub my back and tell me to breathe out the sickness and breathe in the good and the healing. I would obediently follow her instructions and imagine all of my sickness going away.

When I was in grade school I remember being in a reading circle and being too nervous to read aloud. The closer it came to my turn to read, the more and more nervous I would become. The butterflies would be fierce in my tummy and chest. As a mom I remembered well the toll that having to perform publicly had on me then (and to this day), so when my own children would get the butterflies before a piano concert, a play or any other time of performing publicly, I remember my mom's sweet words. I tell them to breathe in the peace and blow out the butterflies. This piece is dedicated to all of us who get the butterflies and need to blow them out and breathe in the peace.

Beyond the Journal

Your work may always feel right at home in an art journal, but maybe you want to go beyond the journal and find different ways to share your story. This next project brings together many of the techniques taught in this book to tell a story outside of the journal.

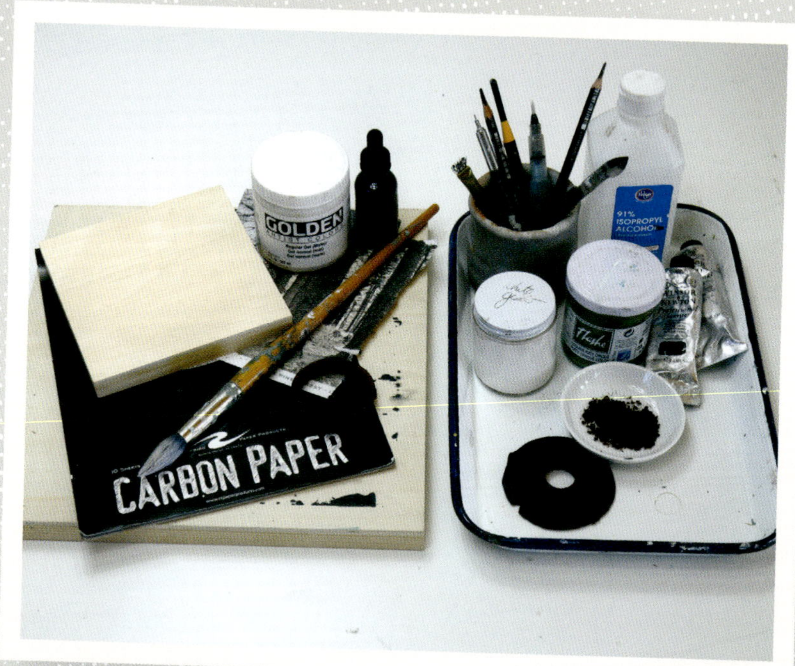

WHAT YOU NEED

- *Black ink with dropper*
- *Carbon paper: black*
- *Ephemera or vintage collage paper*
- *Gesso: white*
- *Golden gel medium*
- *Image*
- *Instant coffee crystals*
- *Mark-making tool*
- *Liquitex matte medium*
- *Paintbrush*
- *Rusty elements*
- *Vinegar + water mixture*
- *Water mister*
- *Wood panel or canvas*

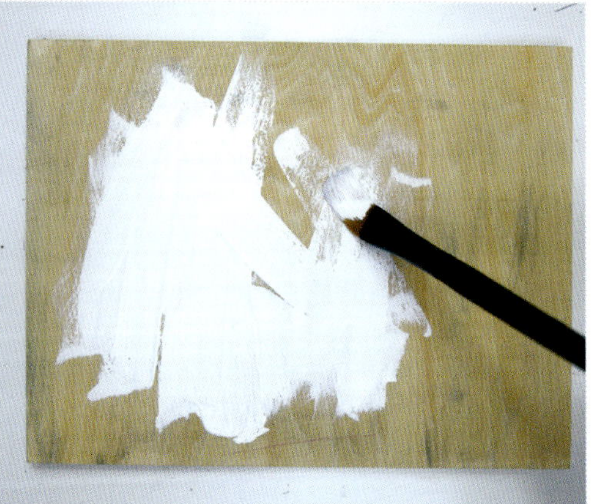

1 Cover your canvas or wood substrate with white gesso and allow it to dry.

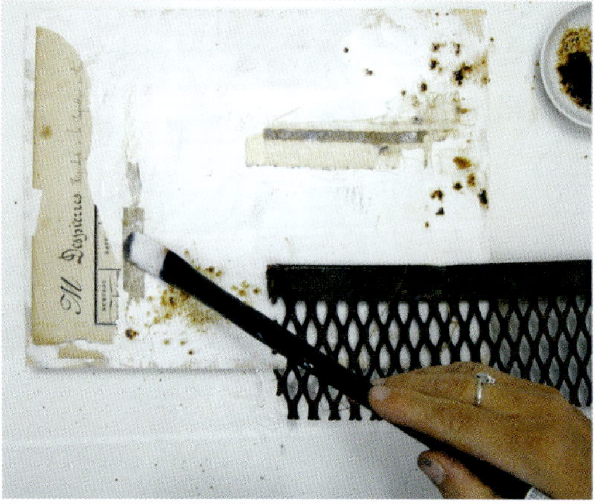

2 Sprinkle instant coffee crystals in a few places and spritz with water. Add vintage ephemera, adhering it with matte medium. While you are working, add some rusty elements in one corner and spray with your vinegar and water mixture taught in Chapter 8.

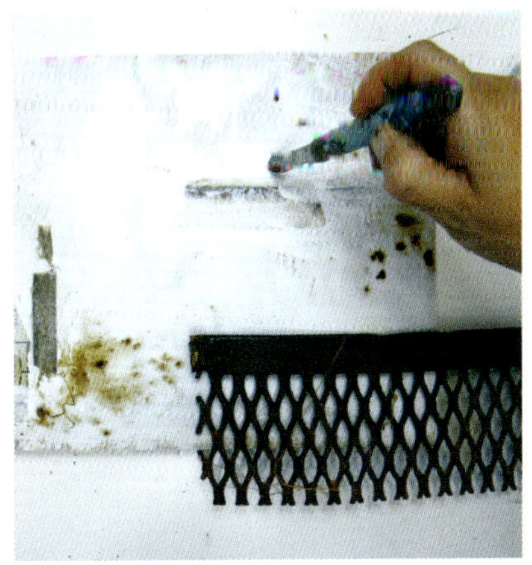

3 Add more white gesso around and over some of the vintage ephemera. While the gesso is wet, come in with a mark-making tool and create lines and repetitive marks.

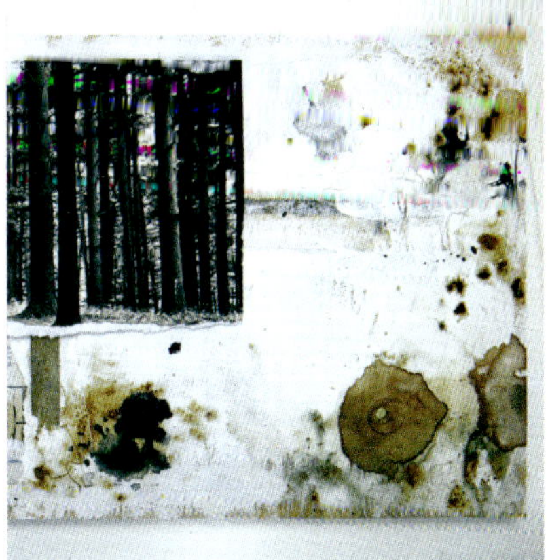

4 Add black ink with a dropper and spray lightly with a spray bottle. Choose an image that will help tell your story and create an image transfer with Golden gel medium. This technique is taught in Chapter 8.

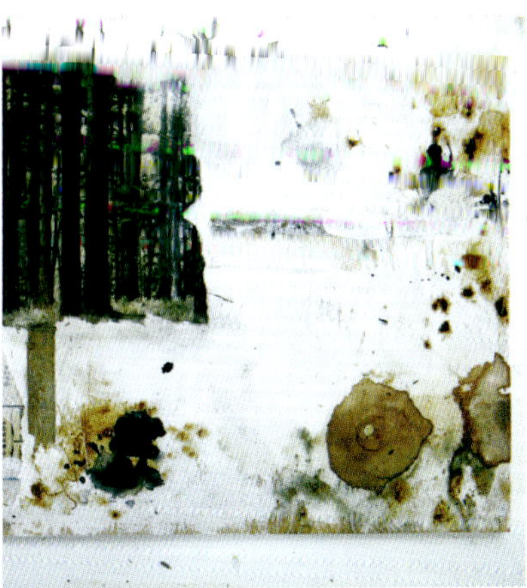

5 Once your image transfer is dry, slowly reveal the image below by lightly rubbing with clean water. While your image is still clear, apply a thin layer of Liquitex matte medium to allow the image to stay clear and dark as it dries.

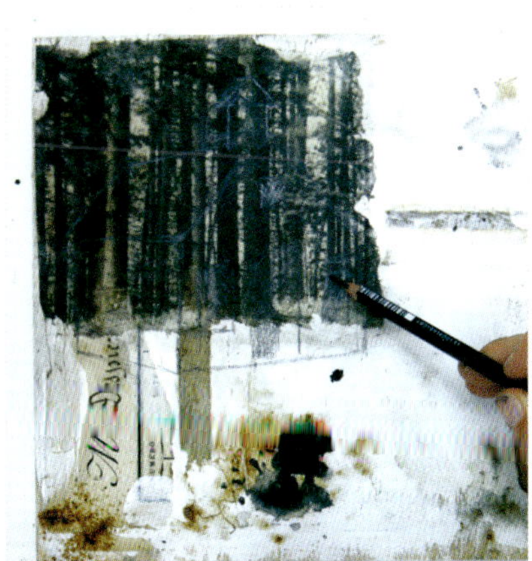

6 Part of the story I am telling here has to do with school, so I incorporated a graphite sketch of an old one-room schoolhouse. You can add elements of your story through sketching, mark making and image transfers.

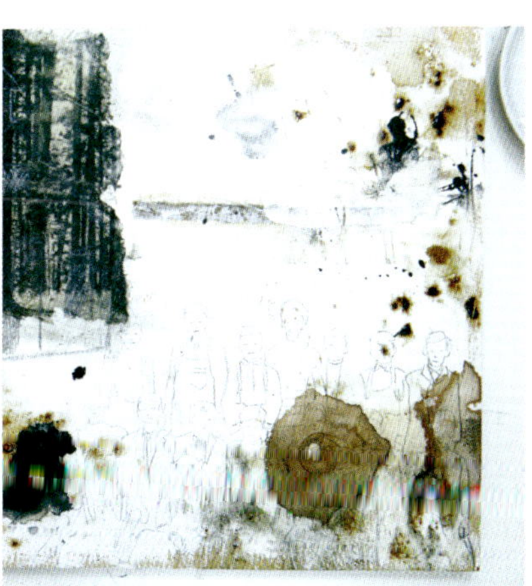

7 Using the image of the school children used in Chapter 15, an image transfer was created using carbon paper. You can create your own carbon paper transfer of a family, home, land or object.

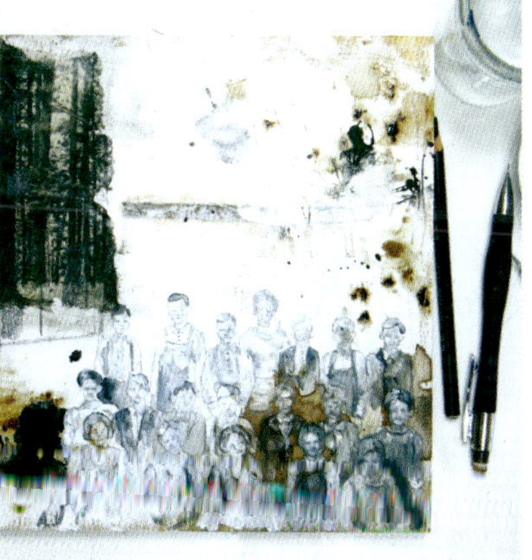

8 All of the children have been "painted" using a Stabilo All pencil, charcoal, graphite and white gesso. This technique was shared in Chapter 15.

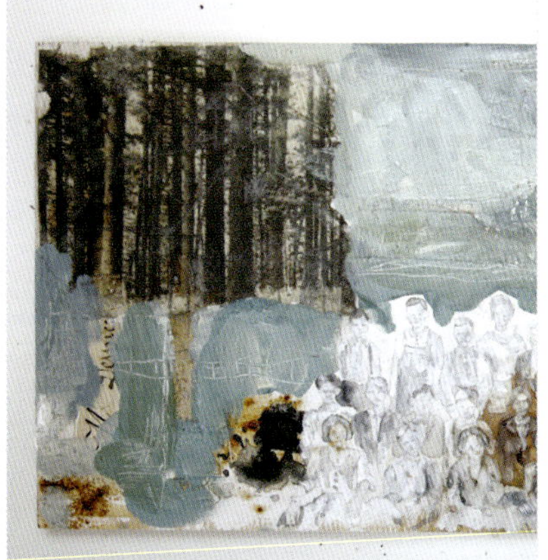 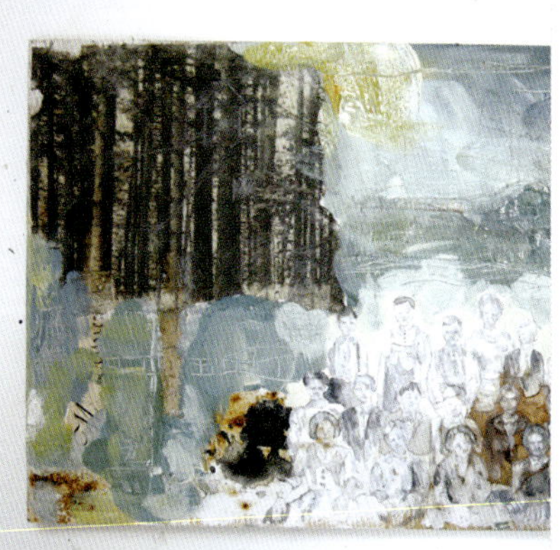 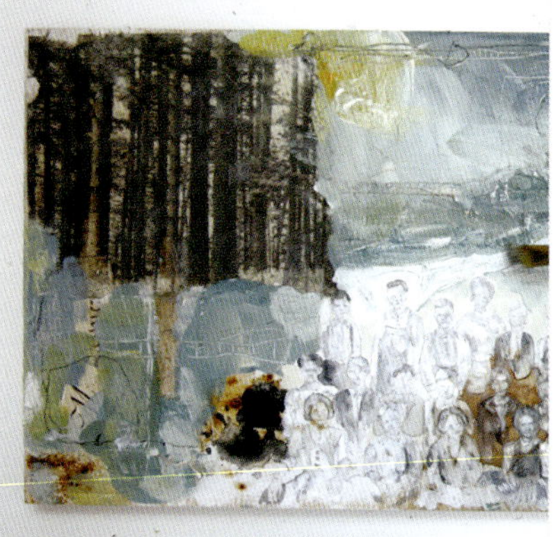

9 I then added different shades of green and blue acrylics from my color palette and lightly blended them without losing the variety of shades. While the paint was wet I used my mark-making tool and etched more lines and symbols. As you bring in colors from your palette, make sure you are adding enough water to allow your paints to blend.

10 I brought in a warm yellow in a few places to complement the palette I had already created and then continued to make marks. What accent colors from your own palette can you add that will create mood and emotion within your piece?

11 Stand back from your work and notice your composition. Now is the time to change where your focal points are resting, to add new marks or design elements if anything appears to be not visually pleasing.

I added a path leading away from the schoolhouse and children to represent their journey to this place. What will you add and how will you direct the eyes of the viewer?

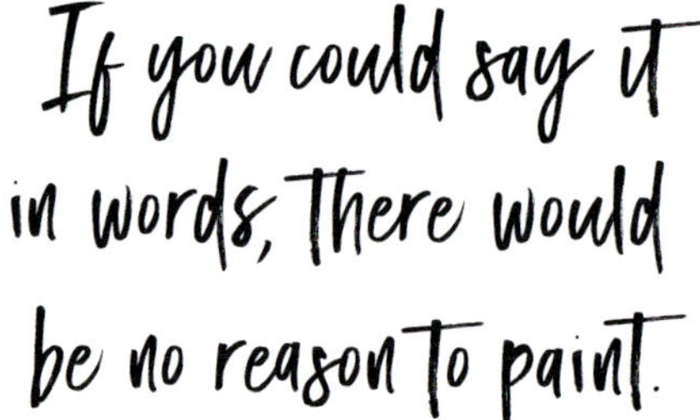

—EDWARD HOPPER

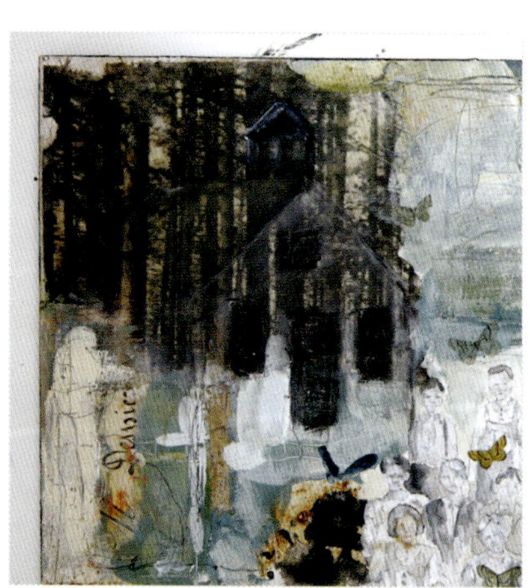

12 I had begun to paint the schoolhouse but liked the composition better when I could see the trees, so I lightly removed most of the paint with rubbing alcohol and smudged the black over the windows and doors to not show the pencil marks. I then went in with a mark-making tool to scuff up the windows and door. In these final stages I added more color sparingly, additional marks and the butterflies throughout the whole piece. I wanted them to look as if they were being breathed out so peace could come.

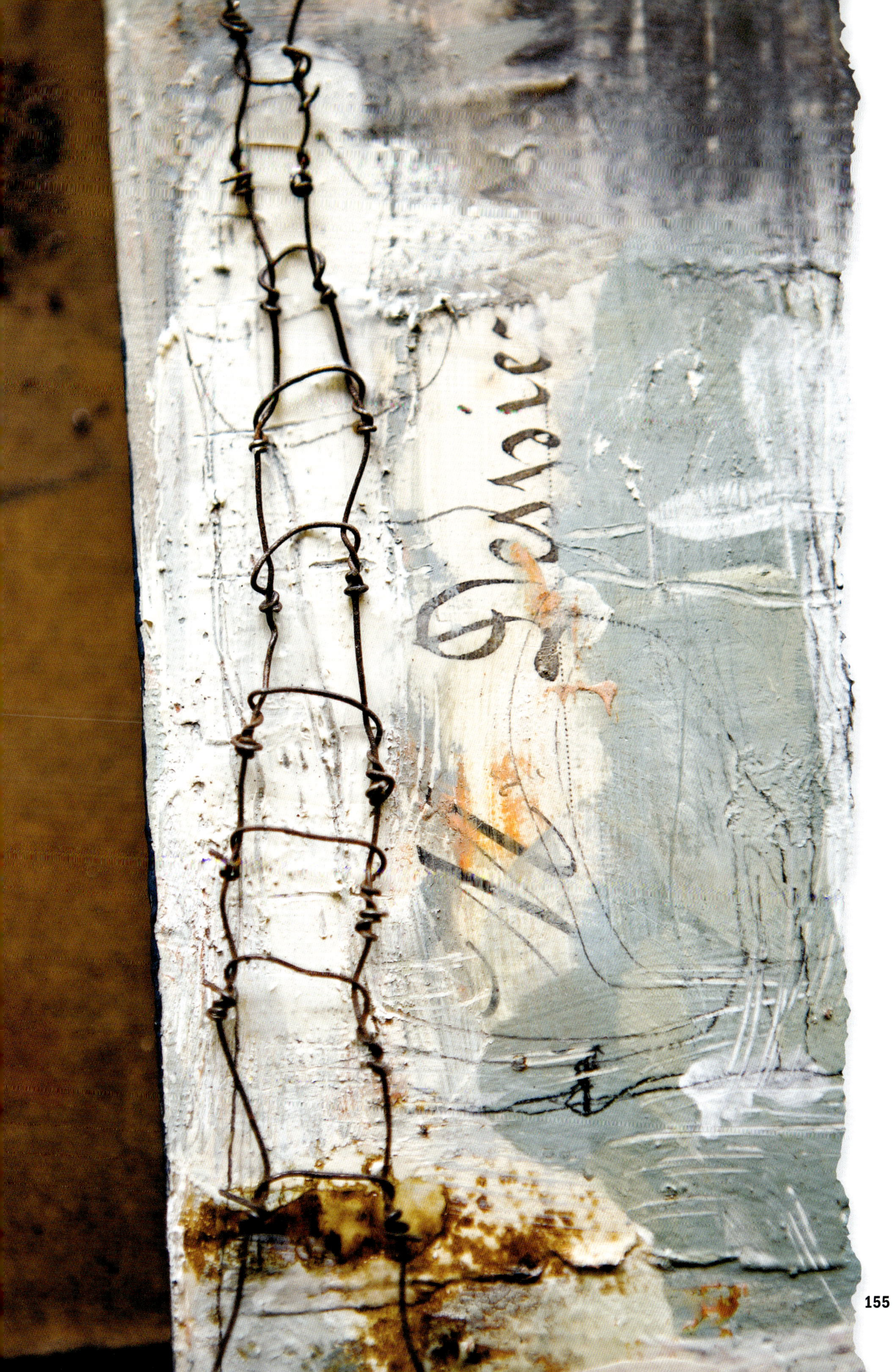

Resources

To view a breakdown of the face, printable art prompts, sticker labels and audio prompts, visit **jeanneoliver.com/the-painted-journal-resources/**.

Art Prompts

- With your arm extended and your body away from your creating surface, begin your mark making.
- With charcoal, add darker values or mark making.
- With your hand or a chamois, smudge your charcoal.
- With whatever medium your are working, use your non-dominant hand.
- Bring in highlights with a white medium.
- For the next 2 minutes, spend time contour drawing with the medium of your choice.
- Create a pattern in your mark making.
- Turn your surface 180-degrees and continue working.
- Place a few drops of ink or paint on your suface, squirt water and let drip.
- Add values or mark making with a soft pastel.
- Create symbolism within your work.
- Put your favorite song on and create to the music.
- Add at least one piece of vintage ephemera to your work.
- Edit out a portion of your work and paint over it.

- Scratch into wet or dry paint with a skewer or craft knife.
- Turn to your symbol and mark-making library and add one element.
- With a dropper, add ink.
- Turn your surface 180-degrees and smudge our a section with your hand or chamois.
- Using a pen or pencil, add words to your surface.
- Step back and look at your work to gain perspective.
- After stepping back from your work, edit out one element.
- With a mechanical pencil, add mark making and scribble elements.
- Add an image transfer or photocopy into your artwork.
- Fill in a shape on your surface with patterned mark making.
- Paint using charcoal, water and white gesso.
- With a larger round brush, add ink to your surface.
- With a mechanical pencil, draw 3-5 lines across your surface.
- Add vintage ephemera to your surface and tear some of it away.

- Paint one larger square within your work or paint an uneven number of smaller squares.
- Using only charcoal and water, create different values.
- Add a darker paint color and scratch mark making into the wet paint.
- Add a complementary color.
- With a flat brush, fill a surface with the same mark making.
- Using gathered words and quotes, create your own poem.
- Spill ink on your surface.
- Stain your surface with coffee or tea.
- Create an image using only charcoal and water.
- Add string.
- Elongate an element in your work.
- Create a horizontal line in your work with scratching, paint or vintage ephemera.
- Create shapes with color within your work, and with a mechanical pencil, scribble around the shape.
- Add texture with plaster, modeling paste, crumpled up paper bag or crumpled up tissue paper.

Index

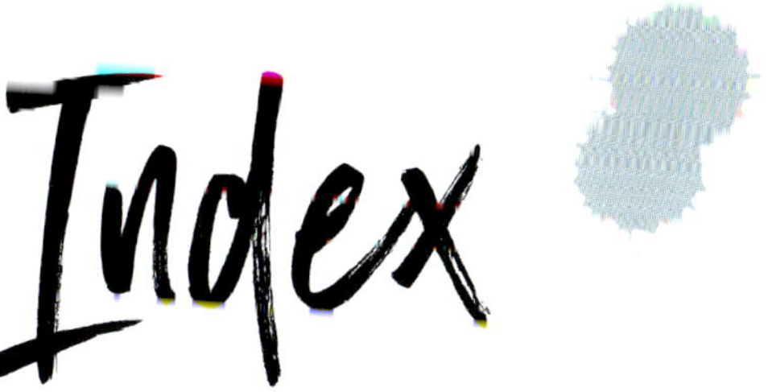

North Light Books
An imprint of Penguin Random House LLC
1745 Broadway, New York, NY 10019
penguinrandomhouse.com

Printed in China
10   9   8   7   6

ISBN: 978-1-4403-5178-5

Edited by Tonia Jenny and Amy Jones
Cover design by Dean Abatemarco
Interior design by Charlene Tiedemann
Photography by Cathy Walters (cathywalters.com)
Pages 90–97: Dixon Silo 2014 © Lance W. Young used with permission.
Page 117: Vintage classroom photograph sourced from McLean County Museum of History, Bloomington, Illinois, used with permission.

The authorized representative in the EU for product safety and compliance is Penguin Random House Ireland, Morrison Chambers, 32 Nassau Street, Dublin D02 YH68, Ireland, https://eu-contact.penguin.ie.

Metric Conversion Chart

TO CONVERT	TO	MULTIPLY BY
Inches	Centimeters	2.54
Centimeters	Inches	0.4
Feet	Centimeters	30.5
Centimeters	Feet	0.03
Yards	Meters	0.9
Meters	Yards	1.1

Acknowledgments

I FEEL LIKE MY WHOLE BUSINESS AND CREATIVITY has been based upon stories, so it is not surprising that I am here as part of my journey. I would like to thank all of the parts of my story for allowing me to gather, elaborate, ignore or honor them in these pages.

This book and this creative life would not be possible without the support and love from my husband, children and family members. You hold me up, cheer me along and are the reason I have stories I want to share. Thank you for giving me the room to try. You make me not afraid to fail. That is the sweetest gift.

Thank you to Tonia Jenny for seeing the value in my story and the stories in others. This book is here because you thought the world would be sweeter with it. Thank you to my editor, Amy Jones, for bringing the book to life.

Dedication

TO MY FAMILY AND THE LAND WHERE I WAS RAISED— I can never thank you enough. For the memories, the joy, the brokenness and the healing, I will forever be grateful.

To the small town of Mt. Morris, Illinois, and the people and land that have made up the core of so much of how I find beauty in the simple and everyday, thank you.

This book is dedicated to my family and my hometown.

About Jeanne Oliver

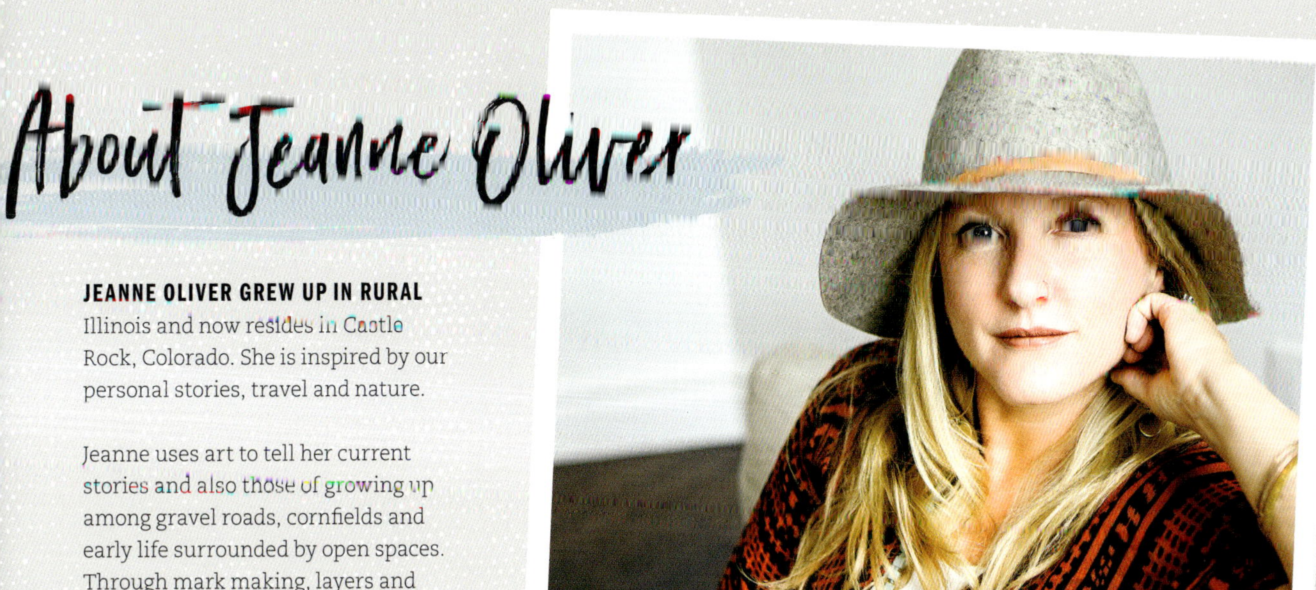

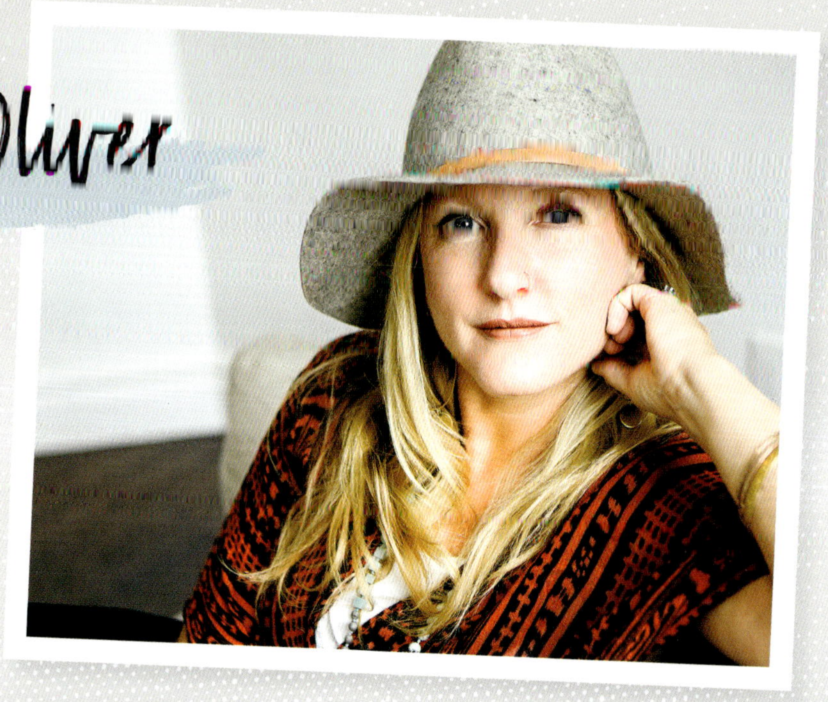

JEANNE OLIVER GREW UP IN RURAL
Illinois and now resides in Castle
Rock, Colorado. She is inspired by our
personal stories, travel and nature.

Jeanne uses art to tell her current
stories and also those of growing up
among gravel roads, cornfields and
early life surrounded by open spaces.
Through mark making, layers and
mixed media, she hopes to convey that
we all have a story to tell.

Jeanne is married to her dream maker,
Kelly, and is the mother of three funny
and creative children. She homeschools
her children even though she has tried
to get out of it a few times. You can
often find her hiking, creating in her
studio and finding an excuse to have
another cup of coffee.

She speaks and teaches all around the
country and sometimes she even gets
to cross the pond. She was told that
she needed to find that One Thing but
she doesn't like listening to directions,
so she embraces many loves and
that has given her a sweet mash-up
of family, art and travel. Connecting
with women and sharing that each
of us has been creatively made is one
of her passions. Visit her website at
JeanneOliver.com.

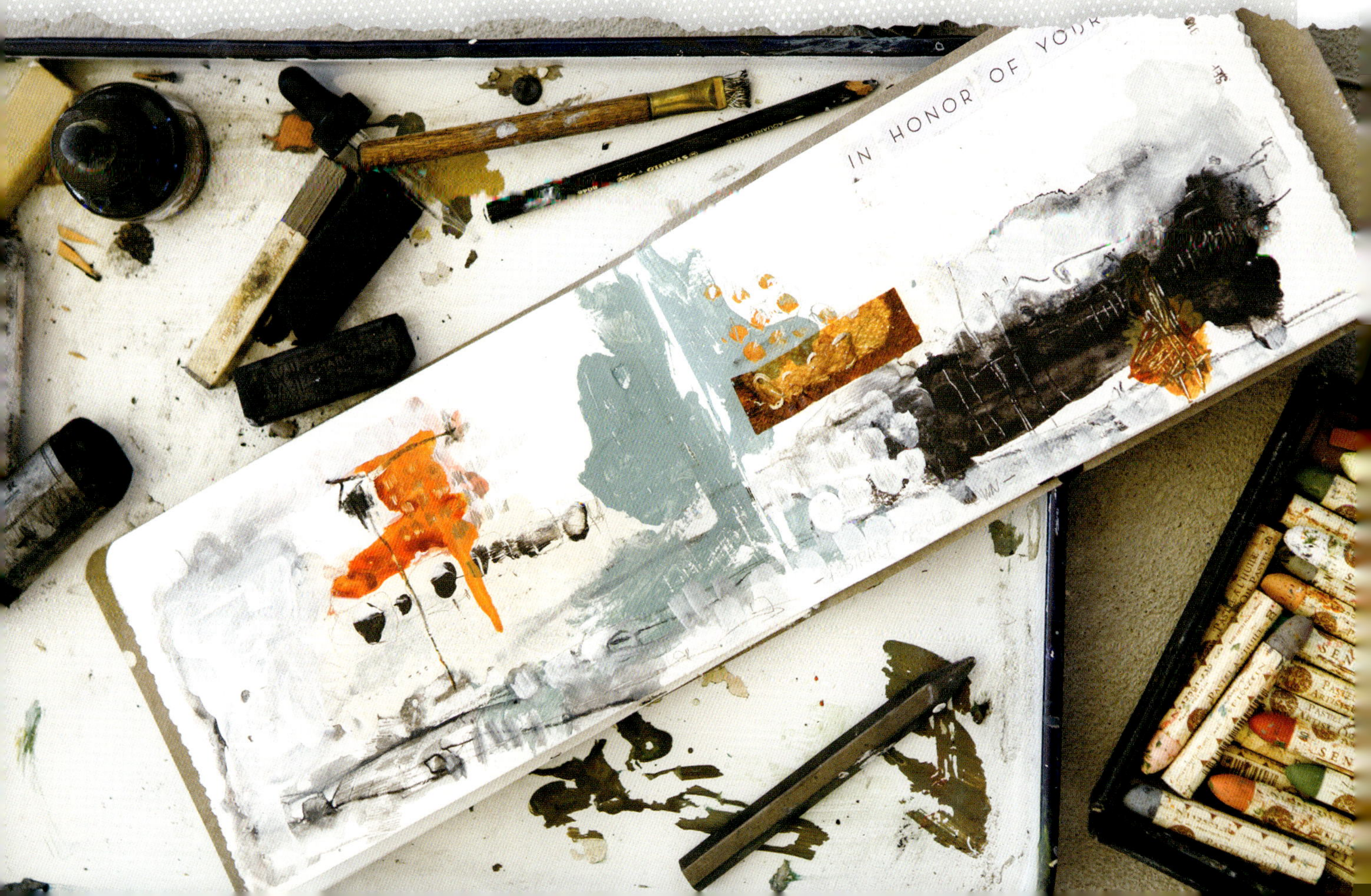